What Did They Mean By That?

A Dictionary of
Historical Terms for Genealogists

Paul Drake, J.D.

Heritage Books, Inc.

Paul Drake is the author of
In Search of Family History: A Starting Place
avaliable from Heritage Books, Inc.

Published 1994 By
HERITAGE BOOKS, INC.
1540-E Pointer Ridge Place, Bowie, Maryland 20716
(301) 390-7709

ISBN 1-55613-944-6

A Complete Catalog Listing Hundreds of Titles on
Genealogy, History, and Americana
Available Free on Request

To dearest Brittany, Bethany, Evan, Diane, Allison,
and those who are destined to follow them.

CONTENTS

Acknowledgements

I very much thank Jo White Linn for her early encouragement and guidance in the project; Karen and Roxanne of Heritage Books, for their uncommon assistance and work with the manuscript; Brittany, Bethany, Evan, Diane and Allison for the inspiration; Paul, Diane, and Cheryl, for the pride shown and help freely given; Marty, for the hours spent alone and the snacks brought to the computer; and finally, the ancestors and others now long gone who wrote words that I did not understand, and the students and fellow researchers who insisted upon knowing what they meant. I am deeply indebted to you all.

P.D.
1994

INTRODUCTION

Since but few of the great mass of ordinary colonial men (and even fewer women) could read and write, paper was very expensive, writing instruments were crude, and postal service was either non-existent or in its infancy, messages over long distances by other than merchants and representatives of government were but few and far between. Moreover, those businessmen and traders who did require knowledge and evidence of transactions from afar had long before developed business forms of sorts - negotiable instruments - and a jargon or vernacular of their trades that required only minimal use of additional written language. For those reasons, one could wander through the streets of colonial America and, save for those in commerce, find virtually no one engaged in writing anything.

Upon entering the courthouses however, all would be different. Virtually every office of government had people working, quill pens in hand; they, the scribes, the scriveners. For a full millennium, the common law, by which all life, business, and - most importantly to those who thought in English - inheritances and real estate transactions were based and determined, had required that decisions affecting rights and duties of rich and poor alike should be memorialized, accessible, and remembered, thus necessitating courts minutes, orders, and records.

Then too, the taxing authorities, without whom there would be no income to support the government and institutions of the day, had to record identity, ownership, and exchanges of monies and credits. Finally, those legislators, who in the name of peace, the public good, and prosperity determined what actions were proper and what were not, were constrained to set forth their mandates with particularity and give notice of those requirements to the whole of society. Otherwise, those governed could not know what was expected of them.

There was yet one more institution where those learned in the 'art and mystery' of writing were to be found - the church. Indeed, in the earliest of times it was only the clerics and the lawmakers who were literate as we know that term today, and, in fact, it may be argued that throughout the long, long 'dark ages' only the church had clinged to, preserved, and sent forward to us what we now call archives.

The language that those myriad now gone used in creating records - that device we call American English - was and remains an incredibly rich and powerful tool. But we must remember that it is not and never has been a static language, and its many variations are not carved in stone somewhere such that we may seek out what is correct or incorrect. Mr. Justice Holmes said it best: "A word is not a crystal, transparent and unchanging. It is, rather, the skin of a living thought, and its meaning may vary greatly with the time and the context in which it is found."

So, while but minimal effort is required to read and understand even the earliest writings of our colonial ancestors, some components have varied over these centuries, and many words - like our ancestors who wrote them - have come upon the stage of the great play of history, and then, as quietly as they arrived, disappeared into the soft black of the past.

The family historian must seek out the records of the merchants, the courts, the legislators, and the churches, all the while striving to remain aware that just as we have created words like television, computer, and space station, and set aside words and expressions such as ticking and ice box, our ancestors had to do the same. While they took up German words like hex, sauerkraut, fresh, hoodlum, and kindergarten, Spanish words such as barbecue, chocolate, and tornado, French sounds like bayou, levee, depot, and chowder, Indian words such as hickory, pecan, hominy, moccasin, and raccoon, and invented the likes of popcorn, sweet potato, eggplant, bullfrog, and backswoodsman, they left behind them that many and more terms and sounds no longer needed in their daily lives, such were improlificate, peel, horse tree and the long "A" sounds of England, such as fahst for fast, dahnce for dance, and hoff for half.

Then too, whether the words be new or of remote origin, spelling and punctuation were not terribly important to our forebears; if the message was a simple one - and most were - a detailed and precise management of words was not called for. To the merchants and scribes of 1725, the esoteric pronouncements of the grammarians of today would have been viewed as but a waste of time and talent.

Just as good researchers never make judgements concerning the conduct, attitudes, and institutions of ancestors, likewise we must make no evaluations of their spelling, punctuation, and grammar. They got along very well without our rules of grammatical propriety, and used, adopted, or invented those words they found necessary. Here are a few of those myriad sounds and expressions.

ABBREVIATIONS

An entry in the early Surry County, Virginia, court records states that a jury

> "...returned for virdt. we find no caus: of accon
> upon ye defdts. motn: the juryes verdt is confirm. the suit
> dismist and the sd Hines ordrd to pay all Costs als exo."

That order meant, simply, that the jury's verdict was that the plaintiff had no cause of action against the defendant. After the verdict the plaintiff moved that the jury confirm (probably by voice) that indeed they had so decided, which they did, whereupon the court dismissed the lawsuit. Hines - the loser - was ordered to pay all court costs, and an execution was ordered in case he failed to pay those sums."

In early times, the difficulty of writing with a quill pen, coupled with the tedium arising from the many repetitive phrases, especially in legal writings, court reports, and in the daily entries of merchants and bookkeepers, considerably more so than today, made it convenient to abbreviate many names, words, and phrases. Such abbreviations were limited only by the imagination of the writer, hence the following are but a few of the more common ones. Notice too, that many given names were written by setting forth a few of the first letters, often followed by a period, colon, or the last letter, e.g, Richard often was Richd, William was Wm. or Wm:, James was Ja: or Jas, Henry was Hen., Elizabeth was Eliz., Catherine was Cath., Edward was Ed:, Law: was Lawrence, Xtoph: and Xor were Christopher, and so on.

Commas and other punctuation marks often were not used by some writers, while others did so with great consistency. Further, there were two (2) symbols commonly used in early days that we no longer employ, namely, the crossed p (𝓅 or 𝓅) and the thorn (🜝) or (𝔶).

As to those, the crossed p was used particularly for the prefixes per, pre, pro, and pur, and generally for any word commencing with a p where the following letters obviously revealed the meaning, e.g, Pish for parish, phaps for perhaps, psnt or psent for present, ppcon for proportion, pservation for preservation, psonal for personal, pbate for probate, ptest for protest, pduce for produce, pticular for particular, and pill meaning peril, etc. The thorn represented the sound th, and commonly appeared as "ye" for "the" (our ancestors were not saying "ye"), yt for it, yat for that, yis or ys for this, yose for those, yer or yere for there, etc. Some of the more common abbreviations follow.

Common Abbreviations

& caske = with cask, container

&c = and so forth, etc.

= a hyphen (-)

@, a) = at, as "at @ 10 cents lb."

10br, Xbr = December

7br:, 7ber = September

8br:, 8ber = October

9br:, 9ber = November

Ab:, Abrhm = Abraham

accot., acct., acompt, accon = account, or action at law

Admr., admr., admr = administrator

Admrx., Admx: = administratrix

aforsd, aforesd: = aforesaid

agt. = against or agent

als., als, alsoe, als. = alius, the second, also

Ano., An. = year, as in "Ano 1683"

appls, applls = appeals, as in law

Apr., Aprill, Abrill = April

att, att. = at or attorney

attachmt, attachm: = attachment, as in law

Augst., Aug., Augs. = August

bal., ball, ball: = an account balance

bbl= barrel

B.L.M.= U.S. Bureau of Land Management

Capt. = Captain

Clke., Clk., Cl., Cl Ct., Cl CT., ClCt: = Clerk (of a court or county)

cold., col.: = abbreviation for negro or black person, often found in legal documents and censuses.

Coll., Colln., Col. = Colonel

complt. = complaint

confest = confessed, as in confession of a judgement

Cort, Crte. = court

Cr or cr. = as now, a credit

cwt. = a hundredweight; one hundred and twelve pounds, e.g., "The inventory revealed three cwt. of bronze."

deced., decd., dcd. = deceased

Decmb., Decmbr., Dec. = December

defendt., defend. defdt. = defendant

demi, demi-, dem.: abbreviation for one half or smaller than.

dep., depty = deputy

D.O.W. = died of wounds

dol, $: abbreviation for U.S. dollar and Spanish milled dollar, and occasionally an early Peso.

dischd, discd. = discharged

Dr., dr. = as now, a debtor, debt, or indebted to, especially in account ledgers

drest = dressed (as in meat)

dyet = food, meals, as in a prisoner's dyet

Esq., esqur = esquire

Ex:, ex., Exx, exx: = executor, executrix

Excelly = Excellancy

exit. atta: = attachment was signed and issued by the court

exit: it goes forth, the issuance of a process, writ, etc., by a court

exon, excn., exec., execn: = execution, as in law suits

F.A.S.G.: a Fellow Of The American Society Of Genealogists, an honor society limited to 50 members.

F.I.G.R.S.: a Fellow Of The Irish Genealogical Research Society (Ireland), an honor awarded those who have made outstanding contributions to Irish research.

F.N.G.S.: a Fellow Of The National Genealogical Society, an honor awarded for outstanding contributions to American or British genealogical research.

F.S.G: a Fellow Of The Society Of Genealogists, an honor awarded for outstanding contributions to British genealogy (London).

Febr., FebR., Feb. = February

fi. fa. = a writ of fieri facias

fiveteen = fifteen

fower = four (4)

gal., gall.: abbreviation for gallon.

Genll. = General, an officer

Govr., Gov:, Govr: = Governor, Royal Governor

grand jur, grnd jur = grand jury

handks, hk, hhk = handkerchief or handkerchiefs

hhd., hd. = *hogshead*, see definition.

Honble = Honorable

importacon = importation

imps.= *imprimis*, see definition.

inqst = inquest, as in coroner's inquest

Janry., JanRy., Jan., Jan = January

Joyne = in litigation, an assertion or claim by one and the response thereto by another

Ju, Ju. = June

judgmt, judgmnt, etc., = judgement, as at law

Jul. = July

Junr., Jr. = junior

K.I.A. = killed in action

lb.= *pound*, see definition.

Lt. = Lieutenant

Lt. Coll., Lt. Col. = Lt. Colonel

m., M = thousand

M.I.A. = missing in action

Madm., Mdm, mdm = Madam

Maj:, Majr. = Major

Mar., Mar, mRch = March

Matys., Mats:, majt. = Majesty's, as in his Majesty's horse

mrkd, mrked = marked, branded, as in cattle

M.T., MT = early, the Michaelmas term of court, November 2 - November 25

N.A. = non allocatur, not allowed

n.o.v., judgment n.o.v. = notwithstanding the verdict of a jury

non est invent, non est inv, non est inventus, N.E.I.: = notation by an officer of court that a person sought was not found; usually meant recently deceased

no. vo. = nolens volens, with or without consent

Novmbr., Novm, Novmb = November

O.C. = Orphan's Court

o.c. = ope consilio, an accessory, usually criminal

Oct. Oct = October

ordrd, ordr = ordered, order

orpht, Orpht, orpns. = orphan, orphans

O.S. = old style calendar (Julian)

o.s.p. = died without issue

P.O.W. = prisoner of war

p: = per, as in an amount chargeable to a purchase

p:pole, p:poll = per person

p:cells = parcels, usually of land (with or without a crossed p)

pds., #, Pounds = pounds of weight

Pish (crossed p), Parsh = parish

plt. = plaintiff

plu., plur., plur: = pluries, a 3rd or subsequent writ, warrant, or court order

powr. = any power to act for another, as in power of attorney

P.P. propria persona, in propria persona = a litigant who represents himself

pr, pr., prs. = two (2) or a pair; a number of pairs

psentmt = a presentment - charge - made by a grand jury

pte. = part

pymt, pymnt = payment

q.e.n. = wherefore *execution* (q.v.) should not issue

qrtr, qtr, qr. = quarter

recd. = received

reffrd = referred

reqt. = request

R. = king or queen

Rt., Rt. Honab: = Right Honorable, a title

rt:, rt. = right, as in a right of dower

rudimnts, rudmnts = rudiments

sd. = said

Senr:, Senr., Sen: = senior

Sept. = September

servt., serv. = servant, indentured or otherwise

sm, sm., sma = small

Sterl. = Sterling

sub-, sub/ = as in sub-Sheriff, a deputy or chief assistant

sufft., sufftly = sufficient, sufficiently

suite = suit, as at law

T = township

to., to-w = to-wit, e.g., "He addressed the petition to the richest residents of the precinct, to., the Parkeses, the Harrisons, and others."

tobo., tob. = tobacco

v., vs., = versus, as in a law suit

virdt:, Virdt:, verd:, verdt = verdict, usually of a jury

Virga:, Virga. = Virginia

W.I.A. = wounded in action

warrt. = warrant

wch. = which

wido:, wido. = widow

wth., wt. = with

xt = next, as in next friend

xt. court, xt. crt. = next term of court

Xtian, xtian = Christian

yds = yards

yre = year

The SAXON AND ENGLISH ALPHABETS.

Ā	A	a	a	O	O	o	o
B	B	b	b	P	P	p	p
C	C	c	c	Q	Q	cp	q
D	D	ƀ	d	R	R	ɲ	r
Є	E	e	e	S	S	ſ	ſ
F	F	ŗ	f	T	T	τ	t
Ⴚ	G	ȝ	g	U	U	u	u
Þ	H	h	h	V	V	v	▼
I	I	ı	i	ɯ	W	ƿ	w
K	K	k	k	X	X	x	x
L	L	l	l	Y	Y	ẏ	y
ⱈ	M	m	m	Z.	Z.	z	z
N	N	ŋ	n				

Th Ð ȣ þ.   That ƀ.   And ȝ

The alphabet as illustrated in Samuel Johnson's famous 1802
Dictionary of the English Language.

A

A.E.F.: See **World War I.**

a- (a prefix): from the Scottish dialect, common in the **Scotch-Irish** (q.v.) settlements of the Southern Appalachians, even now, e.g., "Their expressions such as was a-goin', was a-coming, is a-doing, was a-washin', and goin' a-fishing are typical of the Scotch-Irish influence."

a consilius, a cons.: of counsel, e.g., "A person's name appearing at the end of a legal document or writing, followed by the words 'a consilius' reveals that person to have been an attorney in that matter."

a la daub: food suspended in flavored gelatin; in **jelly** (q.v.), e.g., "Mrs. Connor served pheasants, partridges, quail, and fish a la daub."

a menso et thoro: a separation of husband and wife, literally from table and bed; a separation, not a divorce, e.g., "Early separations a menso et thoro reveal marital differences not legally sufficient for or resulting in divorces." Also see **divorce.**

a posteriori: from or by reason of what follows; where the effect reveals the cause, e.g., "She could not convey the land away, a posteriori the **entailment** (q.v.)."

a vinculo matrimonii: a divorce as we know the term today; a dissolution of the marriage bonds, to be distinguished from a divorce **a mensa et thoro** (q.v.), e.g., "Their Pennsylvania divorce a vinculo matromonii left both parties free to remarry."

ab initio: from the beginning, e.g., "The court ordered the trespasser to pay the fair rental value of the property ab initio, that is, since the first day of his being there without permission."

ab intestato: ownership through the death of another without a will (**intestate**, q.v.), e.g., "The court order related that she owned the land ab intestato."

abandon: a giving up or relinquishment with intent to not ever again take up, e.g., "Since he was said to 'have abandoned' the grant, the researcher knew that Drake was alive at the date of the abandonment."

abate, plea in abatement: a reduction in amount or rights; a request for a reduction or diminution of an amount or quantum of rights, e.g., "The court abated as excessive the damages awarded by the county court"; "Having newly learned of an additional child who went 'West', the lawyer made a plea in abatement that the legacies be reduced proportionately."

abettor: one who aids and encourages another, e.g., "In 1676 William West was one of the abettors of Bacon."

abode: a place of dwelling, residence, "domicile," e.g., "His statement that his abode was in Smith County reveals that he likely was required to vote there."

abolition, Abolitionists: those of the period of the Civil War and the years preceding who actively sought and spoke out for the freedom of slaves and the end of the institution of slavery, e.g., "**Uncle Tom's Cabin** (q.v.) brought the abolitionists to new levels of outcry."

abscess: early, a pocket or site of any infection or undue tenderness, whether inside or without the body, e.g., "In 1852, Asa Sherwood was said to have died of an 'abscess in the side', probably acute appendicitis."

absolution: a remission of sins or penance, e.g., "At the point of death, he requested absolution."

abstract: pertinent or principal portions of documents that tend to prove title to real property; in genealogy, a statement or setting forth of pertinent portions of a writing or document; the act of selecting pertinent portions of a writing, e.g., "She did a scholarly abstract of the Nash County personal property tax records"; "She abstracted the recorded deeds of Rowan County." See also **extract.**

abuse: early, to seduce or attempt to seduce; an unjust censure; an ill use of anything, e.g., "John Drake abused Ann West, and was required to apologize for his actions in open court"; "She abused the privileges given her as an apprentice."

abut: reveals a jointure of tracts of land, e.g., "In early descriptions, the ends of property abutted and sides were said to **adjoin** (q.v.)."

accomplice: one of two or more people who, with knowledge, intentionally and voluntarily undertakes a crime, e.g., "The old entry having recited that he was an accomplice revealed their common plan and execution of the crime."

accompt: early, an account or accretion of debt, e.g., "To his accompt with Wren, he charged 3 **ells** (q.v.) of serge."

accord and satisfaction: a settlement made by one against whom a claim or right of action exists, e.g., "His accord and satisfaction was not considered to be an admission of the debt."

acknowledge, acknowledgement: affirming the truth or validity of an act or words of oneself or of another; that portion of a writing wherein the validity or truth of the document is confirmed, e.g., "At their request, she acknowledged the deed to bear their signatures"; "The acknowledgement in the lease also bore the signature of a neighbor."

acquittance: a deliverance or release from an offense; a determination that one did not act as alleged, e.g., "His acquittance of the charges was noted in the Loose Papers."

acre right: in New England, a varying right to the use and enjoyment of the common land of the town, e.g., "A five acre right in the town was equal to at least fifty acres of upland and five acres of meadow."

acre: a common measure of area; a parcel of land equal to 440 square yards, or 160 perches; 43,560 sq. ft, e.g., "A square mile is 640 acres, a **section** (q.v.) also is a square mile, and 36 square miles - 36 sections - are a **township** (q.v.)."

acta publica: matters well-known to the public or transacted before officers or officials, e.g., "Her acknowledgement before the justice of the peace was said to be acta publica."

actio quod jusso: suit against an owner for a wrongful act of his slave, e.g., "He sued Harrison actio quod jusso by reason of damage done by the slave, Kitt ."

action: now, in genealogy and law, a lawsuit or claim at law or in equity; early, an action personal was a right of one person against another, an action real was by one person against another who possessed some property sued for, and an action mixt was one that sought the recovery of some property, and also was against the person who held it, e.g., "His action was against the administrator and sought a division of the cattle"; "His action mixt was for the return of the three cows and for the profit lost because the defendant refused to return them."

actionable: punishable, redressible, or that which admits of an action at law or in equity, e.g., "His use of the neighbors' land without permission was actionable."

ad litem: for this suit or proceeding, e.g., "Since the person suing was under age, Jones was appointed guardian ad litem." See also **next friend.**

adjoined: reveals a jointure of tracts of land, e.g., "In early descriptions, the ends of property were said to **abut** (q.v.) and sides were said to adjoin."

adjudge: to judge or decree; to declare that one position or contention prevails over another, e.g., "In light of the evidence, she was adjudged insane."

adjudicate: to adjudge, to decide a case or matter involving the law or equity, e.g., "As the one hearing the case, it was his task to adjudicate as to her sanity."

administrator, administratrix: a person, male or female, appointed by a court to administer the estate of one who has died a) without a will, or b) with a will wherein no executor was named, or where he who was named in the will was not qualified or chose not to serve, e.g., The court appointed him and her as administrator and administratrix c.t.a. (**cum testamento annexo,** q.v.), respectively of the estate of John Smith." See also **administrator with will annexed.**

administrator with will annexed, administratrix w.w.a.: a person, male or female, appointed by the court to administer an estate where the will does not control or is defective, e.g., "The will was not witnessed legally, so the court was required to appoint an administrator with the will annexed."

administrators' bonds: See **bonds.**

adoption: A legal process whereby one makes someone else's child legally his or her own; where adoptive parents undertake the duties of natural parents to a child, and the adopted child gains the rights, privileges, and duties of a natural child; judicial or political recognition of an assumption of the duties of parenthood by persons who are not the natural parents. e.g., "They sought a decree of adoption when they assumed parental duties over little John."

adult, adulthood: at Civil Law, a male of fourteen or more or a female of twelve or more years; at common law, twenty one or more years old, however in some jurisdictions eighteen was viewed as adulthood; sometimes early, that age at which one's peers presumed him or her to be able to manage his or her own affairs; not necessarily synonymous with "of age" which carries legal connotations, e.g., "The neighbors considered him to be at adulthood, even though he was but fifteen." Also see *of age.*

adverse possession: an intentional holding of and claiming real property as against the world and the rightful owner, e.g., "Even though he claimed to own it and lived on the land for three years, the claim was denied since the Tennessee State Code required eight years before one could claim ownership through adverse possession."

adze, adz: a tool for different uses with blades of various shapes placed at right angles to the handle, used to shape wood, e.g., "Since the inventory revealed a *cooper's* (q.v.) adze, the researcher had evidence of the occupation of the ancestor."

affiance: an early term meaning to betroth or to bind another through a promise of marriage, e.g., "The court held that he was to pay £50 and costs by reason of the breach of his affiance."

affiant, affidavit: one who, before one authorized to administer oaths, swears or affirms the truth of facts set forth in an affidavit, e.g., "The affiant signed the affidavit and then *acknowledged* (q.v.) the truth of it before a *Notary Public* (q.v.)."

affinity: the relationship between people whose kinship is by marriage, and not "by blood"; the relationship between a husband and his wife's relatives is by affinity, e.g., "The children of her sister-in-law are related to her by affinity." Also see *consanguinity.*

affirmation: a declaration, in lieu of an oath, as to the truth or validity of a fact, signature, or writing, by one whose religious convictions prohibit oaths (Quakers and Mennonites were so prohibited), e.g., "Since Ben Beeson affirmed the deed between John Jennings and Will Beeson, the researcher had a clue to his religious beliefs."

affix: to add to, usually at the end, e.g., "His seal was affixed after the parties executed the deed."

aforesaid, abovesaid, said: words used in legal documents that refer to a person, object, proposition, or premise previously set forth in the same document, e.g., "In the will, she wrote of the 'family farm' and then of several other tracts, and distinguished between them by referring to the former as the 'said family farm'."

A.G.: an Accredited Genealogist; one who has passed the rigorous test administered by Family History Library (FHL) of Salt Lake City.

age of consent: early, that age at which one might marry without the permission of the parents; now, that age is determined by statute, usually eighteen or twenty one, e.g., "In North Carolina, the age of consent for marriage is eighteen."

agothy: thought to be a very expensive fabric, now unknown, "Revealing its quality, John Brown's account related the purchase of 1 3/4 yds of agothy at 10S/6p per yard, while the finest *lawn* (q.v.) sold but for 3S a yard."

ague: an early term meaning any intermittent fever and chills; a fever, early thought to be a disease rather than a symptom of one, e.g., "He suffered from agues over many years."

ague root: black snakeroot, e.g., "In early Virginia, ague root was the most common 'cure' administered for a shivering and shaking accompanied by chills, the ague."

ahnentafel: (Ger., ancestor chart or table) a genealogical numbering system which traces the ancestry of an individual back in time, assigning that individual the number 1. The relationship and sex of any of that individual's ancestors may be determined, since the number of the father is always twice that of the child (thus, always even), and the number of the mother is always twice that of the child, plus one (thus, always odd). "In Bob Jones's ahnentafel, since he is number 1, his father is number 2 and his mother is number 3. His paternal grandfather is 4 and his paternal grandmother is 5. His maternal grandfather is 6 and his maternal grandmother is 7. His paternal great-grandparents are therefore 8, 9, 10, and 11, and his maternal great-grandparents are 12, 13, 14, and 15.

Air Corps: the name given the organization of military aircraft and the crews and adjunct personnel necessary to maintain them, prior to the organization of the U.S. Air Force, e.g., "After World War II, Those pilots who flew for the Army Air Corps found themselves in the U.S. Air Force."

air rifle: See *windgun.*

airs, putting on: referred to those who pretended to an affluence or station above them, e.g., "Driving about in his doored carriage, he was considered to be putting on airs."

Alamo, siege of: that siege, commencing on 23 February, and battle of 6 March, 1836, in which Travis, Crockett, and 188 Texans were killed at the Alamo by General Santa Anna and some 3000 Mexicans, e.g., "Bowie was one of those killed at the Alamo."

Alaska Gold Rush: See *Klondike gold rush.*

Albemarle Colony: that settlement of the mid-1650s of Virginians and Marylanders across the Dismal Swamp in the area east of Chowan River and bordering Albemarle Sound in present day North Carolina, e.g., "Many of the names known to the Albemarle Colony may yet be found in Bertie and Chowan Counties of North Carolina."

alchemy, arkemy: the ancient investigation of chemistry; also, an alloy containing copper or brass, gold in color and often used in tableware or decorative housewares, e.g., "Early alchemists attempted to make gold by mixing chemicals and metals together"; "The mortar and pestle found in the inventory were of alchemy."

alcoholism: as recently, early thought to be a weakness of the body and treated as an ailment, e.g., "For her alcoholism, Dr. Drake prescribed cinchona, opium, zinc oxide, capsicum, and purges."

ale: an ancient intoxicating drink made by introducing malt to hot water, and then allowing fermentation and adding flavoring or sweeteners, e.g., "Barley was a favorite grain from which to make English ale."

alias, als, als, alius dictus: meaning simply, another, but used to mean another or different name either assumed or by which a person is known; frequently used to denote the maiden name of a married daughter, e.g., "The writ referred to her as Jane Parker als Huntt, revealing to the researcher that one was likely her maiden name and the other her married name."

aliquot: any fraction, e.g., "He had an aliquot share of the estate."

alius capius: an order by a court, usually to a sheriff, issued when a prior similar or identical order has failed or not been fulfilled, e.g., "The old order read 'als. capius', so she knew that since a prior capius had gone unsatisfied perhaps the ancestor had not lived there."

All Saints Day: an ancient and religious holiday observed on November 1, e.g., "All Saints Day was celebrated widely in old England and the early American colonies."

All Souls Day: an ancient and religious holiday observed on November 2, the day following All Saints Day, e.g., "In the early colonies, All Saints Day and All Souls Day usually were celebrated together."

allay: See **alloy.**

allopathic medicine: as now, that practice of healing early taught by many physicians and schools; affecting healing and cures through the administration of remedies and medicines, e.g., "Being a practitioner of **homeopathic** (q.v.) medicine, those of the allopathic discipline disapproved of his methods.

alloy: as now, a mixture of metals, e.g., "In early English and very early colonial law, any alloy containing silver could be and often was called lacus."

alms: money or things of value given for the relief of the poor, e.g., "As alms, he bequeathed ten shillings for the poor of the parish."

almshouse: a poorhouse; a residence for those who must rely upon charity, i.e., alms, e.g., "In the 1850 census Martha Drake was revealed to be residing in the almshouse."

alternative writ: an order of a court that a person either do as set forth or show cause to the court why it should not be done, e.g., "The alternative writ provided that he return Kitt to his master or come before the court and show why he should not."

amanuensis: early, a stenographer; one who takes dictation, e.g., "Before literacy was commonplace, the calling of amanuensis was a most worthwhile goal."

ambergris: a secretion from the innards of the sperm whale, long used in perfumery, e.g., "The pantries of the rich of the 17th, 18th, and early 19th centuries usually listed ambergris for the making of colognes, and scented body lotions, etc."

ambrotype: a common, early **picture** (q.v.) created without printing, by placing the negative on a dark background, e.g., "Before the development of the process of printing a photo from a negative, ambrotypes were considered revolutionary."

amenorrhoea: absence of menstrual flow, e.g., "Black snakeroot was thought to have value in curing gout, rheumatism, and amenorrhoea."

American Revolution, The: See *War of Independence*

American War: See *War of Independence*

amicus curiae: literally, friend of the court, e.g., "In order to protect the interests of the community, the judge allowed testimony amicus curiae in the case between the two men."

amulet, periapt: early, an object hung around the neck, thought to affect cures or have medicinal value, e.g., "Her mother made an amulet of herbs thought to cure pleurisy."

anaphrodisia: diminished sexual desire, e.g., "When anaphrodisia was present, the old doctor administered phosphorus, musk, bayberry, and nutmeg."

ancestor: any person from whom one descends, or through whom lineage is traced, e.g., "His most interesting ancestor was his great-great grandfather."

ancient deed: a deed made more than thirty years earlier, and kept in a fashion as to reveal its importance; a deed that appears to be valid and unsuspicious, e.g., "The court ruled it an ancient deed, and ordered it recorded even though the grantor ans the witnesses were dead."

ancient writings: writings at least thirty years old, that bear the marks of age, and were kept with care, thereby manifesting significance, e.g., "Of the two documents, one was a copy, and the other was admitted into evidence as an ancient writing."

ancillary administration: any administration of an estate in a state or jurisdiction other than that in which the decedent resided or was domiciled at the time of death, e.g., "Even though he lived and died in Maine, an ancillary administration was sought in New York because he owned real estate there."

andirons, chimney dogs, dogs, dog irons, fire dogs: heavy iron supports placed in a fireplace in pairs, upon which logs were burned, e.g., "The blacksmith sold heavy chimney dogs, the price being 'two shillings (2S), the pair'"; "He made andirons of old railroad rails."

andromania: nymphomania, e.g., "The entry set forth the cause of her insanity as andromania."

anemia: early often thought to be a disease, rather than a symptom, e.g., "Dr. Lockhart treated anemia with acid tonics, arsenic, iron, manganese, phosphites, and cold sponging."

anesthetics: in the early colonies, only opium and alcoholic beverages were known, then morphine was introduced, and by the early nineteenth century, laughing gas was available, e.g., "There being no morphine or opium at hand, Billy Drake underwent amputation of his leg with only whiskey as an anesthetic."

anil: See **indigo**.

animal dishes: any small covered bowl shaped like an animal or bird, e.g., "She had an animal dish shaped like a dog."

anise seed, aniseed: an ancient spice and seasoning, e.g., "She used the seeds of anise to flavor the brandy."

answer the contrary: or else; means that one will answer at law for a failure to do as ordered, e.g., "The Sussex court ordered that a certain list of people appear at the next court, or answer the contrary."

antebellum, ante-bellum: usually, those years of the nineteenth century shortly prior to the American Civil War; sometimes, any time period prior to that war, e.g., "Of the ante-bellum mansions, perhaps Lee's home at Arlington is the most typical."

anthrax: a common, early, and deadly disease of animals, particularly cattle, but also including man, in whom it was excruciatingly painful, e.g., "Upon the appearance of a carbuncle like swelling and lesion, Dr. Drake knew the patient had contracted the dreaded anthrax."

antichresis: a Civil law device similar to a chattel mortgage; a pledge by which a debtor pledges income from property to a creditor, e.g., "The Louisiana researcher must be aware of the antichresis."

antiseptics: See **vinegar of the 4 thieves**.

anvil: a very heavy iron shaping device, usually mounted on a table or bench, and used by one who shapes metal, e.g., "The blacksmith had anvils of several sizes."

ap-, a Welsh prefix meaning son of or grandson of, e.g., "Owen, a son of John Griffith, was said to be ap-Griffith." Also see **O'-, Mc-, and van -**.

Apache War: those conflicts with the Apaches that occurred between the 1871 Massacre at Camp Grant in Arizona and the capture of Geronimo in 1886, "The U.S. Cavalry was engaged off and on with the Apaches throughout the period known as the Apache War."

apartment: early, a portion of a house set aside for occupation by one person, while the rest was occupied by others, e.g., "Having been said to have a sleeping apartment in the home, it is likely that he was not a member of the family."

aphonia: a loss of one's voice, usually temporary, e.g., "Unless it was known to be cancerous, Dr. Lockhart administered mustard plasters and electricity for aphonia."

apoplexy: "stroke"; cerebral hemorrhage; usually a break or rupture of a blood vessel in the brain, not produced by an external cause, e.g., "He suffered apoplexy ("stroke"), was given **coriander** (q.v.) and crotan oil every hour, and soon died."

apothecary chest: a small, lidded, wooden chest with drawers used to store herbs, chemicals, etc., used by early apothecaries, e.g., "The appraisal listed the value of the apothecary chest as three shillings."

apothecary, pothecary: one who concocted, mixed, and sold medicines and drugs, e.g., "The apothecaries of the seventeenth century often enjoyed a greater respect than did the physicians."

appeals (courts of): See **courts of appeals.**

appraisal, appraisement: an assessment of the value of property, real or personal; in genealogy, usually the evaluation of assets belonging to a **decedent** (q.v.) at the time of death, e.g., The appraisal of the inventory was established at 3000 lbs. of tobacco."

apprentice: in genealogy, one who is bound to another for a set period of time, and who usually exchanged labor and time for sustenance, room, training in some discipline, and very often a measure of education, e.g., "At age twelve, Kersey was apprenticed to Parker to learn the **art and mystery** (q.v.) of the pewterer."

apprenticeships: See **apprentice.**

appurtenance: rights or assets contained upon, or associated or in conjunction with, real property are considered to be of value or worth, e.g., "In the deed for one half of the land, one of the appurtenances was a right to use the road across the other half."

aqua vitae: an intoxicant high in alcohol content; any spirituous liquor, e.g., "The aqua vitae listed in the inventory probably was medicinal brandy or liquor."

arbitrios: in Spanish and Mexican law, taxes imposed upon merchandise by cities and towns, e.g., "In early California and Texas, the researcher will find lists of arbitrios, which are tax lists."

architectural mirror, architectural wardrobe, etc.: any item of furniture built into the walls or basic structure of a house and complimentary to the styling and architecture of the whole, e.g. "Her architectural mirror was in the main hall."

archives, archive: a repository of those documents, writings, mementos, and artifacts that relate to the sponsor of or parental authority over that facility; also, the historic materials making up such a collection, e.g., "The state archives preserves those materials having to do with its formation and its people" "That building contains the archives."

ardent spirits: spirituous liquors, e.g., "Early records often speak of ardent spirits, meaning liquors, rums, and brandies, and not including wines." See **aqua vitae.**

armies, organization of: varied through the centuries, however in the U.S. from largest to smallest, the units of combat soldiers usually have been:

army, the largest self-sustaining unit, usually commanded by a general or lieutenant general, and named for a region or given a number, e.g., (Patton's) Third Army, (Lee's) Army of Northern Virginia;

corps, consisting of two or more *divisions*, and usually given numbers (now Roman Numerals), e.g., First Corps, Fifth Corps, XVIII Corps;

     division, made up of two or more *brigades,* and either numbered or named for the commander who often has been a major general, e.g., Second Division, Hancock's Division;

     brigades, made up of two or more *regiments,* and usually numbered or named for the commander who often was a brigadier general, e.g., Third Brigade, Texas Brigade;

     regiment, usually numbered, commanded by a colonel, and made up of a number of *companies* (8 to 10), e.g., 55th Ohio, 43rd North Carolina, or sometimes given names, e.g., Edenton Blues, Coldstream Guards, 5th U.S. Sharpshooters, 4th Fusiliers;

     battalions, made up of two or more *companies,* commanded by an officer less than a colonel, and usually numbered, e.g., 3rd Battalion;

     companies, usually lettered "A" et seq. (but no "J"), the letter being followed by the regimental name or number, and commanded by a junior officer (lieutenant, cornet, etc.), e.g., Co. K., 1st Infantry, Co. B, 7th Cavalry;

     platoons, usually numbered, commanded by a noncommissioned officer, and consisting of two or more *squads,* e.g., 1st platoon, Co. K.;

     squads, the smallest organizational unit, usually assigned a letter, and consisting of 10 soldiers, e.g., B squad, 2nd Platoon.

armoire: (Fr.) a large cabinet used as a wardrobe; sometimes, a large clothes press, usually of better wood and more or less ornate, e.g., "Since there was both a wardrobe and an armoire listed in the inventory, she might correctly guess that the armoire was more ornate, elaborate, and valuable."

armor: See **coats of arms.**

armorer: one that makes armor or weapons, or one who dresses another in armor, e.g., "In 1725, he was a metal worker and armorer in Virginia."

armorial bearings: See **coats of arms.**

arms: generally, those emblems, insignia, and colors reserved to a person or family of nobility, usually by the Crown, e.g., "His arms were similar to those of the ancient Drakes of Devon." Also see **heraldry.**

army: See **armies, organization of.**

arraign: to bring an accused person before the court and read or state the criminal charge lodged against him, to which he then pleads, e.g., "On the first day of the May court he was brought in to be arraigned and pleaded 'not guilty' "

arrow back chair: any of several styles, usually **primitive** (q.v.) and often plank bottom chairs having arrow shaped spindles, e.g., "Her primitive arrow back chair had a hickory seat and dated to 1820."

art and mystery: an early expression used to describe the knowledge needed to enter some calling, occupation, or profession, e.g., "Kersey was said to have learned the art and mystery of the pewterer."

asafoetida, asfoetida bags, asfetidy: (spelling varied) a gum or extract, originally from the East Indies, which had a strong taste and odor and was thought to have medicinal value; small bags of asfoetida worn around the neck as an **amulet** (q.v.), e.g., "The mother insisted that her children wear asfoetida bags during the winter to ward off diseases of the chest."

ascendants: our ancestors, e.g., "Ascendants are the opposite of descendants."

ascites: accumulation of fluid in the abdominal cavity; dropsy of the stomach, e.g., "An early 'cure' for ascites, usually called dropsy, was a tea of cowslips."

Ash Wednesday: a day of religious significance celebrated on the first Wednesday after Lent, e.g., "The county court was to meet on the first Monday after Ash Wednesday."

assault: a threat of harm to another coupled with the apparent ability and intention to carry it out, e.g., "His statement that unless she stopped shouting he would slap her did not constitute an assault." Also see ***battery.***

assessor: a person or board empowered to determine the value of property for purposes of taxation, e.g., "The assessor determined that the land had a tax value of $6,000.00."

asset: any property, including ***real property*** (q.v.), and ***personalty*** (q.v.), among assets, personalty is all property other than real estate, and in addition to tangible property - cattle, refrigerators, tools, etc. - intangible property, such as stocks, bonds, negotiable writings, legal claims against others, and accounts receivable are also personalty, e.g., "As assets, he had real estate, and personalty consisting of cattle, money, accounts receivable, and stock."

assignment: a transfer to another of any interest in property, e.g., "Many early land warrants were transferred by assignment to someone else, who then ***perfected*** (q.v.) the title."

assignment of dower: the legal act by which a widow's share in her husband's assets is determined in amount and set aside for her, e.g., "Her assignment of dower was made within a few days after the ***inventory*** (q.v.) and ***appraisement*** (q.v.)."

assumpsit on quantum meruit, quantum meruit: an early legal action for work or labor performed pursuant to an unwritten contract, e.g., "His action in quantum meruit sought the money due him for fourteen days' labor in the fields."

astringent bolus: See ***bolus.***

atamita: a third-great grandfather's sister, e.g., "In Louisiana, the term atamita occasionally appears, meaning one's fourth-great aunt."

atavia: one's third-great grandmother, e.g., "The term atavia occasionally appears in early Louisiana records."

atavunculus: the brother of one's third-great grandfather, e.g., "In Louisiana, the term atavunculus occasionally appears, meaning one's fourth-great uncle."

atavus: a third-great grandfather, e.g., "In Louisiana, the term atavus occasionally appears, meaning one's third-great grandfather."

attest: to swear or affirm as to truth or genuineness, e.g., "He attested to the statement that the servant had accidentally drowned." Also see ***acknowledge.***

auction, licitation, outcry: a sale of property, usually public and most often the method chosen by courts, by orally offering it to the highest bidder, usually from the courthouse steps in early times, e.g., "The sheriff was ordered to sell the goods on the courthouse steps by public auction by outcry."

autogiro, autogyro: an airplane with a revolving wing; an early twentieth-century term nearly synonymous with helicopter, e.g., "The invention of the autogiro by Sikorsky and others led to the helicopters of later years."

avunculus: a maternal uncle; one's mother's brother, e.g., "In Louisiana research, one frequently finds the term avunculus."

B

B.B. gun: See **windgun.**

B.C.G.: See **Board of Certification Of Genealogists.**

bachelors' ball: a party or dance for single men and women, e.g., "Being new in town, he was glad to receive the invitation to the bachelors' ball."

backbar: a lug in a chimney, e.g., "The **blacksmith** (q.v.) made the irons and backbars for their new cabin."

backbond: an indemnification bond given, assuring a **surety** (q.v.) that he or she would suffer no loss, e.g., "His sister posted a backbond guaranteeing the surety for the administrator that he would suffer no loss."

Bacon's Rebellion: those actions against the Indians by Nathaniel Bacon and some 500 Virginia and Maryland colonials from May to October, 1676 that were declared as treasonous by Governor Berkeley, and resulted in 23 executions before forgiveness was granted the remainder, e.g., "Bacon's Rebellion collapsed after Bacon's sudden death on 18 October, 1676."

badikins, whippletrees: iron holders or separators used to keep the chains of draft animals from entangling, e.g., "To find badikins in estate inventories is a very common occurrence."

bailiff: an officer of court, early with considerably more authority than now, quite usually appointed and charged with keeping order and assisting the judge, e.g., "The bailiff was directed to bring the witnesses to the court room."

bailiwick: a specific area of jurisdiction or control, particularly of the early bailiffs; also, slang for an area frequented or controlled by someone, e.g., "If John Jones was in his bailiwick, the Sheriff was ordered to bring him in"; "He looked upon the area of Jamestown as his bailiwick."

bake oven: unlike now, a heavy, iron, lidded cooking pot with bails and short legs, usually ten or more inches in diameter, e.g., "The bake oven was placed over hot coals drawn from the fireplace with the **stove rake** (q.v.)."

bake-kettle: a Dutch oven, e.g., "There was a black iron bake-kettle in the inventory."

bale: early, a small bucket; occasionally now, a handle for a bucket or pot; commonly now, drawer pulls, e.g., "There were two copper bales among his belongings"; "the drawer bales were missing."

baler: a machine for binding hay or other plants of long stalk, e.g., "The baler owned by Cole in 1880 was appraised at $6.00."

ball: a round projectile fired in early rifles, e.g., "The ball was placed on a small swatch of cloth and forced down into the barrel with a **ramrod** (q.v.)." Also see **muzzle loader,** , and **cap and ball,.**

balloon back chairs: any of a number of styles and designs of chairs with a rounded and balloon shaped back without splats, e.g., "Her twin balloon back chairs were Victorian and were of walnut."

bandog: See **mastiff.**

bank: to arrange burning fireplace logs so as to gain the maximum benefit and longevity of burning, especially during the night, e.g., "He was careful to bank the fire before retiring."

banns (proclamation of): a requirement of the Church of England and the early Catholic Church that a marriage be announced publicly prior to its solemnization; a frequent term revealing an announcement in a church, on consecutive Sundays, that a marriage was intended, the purpose being to provide an opportunity for legitimate objections, e.g., "There having been no one speaking out against it after banns had been duly published, the priest was free to perform the marriage ceremony."

banquet table: a very long table for dining, usually having three sets of legs or three pedestals, and often with leaves, e.g., "Her mahogany Duncan Phyffe banquet table was on three pedestals."

baptism: an important, widespread, religious service or action by which one (usually, the very young) is committed to church service or thought; in genealogy, an excellent source of dates, names of witnesses, and relatives, e.g., "His great aunt and uncle were witnesses at his baptism."

baptismal bowl: a small bowl, usually of better glass and decorated, in which holy water was placed for a baptism, after which the bowl was presented to the parents or sponsors as a memento, e.g., "She had a baptismal bowl for each of her children."

barbed wire, bobwire: invented in 1874, it was a boon to the cattle business, and solved the enormous problem of fencing, e.g., "With the advent of barbed wire, for the first time in history domesticated animals could be effectively contained."

barberry: a berry of sharp taste used in making pickles, and thought to have medicinal value where an acid was to be administered, e.g., "During late summer, she gathered barberries for pickling"; "Dr. Lockhart administered barberry juice when he believed the stomach not to have sufficient acid."

barbers itch: ringworm; a red itchy, scaly fungi usually spread by the unsanitized tools of early barbers, e.g., "He caught the barber's itch, and never returned to Greer's shop."

barbers' bottles: See **cologne bottles.**

bark, barque: a common tub used to cure and tan skins; a sailing ship with three or more masts, e.g., "The barks and animal skins found in the inventory likely reveal that he was a tanner."

barkeep: an early term (later, bartender); one who tends the bar and dispenses beverages in an **inn** (q.v.), **ordinary** (q.v.), **roadhouse** (q.v.) or **pub** (q.v.), e.g., "Even though early barkeeps were entertainers, joke and tale tellers, and friends to their patrons, most of all they were bearers of the news of the day."

baronage: refers to the entirety of British **peerage** (q.v.), e.g., "The baronage of Britain has its roots in Roman times."

baronet: a commoner, yet a member of Britain's hereditary order of honor and entitled to be addressed as Sir, e.g., "A baronetcy is the rank or patent of a baronet." Also see **knight.**

barrel: 31 1/2 gallons of other than wine or petroleum, e.g., "In early Pennsylvania, oil was stored in wooden casks of 42 gallons, a bit larger than a barrel."

base begotten, base born: usually, an illegitimate birth; one born of low station, yet not illegitimate, e.g., "The support for her base begotten child would be the county"; "Even though base born, he rose to a position of respect in the community."

base fee: a conditional or determinable fee, e.g., "Since the property would revert if she died without male natural children, it was a base or conditional fee."

basin stand: a small, usually well finished stand with a shelf and drawer below, splash boards at the sides and back, and the top cut out to permit the placing therein of a large basin or bowl, e.g., "Since indoor plumbing ended their value, most basin stands ended up being kindling."

basset: a card game similar to faro played in the colonies and in Europe during the early years (1650-1750), e.g., "Maryland colonials liked to gamble, and basset and faro were two of their favorite games."

bat, laundry bat, butter bat: wooden paddles used variously for stirring, e.g., "In addition to her butter bat, she had a laundry bat used to stir clothes while they were in boiling soap water."

bathes: See **take the waters.**

battalion: See **armies, organization of.**

battery: the striking of another, e.g., "He was charged with assault and battery, since he had threatened her (the assault) and then struck her (the battery)." See **assault.**

batting: raw, usually cotton or wool, and sometimes fiber or hair sewn inside or beneath cloth or fabric to add body, thickness, or insulation, e.g., "She used cotton batting in her quilts."

Bay Psalm Book: printed first in 1640, and running through 27 editions before 1750, doubtless the colonial bestseller of all time; a song book of lyrics without music, resulting in different melodies and timing by virtually every congregation, e.g., "While the words were from the Bay Psalm Book in both cases, the New Jerseyites hardly recognized the hymns of Massachusetts."

bay: in genealogy, a color; a brown or dark red-brown horse that is lighter brown and more red than the color chestnut, e.g., "He described the horse bequeathed to his second son as 'a bay named Libby'." Also see *sorrel, chestnut, dun, roan, gray, black, buckskin, Appaloosa,* and *pinto (painted)*.

beaker: a glass or cup used for drinking liquids, e.g., "There were three beakers in the inventory."

beam: a balance or the bar of a balance (beam and balance), from which nothing more."

bearbaiting, bear baiting: the early sport of inducing several dogs to attack a chained bear, e.g., "Incredible as it now seems, bearbaiting was a popular pastime at early fairs and carnivals."

beast: See **work beasts.**

becker: a wooden dish for serving, e.g., "There were two beckers in the inventory."

bed: unlike now, usually a **tick** (q.v.), e.g., "The 1679 inventory listing of a flock bed referred to a rag- and scrapcloth-filled ticking bag - a tick."

bed and furniture: a common early expression meaning a bed (as we know it) and all that usually accompanied it located in a certain room used as a sleeping room, e.g., "The **bequest** (q.v.) of his bed and furniture meant that she was to receive the tick (bed), and the valance bedstead, a chest, the **curtains** (q.v.), a **rug** (q.v.), and a comforter."

bed lounge: See **sofa bed.**

bed warmer: a rather long-handled, metal pan with a lid into which were placed hot coals, the same rubbed over the sheets to warm the bed before retiring, and sometimes left within the bed to provide warmth for the feet, e.g., "To the pleasure of the elders of the family, through the use of the bed warmer the chill was taken from the bed."

Bedlam: originally, the hospital of St. Mary in London (Bethlehem), constructed c1250 and used as an insane asylum after about 1400; the anguish, screaming, and incoherent babbling heard there led to the term, e.g., "The anger vented by the crowd was almost bedlam."

bedroom: early, usually the main sleeping room or rooms on the first floor, e.g., "The head of the household and his wife usually occupied the bedroom, and the children slept in the **chamber** (q.v.) above."

bedside table: now called a nightstand; early, any of the many styles and designs of small, usually rectangular, single-drawered tables placed beside a bed for a lamp, medicines, pictures, etc., e.g., "She had a walnut bedside table for each of the bedsteads."

bedsores: (decubitis) those lesions - often causing deep scars - brought about by the protracted stays in bed early thought necessary to healing, e.g., "Having lain in the bed for six weeks after the amputations, Billy's bedsores were extensive and remained as scars for the rest of his life."

bedstead and cord: now called a bed frame, or simply bed; instead of slats, such bed frames had rope strung horizontally and longitudinally within them, upon which a "bed" (ticking bag, later a mattress) was placed, e.g., "In her inventory were 2 bedsteads and cords, and 2 **rugs** (q.v.)."

bee hives: See **scaps.**

Beecher's Bibles: name given to Sharp's rifles in 1856 by the Free States Party, and used in the Kansas border wars, e.g., "Connor's pioneer relatives of Lawrence, Kansas, were fortunate to avoid the wrath of Beecher's Bibles."

beer: as now, e.g., "In addition to those of today, fermented beers made of spruce oil or extract, molasses, ginger, and roots were common."

Belgian: a breed of heavy, powerful, draft horses, popular in America, and originally bred in Belgium and northern Europe, e.g., "His team was made up of four fine Belgians."

bell glass: a bell-shaped, glass dome used to display mementos; a domed glass used to protect young plants, e.g., "Her wedding shoes were placed in the bell glass, and it, then, displayed on the mantle."

belladonna (deadly nightshade): an extract of belladonna roots and leaves were widely used as an antiseptic or as a heart and respiratory stimulant, e.g., "Dr. Drake regularly administered belladonna for heart palpitations."

bellows: a hinged, sealed device, which, through opening and closing, forced air to a fire, e.g., "Through the use of his large bellows, the **blacksmith** (q.v.) was able to generate enough heat to make iron workable."

belt loom, braid loom: a common small loom used to make belts, headbands, hairbands, straps, and decorative braiding, etc., e.g., "As an old lady, she enjoyed making items for her grandchildren on the belt loom."

bench warrant: a warrant issued from a judge during a session of court, ordering the immediate seizure or arrest of a person, e.g., "The court, upon hearing the witnesses, issued a bench warrant for Parker."

benefice: See **rectory.**

beneficiary: one who benefits from an act of or provision made by another; one who inherits from another is said to be that person's beneficiary, e.g., "She was one of the beneficiaries of his insurance."

benefit of clergy, pleaded their clergy: an ancient exemption from execution granted, first, to members of the clergy even of the lowest station, and later to all who could read (usually the Fifty First Psalm), e.g., "Having 'prayed his clergy' - claimed benefit of clergy - he was ordered transported to the Virginia colony."

bengal: a common, early, striped muslin, e.g., "There was an ell of bengal charged to her 1778 account."

benjamin: a popular tailored man's coat of the Victorian and Edwardian periods, said to be named for Prime Minister Benjamin Disraeli, e.g., "Among his belongings were bands, cravats, knee stockings, and a worsted benjamin."

benzoin: a resin, often used as a stimulant and expectorant and as a base for perfumes and colognes, e.g., "Benzoin was a staple in the medicine chest of the country Doctor"; "As a **perfumer** (q.v.), he maintained a large supply of benzoin to be used as a base."

bequest, bequeath: a will provision directing that ownership in specific personal property be transferred to a named person or persons, e.g., "His bequest was a cow and a calf"; "She **devised** (q.v.) forty acres to her son, and bequeathed her favorite chair to her daughter."

beriberi, beri-beri: a disease caused by a lack of Vitamin B, common among early settlers and sailors, symptoms being emaciation and swollen and painful, sometimes paralyzed, hands and feet, e.g., "Early Virginia settlers frequently had no eggs, vegetables, nor citrus fruits in winter, hence many suffered from beriberi."

beryl: a semi-precious stone used as jewelry, frequently found in early inventories, e.g., "She had two beryls, an amber, and a gold ring."

Bess: See **Good Queen Bess.**

best evidence (rule of): the best evidence of which a certain proposition is susceptible; original, as opposed to that which derives from some original source, e.g., "Rather than one's recollection, a tombstone is the best evidence of the place of burial of that person."

betroth, betrothal, betrothed: an exchange of promises to marry, e.g., "As his intended wife, she was said to be betrothed to him."

betterment: an improvement (beyond a repair) to an estate that increases its value, e.g., "The court decided that the administrator was entitled to be compensated for the betterment of the buildings."

betty lamp, phoebe lamp: betty lamp, pre-kerosene, shallow, open bowl-shaped lamps, with a nipple through which a rag was drawn and lit, the other end resting in grease or **tallow** (q.v.); phoebe lamp, the same but with a dish or small pan to catch the drippings, e.g., "With the advent of kerosene, housewives were glad to be rid of the smoking, dirty, and often stinking, betty and phoebe lamps."

bettys, Betties: See **desserts, early.**

beyond sea, ouster le mer, over sea: beyond the control or jurisdiction - the 'legal reach' - of the British Isles or the colonial government, e.g., "The sheriff had learned that the accused criminal had boarded a sea-going vessel for parts unknown, so the warrant was returned to the court endorsed 'The defendant is beyond sea'."

Bible box: See **Bible stand.**

Bible stand, bible box: a small easel or box-shaped stand used for family devotions, usually made of better wood, strong and wide enough to hold an opened Bible, often with a hinged top revealing a compartment to store the Bible for protection, and often kept in the parlor, better room, or near the dining table, e.g., "Her Bible stand was of walnut and her initials had been inlaid in the surface."

big house: See **plantation house.**

bigamy: the act of entering into a marriage with one person while still legally married to another, where such a marriage is illegal, e.g., "**Polygamy** (q.v.) as practiced by Mormons was not bigamy, since in the latter there is criminal intent."

biggin: a cap or nightcap, e.g., "'...Ma in her kerchief and I in my cap....' could have been written 'kerchief and biggin'."

bile: a body fluid that aids in digestion, early thought to be a critical substance in diagnosing disease and affecting cures, e.g., "Black and yellow bile were thought to cause mental illness."

bilious, biliousness: a condition now known to result from inadequate liver function, but early thought to result from an excess of bile, hence the term, e.g., "The 'bilious plague' that appeared in Connecticut from 1794 through 1796 may have been yellow fever."

bill and crossbill: the method or complaint by which a legal action was commenced, the crossbill (cross petition, cross complaint) being a claim by the defendant against that person filing or bringing the bill (petition, complaint), e.g., "His bill was in **assumpsit** (q.v.), as was the crossbill."

bill of credit: a promissory note usually issued by a government, intended to substitute for money, e.g., "The bills of credit issued by the Continental Congress were viewed with suspicion."

bill of exchange: an order or request by one directing another to pay a certain sum to a third person, often used in the American colonies as money, e.g., "Early planters often used bills of exchange in their commerce with England."

bill of lading: a writing given by a shipper acknowledging his receipt of goods in a certain quantity and condition, often used as money in the early colonies, e.g., "There being a shortage of currency, he used bills of lading as a quite satisfactory substitute."

bill of sale: a written document evidencing the sale of personal property (sometimes including slaves) from one person to another, often recorded and indexed with early deeds, e.g., "I will need a bill of sale to confirm my purchase of the slaves Kitt and Cloe."

billiard and pea: early, a gambling game similar to modern billiards, and played on a flat table with pockets, e.g., "Among the games, the 1679 Judith Parker inventory revealed a billiard and pea."

bird gun: See **shotgun.**

bird spit: a metal pan with feet used to roast small pieces of meat, birds, and animals, e.g., "There were three trivets and a bird spit in the inventory."

birding piece: See **shotgun.**

birds eye: a common cloth (stuff) with a small round pattern similar to the eye of a bird, e.g., "The inventory revealed that she had two summer dresses of birds eye."

biscuit ware, bisque ware: unglazed porcelain, very common through the Victorian era, and even down to now, e.g., "Her collection of biscuit ware had been gathered over many years."

bishop: an intoxicating drink made of wine, oranges, and sugar, e.g., "When oranges were available at the dock, the innkeeper offered bishops at his bar."

bit: that implement (metal, rope, or leather) placed in the mouth of a horse and connected to the reins or harnessing, by which commands are given to the animal; a metal drilling tool turned by a **brace,** q.v., (early) or a drill (now), e.g., "The horse took the bit in his teeth and ran wild"; "Braces and bits were indispensable to the wagonmaker."

bitch: a common term used to describe a female dog, early and now, e.g., "His Red Bone bitch had eight pups." Also see **slut.**

bites (poisonous): animal poisons not being understood, unusual remedies were prescribed, e.g., "His scorpion bite was treated by applying silver nitrate and potassium hydroxide to the wound, and by giving the patient alcohol and ammonia to drink."

bitters: early, a strong intoxicating drink, often taken and prescribed for their supposed (often, pretended) medicinal value; later, strong spices or seasoning made from leaves or roots, usually used in liquors and occasionally in foods, e.g., "After a long day, he always insisted on having his bitters"; "Her fruitcake recipe called for a teaspoon of Angostura bitters."

bittlin: a milk bowl, usually of wood or glass, and occasionally of metal or pewter, e.g., "Among her kitchen utensils was a pewter bittlin."

black betty: a spirituous liquor, given as a reward to participants in a wedding, e.g., "The guests raced on horseback from a point a mile or so away to the bride's house, the winner receiving a bottle of black betty as a prize."

black book: See **liber niger.**

black pudding: See **blood pudding.**

Black Codes: those legislative enactments following the Civil War by which the Southern states sought to subvert the rights of the Negro, e.g., "One of the results of the Black Codes was the **Freedman's Bureau** (q.v.)."

Black Death: See **bubonic plague herein.**

Black Dutch: Sephardie Jews who married Dutch Protestants to escape the Inquisition, many of their descendants later moving to the Americas, the "black" referring to their dark hair and complexions; perhaps rarely, German immigrants from the Black Forest region, e.g., "For the most part, the Black Dutch came after 1740."

Black Hawk War: the name given the defeat of the upper Mississippi Sauk and Fox Indians under Chief Black Hawk in 1832, e.g., "At age 23, Lincoln was a Captain of Volunteers in the Black Hawk War."

black maria: a closed wagon used to move prisoners about; a "paddy wagon", e.g., "References to black marias are not uncommon in early New Jersey records."

black pudding: a common pudding made of corn meal, blood from swine or cattle, and seasoning, e.g., "Black pudding was a common dish in both the British Isles and the early American colonies."

black sheep: a reprobate or person thought to have a undesirable or reprehensible character, e.g., "Having been jailed twice, he was the family black sheep."

Black Thursday: See **Roaring Twenties.**

Blackbeard: See **pirates.**

blacking case, blacking cabinet: a small, usually ornate, wooden box seat, with a raisable top concealing a compartment for storage of materials used to clean and shine - "blacken" - shoes and boots, e.g., "Only the wealthy had such extravagances as a blacking case."

blackleg: early expression referring to those who made a living by sharp practices, especially at gambling at racetracks, e.g., "His blackleg actions were not quite illegal, but surely were not acceptable to the gentlemen of the town."

blacksmith: one who works with iron, e.g., "The village blacksmith was a most important member of the community."

blacktongue: pellagra; caused by a niacin deficiency, a disease causing severe diarrhea, nervous disorder, and blotches and scaling of the skin, e.g., "The often fatal blacktongue ravaged the neighborhood of Tarboro in 1844 and 1845."

blain: very early, a "pustule"; an early term for any blister or seeping swelling in the skin, e.g., "Since she thought the swelling had been caused by the cold, wet weather, she described it as a chillblain."

blanket box: a common item of early furniture; a lidded chest with no drawers used to store blankets and clothes, and to protect the same against insects and moths, e.g., "As was to be expected, the inventory listed two blanket boxes."

blanket chest: usually, a short-legged chest with a top hinged upward, and often with a cedar lining, designed to store blankets safe from insects, mice, etc., e.g., "Her walnut blanket chest was lined with cedar."

blast, black stem rust: a fungus that often ddestroyed early Northeast and Midwest wheat crops, e.g., "Before learning that blast resulted from planting wheat near the fungus-bearing barberry, farmers thought the disease was caused by a "vapor breaking out of the Earth."

bleeding, phlebotomy: the process of letting blood by opening a vein or artery, the same thought to have medicinal value through the reduction of internal pressures, e.g., "The **chirurgeons** (q.v.) bled Washington many times before his death of pneumonia, which actions greatly weakened him." Also see **cupping.**

blind tiger: the house of a bootlegger who permitted drinking on the premises, e.g., "He was said to spend every evening with the blind tiger."

blinders: that part of animal harnessing that limits peripheral vision, and so forces their attention forward, e.g., "He used blinders on the team to prevent them from being distracted."

blister: See **poultice.**

blistering: one of the methods, along with bleeding, vomiting, and sweating, by which the bodily humours were thought to be purged, adjusted, or balanced, e.g., "Blistering was prescribed when it was thought that an excess of certain humours was the cause of some ailment."

blocks and tackle, block and tackle: pulleys (blocks) and rope (tackle) so arranged as to gain mechanical advantage, common in early rural and work settings, e.g., "With the blocks and tackle, one man could easily move a thousand pounds."

bloodletter, bloodlet: one who was knowledgeable in phlebotomy, e.g., "The old woman was the family bloodletter." See **cupping,** and **bleeding.**

bloodstone: a deep green and blood-red semi-precious stone used as jewelry, often found in early inventories, e.g., "She had an amber necklace, a silver pin, and a bloodstone ring."

bloody flux, flux: See **dysentery.**

blubber: whale flesh, which, upon rendering, yields whale oil, e.g., "Blubber had many uses, including the dressing of leather."

blue: other than the common meaning, a slate, dark gray, or dove colored horse, dog, or (occasionally) a cow, e.g., "His will described the gelding as a blue."

bluing: (blue) indigo dissolved in water and used in dying cloth, e.g.,"Indigo was the prime source of bluing available in the early days, and when not available, berries were used."

blunderbuss: an early firearm of large caliber; a firearm with a bell shaped muzzle, often depicted with early colonials, e.g., "The Pilgrims of New England often are portrayed hunting with blunderbusses."

boar: See **swine.**

board, boarding house, boarder, room and board: food, drink, and entertainment provided a guest at an inn, along with **room** (q.v.); that amount paid for food and drink in an inn or "boarding house"; any person, other than immediate family, residing within a household, e.g., "As room and board, his sleeping room was $1.50 per week, and his food and drink twice a day were an additional $1.75"; "In the census of 1870, the farm hand was shown as a boarder."

board cloth: a tablecloth; a cloth placed on the eating boards, e.g., "The inventory listed a 'deble' (table) and 3 board cloths."

Board For Certification Of Genealogists (B.C.G.): a non-profit organization of genealogists, having as its principal purpose to insure a measure of quality and competence in both the hobby and the field of professional genealogy, e.g., "B.C.G. offers voluntary certification in six (6) categories, i.e., Certified Genealogical Record Searcher (C.G.R.S.); Certified American Lineage Specialist (C.A.L.S.); Certified American Indian Lineage Specialist (C.A.I.L.S.); Certified Genealogist (C.G.); Certified Genealogical Lecturer (C.G.L.); and Certified Genealogical Instructor (C.G.I.)."

boarders: See **board, etc.**

boarding house: See **board, etc.**

boards: a dance floor, e.g., "He spent most of the evening on the boards."

bob: a short women's hairstyle, dating from the Civil War, and still fashionable from time to time; a bunch of flowers or ribbons worn as a corsage, e.g., "The bob was seen in fashion publications of the 1860s"; "She wore a bob of pink flowers and fern."

bobcherry: an early child's game played without the use of hands, wherein a cherry or piece of candy was dangled and moved about at mouth level, and children sought to seize it with their mouths, e.g., "They played **grey wooley** (q.v.) and bobcherry."

bobs, ear bobs: ear rings, e.g., "Ear bobs were not commonly worn by other than women of affluence."

bobtail driver: early, a co-venturer in hauling goods by wagon; one who drives a wagon partially at the direction and profit of the owner and partly on his own account; also, occasionally one who drove a laundry wagon, e.g., "He was described as a bobtail driver, and worked for Jones and himself."

bodice: early, a quilted waistcoat, often with whalebone stays; a corset; a woman's undergarment extending from the neck to the waist, e.g., "There were two linen bodices listed in the inventory."

bodkin: a small, sharp-pointed tool similar to an awl; sometimes, a dagger, e.g., "The shoemaker's belongings included two bodkins."

Bohea: a popular variety of tea from India, commonly consumed by the wealthy of the colonies, e.g., "The ship *Lion* brought spices and Bohea on its return from Singapore."

bole: a measure of grain equaling six bushels, e.g., "He sold eight boles of corn at one shilling (1S) the bole."

bolster, boulster, bed and bolster: a thin pad for lounging or resting, sometimes used as a pad under **ticks** (q.v.), and often used on **daybeds** (q.v.), e.g., "Virtually every inventory of the seventeenth century included at least one boulster."

bolter: See **searce.**

bolus: medicine taken internally, made into a soft mass larger than a pill, as in **cordial** (q.v.) (stimulative) or astringent (constrictive) boluses, e.g., "She made a cordial bolus of brandy, herbs, and honey, and an astringent bolus of zinc and copper sulfate."

bombard: a large wine barrel or large drinking utensil; a very large **jack** (q.v.), e.g., "The 1703 list of his belongings included a jack with gold decoration, several flagons, and a bombard, the last doubtless a large mug."

bona fides, mala fides: in good or bad faith, e.g., "His actions, though illegal, were bona fides in the eyes of the court."

bond: a sum of money, pledge of credit, insurance guaranty, or other thing of value deposited, usually with a court, as assurance that one will faithfully perform certain duties, e.g., "As was expected, the administrator was required to post a bond equal to twice the value of the **assets** (q.v.)."

bondmaid, bondman: one who is bound to another, quite usually as a servant, e.g., "The bondmaid was fourteen, and was bound to serve until her twenty-fifth birthday."

bondwoman: an early term often meaning a female slave, e.g., "Old Judy was a bondwoman, and was valued at but L8 Sterling."

bonesetter: early term for a surgeon (**chirurgeon,** q.v.), e.g., "They went to the bonesetter for broken limbs and dislocations."

bonnet box, bride's bonnet box, ladies' hat box: a small, lidded, wooden box in which to store a lady's hat (a bonnet), lined and often cloth-covered with decorative sewing as adornment, e.g., "She had done the needlepoint work for the cover of her bonnet box."

Bonnet, Stede: See *pirates.*

bookcase: any of the many styles and shapes of cabinets designed for the storage or display (or both) of books, the single common design feature being a writing surface, either flat or on a hinged leaf, e.g., "He had two bookcases, one a walnut cabinet with shelves above and below the writing surface, and the other, a drop front cabinet with three drawers below, and a single shelf above." Also see *side by side* and *stack bookcase.*

Boomers: name given those under Payne and Couch who sought to settle in Oklahoma in 1884, and were ousted by the U.S. Cavalry, e.g., "Some of the Boomers returned, participated in, and settled lands opened up by the **Oklahoma Land Rush** (q.v.) of 1890."

bootjack: a wooden or metal device shaped like the letter "V" so designed as to permit removal of boots without bending over or dirtying one's hands, e.g., "A bootjack often was near the door leading to the kitchen."

bootlegger, jointist: one who sells liquor or other intoxicating beverages without a license or contrary to law, e.g., "Every town in **dry** (q.v.) states has its bootleggers."

boots: See *shoes.*

boot tree: a common wooden form, shaped like a leg and foot, over which boots were placed for drying, shaping, or stretching, e.g., "There were both small and large boot trees in the inventory."

Bordelais, Burdelais: wine made of grapes of the same name, popular since the eighteenth century, e.g., "Washington often served Bordelais and Madeira."

bordello, bordel: as now, a house of prostitution, e.g., "Every colony had its bordellos."

boree: an early dance, e.g., "At parties they often danced the reels and borees."

borough, -boro: a town or small city; a portion of a city or municipality; in Pennsylvania, New Jersey, and Connecticut, that portion of a township that has been chartered as a municipality, e.g., "In some states, by definition boroughs were incorporated"; "The borough of Queens is part of New York City."

borrow fire, carry fire: to gain coals or fire from another, e.g., "Before matches, if the household fires were allowed to go completely out and one had no flint, steel and tinder, it was necessary to go to another house and borrow fire."

boss: usually, very large or fine, e.g., "They came from the woods with a boss log of walnut."

Boston Rocker: a typically American variation of the Windsor chair that first appeared in New England, and consisted of a shaped seat, a tall back with usually seven or more upright spindles, curved arms, and medium-length rockers, e.g., "Her Boston Rocker had remained in the corner of the parlor for all the seventy years since she had died."

bottle: early, one quart of wine; a small glass container with a narrow neck, e.g., "He had four bottles of Madeira."

bound servants: early, either indentured servants or negroes, later, referred to indentured servants only, e.g., "The first negroes came to the **Virginia Colony** (q.v.) in 1619 as 'bound servants'." Also see **indentured servants.**

bounded tree, boundary tree: a tree marking the corner or sometimes a boundary line of a tract of land, e.g., "The bounded tree marked the point at which the Fleming land joined the Meeting House Road."

bounders: marks or monuments (sometimes trees) at turns in or the ends of surveyed lines, e.g., "The bounders on the north and west lines were piles of stones, and that on the southwest corner was an oak tree."

bounty: usually, money paid by a government for the capture or killing of **varmints** (q.v.) and pests, e.g., "Bounties were paid on crows' heads as late as 1960."

bounty jumpers: the name given those who, after accepting a bounty for enlistment during the Civil War, would go to another town, perhaps change their name, and again enlist and accept a bounty payment, e.g., "John Arnold was one of the many bounty jumpers in Civil War Ohio."

bounty lands: lands from the public domain given or granted, commencing in 1776 as a reward for desertion from the British Army, as compensation for military service or goods or equipment supplied to early governments or armies, e.g., "The bounty lands awarded by Connecticut after the Revolution, in part, were for horses, guns, clothing, and blankets supplied to the army units from Connecticut."

bousy: an early term for drunkenness, e.g., "He was bousy most of the time, even at services."

bouwerye: in old Dutch New York, a farm occupied by the owner, e.g., "Old man In den Hoffen was proud of his bouwerye."

bowie knife: a long, heavy, single-edged working knife, named for wilderness scout Jim Bowie, who is said to have designed it, e.g., "The bowie knife was eminently practical for the woodsman and hunter."

bowls: a game of bowling played out of doors on grass, e.g., "Sir Francis Drake is said to have being playing at bowls when he learned of the approach of the Spanish Armada." See **games.**

box: apparently, a measure of unknown quantity or weight of iron or metal, e.g., "Early store ledgers occasionally list boxes of iron."

box iron: a smoothing iron with a closable inner container for hot coals, e.g., "One of the most difficult tasks of the early housewife was the requirement that she spend hours over a box iron or a **sadiron** (q.v.)."

Boys in Blue: See **Union Army.**

Boys in Gray: See **Confederate Army.**

brace, brace and bit: that hand-operated device in which **bits** (q.v.) are mounted for boring holes, e.g., "Building barns would have been almost impossible without braces and bits."

braced-back chair: a common, early, spindle-backed chair, with two or occasionally three additional vertical braces extending into a neck or protrusion at the back of the seat, e.g., "His braced-back chair was of ***American Windsor*** (q.v.) style, except for the extra braces."

bracer: early tincture or bandage, e.g., "To treat the wound, she made a bracer of iodine."

Braddocks Road: See ***roads, early.***

braid loom: See **belt loom.**

brain, diseases of: The brain not having been understood, devastating remedies often were employed when the symptoms of "brain disease" appeared, e.g., "For anemia of the brain (meaning now lost), eucalyptus, phosphorus and camphor were popular remedies; for hyperaemia of the brain (excess blood in the brain), **bleeding** (q.v.), cold to the head, and anal injections were used; for inflammation of the brain, **cupping** (q.v.), bleeding, and **blisters** (q.v.); for overtaxed brain, bromides and phosphorus, and for softening of the brain, tincture of phosphorus."

brain, softening of the: See **brain, diseases of.**

braising pan: open, metal (usually iron) pan with short legs, used for braising, e.g., "In the list of **personalty** (q.v.) were three 'kittles' and a braising pan."

bramble: blackberry, raspberry, or dewberry bush, e.g., "The fruits of the many brambles said to have been growing on the property probably were used to make wines."

branch: a candle stand for more than one candle; also sometimes a part of a chandelier, e.g., "Whether the branch found in the inventory was a multiple candlestand or a part of a chandelier could not be ascertained."

brandlet: a common large trivet; a legged, black iron stand placed over coals and embers, and upon which were placed kettles and large pots, e.g., "The kitchen inventory revealed two trivets and a brandlet."

brandy: a common, strong liquor distilled from any wine, e.g., "The brandy in the inventory may have been made on the property."

brasier, brassier, brazier: a metal pan designed to hold coals and embers over which cooking was done; one who worked with brass, bronze, and similar metals, e.g., "There were two small brasiers listed in the estate inventory"; "Parker was variously described as a pewterer and a brazier"

breakbone fever: See **dengue.**

breakfront: any of the many designs and styles of large wooden cabinets with a center section that extends further forward than the two sides, or with a top section not extending to the fron endge of the bottom section, e.g., "Her walnut breakfront, made in 1836, was valued at $4000.00."

break the Pope's neck: a game of adults or older children of both sexes, the rules having been forgotten, e.g., "Virginians of the pre-Revolutionary period played break the Pope's neck." See also, **games.**

break wind: to flatulate, e.g., "Heavy diets often caused indigestion and gas on the stomach then called wind, hence came the phrase to break wind."

breast knot: intertwined ribbons worn by women as decorations at the breast, e.g., "The old photo of her revealed a pretty breast knot."

breast plate: very common, early, sleeveless and backless armor made of metal or heavy leather; sometimes, a small decorative leather pad or disc attached to the harnessing and hung at the breast of a horse, e.g., "Probably the last armor to be found in the colonies and used in war was the breast plate."

breeches, britches: common early item of male clothing usually extending to just below the knee and tied there; now, any men's pants, e.g., "Breeches were found in most inventories of eighteenth-century men."

Brewster chair: a massive chair found throughout the seventeenth century, usually with turned spindles at the back and beneath the seat, almost indistinguishable from the Carver chair of the same period, e.g., "Thorowgood's seventeenth-century home contains a beautiful example of a Brewster chair."

brickbat: a brick, or piece of brick used as a weapon, e.g., "He hit him with a brickbat."

bride's basket: thought to be an expensive, highly decorated or ornate, small, metal frame holding an ornate bowl, and used for sweetmeats or candies, e.g., "The inventory spoke of a *chased* (q.v.) silver bride's basket."

bridle, bridle path: harnessing, including the bit, placed on the head of a horse, by which it is controlled; an early (and now) path or way only wide enough for a horse and rider, e.g., "Virtually every farm inventory before 1930 contained one or more bridles"; "Most travel in early seventeenth-century Virginia was via bridle paths."

brigade: See **armies, organization of.**

Bright's disease: nephritis or kidney disease; an extremely painful, dreaded, and common disease for which no cures were known, e.g., "There being no dialysis, old Dan Carner suffered terribly before dying of Bright's disease." Also see **kidney disease.**

brimstone: sulphur, used for the burning of waste, in making gunpowder and explosives, and thought to have extensive medicinal value, e.g., "The armory might be expected always to have brimstone on hand"; "Flowers of sulphur, also called brimstone, was a mainstay of the apothecary trade."

brindle: a color of an animal, usually a dog or horse, dark over gray or buff, e.g., "His brindle dog was his constant companion."

bristle: the coarse, stiff hair of swine, widely used for early brushes, e.g., "At his death, there were several bristle brushes in his shop."

Bristol blue: a fine, dark blue, early, transparent or translucent glass used in better and usually decorative glassware, e.g., "Her Bristol blue candy dish was superb."

Bristol glass: an early, opaque, white glass similar to milk glass, popular for decorative glassware, e.g., "She had a butter dish of Bristol."

broadaxe, goosewing: a common axe with a broad, flat blade, chisel-shaped on one side only, and used widely for working logs into beams, e.g., "The beams had been hewn with a broad axe."

broadcasting: See **sow.**

broadcloth: a closely woven fabric, usually of cotton, linen, or silk, and used for lighter clothes, e.g., "The tailor made the gentlemens' shirts of broadcloth."

brocade: a variegated cloth, usually of silk, e.g., "He had three brocade waistcoats."

broiler: unlike now, a long-handled, hinged, scissor-shaped kitchen utensil made of corrugated and perforated metal, usually iron, with a removable bottom, e.g., "Meat to be broiled was placed between the perforated jaws of the broiler and held in the fire until done."

brothers: as now, a sibling; a member of a religious order, particularly Catholic; the terms often were used in the Biblical sense, e.g., "Care must be exercised since the records of old churches often refer to unrelated members of the congregation as brothers and sisters." Also see **sisters,** and **siblings.**

brougham, brome, broom: a closed carriage, usually seating four, with the driver high outside, e.g., "His wealth was reflected in his beautiful brougham with a **liveried** (q.v.) driver."

Brown Bess: flintlock muskets used by British forces in the eighteenth century, so called after Queen Elizabeth I and by reason of the metal being 'browned' and not 'blued', e.g., "A majority of the British soldiers carried Brown Besses during the **French and Indian War** (q.v.)."

brushes, scrub: See **clamps.**

bub: very strong beer, ale, or other malt liquor, e.g., "The New England colonists very much enjoyed their bub."

bubo: any swelling of the lymph glands, especially in the groin and armpits, e.g., "Dr. Lockhart applied ice and poultices to try to cure bubo."

bubonic plague, Black Death: that disease, probably carried by fleas and rats, that killed perhaps one third of the populace of England and Europe during the middle ages, e.g., "The 'plague' reported by chirurgeon Stringer as the cause of death of Richard and Edward Newport very likely was bubonic plague."

Buccaneer musket, Buckaneer gun: a common long **musket** (q.v.) of the seventeenth and early eighteenth centuries, e.g., "In 1698, Owen Griffith bequeathed his 'pistoll, houlster, and Buckaneer gun' to his eldest son."

buck: the chassis of a simple utility wagon, yet when a plain wooden seat was added, the wagon was called a buckboard; lye, a buck tub was a tub in which cloth and yarn were cleaned and bleached with lye; a male animal, e.g., "The buck deer dressed out at 165 pounds."

bucket bench: a cupboard of much utility, usually with doors below and a rimmed, shallow shelf and work surface above, e.g., "As were most, the bucket bench was made of ash and maple."

buckles: common types in inventories were 'shoe', 'belt', 'hat', and 'spur', e.g., "The pilgrims often mistakenly are depicted with shiny, silver shoe buckles." See also **desserts, early.**

buckram: formerly, a strong, coarse, stiffened linen cloth, widely used for book binding, e.g., "Books not bound in leather usually were done in buckram."

buckskin: deer skin; a very light brown or tan horse, e.g., e wore a buckskin coat"; "Diane was very proud of her buckskin mare."

buff: coarse leather prepared from buffalo skin and often used for belts or harnessing, e.g., "Buff belts and moccasins were very common in the early west."

buffet: curiously, sometimes the name given a **side by side** (q.v.); a long, rather narrow, waist-high serving piece, usually made of better-quality, highly-finished wood, with several drawers and one or two doored compartments below the top on either end of the drawers, used to serve a variety of foods, "buffet style," e.g., "Her Victorian walnut buffet had belonged to her grandmother."

bugger: See **cover.**

buggy: a light, four-wheeled carriage having one seat, and often with a removable top, e.g., "Dr. Drake's buggy and his old dog 'Watch' were well known in the little town." Also see **road wagon.**

bullet mold, pincer mold: a metal mold into which melted lead was poured to form bullets; a mold was needed for each caliber of weapon, e.g., "His grandfather's 57-caliber bullet mold was a prized memento."

bullseye lamp: a wicked, oil lamp with directional reflectors; a lamp that reflects light in a certain direction, e.g., "In his work as a clockmaker, his bullseye lamp was invaluable."

bumper: a large metal or glass drinking utensil; any filled cup, e.g., "The tavernkeeper kept his patron's bumpers displayed on the backbar"; "They raised their bumpers in a toast."

bundle, bundling: the little-understood eighteenth-century practice of young lovers sleeping or being in bed together with their clothes on, usually separated by a low board, e.g., "English ladies and gentlemen were shocked by the widespread New England practice of bundling."

bureau: See **chiffonier.**

Bureaus of Vital Statistics: See **vital statistics.**

burgess: as in Pennsylvania, the chief executive officer of a borough, having generally the same duties as a mayor of a city; in Connecticut, comparable to trustees or commissioners in other states; in early Virginia, freemen elected to the House of Burgesses (legislature) commencing in 1619, e.g., "She learned that her ancestor was the burgess of the borough of Coxetown."

burglary: originally, breaking into and entering the home of another at night with felonious intentions; later, any breaking and entering with felonious intent, day or night, e.g., "He was found guilty of burglary and was ordered transported to the colonies."

Burgundy: a dark red, sweet wine, very popular in the eighteenth and nineteenth centuries, and named for the province of Burgundy in France, e.g., "There was a hogshead of Burgundy shown on his **accompt** (q.v.)."

burl grain: now quite rare, speckled, beautiful graining created in a burl (growth) on the side of a tree, e.g., "Almost all burls were and are cut into veneer in order that the most use could be made of them."

burlap sack, burlap bag: See **gunny sack.**

burning glass: a magnifying glass; a glass used to concentrate heat to bring ignition and often, before matches, used to start fires, e.g., "Early inventories occasionally reveal burning glasses."

bushel: a measure of volume of weight (four pecks, eight gallons, or thirty-two quarts); a large basket, e.g., "A favored way of telling one that talents or knowledge should be used and openly displayed was 'Don't hide your light under a bushel'"; "His harvest consisted of two hundred bushels of wheat and sixty bushels of barley."

business wagon: any wagon for hauling, but usually a **buckboard** (q.v.) for hire, e.g., "The livery stable advertised **hacks** (q.v.) and business wagons for hire."

busk: steel or whalebone braces to strengthen a woman's stays, as in a corset, e.g., "Fashions of the 19th century often required the wearing of busks."

buskins: See **shoes.**

bussened: probably meant ruptured, or a male made incapable of sexual activity by reason of injury to the genitalia, e.g., "He returned from the Civil War bussened."

bustard: early name for wild turkeys, e.g., "The early settlers were grateful for the bustards provided by the Indians."

butler's desk: a three- or four-drawered cabinet, with a flat top, appearing like a chest of drawers, with what appears to be the top drawer-front hinged so as to drop down and reveal **pigeon holes** (q.v.), small drawers, and a writing surface, e.g., "The elegant Empire butler's desk was **flame grain** (q.v.) mahogany."

butler's sideboard, butler sideboard: a common item of furniture among the more affluent; a sideboard, usually with a two-doored china or glass compartment above, two or three drawers below, with a fall-front revealing **pigeon holes** (q.v.) and a writing surface, e.g., "His walnut butler's sideboard had belonged to his great-grandfather."

butter bat: a small, flat, wooden utensil used to work butter, e.g., "Her inventory listed a butter bat and a **butter churn** (q.v.)." Also see **bat.**

butter churn, churn (and dasher): a cylindrical, usually earthen container of 2 to 5 or more gallons, in which is placed fresh whole milk, the same then churned (dashed) by rapidly moving the dasher up and down, thereby separating butter from the non-fat liquids (buttermilk), e.g., "While churns are often available in antique shops, few original dashers have survived."

butter mold: a wooden mold, into which bulk butter was placed and then pressed out with a plunger, thereby measuring and shaping it, usually with a decorative design in the head of the plunger, e.g., "Her favorite butter mold pressed her initials into the butter."

buttermilk paint: See **milk paint.**

buttery: a pantry; a cool place of storage for cheese, butter, sauces, etc.; e.g., "Her buttery was in the coolest part of the winter kitchen." Also see **fruitery.**

button: unknown, a child's game, e.g., "Early Appalachian records reveal children playing button."

butts and bounds: See **metes and bounds.**

by blood: See **consanguinity.**

byroad: a neighborhood road or lane of early New Jersey, legally recognized, yet not public and not private in that the public was authorized to use it irregularly, e.g., "His land was traversed by a byroad, and the county helped maintain it by requiring road work."

C

C.G.: See **Certified Genealogist.**

cabbage chopper, cabbage cutter, kraut cutter: a common wooden kitchen utensil, usually from 18 to 36 inches long and 6 to 9 inches wide, having a sliding platform that moved to and fro across a sharp blade, thereby shredding cabbage, e.g., "Virtually every early housewife had a cabbage chopper or kraut cutter."

cabin: a small, often windowless structure with none or minimal plumbing, used as a crude residence, e.g., "In 1856 Arnold moved Rebecca and her children into a cabin valued at $20.00."

cabinetmaker, cabinetmaking: as distinguished from a carpenter, a cabinetmaker was one who made fine, small, wooden cabinets, chests, and boxes; later, one who made fine wooden furniture and cabinets of any size, e.g., "Her elegant Empire **chest on chest** (q.v.) was made by the local cabinetmaker."

caboose: formerly, a railroad car at the end of a freight train in which rode the conductor and other of the train crew; a free-standing bake oven, e.g., "The use of cabooses on trains ended in the 1980s"; "The caboose in the inventory was an oven, and had nothing to do with trains."

cabriolet: early, a one-horse, single-seated, two-wheeled carriage; later, a one-horse, four-passenger carriage with a canopy, e.g., "In the 1846 sale of Cole's **personalty,** (q.v.) his cabriolet brought $40.00."

cachexes, cachexia: chronic ill health, accompanied with emaciation, e.g., "Dr. Lockhart administered tonics, usually with a high alcohol content, for cachexia, especially if it was the result of cancer."

cag: See **keg.**

cairn: a pile of rocks used to cover and mark a burial place; a pile of rocks designating a corner or turning point in a survey, e.g., "The cairn of the commanding officer may yet be seen at King's Mountain battlefield"; "The northwest corner was marked by a tree and the northeast corner was marked by a cairn."

caisson: a wheeled box or chest used to haul powder, shot, and supplies for a cannon, e.g., "Traditionally, the body of an army officer is transported to the cemetery on a caisson."

Cajuns: the name given those descendants of the French settlers of Acadia and New Brunswick, who transported to Louisiana; the name probably was corrupted from Acadians, to Cadians, to Cadyans, to Cajuns, e.g., "The Cajuns brought great food and the Civil Law to Louisiana."

calabash: a gourd; a drinking or eating utensil made from a dried gourd, e.g., "Every summer she dried gourds to be used for calabashes."

calamine, calamine brass: as now, a lotion for insect bites and burns made from oxides of zinc and iron, an alloy, e.g., "Calamine lotion was in use before 1880"; "Calamine brass, used as an imitation for gold, was an alloy of zinc carbonate and copper."

calculi, calculus: as with pebbles; the formation of stones within the bladder or kidneys, e.g., "Stewart's Pocket Therapeutics suggests that the treatment for calculi - 'the stone' - should be alkalies, 'mineral acids', narcotics, and nitric acid if renal, and, if biliary, should be anesthetics, ice bags, morphine, and a mixture of turpentine and ether."

caldron: See ***cauldron.***

calenture: yellow fever; the violent and delirious fever that attacked people on shipboard, especially sailors in the tropics. Early epidemics of calenture occurred in New York in 1668, Boston in 1691, and Charleston in 1699, e.g., "In the early colonies, calenture quite usually resulted in death."

caliber: the bore or diameter of the projectile of a firearm, usually given in percentages of inches, e.g., "The muskets carried in the Civil War were of several calibers, including .45, .57, and .69."

calico, callaco: a common cotton cloth, originally from India; a yellow, black and red-brown, large-spotted cat, e.g., "She made their aprons of calico"; "The poem described the dog as gingham, and the cat as calico."

California gold rush: See ***Forty-niners.***

caliver: an early, hand-held firearm, e.g., "The militia was armed with only blunderbusses and a few calivers."

callosity: early word for any hardened, thickened, or (sometimes) swollen portion of the body that was not accompanied by pain, e.g., "He had a large red callosity on his abdomen."

calomel: mercuric chloride; a widely used purge (laxative), also thought to have medicinal value in curing syphilis, yellow fever, and many other ailments e.g., "The old country doctor was sure to have calomel in his medicine satchel."

camel back trunk: so called by reason of the humped appearance of the hinged top, such trunks were very sturdy, made of wood, leather, and metal, with hasps and locks, and had compartments and removable trays within, e.g., "He had two camel back trunks that dated from 1870."

camlet: an expensive fabric made of silk and camel hair, e.g., "The inventory revealed a camlet coat."

camphor, camphire: that sap or material extruded by the tree of the same name and widely thought to have medicinal value, e.g., "In early times, camphor was used by nearly all physicians."

camus: a thin dress, e.g., "She had several camuses for warm weather wear."

can: originally, a cup made of tin or copper, e.g., "The cans listed in the inventory probably were drinking cups."

canal boat: a wide, shallow-draft barge, pulled by mules driven along the causeway or bank, e.g., "Many of the young men of old Holidaysburg gained employment as drivers of the mules used to pull canal boats."

canal horn: a brass horn used to call attention to the presence of canal and river boats, e.g., "The inventory of property of the old captain revealed a canal horn."

canals, well known: commencing in 1817 with the authorization of the Erie Canal linking Albany with Buffalo, and lasting through the coming of the railroad, some better known were *Morris Co.* across New Jersey, *Delaware and Hudson* connecting Homesdale, Pennsylvania, with Kingston, New York; *James River and Kanawha* from Richmond to Buchanan, Virginia; *Chesapeake and Ohio,* and *Pennsylvania Portage and Canal System* from Philadelphia to Pittsburgh; *Welland* connecting Lakes Erie and Ontario; *Wabash and Erie* between Toledo and Evansville, Indiana; and the *Illinois and Michigan* between Lake Michigan and the Illinois River.

Canary, Tenerife: sweet wines from the Canary Islands, and very popular in the colonies, e.g., "The Boston Rocker served Madeira, Burgundy, and Canary."

cancer: as now, but early not at all understood, e.g., "For 'a cancer' of the stomach, he administered arsenic and carbon bisulphide, and for other internal cancers he often gave prescribed carbolic acid, chromic acid, zinc sulphide or zinc chloride."

candle arm: a small holder for one, two, or three candles, usually suspended against the wall; a *sconce* (q.v.), e.g., "There were two candle arms and two *chandeliers* (q.v.) in the inventory."

candle beam: a crude, roughly made, candle chandelier, e.g., "Being a blacksmith, he made the candle beam from black iron."

candle mold: metal (usually tin) tubes, open at the top and having a string hole at the bottom, several of which were mounted in a holder or rack. A string wick was placed through the hole and the tube, and then the latter was filled with molten wax or tallow, e.g., "Before lamp oil, nearly all homes had one or more candle molds."

candlebox: a container, widely varying in size and usually wooden, used to store 6 to 20 candles, e.g., "Their candlebox was about fourteen inches long, eight inches wide and six inches deep, and held sixteen candles."

candlelight: the end of the day; near dark, e.g., "He came to call at candlelight."

Candlemas: an ancient English holiday held on February 2; the feast of the purification of the Virgin Mary celebrated in the church with many candles, e.g., "Wherever the Church of England was found, Candlemas was celebrated with regularity ."

candler, chandler: one who makes candles; that occupation or calling that gave rise to the surname Chandler, e.g., "Knowledge of the many waxes and tallows, their sources, methods of molding, and the several additives used to vary burning time or to add colors gave rise to the ancient calling of the candler."

candles: as now, e.g., "Her recipe for candles was '...cut tallow into small pieces, put into a tin vessel with a spout, and set it in boiling water, stir until tallow is melted but do not boil as it will flake, pour into molds'."

candlestand: any of the many shapes and styles of small, lightweight, easily movable stands for two or more candles, usually of wood, and designed to stand on the floor and provide illumination, e.g., "Her affluence made it possible for her to have candlestands of walnut, cherry, and mahogany."

candy: as now, confections were known and enjoyed, e.g., "Of the many candies, rock candy was sugar crystallized on a string, suckets were hard candies to be dissolved in the mouth, toffee (taffy) was as now, sweetmeats were candied fruits, often eaten with the hands, and sugar plums were lumps of crystallized sugar dipped in fruit juices."

candy pull, candy stew, candy boil, toffee pull, taffy pull: a social gathering of folks, usually young, for the purpose of enjoying the company of each other and making candy, e.g., "Being new in town, he was happy to gain an invitation to the candy pull."

candy stew: See **candy pull.**

cannister: very early, a small basket; in the 17th, 18th, and 19th centuries, artillery projectiles shaped like a basket and containing numerous smaller projectiles, the same designed to burst apart upon impact, e.g., "Through the use of cannister the Union artillery is said to have devastated the ranks of men in Pickett's Assault."

cannonball bed: a bedstead, common after the Civil War, with posts, the tops of which were decorated with cannonball-shaped carvings, e.g., "The walnut cannonball bed was beautiful."

canoe: a common boat, pointed at both ends, considerably larger than those in use today, used on shallow rivers to haul freight, e.g., "By 1750, there were many small boats and canoes plying the Blackwater, Meharrin, and Chowan rivers."

canon: law set forth by ecclesiastical councils or bodies, e.g., "The canon law provided rules of religious conduct for the early settlers."

canopy bed: See **poster bed.**

canter: See **gaits.**

cap and ball: an ignition cap and a projectile, however the term described rifles, pistols, or shot guns that succeeded **flintlocks** (q.v.) and preceded breech-loaded arms, and were fired by a springed hammer striking a small explosive ignition "cap" placed over a small tube (nipple) leading to the powder propellant, the ignition of which propelled the "ball", e.g., "The cap and ball rifles were vastly more reliable than the old flintlocks, especially in damp weather."

caparison: a cover for a horse, e.g., "There was substantial **harnessing** (q.v.) and three caparisons in the inventory."

capitation tax: See **poll tax.**

capius: literally, "take that"; a term used variously for writs or orders to an officer of a court directing arrest, notification, confiscation, attachment, etc.; should the first capius fail in its purpose, an alias capius would issue, and should it fail, a third, it known as a pluries capius was issued, e.g., "A capius and then an alius capius was issued to Sheriff Massenburg ordering the gathering and sale of the **assets** (q.v.) of Jones."

caps: See **cap and ball.**

capuchin: a woman's hooded cloak made in the style of the Capuchin monks, e.g., "On chilly days, she wore a fine wool capuchin."

caraco: a short woman's jacket, e.g., "In her inventory were two dresses, three gowns, and a caraco.

carat, caract: a measure of weight, quite usually of gemstones, equaling four grains; also, a measure of the fineness of gold, whereby the whole is divided into twenty-four parts and those parts that are pure gold are the caratage, e.g., "His wife's diamond weighed six grains, thus was one and one half carats"; "The base metal made up six parts and the gold, eighteen, so the alloy was eighteen carat gold."

caraway seeds: as now, used for gas, flatulence, colic, hiccups, and, interestingly, loss of hair, e.g., "The housewife of the early years always planted caraway in the **kitchen garden** (q.v.)."

carbine: a short-barreled firearm, designed to be easily carried on horseback or through a heavily wooded area, and usually having a rifled barrel, e.g., "Cavalrymen usually were armed with carbines."

carboy: a large glass container around which a wooden framework was built, e.g., "By the year 1825 many acids and embalmers' and tanning fluids were shipped in carboys."

carbuncle: a painful inflammation and swelling under the skin, more serious than a boil, e.g., "The carbuncle was lanced and **turpentine** (q.v.) was applied."

card: a small, handled, wooden or leather tool with fine wire teeth, used to separate the fibers of wool and other animal hair, flax, or cotton, e.g., "Few were the 18th- or early 19th-century households that did not possess several cards."

card catalog: a listing of books and materials arranged alphabetically by title, name, category, subject, and author, and a "must" for the researcher, e.g., "The 'maps' listed in the card catalog were valuable research tools for her."

card table: unlike now, a small table with a drop leaf, usually supported by a hinged leg, e.g., "There was a card table and a **center table** (q.v.) in the inventory."

cardinal: a woman's hooded cloak, named after the garb of a Roman Catholic Cardinal, e.g., "She wore her wool and cotton cardinal on chilly days."

caries: early, a decay of teeth or bones; now a decay of teeth, e.g., "Dr. Lockhart viewed the withering and loss of bone in his arm as a caries."

carmine: a color, crimson or bright red, e.g., "She made carmine by adding powdered insects called cochineal to vinegar and hot water."

Carolina Parakeets, Carolina Parrots: yellow, orange, with green and white, small, gregarious, the only native parrot of what now is the United States; now extinct, but common and popular as pets in the 17th, 18th and first half of the 19th centuries, e.g., "The Carolina parakeet went the way of the passenger pigeon, likely by reason of its propensity to eat fresh fruit from colonial orchards." Also see ***pigeon.***

carpenter: one who does heavy construction with wood, usually houses, barns, other buildings, shelves, etc., e.g., "While he was a well-known carpenter, he did not have the skills of a cabinetmaker."

carpet: early, any colored covering for floors or otherwise, e.g., "He had a carpet to cover the carriage seats."

carpetbaggers: so-called by reason of their belongings often being placed in a bag made of old carpeting, they went South during **Reconstruction** (q.v.) hoping to gain office or otherwise take advantage of the disrupted institutions, e.g., "Those who seek ancestors who emigrated to the South during the period 1867-1885 often will find that they are hunting for carpetbaggers."

carriage: a general term for any of many styles and sizes of horse-drawn vehicles for business and pleasure, with or without tops and, unlike ***wagons*** (q.v.), with but limited space for luggage or light hauling, i.e., ***cart, gig, chaise,*** etc., e.g., "Ida was quite conscious of the fact that her father could afford a carriage, while the fathers of most of her friends could not." "Some of the many horse drawn vehicles were omnibus, wagonette, ***surrey*** (q.v.), ***cutter*** (q.v.), ***sleigh*** (q.v.), top buggy, ***runabout*** (q.v.), road wagon (q.v.), and ***chaise (shay)***, (q.v.)"

carriage horses: light horses used to pull carriages, gigs, and other light vehicles, e.g., "Her pair of chestnut carriage horses were her pride and joy." Also see ***draft horses.***

carry: to take someone someplace, e.g., "He asked if the neighbor might carry his son to school."

cart: a two-wheeled, animal-drawn vehicle used to haul all manner of materials, very common in the 17th and 18th centuries because of the poor roads on this continent, e.g., "In early New York, there were myriad carts, yet only a few four-wheeled vehicles."

carte de visite: (French; cards of or for the visit or call - calling cards); in the U.S., photographs small enough to be carried on the person; small

pictures (q.v.) widely made and sold during and for 30 years after the Civil War and, as today, given as remembrances, e.g., "Cartes de visite of General Sherman were being advertised within a few weeks after the March To The Sea."

cartouche: variously, a paper box for cartridges, or individual small thin paper containers holding the ball and powder necessary to load one round in a firearm, e.g., "The '200 cartouches' in his list doubtless were individually wrapped rounds of powder and ball for his musket."

cartridge box: a small, closable, cloth or leather box, usually hung from the waist by a beltloop, the same holding **cartouches** (q.v.) and, later, metal cartridges, e.g., "The cartridge box usually issued to Union soldiers was made of black leather."

Carver chair: now, virtually indistinguishable from the **Brewster chair** (q.v.).

case: early, a box of nearly any size; later, a trunk, or a medium to large chest with drawers (**chest of drawers,** q.v.); a common early abbreviation for trespass on the case, a legal action providing a remedy where injury arose through the acts of another, even though there was no force applied nor intended against the injured, e.g., "There were two (2) 'old cases' listed in the inventory."; e.g., "His action on the case arose out of his injuries sustained when the neighbor's rickety barn collapsed upon him."

case drink, English: unknown, apparently an intoxicating liquor, e.g., "An old Isle of Wight record reveals a debt for a shipment of English Case Drink."

case knife: early, a large kitchen knife; later, any small knife with a folding blade; presently, any small, pocket knife, e.g., "There were three **slicers** (q.v.) and two case knives in the inventory."

casement cloth: a light, loosely woven cloth used to make curtains for windows and beds, e.g., Her account revealed three **ells** (q.v.) of casement cloth."

casing: the thin membrane from the intestines of hogs and sheep, stuffed with bulk sausage creating "link sausages", e.g., "Casing was much in demand at **killing time** (q.v.) as sausages of many varieties were universally made."

cask: a medium to large barrel of any measure, e.g., "There were several casks of tobacco in the inventory."

casket supports: sturdy, well finished, splayed leg, supports for caskets, e.g., "In early times when the dead were shown in the home, casket supports were common and shared among neighbors."

cassia: a rather uncommon sweet cooking spice, occasionally made into a liqueur, e.g., "Her purchase of a small amount of cassia appeared was revealed in the account ledger."

caster, caster set: a small wheel, such as used on the legs of chests, cabinets, commodes, washstands, and bedsteads; a small, usually metal holder for cruets of condiments and spices, placed at the table while eating; a stand to hold four to seven cruets, e.g., "The casters of the walnut commode were of white porcelain"; "The cruets were of cut glass and the caster was of silver plate."

castor set: See **caster.**

casualty, casualties: early, any loss of military personnel that decreased the numbers of those present for duty, including loses by death, wounds, capture, disease, desertion, and sometimes even discharge; recently and now, one who has been killed or wounded even slightly, while engaged in armed military service, whether through battle or otherwise, e.g., "During the Civil War, the 1st Maine Heavy Artillery suffered the highest casualties of all units in the Federal Army."

cataplasm: See **poultice.**

catarrh, coryza: almost any inflammation or disease of the respiratory tract, e.g., "Hot spirituous **cordials** (q.v.) at bedtime and the inhalation of ammonia and camphor were often administered for catarrh."

cathartics: See **purge, purgatives, cathartics.**

Catholic school recores: See **Orders of Nuns.**

Cato conspiracy: the most serious (Sept. 9, 1739) of slave uprisings in and near Charleston, SC, resulting in 30 white and 44 black deaths, and the hanging of some 50 blacks thought to be participants, e.g., "Genealogists have uncovered the names of many of those involved, both black and white, in the Stono Cato conspiracy." Also see **Nat Turner Uprising.**

catsup: unlike now, a condiment with a walnut or mushroom base, e.g., "Until the 19th century, catsup found in recipes contained no tomatoes."

cattail: a tall plant that grows in moist soil, the leaves of which were used in basketry and the tops as **ticking** (q.v.), e.g., "The cattails that grew in the marsh below the house provided material for her basket making and their bedding, as well."

caudle: a warm mixture for the sick, and usually containing food and wine, beer, or other intoxicant; the root for our word "coddle", e.g., "When her children had the chills she gave them a caudle of warm wine and cooked oatmeal.";

cauldron, caldron: any large boiling pot or kettle, usually with three legs, e.g., "The inventory revealed a number of kettles and a caldron."

cauterization, cauterizing: bringing about a cessation of bleeding through searing or burning of the exposed open blood vessels, e.g., "After amputation of Billy Drake's arm, the bleeding was stopped by cauterization."

Cavaliers: whether of high station or common tenant farmers, those followers of Charles I in his differences with Parliament (as opposed to the "Roundheads" who were pro-Parliament) who, when he was beheaded in 1649, sought refuge in the American colonies, particularly pro-Royalist Virginia, e.g., "The erroneous notion that most or all Cavaliers were of high station and wealth arose in the 19th century."

caveat, caveat to a will: literally, "beware"; the filing of a document stating a claim of rights in land, the purpose being to prevent the issuance of a patent or grant for the same tract to another person; a legal attack upon the validity of a will; a demand upon an administrator or apparent heirs that a will be produced and probated; e.g., "His caveat stated that his survey showed part of the tract about to be patented to Smith"; "Her caveat to the will stated that the heirs knew the will not to be the last one written."

celice: See **horsehair upholstery.**

cellar: a cool space, usually under the house or below ground, where vegetables, fruits, and other perishable foods were kept, as in "cold cellar"; a small container for salt, etc., as in salt cellar (salt shaker); a large container, box, or storage space used for any number of commodities, as in oil cellar, wine cellar, or tool cellar, e.g., "The salt cellars were of cut glass."

cellaret: a small rack or case, usually kept near the place of taking meals, and designed to hold several bottles of wine, e.g., "Her cellaret was placed beside the **sideboard** (q.v.).

cemetery: while common in old England and the colonies before 1700, the early South seems to have commonly preferred "church yard", e.g., "Some residents of the antebellum South were unfamiliar with the word *cemetery*." Also see **church yard.**

cenotaph: a monument to one who is buried elsewhere, e.g., "Colonel Wilson's cenotaph is in Bowling Green; his burial place is unknown."

censer: a container or dish in which incense is burned, e.g., "Marty had a silver plated censer that had belonged to her mother-in-law."

census, census taker: usually, an official listing of all persons within a political subdivision (precinct, city, county, state, nation); formerly, a census was taken solely by census-takers who went from door to door listing the names, ages, occupations, etc., of the occupants of each dwelling; most commonly the Decennial Censuses taken by the U.S. Government every ten years commencing in 1790; often imprecisely used interchangeably with **enumeration** (q.v.) e.g., "The Eighth Decennial Census of the U.S. was taken in 1860"; "The censuses taken before 1850 are more properly called enumerations." Also see **enumerations.**

center table: See **parlor table.**

century, centuries: 100-year periods, the 1800s being the 19th century, the 1700s being the 18th century, etc., e.g., "She was born in 1701, the beginning of the 18th century."

cephalgy: early, a severe headache, probably the modern "migraine", e.g., "The diary stated that he often suffered from cephalgy."

cephalic, cephalick: any medicine used to relieve a headache, e.g., "Maggie often administered sassafras tea and honey as a cephalick."

cepi: (I have taken or done) a common return written on a **capius** (q.v.) by the officer serving the same, e.g., "The capius in the loose papers was endorsed 'cepi corpus', meaning he had taken the defendant into custody."

certificate: in legal records, any written evidence that the county, etc., owes the holder, e.g., "He had a 'certificate for a bear's head', meaning that he was to be paid a bounty upon presentation of that writing."

certificate land: usually, land granted anew to a different owner through a certification by a clerk of the court that a prior owner had abandoned the premises, had failed to **seat** (q.v.) the property, or otherwise had lost rights of ownership; those lands in Pennsylvania that veterans or their assignees could buy with the certificates issued to them in lieu of pay during the Revolution, e.g., "The are many examples of certifications in the early Virginia patent lists"; "Carner had sixty acres of certificate land." Also see **land grants.**

Certified American Indian Lineage Specialist (C.A.I.L.S.): See **Board of Certification Of Genealogists.**

Certified American Lineage Specialist (C.A.L.S.): See **Board of Certification Of Genealogists.**

Certified Genealogical Instructor (C.G.I.): See **Board of Certification Of Genealogists.**

Certified Genealogical Lecturer (C.G.L.): See **Board of Certification Of Genealogists.**

Certified Genealogical Record Searcher (C.G.R.S.): See **Board of Certification Of Genealogists.**

Certified Genealogist (C.G.): See **Board of Certification Of Genealogists.**

certiorari, writ of: an ancient writ from a higher court ordering a lower court to certify and forward the record of a prior proceeding, e.g., "When the Supreme Court denies certiorari, the effect is that the decision of the lower court stands."

cerulean: blue, the color of the sky; a very popular early color for ladies' clothing, e.g., "She wore a cerulean shawl of fine linen."

cesset executio: a term often endorsed on early court orders, meaning cease or stay the execution of that order, e.g., "The capius bore the words cesset executio, so she knew the court had withdrawn the order of arrest of the ancestor."

chafe, chafing dish: to warm or sear food, e.g., "When she said she had chafed it, she meant that she had seared the meat."

chaff bed: a ticking bag stuffed with chaff and used as a mattress, e.g., "While many **ticks** (q.v.) contained chaff, straw, or even grass, the better ones were of feathers."

chaffern: See **chafe, chafing dish.**

chain: a common, early term of surveying; a measurement of length, being sixty-six (66) feet, e.g., "The old description revealed that the property was rectangular; four chains wide and seven chains long." Also see **furlong** and **pole** .

chain carrier, chainbearer, sworn chain carrier: the ancient term for one who assists a surveyor in establishing boundaries by carrying the measuring chain from point to point; a surveyor's assistant, e.g., "The chain carrier hoped one day to become a county surveyor."

chain of title: documents or writings showing the chronological sequence of ownership of land through which present title has devolved, e.g., "With the deed a statement showing chain of title from the original land grant down to the new owner."

chair table: a table with a top hinged so as to raise to an upright position and thereby serve as the back for a seat hidden when the table is in the horizontal position, e.g., "Chair tables saved much needed space in the small homes of past centuries."

chair wheel: a spinning wheel with a seat facilitating the use of double or divided treadles, e.g., "Divided treeadles required a chair wheel."

chaise, shay: a two-wheeled carriage, pulled by one horse and seating two people, usually with a top that opened and closed, e.g., "The famous 19th -century poem 'The One Horse Shay' spoke of the construction of a chaise." Also see ***carriage.***

Chamber of Commerce: a non-profit organization of those who would further the welfare of a community, state and nation, e.g., "She located the ancestral property with the help of maps she procured from the Chamber of Commerce."

chamber: a sleeping room, usually on the second floor and named according to the room over which it was situated, e.g., "She slept in the parlor chamber, and the two youngest children were placed in the kitchen chamber."

chamber pot, thundermug: a pot used for relieving oneself, usually of a capacity of a gallon or more, and stored in a commode in a sleeping room, e.g., "Better 18th-century chamber pots were made of porcelain."

chambray: a two-colored fabric made of any material, e.g., "The chambray dress was pink and violet."

chancel: early, the eastern end of a church; the end of a church building where is found the alter or communion table, e.g., "Early Episcopal churches almost always had the chancel on the east end of the building."

chancellor(s): early, those judges with the authority to moderate the law when conscience or fairness required it, e.g., "In some states, such as Tennessee, the distinction between chancellors and judges at law has been maintained down to the present time."

chancery, courts of: except in a few states, no longer distinguished from courts of law; a court having general equity powers as distinguished from those at law, e.g., "In early times, courts of chancery universally were separate and distinct from law courts."

chancre, chancroid: a sore arising from a venereal disease, e.g., "The chancres described in early medical records were caused by the 'secret diseases'."

chandelier: early, any hanging fixture designed to hold candles or lamps, e.g., "Only better homes had other than the crudest of chandeliers." Also see ***chandler.***

chandler, candler: the occupation of one who makes and sells candles; occasionally one who sells trinkets, curios, gewgaws, etc., e.g., "Until the advent of lamp oil, one might earn a living as a chandler"; "The local chandler also sold toys."

charbon: See ***anthrax.***

charcoal irons: smoothing tools (now, "irons") into which coals were placed to maintain heat for a long period, e.g., "Her charcoal irons were very heavy and exhausting to use."

charger: a large, flat, shallow metal or wooden dish used for serving meats and poultry, e.g., "Chargers are common items in early inventories."

charter: in genealogy, any writing by which government bestows rights or privileges, e.g., "The charter of the Ohio Company granted extensive rights to the use of land in the Northwest Territory."

charwoman: a woman hired for menial housework, e.g., "The record of Susan working as a charwoman reveals her low station in the community."

chase, chaser, chased: usually, to engrave metal, or to decorate one metal with another; one who is skilled in chasing metals; a metal object that has been decorated or embossed with another metal or gemstones, e.g., "The caster was brass chased with silver"; "Her brooch was silver plate chased with a beryl."

chatelaine: a pin or brooch-like clasp, worn at the waist by women, e.g., "Her chatelaine was of red gold with seed pearls."

chattel: any tangible, movable personal property; rarely, "chattels personal" referring to intangibles that are negotiable instruments or evidence of debt, or "chattels real" referring to an interest in realty less than a *freehold* (q.v.), e.g., "Among his chattels were farm implements and tools."

chebobbin: a "drag sled"; a large, sturdy, sled used to haul logs and other heavy loads, e.g., "With an axe, two horses, an old chebobbin, and an enormous effort, he cut and sold enough logs to feed his family that winter."

cheap: unlike now, inexpensive, e.g., "Currier and Ives advertised that their prints were fine and cheap."

checkers: See **pool checkers.**

checks: See **games of children.**

chect linen, checked linen: a common early linen cloth made with various colors woven in the shape of a checkerboard, e.g., William Parham's store stocked chect linen."

cheese press: used in making cheese by pressing liquids (whey) from milk curds, e.g., "The housewife put the cheese press to good use each autumn."

cheesemonger: a merchant or one who deals in cheese, e.g., "There were several cheesemongers listed in early New York City."

chemise, chemmy: a long, straight, loose undergarment or night gown; a long, straight, plain dress with sleeves, e.g., "At her death, Susannah had two chemises." Also see **mother hubbard.**

cherriderry: rather rough, calico-like cotton cloth used to make clothes for work and for children, e.g., "Because of the hard use that his work clothes had to bear, she made his cool-weather shirts of cherriderry."

Cherry Valley and Wyoming Valley Massacres: July 3, and Nov. 11, 1778, the name given those murders of New York and Pennsylvania settlers by Loyalists and Indians under Butler and Johnson, e.g., "The Pennsylvania county histories contain many tales of the Cherry Valley and Wyoming Valley Massacres."

chessart: a vat used for making cheese, e.g., "The chessart listed in the inventory revealed that the family probably made cheese enough for sale to the townspeople."

chest: early, any medium to large wooden box without drawers, but often with a hinged lid, sometimes made of sassafras, redwood, or cedar in order to discourage insects, e.g., "Two 'old chests' appeared in the 1691 list of furniture."

chest of drawers: any of several designs and shapes, with and without legs, of chests containing drawers, e.g., "Most country folks spoke only of chests of drawers, having never owned **highboys** (q.v.), **chests on chests** (q.v.), **chests on frames** (q.v.), etc." Also see **chiffonier.**

chest, chest of tea: usually 100 lbs, sometimes apparently 120 lbs, e.g., "The chests of tea thrown overboard during the **Boston Tea Party** (q.v.) weighed 100 or more lbs each."

chest on chest: appearing to be two "chests" of drawers on legs, one atop the other, with the upper usually being narrower with slightly smaller drawers, e.g., "The chest on chest was made of bird's-eye maple, as was common in early times."

chest on frame: a chest of two or three drawers having the appearance of a chest of drawers placed on a legged frame, e.g., "Her Chippendale chest on frame was truly elegant."

chest over drawers: a seldom-used term to describe a chest of drawers with a hinged lid over a box-shaped compartment in the top, e.g., "Chests over drawers were not common in the early days."

chestnut: as now, a nut-bearing tree; in genealogy, a color; a horse of deep, rich chocolate brown color, e.g., "She had a bay mare and a chestnut colt."

chicken pox: a disease, now principally of children, that lasted for six to eight days, brought a fever and a red rash, which, if disturbed, left minor scarring, e.g., "Before the advent of inoculations for the disease, virtually all children contracted chicken pox."

chickens, dungle fowl: early, meant young hens, as distinguished from roosters, especially of **dungle fowl** (q.v.), e.g., "She had several capons and ten chickens."

chiffonier, bureau: a short-legged chest, usually of four drawers, with a mirror mounted in the bonnet, and of many styles, e.g., "She had purchased the oak chiffonier from the local cabinetmaker.

chigger, harvest mite: a common mite causing severe itching, particularly aggravating at harvest season when men were required to handle grain crops extensively, e.g., "The chiggers were very annoying, especially at **haying time** (q.v.)."

child's part, child's portion: that portion to which a widow is entitled in lieu of dower or of a provision of a will, and equal to the intestate interest of any child of the decedent, it was subject to its prorata share of expenses down to final distribution, e.g., "The court set off her child's part of the estate of her husband."

chills and fevers: a common expression meaning any chilling and feverish condition thought to be a disease rather than a symptom, e.g., "For chills and fevers the pioneer mother often made a tea of redbud bark."

chimney board, fire fender, fender: a low shield placed before the fire, especially at night, to prevent hot coals from being ejected into the room, "Because of her fear of fire, she always had the chimney board in place."

chimney corner: a place by the fire; often used as a description of the place where would be found loafers or the indolent, e.g., "Byrd referred to North Carolina men as likely to be found in the chimney corner while their wives did the work."

chimney hooks: iron hooks, attached to the sides of the fireplace, from which stew pots and kettles were hung, e.g., "The blacksmith made the fireplace tools for the village, including **lugs** (q.v.) and chimney hooks."

chimney jack: See **smoke jack.**

china cabinet, china closet, curio: a medium sized, usually well-finished, doored cabinet with glass on the sides and in the doors, sometimes designed as a corner cabinet, and used to display and store glassware, china, and curios, e.g., "Her walnut china cabinet had a small mirror mounted on the bonnet."

china closet: See **china cabinet.**

china root: a root thought to have medicinal value, originally imported from China, e.g., "The apothecary maintained a supply of china root."

chintz, chints: a simple, inexpensive, printed cotton cloth, from which came the term "chincy" meaning cheaply made, e.g., "She made the children's everyday shirts and blouses from chintz."

chip hat: a straw hat; a warm weather hat for men or women, made of woven straw, hemp, etc., "They wore chip hats to keep the hot sun off their faces."

chirurgeon: a surgeon; one who through manual dexterity and training set bones, extracted teeth, and performed the limited surgery of early days, always distinguished from physicians, who sought to heal others through the use of concoctions and medications, e.g., "The ship's chirurgeon set his broken arm." Also see **physicians.**

chitlings, chitlins: muscles surrounding the intestines of hogs, deep fried and salted, e.g., "Chitlins were not eaten by upper class Southerners."

chivalry, chivalrous: early, having to do only with knights, and not used to refer to matters pertaining to inheritable nobility; later, any noble or gentlemanly conduct; e.g., "As a knight, he was expected to display the traits of chivalry."

chlorosis: anemia resulting from iron deficiency, the symptoms being dull yellow-green skin and complexion, e.g., "Arsenic mistakenly was thought to assist in curing chlorosis."

chocolate: other than as now, a pan used to melt chocolate, e.g., "There was a chocolate listed in the appraisal, meaning a pan."

cholera: an acute, terribly painful, and, in early days, usually fatal disease, symptoms of which were extreme vomiting, diarrhea, and horrendous cramps, e.g., "An epidemic of cholera ravaged central Ohio in the early 1850s, for which physicians administered calomel, silver nitrate, chloroform, ice, tea and coffee, and even strychnine and arsenic."

chologogues: those medications used to purge one of "bile", e.g., "In early Virginia, chologogues were used along with blistering and bleeding."

cholor: bile; the bodily liquid formerly thought to cause irascibility, e.g., "The doctor thought his frequent anger revealed an excess of cholor."

chop house: a low class house of entertainment, e.g., "The chop house was not attended by the upper class of Charlestonians."

chordee: a downward bending of the penis, congenital or more often resulting from gonorrhea, e.g., "For chordee, Dr. Lockhart administered aconite, belladonna and camphor."

chore: early and now, those daily or regular tasks assigned to some member of the family, e.g., "The little girls' daily chores included feeding the chickens and gathering eggs."

chorea, St. Vitus' Dance: early, a usually fatal disease of the central nervous system, the principle symptom of which is twitching, shaking, and involuntary movements, e.g., "Aconite and arsenic both were thought to assist in treating the deadly chorea."

christening: a religious ceremony by which one (usually a child) is admitted to a church; the naming of a son or daughter for a church official; quite usually, such ceremonies include **dedications** (q.v.), e.g., "In 1807, he was christened "Johannes George Schnyder, Jr."

chronological: a listing or ordering of events by date, e.g., "She set forth the births of her nieces and nephews in chronological order."

churches, Revolutionary period: religion was widespread and varied, even very early, e.g., "Paulin and Wright in *Atlas of Historical Geography of the U.S.* (Greenwood Press, 1975) found that of the faiths represented in 1775, Congregational churches numbered 668; Presbyterian numbered 558; Episcopal, 495; Baptist, 494; Friends, 310; German Reformed, 159; Lutheran, 150; Dutch Reformed, 120; Methodist, 65; Catholic, 56; and all others totaled 120 churches."

church yard, churchyard: a cemetery; early, the cemetery adjoining a church, quite usually reserved for members of that congregation; now, the environs of a church, e.g., "We found his grave in the Primitive Baptist churchyard." However, very early all but criminals and the excommunicated were buried in a church, church yard, or on private property, and criminals were buried out of the sight of God, in a "cemetery", e.g., "Since the preferred place of burial was near the church - in the church yard - until the twentieth century that term often was preferred over cemetery."

chymical: common, early form of "chemical", e.g., "The medication was made of a mixture of chymicals."

cicatrix, cicatrice, cicatrize: a scar left from a wound; the actions of a body in healing a wound, e.g., "The cicatrix from the musket ball was very large."

cinchona, Peruvian bark: the medically prized bark of the cinchona tree, from which was made quinine, tonics, salves, etc., e.g., "In his inventory, the old doctor had several pounds of cinchona bark."

Cincinnati, Order of: See **Order of the Cincinnati.**

cinnabar: mercuric sulfide, that mineral from which is extracted mercury, e.g., "The earliest physicians thought the medicinal value of cinnabar and the mercury extracted from it to be very great."

cinnamon, spirits of, oil of: a spice, thought to have medicinal value, e.g., "Dr. Knight prescribed **cordial** (q.v.) waters and spirits of cinnamon."

cipher, ciphered: to do arithmetical calculations; initials or letters embroidered on cloth, e.g., "He was not good at his ciphers"; "She had three ciphered handkerchiefs."

circa, ca., c., c: approximately; chronologically near to; in genealogy, a term used when a precise date or year is unknown, yet the date given is thought to be nearly accurate, e.g., "He knew she was born after 1820 yet before 1824, so he listed her birth year as circa 1822 (c1822)."

circuit courts: See **courts (circuit).**

cista: See **deed box.**

cistern: a large, usually lined and lidded hole in the ground in which rainwater was caught and stored for household use; any large container for liquids, e.g., "The cistern was at the corner of the house and was about eight feet deep."

citation: in genealogy, those words that reveal the source from which stated information was gained, e.g., "The citation set forth for the treaty date was, Richard L. Morton, Colonial Virginia, 2 Vols. (Univ. of N.C. Press, 1960), vol. 1, pp. 216."

citrine: an early known semi-precious stone, amber or yellow/orange in color, e.g., "She had a ring of citrine and two of opal."

city: in the U.S., usually a municipality, larger than a town or village, that governs itself under a charter granted by a state, e.g., "A city is not part of a county, yet governs itself in much the same way."

Civil Law: in genealogy, a system of laws not arising out of the common and ecclesiastical law, and adopted in early Louisiana by reason of the French citizenry and influence, e.g., "The use of the Civil Law makes Louisiana research in courts' records different from Virginia research."

Civil War (American): that armed conflict that took place between the South and the North during the years 1861- 1865; sometimes called the War between the States, or, by the North, the "War of the Rebellion" and, by the South, the "War of Southern Independence", and in which there were some 625,000 casualties, e.g., "The bloodiest single day of the Civil War, and probably of U.S. History, was September 17, 1862, the Battle of Antietam or Sharpsburg."

clamps: thought to be large scrub brushes such as were used on floors, e.g., "References to clamps usually appear in association with scrub water containers such as large buckets or kettles."

clap: See **gonorrhea.**

claret: a red wine, originally French; the color red, e.g., "It was considered appropriate, then and now, to serve claret with lamb."

claricord: a stringed instrument built in the shape of a spinet, e.g., "The claricord in the inventory probably revealed a measure of appreciation of music."

claspknife: early, any knife in which the blade folded into the handle, e.g., "His large claspknife was unusual for the 17th century."

clear and convincing: a measure of proof beyond that called *"preponderance of the evidence,"*(q.v.) but not as stringent as *"beyond a reasonable doubt"*, (q.v.); in genealogy, that quantum of evidence that leaves the researcher satisfied that one hypothesis is almost certainly correct as against all others, or that no other solution is likely to be found, e.g., "Clear and convincing usually is the measure of proof required by courts in matters akin to genealogy, such as dealing with wills, deeds, and explaining words used in other than ordinary ways."

cleaver: a large, heavy-bladed, handled knife, used to chop small bones within meat, e.g., "The expression 'pork chops' and 'veal chops' arose from the need to use a cleaver to chop the rib bones in those cuts of meat."

clerk's desk: See *schoolmaster's desk.*

clerk: in genealogy, that person acting as the keeper of records (and early, the scribe) of a political subdivision or court, usually the latter, e.g., "Gary Williams has been the Clerk of and to the Circuit Court of Sussex for twenty years."

clevis, clovis: a common tool of many uses; a heavy wooden or iron "U" with holes in both ends through which an iron or heavy wooden pin was placed in order to secure ropes, hitches, etc., "In the inventory were several clevises."

clicket: a doorknocker, e.g., "The brass clicket was most unusual."

clipper ships: the very fast, beautiful, and usually three-masted ships designed for speed, and in common use from 1845 or so until the 1870s, e.g., "After the magnificent clipper ships came the unwieldy appearing, steam-driven vessels."

clocks: as now; early, unlike now, decorations, usually on stockings of gentlemen and sometimes ladies, found at or near the ankle, e.g., "His worsted stockings were said to have had decorative clocks."

clogs: See *shoes.*

cloisonne: colorful oil decoration and painting where the colors are separated by metal or metallic paint, e.g., "She had both jewelry and vases of cloisonne."

close: early, the entirety of the inside of a dwelling house; later, a small, fenced field, e.g., "To enter the close without permission was a trespass"; "There was a close just outside the door to the kitchen."

closestool: a potty chair; a box, chair, or stool with a hole in the seat designed to hold a *chamber pot,* (q.v.), e.g., "The closestool was of cherry and very well made."

closet: early, a small room; now, a cabinet or recessed, doored storage space, e.g., "Her jelly closet was kept in a corner of the *cold cellar* (q.v.)."

clothes press, press, linen press: a doored chest of drawers in which clothes could be stored flat - 'pressed'; occasionally, a wardrobe or armoire, e.g., "Her clothes press was of cherry and had four drawers."

clothes smoothers: See **iron (to), etc.**

clothes squeezer: See **wringer.**

clove: a frequently used spice; a bud from which oil of cloves is pressed, the same used to flavor foods and medicines, e.g., "She mixed clove oil with chloroform, and applied it to the child's sore tooth."

clustergrape: a black currant, e.g., "What Maggie called clustergrape jelly was made from black currants, sugar, lemon juice, and gelatin."

Clydesdales: a breed of heavy, powerful, draft horses, popular in America early and now, and originally bred in Scotland, noted for long hair (feathers) on the backs of the legs and hoofs, e.g., "Budweiser Brewery introduced the long-popular Clydesdales to the modern business world."

clyster, glyster: an enema; any injection through the anus; a very common curative procedure until well into the twentieth century, e.g., "During the 17th century, clyster syringes often were listed in inventories."

coach: a common term for any closed, four-wheeled vehicle with seats facing each other, used for pleasure or ceremonies of state, e.g., "The coaches offered for hire usually were well-kept and clean."

coal oil lamps: See **lamps.**

coal oil, lamp oil: a common term, usually meaning the petroleum distillate kerosene; the term coal oil derived from the erroneous notion that kerosene was a by-product of or found in conjunction with coal; early, "lamp oil" often referred to whale oil, e.g., "The ready availability of coal oil in the 1860s brought the death of candles for illumination."

coaster: a small to medium size ship moving and trading between coastal ports, e.g., "Coasters were active in Albemarle Sound."

coats of arms, coat armor, armor: heraldic ensigns and emblems, originally painted on shields, "His coat armor bore lions rampant." Also see **heraldry.**

cobbler: one who repairs shoes, boots, harnessing, and leather goods, e.g., "Even though the distinction was often clouded, a **shoemaker** (q.v.) or **cordwainer** (q.v.) made shoes, and the less-skilled cobblers repaired them."

cochineal: early, a color; a dye made from the ground bodies of cochineal bugs, e.g., "The red dye in common cloth usually was made of cochineal."

cock: a rooster; a male of any large species of birds; a decorative weathervane in the shape of a rooster, as in weathercock; an iron projection from a plow blade; the hammer, spring, and latchback in the lock of a firearm, e.g., "She had several cocks and three dozen hens"; ""The blacksmith made him a new plow blade as he had broken off the cock"; "The gunsmith made a new cock for the old man's gun."

cocked hat: a man's jaunty pointed hat with a large stiff brim turned up, e.g., "He was the town dandy and was said to 'wear a cocked hat'."

cocklestairs: an early term for a spiral staircase, e.g., "Cocklestairs were common in the homes of the wealthy of early Virginia."

cockloft: derives from a high place where might be found roosters or birds crowing; a room in the **garret** (q.v.), e.g., "She had placed two old chairs and an old **chest** (q.v.) in the cockloft."

cockney: early, a citizen of the East End of London; now, an English dialect characterized by rhymes or limericks, e.g., "He spoke cockney, and was proud of it." See also **King's English.**

coddle: See **caudle.**

codicil: usually, an amendment to a provision or term of a will (dated, signed and witnessed), and added thereto subsequent to the signing of the original will, e.g., "The codicil added her youngest granddaughter to the list of beneficiaries."

coffee mill: any of the small household coffee grinders, widely used to grind coffee beans before modern sealed canning permitted the purchase of ground coffee; a large coffee grinder such as was used in stores, e.g., "By not grinding the beans in the coffee mill until time for its use, she kept her coffee much fresher."

coffer: a small chest or closable box used for valuables, e.g., "His coffer was full of silver coins."

cognac: originally, a brandy from the region of Cognac in France; later and now, any good brandy, e.g., "The cognac listed in the inventory probably was imported from France."

cognation: in **Civil law** (q.v.), any relationship, whether by blood or family, e.g., "The relationship between brothers may be called cognation in Louisiana."

cohabitation bond: official records created after the Civil War that legitimized marriages and the issue of slaves who had lived together, e.g., "Bill and Mary were happy to sign the cohabitation bond and so be married in the eyes of the church and the state."

cohabitation: literally, living together; in genealogy, a man and woman, either or both unmarried, conducting themselves as a family unit, e.g., "They had cohabited on the frontier for many years, and were married when the church was established there."

coin silver: silver of coin quality; fine alloy, very high in silver, e.g., "Evan has the coin silver watch that Tom Roberts bought in 1878."

colander: as now, a sieve-like pan or bowl with small holes in the bottom, used to drain and strain food, e.g., "Her colander was very important to making foods for the very young or the very old." Also see **riddle,** and **tea strainer.**

cold., col.: abbreviation for negro or black person, often found in legal documents and censuses.

cole: Saxon for cabbage, from whence derives "cole slaw", *slaw* meaning salad, (also see **cabbage chopper**); e.g., "She bought cabbage at the weekly market and made cole slaw."

colic, colick, colicky: as now, any discomfort of the stomach, usually in the very young, e.g., "Very early, it was thought that wolf dung carried about would aid one suffering from colic, and pioneer remedies for the colic included vinegar and water, Crawley root tea, nitroglycerin, calomel, and asafoetida."

collar: usually that padded portion of **harness** (q.v.) attached to the **hames** (q.v.) and against which the horse pushes to move a load, e.g., "The collar and hames are under great stress when a draft horse is moving a heavy load."

collateral lines, collateral branches: all relatives who are not directly (lineally) related; those families and persons related to the subject person through brothers or sisters of ancestors, or through marriages to such brothers or sisters, e.g., "The children of his great grandfather's brother were collateral lines in which he was interested."

collier: early, anyone who digs coal; later, one who digs, processes, or sells coal, e.g., "Thomas Baynham was a collier in Leicestershire and continued in that occupation in early Ohio."

collop: a small piece of meat broiled over open coals, e.g., "They had veal collops."

collyrium: an ointment for the eyes, e.g., "Dr. Drake made up a boric acid collyrium for his patients with **redeye** (q.v.)."

cologne, cologne water, foo-foo: unlike now, made at home, e.g., "Her recipe for 'cologne water' was '3 qts. spirits of wine, 6 drachms oil of lavender, 1 drachm of rosemary, 3 drams lemon oil, 10 drops cinnamon oil, mix well'."

cologne bottles, barbers' bottles: any of the many small, necked, ornate or decorated glass or ceramic bottles, often with a glass stopper, in which were stored colognes and perfumes, e.g., "Some of the cologne bottles are works of art."

Cologneware: any stoneware or crockery, so-called by reason of the early quality of such wares made in Cologne, Germany, e.g., "Being Pennsylvania Dutch, she called her best crockery Cologneware even though it had been made locally."

colonial: those years before the American Revolution during which the American states-to-be were colonies of England, France, Spain, etc., e.g., "By the 1750s, many colonials had begun to refer to themselves as Americans."

colonial churches: See **churches, Revolutionary period.**

colors: the flag or pennant bearing the symbols and colors chosen to represent a specific military unit, usually a regiment, originally carried into battle by a junior officer known as a cornet, e.g., "The loss of their colors in the Cornfield at Antietam caused great consternation among the Texans."

colt: See **horse.**

colter: See **coulter.**

coma: as now, a state of unconsciousness from which one seems incapable of awakening, e.g., "Dr. Lockhart administered blisters and mustard plasters, croton oil, and cathartics for coma."

comb-back chair: a variation of the **Windsor chair** (q.v.); a chair with thin vertical back slats set nearly parallel to each other and resembling a large comb, e.g., "She had a beautiful walnut comb-back chair."

combing jackets: a lacy or sheer, full ladies' cape worn about the home or while dressing the hair, e.g., "Only very wealthy ladies ever owned or dared to wear a combing jacket."

comfit: See **confiture.**

comfortable drinks: intoxicating liquors or beverages, e.g., "The early distrust in native water led to an increased consumption of comfortable drinks."

comforter: a quilt; a heavy cover, usually quilted or of wool; occasionally, a woolen scarf, e.g., "She made a big comforter for use on cold nights."

commission of administration: See **letters of administration.**

commitment: early, incarceration; later incarceration in a penal or lunatic asylum, e.g., "The sheriff was ordered to enforce the order of commitment for lunacy."

Committees of Safety: those citizens locally appointed in Revolutionary times and having the authority to call out the militia as danger approached, e.g., "When Cornwallis neared Tarboro, the Committees of Safety alerted the militia and the citizenry."

commode: in England early, a headdress of women; in the American colonies, a small cabinet with one or more small drawers for towels, etc., and a small doored compartment in which to place a **chamber pot,** (q.v.), e.g., "Most 19th-century commodes were made of oak or poplar, and only a few were of walnut or mahogany."

common: of low class, e.g., "She often referred to those of low station and manners as common"; "Indeed, those people are common."

common law: those customs and court decisions that through long use and recognition have gained the strength of law, as opposed to statutory law, which gains its authority from the legislative and executive branches of government, e.g., "**Primogeniture** (q.v.) had its roots in the common law." Also see **Civil Law.**

common-law marriage: an agreement to marry, followed by cohabitation, which arrangement has not been formalized in any legally accepted manner, and as to which relationship there was required a continued, not occasional, recognition by the parties, e. g, "By reason of their common-law marriage, she asserted a claim to a widow's share of his estate."

common pleas (courts of): early, the name given the lowest court of general jurisdiction in some states, while other names have come into use elsewhere, e.g., "While in Ohio and South Carolina the first court of general jurisdiction is Common Pleas, in North Carolina it is called Pleas and Quarter Sessions, and in Virginia is known as Circuit Court."

Common Prayer, Book Of: the printed liturgy and approved public form of prayer prescribed by the Church of England; widely circulated, used and read throughout the early colonies, e.g., "The Book of Common Prayer was in virtually every colonial household that had a literate master."

common scold: See **scold.**

community property: property owned in common by husband and wife; property gained by a husband or wife during marriage, not intended by the couple to be owned singly, e.g., "Their furniture was viewed by the court as community property, even though she had purchased and paid for it when he was not present."

company: See **armies, organization of.**

compilation: a literary writing or recording formed by the collection and assembling of "...preexisting materials... that are selected, coordinated, or arranged in such a way that the resulting work constitutes an original work of authorship." 17 U.S.C. 101, e.g., "Margaret's compilation of 17th-century records required that she be very selective."

complainant: one who brings suit; a **plaintiff** (q.v.) in an action at law or in equity, e.g., "The plaintiff is called a complainant in many jurisdictions."

compote, compotier: occasionally, a cooked, sweetened, fruit dessert; usually, a stemmed, lidded glass bowl in which to serve nuts, candies, or small confections, e.g., "The compote was of **milk glass** (q.v.)."

Compromise of 1850: those five acts of Congress designed to quell unrest over slavery and territorial admissions either imminent or projected, they brought together for the last time the oratory of Clay, Calhoun and Webster, and resulted in the admission of California as free, permitted Texas, Utah, and New Mexico to choose, continued the several fugitive slave acts, and abolished slavery in the District of Columbia, e.g., "The legislation called the Compromise of 1850 would not last much beyond the deaths of the great orators."

compt, accompt: early term for an account or computation, e.g., "He kept compts for most of his customers."

compurge, compurgation, compurgators: the act of attesting to the credibility, veracity, or truthfulness of another, e.g., "In early courts' records trials, character witnesses were called compurgators."

conceits: fancy desserts or confections, e.g., "Mrs. Randolph wrote of a conceit called a 'Hens' Nest', made of sweetened lemon and blanc mange."

concoction: an early term for any mixture, usually having medicinal purposes, e.g., "Physicians mixed concoctions to aid in healing."

condemnation: a taking of private property by government where the owner is not compensated, e.g., "His tavern was declared a public nuisance and was condemned and closed by the colony." Also see **eminent domain.**

condiment: as now, seasoning or sauce used with other food, e.g., "She kept condiments at the table in her **caster** (q.v.) and **cruets** (q.v.)."

condylomata: a wartlike growth in the area of the genitals, e.g., "He suffered greatly from a condyloma, and treated it with calomel and weak nitric acid."

Conestoga: a large wagon, ribbed and canvas covered, with huge wheels, designed for transportation of freight, heavy goods, and large loads, first made in Conestoga, Lancaster County, Pennsylvania, and thereafter in many places; a large, heavy and powerful strain of draft horses, so named by reason of their use with large wagons, such as the Conestoga, e.g., "He rented Conestogas and wagons in Lancaster." "There were hundreds of Conestoga wagons travelling the Philadelphia Wagon Road."

confections: See **desserts,** and **candy.**

Confederate Army, Boys in Gray, Rebels: the armed forces of the Southern states during the Civil War, e.g., "The last survivor of the Confederate Army was John Salling of Virginia."

Confederate States Of America, Southern Confederacy: See **secession.**

confess: to consent to a legal remedy sought, or to admit the truth of an allegation, e.g., "He confessed judgment in favor of Hunt."

confirmation: in genealogy, a religious service by which one who is of the age of discretion is established (confirmed) as a member or participant in a chosen faith, e.g., "His confirmation took place on 17 August 1814." Also see **baptism** and **christening.**

confiture, comfit: a sweetmeat, confection or candy, usually of fruit preserved in sugar, e.g., "She had confitures of both raspberries and strawberries"; "The comfits she made were fit for the King."

conjugal rights: the right of a husband or wife to the companionship and affection of the other; often used to describe the rights of a spouse to sexual relations, e.g., "He was deprived of his conjugal rights by reason of her protracted mental illness."

conniption, conniption fit: hysteria, involuntary shaking or jerking; often used as a humorous and exaggerated description of the effect one's actions would have upon another, e.g., "If you dirty your Sunday clothes, your mother will have a conniption fit."

connubial: matrimonial, e.g., "The newspaper account revealing Ida and Bill's marriage spoke of their entering into a state of connubial bliss."

consanguinity: of the same blood; relationship to another through birth or 'blood'; the relationship between one and those related to him or her through ancestry or descendency, e.g., "His great aunt's grandchildren were his second cousins through consanguinity." Also see **affinity,** and **collateral lines.**

conscription, conscripts: an enrollment of persons, usually into a military unit, e.g., "The Civil War was the first utilizing American conscripts."

conservator: a protector of assets or property, e.g., "She was no longer able to care for her interests, so a conservator was appointed."

consideration: in law and genealogy, the reason or motivation by which a sale, bargain, or contract are entered upon; that asset or thing considered by the parties to be of value and given over in exchange for something else, e.g., "In his deed to her the consideration for the 300 acres was 200 dollars Proclamation money and 'love and affection'." See also **deed of gift.**

console table, half-table: a small side or **lamp table** (q.v.), or a table with a half-round top, e.g., "She had a mahogany console table that she kept against the wall in the main hall."

consort: a non-specific term designating a husband or wife when the other spouse is still living, e.g., "The consort of Queen Elizabeth II was

Prince Philip."

constable: a public officer of a town or section of a county whose duties include matters of the peace, the service of writs, and the custody of jurors, and whose powers vary, and are less than those of a sheriff; early, a more important officer of the law than now, hence the title and office were actively sought, e.g., "Constables of the 18th century usually had the same duties as today, however their positions then carried a greater measure of respect."

consumption, phthisis: often, any disease accompanied by great weight loss or loss of muscular tissue and associated with racking coughs, pleurisy, fever, and cancers, e.g., "**Tuberculosis** (q.v.) caused a rapid and severe deterioration of the body of its victim, hence was one of the diseases called quick consumption."

contemplation of death: See **in contemplation of death.**

contemporary, contemporaries: as now, at the same time; a record created at the time of the event it memorializes, e.g., "Pepys' Diary is a classic example of a contemporary record, it having been kept by him throughout the 1660s."

contiguous: in quite close proximity, yet unlike now usually not connecting or touching, e.g., "While the tracts of his sons were said to be contiguous, they may not have adjoined his."

Continental Line: soldiers of the Revolutionary War who served at least two years and were of the so-called **regular army** (q.v.), i.e., were other than State **militia** (q.v.) and **conscripts** (q.v.), e.g., "He served in the Continental Line from October of 1778 until February of 1781, and then in the Virginia State Militia until the surrender at Yorktown."

contrat: (Fr.) contract, e.g., "The Louisiana records revealed that the matter was in the nature of contrat."

conversation, conversacon: to keep the company of another, usually of the opposite sex, for illicit or immoral purposes, e.g., "Thomas Hunt was said to have been 'of lewd life and conversacon'."

convey, conveyance: to transfer certain rights or a measure of title or ownership to another, e.g., "He conveyed 640 acres and a cow to his son Moses."

cookstove: usually a cast iron stove, burning wood or coal, and used in a kitchen. Also see **four-plated stove.**

cooley can: a ten- to twenty-quart metal container for cold water, having an insert into which whole milk was poured for cooling and so causing the cream to rise to the top for removal, sometimes with a spigot at the bottom to draw off the milk, e.g., "Most poor farmers did not spend the money for a cooley can."

coop: a cage for small animals, especially fowl and rabbits, e.g., "There were several coops revealed by the appraisal."

cooper: a maker of barrels and other round wooden containers; e.g., "He worked both as a slack cooper, making barrels for liquids, and as a dry cooper, making containers for dry substances."

cooperage: a term of trade meaning the cost of the barrels or containers required to deliver the product bought or sold, e.g., "In 1700, the flour was priced at nine Shillings (9S) per hundredweight and the cooperage was agreed to be two pence (2p).

coparcenary, coparceners: joint inheritance; those who jointly inherit some property, e.g., "The property of the intestate went to his brothers and sisters as coparceners."

copper: early, a very large pot or kettle; later, a copper, brass or bronze coin of small denomination, usually a penny, e.g., "The little child was proud of the three coppers he had saved."

copperas: iron sulphate; a common yellow dye, e.g., "She kept copperas in order that she might dye cloth yellow."

coppersmith: one who manufactures or works with copper, e.g., "Paul Revere was one of the most famous of American coppersmiths."

copyright: the title for that U.S. government recognition accorded an author of a literary product; that Constitutionally based statutory right to gain protection for writings and other products of the intellect. See Harper and Row, etc. vs. Nation Enterprises (1985) 471 U.S. 539; 85 L. Ed. 2nd 588; 105 S. Ct. 2218. Time limits 17 U.S.C. Sections 301, 3021, e.g., "Jo was granted a copyright for her Rowan County record abstracts"; "He knew that he could copyright his work if it was original."

coracle: a small, usually round fishing boat made of leather or skins stretched over a wooden framework, e.g., "Early Welsh fishermen made their own coracles."

coram nobis: literally, before us; a finding of error by an equal court; refers to a writ setting forth an error of another court of equal jurisdiction, e.g., "The writ of coram nobis was directed from the full court to the court at ***nisi prius*** (q.v.)."

coram non judice: refers to a matter heard by a court that had no jurisdiction in the matter, e.g., "Despite its lack of jurisdiction, the Ohio county court found him guilty of a felony, so a writ of coram non judice was issued."

coram vobis: an order from a higher court to a lower, ordering a correction of a prior error by the lower court; refers to a review by a higher court of a decision of a lower court, e.g., "The writ of coram vobis from the ***court of appeals*** (q.v.) ordered the ***circuit court*** (q.v.) to correct its error."

coram, coram me: meaning in the presence of, or in my presence, e.g., "The indenture was executed by the parties and the witnesses signed their names followed by the words coram me."

cord: usually, a measure of firewood equalling 128 cu. ft. (8' X 4' X 4'); two (2) ***ricks*** (q.v.) of wood, e.g., "In 1850, the price in Ohio for a cord of good fireplace oak was less than $1.00."

cordial bolus: See ***bolus.***

cordial: early, a stimulant, especially for the heart, and containing alcohol; sometimes in ***bolus*** (q.v.) form, and made from common compounds, including mace, nutmeg, licorice, rhubarb, barley and oil of roses, e.g., "The early physician mixed a powerful cordial of iodides and alcohol."

cordiner: See ***cordwainer.***

cordovan, cordwain: soft, fine-grained, highly finished leather, usually of brown or red brown color, e.g., "His best boots were of cordovan." See also **cordwainer, cordiner.**

cordwainer, cordiner: one who makes shoes, boots, wallets, etc., from fine leather, e.g., "Being a cordwainer, he was quick to distinguish himself from a mere **cobbler** (q.v.)."

coriander: as now, a seasoning; a popular early medication for palsy and **apoplexy** (q.v.), e.g., "She kept coriander both for cooking and for making medicines."

corn, maize: early, maize was known to the American Indians but not in England; any grain that did not grow in pods; any unharvested feed grain, such as wheat, barley, oats, and rye, e.g. "The 1666 Joyner 'corn mill' probably rarely saw what we call corn (maize)."

corn husking bee: a game of harvest season in which the winner was he or she who husked the most corn in a given time period or finished a given row or section in the least time, e.g., "Autumn was made enjoyable by pastimes such as corn husking bees."

corn meal mush: See **mush.**

corn whiskey, corn liqour, corn likker, corn, moonshine, hooch, white lightning, white mule: whiskey made from fermented corn, e.g., "Corn whiskey, often called moonshine after it became illegal, was (and is) manufactured throughout the Appalachian Mountains."

corner chair: a free-standing chair, wherein the back is on two sides, divided and at right angles permitting the same to be used in a corner, thus saving space, e.g., "There was a padded corner chair in the corner of the small library."

Cornet, cornet: an honor; that person, usually commissioned to do so, who carried the colors or guidon of a troop of cavalry, e.g., "He was a Cornet in the **horse** (q.v.) of Charles I."

cornice: a shield or cover, so hung as to cover the rods, hooks, and hangers upon which drapes and curtains were suspended, e.g., "Her bed cornices were painted with blue buttermilk paint."

coroner's inquest: an examination or investigation by a coroner and a jury summoned for purpose into the cause of a death occurring under suspicious or undeterminable circumstances, e.g., "In the early colonies there were many records of coroner's inquests."

coroner: an ancient office; a county officer whose duty it is to inquire into any violent, unexplained, or sudden death; in some jurisdictions the coroner still assumes the duties of the sheriff upon any disability of that officer, e.g., "After causing the suspected persons to **'stroke the body'** (q.v.), the coroner determined that the death was accidental."

corporeal property: material objects, usually **personal property** (q.v.), e.g., "While the building was corporeal property, the income from it was incorporeal."

corps: See **armies, organization of.**

corpse: See **stroking of a corps(e).**

corroborating evidence: in genealogy, that evidence which confirms or strengthens prior or other evidentiary material, e.g., "The entry in the Bible corroborated the facts stated in the newspaper column."

corsair: a privateer, e.g., "During the 16th and 17th centuries, the **Spanish Main** (q.v.) abounded in corsairs. Also see **pirate.**

cosmopathic: healing by appeal to some supernormal or extraordinary power or force, e.g., "In our early days, some folks believed that comets had cosmopathic powers." See also **homeopathic.**

costrel: a drinking bag or container, made of skin or leather, with handles, e.g., "Costrels were seldom used in the colonies, except on the frontier." See also **jack.**

cotenancy, cotenants: a tenancy of owners having distinct and varying titles, yet sharing enjoyment of the premises either physically or in income, e.g., "She had an interest by **devise** (q.v.) and he a lesser one through purchase, so, even though unequal they were cotenants."

cotter pole: an iron bar in the fireplace over which pots and kettles are hung, e.g., "The blacksmith made the cotter poles for most everybody."

cotton batting: See **batting.**

cotton notes: warehouse receipts given for bales of cotton stored in a public warehouse, often used as early currency, e.g., "His estate contained cotton notes of substantial worth."

couch: unlike now, an upholstered, long couch without a back, and having an elevated end designed as a headrest; sometimes early, a large bed for but one person, e.g., "The couch was of tufted wool and Victorian in styling"; "A couch and two **bedsteads** (q.v.) were listed with other **chamber furniture** (q.v.)." Also see **lounge.**

coulter: a knife-like piece of iron (early) or steel (later), 8 to 10 inches long, mounted ahead and in the path of a plow point, designed to cut roots while breaking new land, e.g., "The two coulters in the inventory revealed that he may have broken new land to the plow."

count, countess: early terms; now, in Britain, an earl and his lady, e.g., "Of the **nobility** (q.v.) present, the count - earl - and his lady enjoyed the greatest wealth."

counterpane: a coverlet, formerly sewn in squares resembling window panes, now of any pattern, e.g., "The counterpane in the master bedroom was of many colors."

country, pais (Fr.), pays: unlike now, everyone of the nation, the populous of the nationality, e.g., "A trial per pays or trial by the country both mean trial by jury, by one's peers."

country furniture: refers, not to quality, but to any early furniture made by other than well-known cabinetmakers, e.g., "Even though country furniture, the walnut table and chairs made by the early Vermont cabinetmaker were exquisite."

country linen: rough, sturdy, homespun fabric, made of flax and used in clothes of heaviest wear, e.g., "Their station in life was apparent by their use of country linen clothes for church wear."

county: next to colonial governments and later the States of the Union, the most important subdivisions of early America, and the principal political subdivision within a state, each county maintaining a court of general jurisdiction, the taxing authority, a repository for documents, law enforcement officers, and a treasurer, e.g., "Our pioneer ancestors looked mostly to the county for both the benefits of and the restrictions issuing from government." See also ***precinct, town,*** and ***manor.***

county courts: courts of record having jurisdiction at ***nisi prius,*** (q.v.) guardianships, limited criminal jurisdiction, and usually hearing appeals from the justices of the peace, e. g, "Judge Richeson was a very able Ohio county court judge even though he had no legal education."

county history (-ies): refers to those many late 19th-century publications of varying quality that told of specific counties, their people, politics and happenings, subscriptions for which usually were gained prior to publication, the subscribers submitting information of genealogical interest, e.g., "In the Blair County History he found a map and an early tax list that revealed the presence of his ancestor."

county seat: that designated community or place within a county where court regularly is held, deeds recorded, and taxes paid; the term is very old, and referred to the place where the judges literally sat and dispensed justice and where ***court days*** (q.v.) were celebrated, e.g., "He went over to Findlay, the county seat, to pay his taxes."

county town: the county seat of a county or ***shire*** (q.v.), e.g., "Our county seats are called county towns in Great Britain."

courses and distances: land boundaries set forth in compass points and measured distances, e.g., "Beginning at the southwest corner, the course and distance of the west line was 'north 10 degrees east, a distance of 310 feet'." Also see ***metes and bounds.***

court: in genealogy, either a judge or the judicial office of judges; an officer appointed or elected to make decisions at law or in equity; early, a judge of cases at law, as opposed to in equity which latter were decided 'in chancery' by ***chancellors*** (q.v.), e.g., "The court decided that the case was one of assault and battery"; "The summer session of the court of pleas and quarter sessions commenced in early June."

court cupboard: a cupboard with an open bottom, a shelf, and hinged doors concealing shelves at the top, e.g., "Her old court cupboard was made of yellow poplar."

court days: those predetermined dates during which the regular court sessions were held, usually quarterly, and during which celebration and games, shopping, trading, meetings, and elections were held, e.g., "The horse races will be held in May during court days."

court of chancery: See ***chancery (court of).***

court of common pleas: See ***common pleas (courts of).***

court of oyer and terminer: See ***oyer and terminer, (courts of).***

court of pleas and quarter sessions: See ***pleas and quarter sessions (courts of).***

court of probate: See ***probate courts.***

court of quarter sessions of the peace: See ***quarter sessions of the peace (courts of).***

courtesy: See ***curtesy.***

courting chair: See **love seat.**

courts of appeals: in the courts of the United States, those courts of three judges each, established for each of the nine U.S. circuits; in D.C., Kentucky, Maryland and New York, meaning the court of last resort; the next highest court in all other states, as well as in Connecticut, Virginia and West Virginia, however in Connecticut the highest court is the Supreme Court of Errors, and in the Virginia the highest is known as the Supreme Court of Appeals, e.g., "His appeal was heard in the Court of Appeals for the Third Circuit"; "She was careful to note the precise name given the court of appeals in states with which she was not familiar."

courts, circuit: those courts called common pleas in Ohio and South Carolina are the equivalent of the circuit courts in Virginia, "Sterritt, a Clerk of Courts in Ohio, and Williams, a Clerk to the Circuit Court in Virginia, hold almost identical positions."

cousins, once removed, twice removed, etc.: descendants of one's cousins, e.g., "His second cousin's son was his second cousin, once removed"; "His third cousin's grandson was his third cousin, twice removed."

cousins: early, any person related by blood who was not an ancestor, aunt or uncle, or a brother or sister; later and now, those blood relatives who descend from siblings of an ancestor, e.g., "His third cousins were descended from the siblings of his great grandfather."

covenant: early, a formal enforceable pledge to do something or pay over money or other thing of value; in common parlance, an agreement or compact, written or unwritten, e.g., "In a deed the covenant of seisin provides guaranties of the grantee's rights to possession."

cover, roger, cut: vulgar terms, meaning to have intercourse; breeding stallions were said to "cover" a mare, hence the application of the term to humans, e.g., "In confidence, she told her friend that he had covered her the night before"; "Samuel Pepys wrote of rogering his female acquaintances."

coverlet: as now, a bedspread; the outermost covering of a bed, e.g., "There were but two coverlets in the inventory, even though there were five beds."

coverture: the state and legal condition of a married woman, e.g., "During coverture, without his permission she had no right of sale in her own real estate."

cow doctors: a veterinarian; physicians also often acted as veterinarians during early times, e.g., "William Carter was a cow doctor who lived in Jamestown in 1625."

cowcatcher: the steel scoop or V-shaped ram placed a few inches above the track on the front of all early locomotives, designed to push animals, trees, and other debris from the tracks, e.g., "With the coming of the twentieth century, the cowcatcher was doomed."

cowl: a large vessel or kettle on a pole held between two persons, and in which liquids are carried; a large tub, e.g., "The two men carried the cowl of water to the slaughter area"; "She made up the dye and poured it into the cowl."

cowle, cowl: a thick, heavy linen fabric, such as used in the garb of a monk, e.g., "Early records reveal the presence of cowle for use in outerwear."

cozy: a padded cover to maintain warmth of a chocolate, tea, or other drink pot, e.g., "She had several cozies for use on the ***huntboard*** (q.v.)."

cracker, crackers: originally in England, a noisy, boisterous person; in the early states, illiterate country people, e.g., "Townspeople referred to uneducated farmers as crackers, and many often so spoke of all Georgians."

cracklins: apparently never pronounced cracklings; those small pieces of meat, skin, etc., that surface as the lard is rendered, e.g., "She always skimmed off, cooled, and gave the cracklins to the children as treats." Also see ***render.***

cradle: a bed for an infant; a narrow, slatted, platform attached to the foot of a scythe, the same used to catch the stalks or stems of grain, e.g., "Without the cradle, the harvesting would have been much more time consuming."

crane: a crooked pipe or siphon for drawing liquors from a cask or barrel; the iron hook from which kettles were suspended in a fireplace, e.g., "The innkeeper used a crane to gain wine from the big casks"; "The crane was of black iron, and held a stew pot throughout the winter." Also see ***crook.***

cravat: early called a neckcloth, cravats were both decorative and provided warmth, e.g., "The cravats of the early days became the neckties of today."

craze: to cause the appearance of myriad cracks in the glazing of pottery or glassware, e.g., "Crazed vases were very popular at the turn of the twentieth century."

crazy quilt: a quilt made of many different patterns and fabrics placed in random order, e.g., "Brittany received a crazy quilt made from the clothes of her ancestors." Also see ***linsey-woolsey.***

creamware: any buff-, oyster-, or cream-colored pottery, crockery or earthenware, e.g., "Beth had a creamware bowl that had belonged to her grandmother."

Creek War: that series of conflicts in Alabama and present Mississippi between the Creek Indians and the frontiersmen and Tennessee militiamen under Andrew Jackson that ended at the Battle of Horseshoe Bend, and resulted in the cession to the U.S. of most of the Creek lands, e.g., "James Findlay was a Captain of Volunteers in the Creek War."

creepers: small, low, black iron racks to hold burning logs, e.g., "The creepers were used in the parlor fireplace." Also see ***andirons.***

cresset, cressets, crussie: very large lamps or lights on metal poles or high pedestals, used as a beacons; a black iron basket in which were burned oil, ***pitch*** (q.v.), ***faggots*** (q.v.), small logs, or other combustibles, the same used for illumination, e.g., "Cressets are yet used as street lamps at Colonial Williamsburg."

crest: a term of ***heraldry*** (q.v.); the devices or designs designating a certain person or family, set over a coat of arms, and often mounted on helmets, etc., e.g., "Evan's crest, in part bearing two falcons, was known to all."

cricket: See *footstool.*

crisps: See *desserts, early.*

Crotoan inscription: the letters "CRO" on a rock and the word "Cro-toan" on a post were the sole evidence remaining of Raleigh's Colony that disappeared between mid summer of 1586 and 22 July 1587, e.g., "The Crotoan inscriptions perhaps revealed the island called Crotoan as the destination of the settlers when the Indian difficulties forced them to abandon Raleigh's Colony."

crock, crockery, crock jug: any container or dish made of clay; earthenware; a handled clay container for liquids, e.g., "Diane had several crocks, including one for butter"; "Cheryl referred to her clay water pitcher as a crock jug."

crome: a pitchfork with downturned tines used to unload a manure cart or wagon, e.g., "The crome was used to pull the manure along the bed and off the wagon."

crook: a pot hook, quite usually of iron, e.g., "Every home had several crooks." Also see **chimney hook** and **crane.**

cropper, share cropper: one who, though he has no interest in the land, farms the same in exchange for a share of the crop produced, e.g., "In the post-Civil War South, many who previously had owned substantial land worked as croppers."

crossbill: See **bill and crossbill.**

crossed "p" (𝒫): that character found in early English writings that appears like an ornate letter "p"; usually meaning "per-" or "pre-", e.g., "At the end of the 1680 inventory appeared the words '**Vera** (q.v.) 𝒫 W. E. ClCt', meaning verified by W. E., Clerk of the Court."

crotch grain: See *flame grain.*

croup: early and now, a severe infection of the larynx or throat, usually accompanied with congestion, in early times often fatal to children, e.g., "The early reports reveal that croup and whooping cough brought death to many children."

crow, crow bar: a metal door knocker, usually of brass or iron; a pry bar; a steel or iron bar with a bent, pointed tip, used to shift, raise, or move heavy items, e.g., "She had a pretty brass crow at the parlor door"; "Without the crow bar, the task of the wagonmaker would have been much more difficult. Also see **clicket.**

Crown: early, often called a dollar; a British silver or gold coin worth 5 shillings or one quarter **Pound (£)** (q.v.), e.g., "The Crown was probably the most common coin in colonial America."

crownglass: the finest of window glass, e.g., "Some of the finest of the early plantations had windows of crownglass."

cruet, cruets, cruet holder, cruet rack: small closable bottles used for condiments, and placed at the dining table; a caster or decorative metal (often silver or brass) stand or rack placed on the table, into which were placed individual cruets, e.g., "Her cut-glass cruets were kept in a solid silver cruet holder." Also see **caster.**

crumbcloth: a tablecloth; a cloth placed upon the table to facilitate removal of crumbs and to protect the wooden surface, etc., "Her everyday crumbcloths were made of pink cotton."

cruse, cruskin: in England, a small cup; in the colonies, a large kettle or pot with a handle and a spout for pouring, e.g., "Martha boiled the soap in a cruse, and carried it to the yard for the laundry."

cruset: a melting pot of a goldsmith, e.g., "The appearance of a cruset in the inventory made her suspect that the ancestor worked with gold."

cryer: an auctioneer, e.g., "The court ordered the sheriff to contract with a cryer for the sale."

crystal: glass of the finest quality, without blemish or discoloration, e.g., "The crystal wine glasses in the inventory probably were made in England." Also see **leaded glass.**

cubbies: See **pigeon holes.**

cubby holes: See **pigeon holes.**

cubs: in the Americas, the young of bears and foxes, e.g., "There were six fox cubs in the den."

cultivator: an implement used to work soil after plowing and before harrowing, e.g., "After the plow had opened the ground, the cultivator was the next step in the preparation."

cum testamento annexo: literally, with the will annexed; an administration of an estate where one dies with a will, however no executor was named in it, or the executor named in the will was not qualified or chose not to serve, e.g., "The will named Parker as the executor, however the bond named Hunt as executor cum testamento annexo." See **administrator.**

Cumberland Gap: that pass in the mountains between what is now northeast Tennessee and southeast Kentucky, through which passed myriad of our ancestors on their migration west, after the passage of which the immigrants went west and south to Tennessee and beyond, or north and west to Danville, Harrodsburg, Louisville and the **Ohio Country** (q.v.), e.g., "Many of the settlers on the Ohio River at Evansville had their roots in the Carolinas south and east of Cumberland Gap."

cup, cupping: in addition to the common meaning, the act of bleeding someone through an incision by placing a warmed glass cup over the wound and then cooling the glass and so creating a partial vacuum; phlebotomy, e.g., "Most planters cupped themselves and their families, rather than call a physician or chirurgeon." Also see **cupping glass.**

cupboard, step back cupboard: any of many cabinets, usually having set-back, open shelves above, creating a shallow work space, and doored compartments below, e.g., "The word cupboard originally meant board for cups."

cupping glass: a small glass vessel with a smooth top used to **cup** (q.v.) e.g., "Seventeenth-century inventories often reveal cupping glasses."

curator, curatrix: In civil law, a guardian, male or female; one who is appointed by a court to attend to the affairs of another, e.g., "While in Texas and Louisiana curators were appointed, in Tennessee, Virginia, Ohio that person was called a guardian."

curds: as now, as in 'curds and whey', e.g., "Curds and cream was a favorite Southern dish, made of curds 'carefully spooned to remove the whey', laid in a shallow dish, 'surrounded with thick cream', and eaten with powdered sugar'."

curio: any small memento or **pretty** (q.v.); any curiosity or heirloom, especially if made of glass or fabric; frequently, a paned, doored cabinet designed to hold mementos, e.g., "Diane kept a dozen or so curios in her grandmother's **side by side** (q.v.)." Also see **china cabinet.**

curricle: an uncommon, light, two-wheeled carriage or chaise drawn by two horses side by side, e.g., "He used the curricle for business trips of some distance."

Currier and Ives: that very well known, mid to late 19th-century manufacturer of colored prints and etchings, often idyllic, and usually of stylized home settings, but also of horses, transportation, trains, farms, and scenery, e.g., "Currier and Ives brought color and pleasure to millions of otherwise drab and somber rooms."

currier: one who prepares and dresses leather for use by other trades, e.g., "The currier's task well done resulted in beautiful shoes, boots, and fine harnessing."

curry: a brush or scratcher used to smooth the coat of a horse or mule, e.g., "Mrs. Bater carefully curried her horse every day in order to rid it of parasites and dirt."

curtain top desk: See **roll-type desk.**

curtains, curtins: early, usually the filmy or gauze-like hangings that surrounded a **bed** (q.v.); and used in summer to keep insects from sleepers, and, when more heavily textured, used in winter to prevent drafts or provide a measure of privacy, e.g., "The inventory revealed 2 **valance beds** (q.v.) and the curtains and **rugs** (q.v.) to go with them."

curtesy: early, the life estate in the real property of a deceased wife to which a husband was entitled if the couple had lawful children born alive, e.g., "Through the law of curtesy, at the death of his wife Mr. Haskins became the owner of the forty acres she had inherited from her father."

curtins: See **curtains.**

customhouse: that facility at which taxes were collected on goods being imported or exported, e.g., "The first customhouse for the Virginia colony was located at Jamestown."

custrel: a wine glass, e.g., "There were several custrels in the inventory."

cut (to): See **cover.**

cut: a unit of length equal to 900 feet or 300 yards, e.g., "The factory made one half cut of serge per day."

cut in: as now, to interrupt a dancing couple and take one of the partners as one's own.

cut out: See **cut in.**

cutlass, cutlace, cutlash, cutilax, kutlass: a broad, usually short, single-edged sword, generally thought of as the weapon of gentlemen, e.g.,

"In 1698 Owen Griffith, a former **Cavalier** (q.v.), bequeathed his kutlass to his youngest son."

cutler: early and now, one who makes or sells knives, or sometimes swords, sabers, etc., e.g., "He was a cutler by trade."

cutter: a small, light, usually one-horsed sleigh, seating two persons; a fast, light sailing ship used for near-shore and coastal waters, e.g., "During the long Vermont winters, the old doctor used the cutter to be about Burlington"; "By reason of its handling qualities, the cutter *Phoenix* was a favorite of the old sailors."

cutting horse: an agile horse of great endurance used by cattlemen to work within a herd, e.g., "His preferred his black cutting horse when cattle were to be worked."

cylinder top desk, cylinder desk, cylinder front desk: usually a good to fine quality, medium to large desk, with a recessing top shaped like a quarter circle or quarter barrel, e.g., "His cylinder desk was of solid walnut."

cynanthrophy: mental illness; madness, e.g., "It was said that one who suffered from cynanthrophy acted like a dog."

cypher, cipher: to do simple arithmetic, e.g., "The older children did their cyphering at the back of the one-room schoolhouse, thereby not being distracted by the teaching taking place at the front." Also see **rule of three.**

D

d (preceded by a number): abbreviation for pence or penny; a designator of the size of nails, e.g., "There were twelve pence (12d) in a Shilling"; "There were '1500 9d nails' in the 1679 Parker inventory."

d.s.p.: (Latin) decessit sine prole meaning that a person died without having had children; often seen in genealogies or genealogy charts, e.g., "Elizabeth Carner, 1831-1917, d.s.p."

daguerreotype: named for Louis Daguerre in 1839, a process by which a picture was made through exposure to the vapors of mercury of a silver surface made sensitive by iodine, e.g., "Many old daguerreotypes still exist in museums and private collections." Also see **ambrotype.**

dam: usually, a female equine parent; a term of breeders and owners of horses, e.g., "The Belgian dam and sire both were of the finest bloodlines."

damages: in the law, that money or thing of value ordered paid to compensate one who, through action, inaction or negligence of another, has suffered loss, detriment or injury to person, estate, family, or property, e.g., "To compensate Bater for the injury to his person and reputation, the court awarded him damages in the amount of £5."

damask: linen or silk woven with a texture, e.g., "The **weskit** (q.v.) of linen damask was most elegant."

damps, damp: it was early thought that noxious vapors arose from lowlands and swamps, especially at night, and that the same were infectious, e.g., "All mothers were careful that their children avoided the damps." Also see **drafts.**

damnified: to be damaged, as at law, e.g., "Early court records make many references to plaintiffs being damnified."

dances: as now, e.g., "Some early popular dances, other than dances traditional to specific nations, included **Virginia reels** (q.v.), polkas, minuets, giggs (jigs), square dances and **borees** (q.v.)."

dandy: slang, meaning splendid; a less than complimentary manner of referring to a young man known for overly stylish dress and partying, e.g., "He was the town dandy, and preferred the company of young women to gainful employment."

Danzik, Danzig: an early, better brandy, e.g., "The innkeeper listed two quarts of Danzig and a barrel of apple jack."

dapple gray: a color, gray with spots or splotches of lighter gray or white, usually of a horse, e.g., "His dapple gray **Percherons** (q.v.) were the largest in the show."

dasher (a person): a young person known for partying and light revelry, e.g., "She spoke of encountering a handsome dasher."

dasher (a utensil): See **butter churn.**

Daughters of the American Revolution, (Society of The, D. A. R.): a patriotic, hereditary, and charitable organization of women descended from men and women who performed patriotic or military service during the American Revolution, e.g., "Since her fourth-great grandfather had served in the Continental Line of Pennsylvania, she was eligible for membership in The Daughters of the American Revolution."

Daughters of the Confederacy (The United, U. D. C): a patriotic, hereditary, and non-profit society of women descended lineally or collaterally from persons who served honorably in either Confederate government service or in the armed forces of the Confederacy, e.g., "Since her great grandfather was an Asst. Adjutant General under President Davis, she was eligible for membership in The United Daughters of the Confederacy."

daybed: a narrow single bed, usually used for daytime naps; a chaise lounge; a long, padded seat, usually with a low back, the same for lounging or napping, e.g., "Except when guests were expected, Maggie kept their daybed in the corner of the parlor."

dead man's hand: the poker hand held by Hickok when he was shot dead, e.g., "Aces and eights with a nine has been the dead man's hand since 1892."

dead run: top running speed of an animal, usually a horse, and derived from the fact that a horse often will continue at its fastest pace until it collapses and dies, e.g., "Even at a dead run, his horse was no match for that of his opponent."

de bonis asportatis: an early action at law in trespass seeking the return of personal property taken away unlawfully, e.g., "The early records reveal many cases in trespass de bonis asportatis."

de bonis non (administratis): a successor or subsequent administrator of assets not previously administered, e.g., "When a previously unknown or undiscovered asset was uncovered after an estate had been closed, it was necessary for the courts to appoint administrators or administratrixes de bonis non."

de novo: of new; again; a second time, e.g., "The court issued a **venire** de novo summoning a jury for a new trial of the case."

deal, standard deal, slit deal, whole deal and deal ends: early units of measurement of unfinished lumber, a standard deal was 3" ('12/4') X 9" X 12', from which term and from card playing came the expression "good deal," "fine deal," "fast deal," etc., e.g., "There was forty deal(s) of poplar in that load."

death, contemplations of: See **in contemplation of death.**

debility: early ailments were thought to be diseases rather than series of symptoms of other diseases, and were so called, e.g., "For many debilities, Dr. Drake prescribed cinchona, eucalyptus, quinine, bitters and alcoholic stimulants."

debt, bondage for: See **peonage.**

debt, imprisonment for: See **debtors' prisons.**

debtors' prisons: early, imprisonment often was ordered where one failed to pay debts without legal justification for that failure, the records of which are valuable research tools, e.g., "Debtors' prisons were eliminated commencing in 1817, some of the last to do so having been Kentucky in 1821, Ohio in 1828, Vermont and New Jersey in 1830, New York in 1832, Connecticut in 1837, Louisiana in 1840, Missouri in 1845, and Alabama in 1848. Also see **peonage.**

decedent: usually, one who has lately died, either with or without a will, e.g., "Since her ancestor was described in the record as a decedent, she knew that he probably had died shortly before that entry."

decessit sine prole: See **d.s.p.**

decoct, decoction: to boil or dissolve in hot water, e.g., "Early physicians often wrote of their decoctions."

decoy: as now, and see **shawfowl.**

dedication: similar to baptism, but without the use of water; a "conscious" proclamation or devotion; a Baptist religious service having as its objective a commitment of thought and action to religious purposes, e.g., "At his dedication, he pledged his life to good works."

dedimus potestatum: a commission, usually temporary, granted to take testimony or to perform acts in behalf the court, usually at some distance, e.g. "The court record stated that a dedimus postatum had issued to Huntt to gain the testimony of Newsom."

deed: a formal written document that provides the evidence of a transfer of ownership of property (quite usually real estate) from one person to another; when imprecisely used as a verb, the act of transferring interests in land, e.g., "He executed a deed to John for the 100 acres"; "He deeded the property to his son."

deed box, cista: a small box with a lid and usually a lock in which were kept valuable papers, wills, documents,. deeds, etc., e.g., "His deed box was made of mahogany." Also see **strong box.**

deed of gift: a document by which something thought to be of value is transferred to another with the intention that nothing of value be given in return, e.g., "The deed of gift transferred a horse and **buggy** (q.v.) to her and mentioned his fatherly love."

defendant: as in the law, any person against whom an indictment, information, charge, or claim has been filed in a court, e.g., "As a defendant charged with a crime, he had the ages old right to confront his accusers."

defensives: an early general term referring to medicines and concoctions believed to prevent various ailments, e.g., "Ben Franklin advised hot bathes as defensives against many ailments."

defluxion: early, a description of what was thought to be the flow of bodily **humours** (q.v.) downward, e.g., "The swelling of her legs and feet was saind to result from a defluxion."

delftware, Delftware, Delfware, Holland china: better quality, glazed earthenware from Holland, the glazing often of tin, e.g., "Dr. Bater had two large delftware bowls."

delirium: mental illness not being understood, fevers associated with hysteria, lack of consciousness as to surroundings or actions, or nonsensical babbling were treated as ailments, e.g., "For delirium, he prescribed belladonna, digitalis, opiates, quinine and several different herbs."

demand note: a promissory note that the holder, at his election, may declare due and payable anytime after its execution, e.g., "Early extensions of credit, as now, often were in the form of demand notes."

dementia praecox: (also known as adolescent insanity) an ill-defined term used to describe any of several varieties of mental illness, e.g., "Dr. Lockhart treated her dementia praecox with hot and cold compresses."

demi-boots: See **shoes.**

demi-sangue: (Fr.) of half blood, e.g., "Early Louisiana records speak of mulattoes as demi-sangue."

demijohn: a large, small-necked glass container, usually protected by an open wooden encasement or a wicker jacket, e.g., "General Washington kept demijohns of favorite wines."

demise: death or an end of some action, e.g., "Shortly before Luke's demise in 1672, he leased the tract for twenty years."

Democrats: See **Whigs.**

dengue: breakbone fever; a severe and painful disease of the joints and muscles, peculiar to the South and not appearing in the records until after the beginning of the eighteenth century, e.g., "The dengue was similar to severe arthritis, however after a few weeks the disease subsided, apparently with no after effects."

denomination: an intended worth or value stated and set forth on the surface of coin or paper currency; a faith or religious discipline claiming an allegiance by a group of persons, e.g., "The bills were in two, three, five, and ten dollar denominations"; "The old church was attended by those of the Baptist denomination."

deodand: an ancient term meaning something given to the church in the name of God to pacify wrath, e.g., "Some early colonials offered deodands, hoping thereby to prevent epidemics."

depose, deponent, deposition: the taking of a statement of facts from one who is under oath, usually in response to questions; one who gives testimony under oath in other than open court concerning the truth of some matter, which testimony is reduced to a writing called a deposition; the word **affiant** (q.v.) is often imprecisely used when referring to a deponent, e.g., "The deposition consisted of the statements of three deponents, all sworn and deposed together." (also see **affidavit.**)

depressions: See **panics.**

deputy: a person empowered to act in behalf of another, usually refers to an officer of government, e.g., "In the absence of the coroner, the deputy coroner exercised the duties of the former."

derringer: named for 1850s **gunsmith** (q.v.) Henry Derringer, a common short-barreled pistol carried in a purse, pocket, or hidden on the person, e.g., "It was a bullett from a derringer that killed Abraham Lincoln." Also see **revolver.**

descend: real property (real estate) passing by operation of law at the moment of death, e.g., "The land descended to him in accordance with the statutes of **descent and distribution** (q.v.)."

descendant: one who lineally descends from another, no matter through how many generations; occasionally, those to whom property descends at a death, no matter of what kinship, e.g., "He was a descendent of a Mayflower passenger"; "There being no other known heirs, the land descended to his aunt's grandson."

descent and distribution: the effect of statutory and case law directing the disposition of property upon **intestate** (q.v.) death, e.g., "Since, at death, **realty** (q.v.) is said to descend and **personalty** (q.v.) is said to be distributed, laws controlling such activity are said to be of descent and distribution."

descent: hereditary succession; that land received by virtue of being an heir at law of another, e.g., "Being the only child, upon the death of his parents **intestate** (q.v.), he became the owner of the land by descent."

deshabille, dishabille: a negligee, e.g., "Only the most stylish and affluent colonial women spoke of their nightgowns as deshabilles."

desiccants, desiccatives: concoctions used to dry up sores or wounds, e.g., "The American Indians used various herbs as desiccants."

desk box: a lap-size wooden box with a hinged lid, used for writing, the supplies for which were kept inside, e.g., "As a planter who took long coach trips, he used his desk box frequently."

desk, slant-top desk, drop-leaf desk, drop-front desk, fall-front

desk: a **chest** (q.v.) with a writing surface; early, any of several designs and styles, usually with an angled drop-leaf writing surface, behind which were pigeon holes, a small drawer or two, having 2 or 3 drawers below the writing surface, and often with glass-paned, doored shelves above; later, any furniture designed for writing or working and having drawers, e.g., "Her desk was mahogany, with ball-and-claw feet and brass typical of the period." Also see **knee-hole desk,** and **cylinder-top desk.**

desserts, early: as now, fruit was a popular ingredient for sweet dishes of many varieties, e.g., "In addition to **sweetmeats** (q.v., candied fruits) and **suckets** (q.v., hard candy), patties were little sweet cakes; fried pies were spiced and sugared fruit in a fold of crust fried in a skillet; chess pie was a single crust pie of molasses, eggs, and flour, and henrietta pudding was similar with brandy added but without a crust ; bettys were sweetened fruit between crumb, shortening, and sugar crusts, while dowdies (pan dowdies) were bettys with a cream and fruit filling; if the top was of spices, sugar and flour, and it had no bottom or the bottom was of crumb, shortening, and sugar crust, it was a crisp; if fruit was covered with a layer of cake and then topped with flour, sugar, and spices before baking, it was a buckle; a cobbler was spiced fruit with a baked biscuit dough or other pastry top; if steamed, cobblers were called grunts, and if turned upside down for serving they became slumps; others were cheese cake, jumbals, flummeries, transparent, and pumpkin puddings."

detainer: usually, a legal action used where one who was legally in possession refused to give over land at the end of a lease term; or where one assumes an appearance of ownership or undertakes a possessory interest to which he has no legal right, "When Jones refused to give up the land at the end of his lease, Smith filed an **action** (q.v.) in detainer." (see **forcible entry** and **detainer.**)

determinable fee: See **fee determinable.**

detinue: writ of, or action in or of; an ancient common law **action** (q.v.) by which one sought to recover personal property lawfully obtained in the first instance, yet unlawfully later withheld from the owner, e.g., "When Smith would not surrender the merchandise Jones had paid him to store, Jones filed an action in detinue."

Deutsch: as in "Pennsylvania Dutch," See **Dutch.**

Devil's grip: See **pleurodynia.**

deviner: See **dowser, etc.**

devise, devisor, devisee: to give or grant land (real estate) to another by will, e.g., "He devised 100 acres to her"; "He was the devisor of the tract"; "As one of his devisees, she received forty acres." Also see **bequest.**

dewberry: raspberries, e.g., "Some early cookbooks spoke of dewberries when referring to raspberries."

diacodium: the oil from poppies and poppy seeds; an opiate, e.g., "The old doctor gave diacodium for most nervous disorders."

diaper: early, linen woven into floral patterns; a napkin, e.g., "The mention of diaper in early inventories has nothing to do with infants."

diaphoretic, diarrhoetick: as now, a purge; also, a concoction that promoted perspiring, hence was thought useful in **balancing the humours** (q.v.), e.g., "Dr. Drake prescribed hot, bitter diaphoretic cordials."

diarrhea: as now, e.g., "Early remedies for common stomach complaints accompanied by diarrhea included teas made of whole geraniums and black raspberry bark, and bark of the roots of Red oak." Also see **dysentery, flux.**

dibble, dibbele: a small spade, e.g., "The inventory revealed a **mattock** (q.v.), a **dung fork** (q.v.), and a dibble."

dice box: a box from which dice were rolled in games, e.g., "The presence of a dice box revealed time dedicated to games by children and gambling by adults." Also see **billiard and pea.**

diet-drink: early, a medicated liquor, usually prescribed to promote general well-being, e.g., "His prescription of diet-drinks had nothing to do with obesity."

digit: a measure of length equalling .75 inches, and supposedly the breadth of a man's finger, e.g., "The musket was bored a bit less than a digit."

digitalis: used since early times, a widely used and effective stimulant for the heart made from the dried leaves of the Purple Foxglove plant, e.g., "The 19th-century physician always carried digitalis for his heart patients."

dimity: early, common, fine cotton cloth, e.g., "She carried handkerchiefs of laced dimity."

dinner bell, dinner horn, dinner chime: a bell or horn rung or blown and used to summon to a meal those workers in the fields or at a distance, e.g., "Virtually every American farm of the 19th century had a dinner bell or horn." Also see **dinner.**

dinner pot: that large, often 2-to 10-gallon, kettle, usually hung in the fireplace on a **crane** (q.v.) and in which meat and vegetables were cooked into a stew, e.g., "In order that family members coming in from the cold might be warmed and nourished, the dinner pot was kept warm throughout the winter."

dip, dipping: early, as now, the practice of placing small amounts of chopped, smokeless tobacco (**snuff,** q.v.) between the teeth and cheek, e.g., "The practice by both men and women of dipping snuff was widespread in the old South."

diptheria: a dreaded, acute, and usually fatal bacterial disease, for which there was no inoculation until 1895, the symptoms of which were a raging fever, extreme sore throat, and severe congestion, e.g. "During the 1860s, as a cure for diptheria, Dr. Drake administered a gargle of honey, vinegar and alum, and stimulants such as alum and sulphur, lactic acid, and ice, none of which were of assistance."

direct indexes, reverse indexes: indexes to deeds and mortgages compiled in alphabetical order by surnames of grantors or mortgagors and grantees or mortgagees; often called grantor or grantee indexes, e.g., "She knew that the direct indices found in Tennessee registers offices served the same purpose as the grantor indices of Ohio." Also see **grantor indexes.**

dirk: a dagger; a common, small, knife-like weapon, usually carried hidden on the person, e.g., "The inventory included a dirk and a **case knife** (q.v.)."

disc: See **harrow.**

discharge: the release of a person from military obligation, may be "honorable", "dishonorable" or other; that written document intended to provide proof of the release of someone from a military unit, e.g., "She found his Civil War Discharge among his papers."

discutient: any early application of medication thought to have preventative qualities, e.g., "For a discutient, she prepared a garlic amulet."

disentailment: the legal result of those statutes of and after William IV by which **entailments** (q.v.) were extinguished, e.g., "Even though the deed to Sarah was in **fee tail** (q.v.), the statute disentailed the land."

dish: unlike now, a broad, wide container or platter from which solid food was served; sometimes, a rather deep, hollow container from which liquid food was served, e.g., "While the inventory listed only two dishes, the reason was that the word then had a different meaning."

dish-top table: any of several popular styles of small tables, including **tilt tops** (q.v.) that have a slightly depressed top or a rim around the top creating an appearance of depression, e.g., "Her tilt dish-top table was mahogany and of Victorian styling."

disinherited, disherison, disinherison: the state of being deliberately excluded from an estate - inheritance - in which one would expect and otherwise legally be entitled to share; e.g., "In his will, the father mentioned the son's supposed transgressions, and then specifically disinherited him"; "Early Oregon and Louisiana records sometimes speak of the disherison of children."

dissent: when the provisions of a will gave a widow less than she would have received by law had there been no will, she could dissent from the will and the courts would award her that portion she would have otherwise gained. "Having given her but the income from one fourth of his estate, upon her dissent the court raised the income to that received from one third of it."

distemper: a common term used until the mid-nineteenth century to describe almost any disease or sickness; nervous disorders, usually thought to emanate from the brain or central nervous system, e.g., "The mother would describe as a distemper almost any ailment that she did not understand"; "For distempers, he often administered oils of plants such as of cloves, cinnamon, and cassia, or penny royal or wintergreen, and even turpentine"

distress, make distress: a court-ordered seizure and assumption of ownership of assets to pay some debt or obligation, e.g., "The court ordered the sheriff to 'make distress' and seize the property of any person who failed to pay the new tax levy."

dittany: an plant with purple flowers, common to the eastern U.S., thought to have great medicinal value and used widely by early physicians and healers, e.g., "For snakebites, Dr. Lockhart often prescribed a decoction of dittany.

divers: diverse, various, sometimes "many different" e.g., "He gave divers reasons for his criminal acts."

divining rod: See **dowser, etc.**

division: See **armies, organization of.**

divorce: formerly, either the dissolution of marriage by a divorce **a vinculo matromonii** (q.v.) ('from the bonds of matrimony'), or a separation by divorce **a mensa et thoro** (q.v.) (from 'table and bed' or 'bed and board'), the latter being a suspension of duties that usually left the marriage in full force and effect; now, the word applies to all forms, e.g., "A divorce a vinculo matromonii left the parties free to remarry, while divorces a mensa et thoro were similar to modern legal separations and forbade cohabitation, yet left the marriage and property rights arising therefrom intact."

Dobra, double johannes: also Johannes, double joe, etc., a Portuguese coin equalling about four Pounds Sterling (£3/18S/5p), e.g., "There being very little currency available in the colonies, the merchants accepted the coin of many countries, including the sailors' gold Dobras, often called 'double joes'."

dock, docking: the stump that remains after a tail has been removed; to cut an animals tail, e.g., "She thought her **filly** (q.v.) would be a prettier **mare** (q.v.) if her tail was docked."

dog dollar, lion dollar: an early Dutch coin, so called by reason of a lion imprinted thereon that had the appearance of a dog, e.g., "By reason of the lack of currency, New York and Philadelphia merchants were happy to accept dog dollars from immigrating Hollanders."

dog fox: a male fox, e.g., "There were 2 **vixens** (q.v.), 6 **cubs** (q.v.), and a dog fox in the group."

dog irons: See **andirons.**

dog lock: a flintlock with a hammer of a design appearing like a dog's shoulders and head, e.g., "A few mentions of dog locks appeared in early New England writings."

dog, bench dog: a simple device tapped down into a work surface, designed to hold material being shaped or worked, e.g., "He had several bench dogs in his workshop."

dogdays: July 3 until August 11; those days during which Sirius, the 'Dog Star', rises and sets with the sun, e.g., "Dogdays were thought to bring distempers, especially of a mental sort."

dogs: See **andirons, etc.**

dogie, dogey, dogy: apparently unknown in England; in the American colonies, especially in the 19th-century West, an orphaned calf, e.g., "The lyrics in the old cowboy song, "...get along little dogey..." had nothing to do with canines."

dogtrot: a walkway; a hallway, openable on both ends and usually extending from one end of the house to the other, the same providing air circulation, e.g., "On rainy days, the dogtrot provided a safe place of play for small children."

doily: early, thin, cotton or woolen cloth or **napkin** (q.v.); later, as now, any small piece of cloth used as a pad or decoration under some small object, e.g., "The ell of doily listed in the ledger revealed that napkins likely would be made."

dollar: at the turn of the nineteenth century, a Dutch or German coin, e.g., "If an early reference to a dollar was in a neighborhood of Hollanders or Pennsylvania Dutch, the meaning may have been different from now." Also see **milled dollar.**

dolly stick, dolly tub: a narrow, wooden paddle or wide stick used to agitate clothes during laundering in a large kettle called the dolly tub, e.g., "One of the chores of the little girls was to help by working the dolly stick."

dome-top trunk: See **camel-back trunk.**

Domesday Book: that most revealing and incredibly detailed and accurate effort commissioned by William I - "the Conqueror" - and undertaken by five justices within each county in England commencing in 1081 and ending in 1086, e.g., "The Domesday Book consisted of two volumes, and in all of English history is probably the most valuable series of extant writings touching upon early life."

domicile: that place that one considers "home", and to which one would choose to return over any other residences; that place where one has chosen to live and vote, e.g., "During the work week, he lived in New York City, however his home in New Jersey was his domicile."

donatio causa mortis: a gift of personal property in anticipation or apprehension of death, with the understanding that should the giver survive, the asset again will be his or her property, e.g., "His gift to the child of two steers was donatio causa mortis." Also see **in contemplation of death.**

dornick: Scottish linen cloth used on a table or as napkins, e.g., "The inventory listing of dornick revealed a genteel lifestyle or background."

dory: early and now, a flat-bottomed rowboat with high sides, popular as a fishing boat, e.g., "In early times there were many dories in and about the fishing grounds of Chesapeake Bay."

dotage: a loss of understanding upon attaing old age; childlike actions sometimes seen in the very old, e.g., "In the 1844 lawsuit, Jacob Kistler was said to be a dotard, i.e., he was in his dotage."

Double Eagle: a $20.00 U.S. gold coin, e.g., "The inventory mentioned two double eagles kept in the house."

doublet: a close-fitting, vest-like garment, having a tail around like a very short skirt, usually without sleeves, e.g., "Both men and women regularly wore doublets during early colonial times." Also see **jerkin.**

doubletree: See **swingletree.**

dowdies: See **desserts, early.**

doubloon, doublon: a Spanish coin equalling two pistoles, e.g., "It is common to find mention of doublons in early southwestern records."

dough table, dough box: a small table or bin of women's waist height, "V"-shaped, usually with a shallow-lidded top; a dough box having a compartment under the hinged top surface; the same used to knead and work dough, and then place it beneath the top for rising, e.g., "Her dough table was kept in the corner of the winter kitchen near the stove."

Dover's Powder: the well known medication of Dr. Thomas Dover; a mixture of opium and ipecac, after 400 years still used as a diaphoretic, e.g., "The inventor of Dover's Powder had been a pirate."

dovetail: a widely used method to join corners of furniture or drawers, the cuts being shaped like the tail of a dove and then interlocked, hence the name, e.g., "The drawers were hand dovetailed both front and back, thereby revealing the high quality of the early workmanship."

dowager: early, a title of respect given to ladies (as opposed to women) who survived their husbands, e.g., "Her husband having been a gentleman, she was referred to as a dowager."

dower: that portion of the estate of a decedent that is reserved by law for the maintenance and support of the surviving spouse and their children; originally referred to funds to be derived or produced from any real estate gained by the deceased during marriage and which his children might have inherited; rights of a widow in real property of her deceased husband that varied from state to state, e.g., "At his death, the court ordered her dower to be set aside in cash."

dower chest: a decorated, usually well-made **chest of drawers** (q.v.), e.g., "In many families, each daughter was given a dower chest."

dowry: that property brought to the marriage by the bride, that early became the property of the husband, e.g., "As her dowry she brought sixteen head of **neat cattle** (q.v.)."

dowser, deviner, water witch, divining rod: one who is thought able to detect water, minerals, oil, etc., by use of a divining rod; a small fork of wood peach, apple, cherry, plum, witch hazel (particularly), thought to have magical powers to reveal water, oil, or treasure if used by one who has knowledge of such matters, e.g., "He was widely known for his powers as a deviner or water witch"; "Many was the dowser who, peach fork in hand, selected the spot to drill for water."

drab: thick, usually coarse woolen cloth, generally dyed yellow-brown, from which our current word 'drab' derives, e.g., "His overcoat was drab."

draft: conscription (q.v.) into military service, common in the U.S. during all wars after the Mexican War, e.g., "They failed to volunteer, hence were in the first local draft."

draft age: See **military age.**

draft horses, draught horses: heavy, powerful horses widely used for work, plowing, pulling heavy loads, turning stiles, etc., e.g., "His team of **Belgian** (q.v.) draft horses weighed 3800 pounds." Also see **Clydesdale, Conestoga, Percheron.**

drafts, draughts: slight, cool or cold breezes or movements of air, early thought to be a cause of many and various maladies; also, the game of checkers, e.g., "She sought to keep drafts from sleeping children"; "Draughts was a popular pub game in England." Also see *damps.*

drag sled, drag sledge: a wide-runnered, heavy, flat-bedded wooden sled, usually pulled by 1 or 2 horses, and used for heavy hauling about a farm, e.g., "In the winter, Mr. Keener would hitch the mare to the drag sled, spread straw on it, and permit the young folks to take it to the fields for play."

dragoon, dragoons: a soldier taught, equipped, and prepared to fight, usually on horseback but sometimes on foot, e.g., "At the Battle of Bunker Hill, the dragoons were dismounted."

dram or drachm: an eighth of an ounce; 3.89 grams; a small drink of any intoxicating liquor, e.g., "He took his drams with great pleasure"; "Early apothecaries and physicians very often referred to and wrote of drachms of medications"

dram shop: occasionally, drinking shop; a place where liquor was sold for consumption on the premises, e.g., "There was a dram shop near the Governor's Palace."

draper: one who makes or sells (or both) cloth for better clothing, e.g., "The old deed revealed that Griffith was a London draper."

draw knife, drawknife: a bladed tool with handles on both ends, so designed as to cut when the tool is drawn toward the body, e.g., "Every carpenter and cabinetmaker had drawknives."

drawers, long johns: as now, undergarments, usually covering the legs and lower part of the body, e.g., "His drawers were of cotton."

draws: an early word referring to drawers of a *chest* (q.v.), e.g., "She had a *chest on chest* (q.v.) with three draws above and two below."

dray, dray cart: very early, a two-wheeled cart used to haul beer; later, any sturdily built cart or wagon used for the transport of goods, especially for hire, e.g., ""The Capitol City Line had 8 drays and 14 draymen in its employ."

Dred Scott Case, Dred Scott vs. Sandford: that classic and much studied Supreme Court decision of 1857 that deeply angered the North by determining generally that Scott, a slave, by residing for a period in a "free" State, was not himself thereby free, and that the *Missouri Compromise* (q.v.), insofar as it declared him free, was unconstitutional on the grounds that it deprived persons of owning property in the form of slaves without due process, and so was contrary to the 14th Amendment, e.g., "For the first time since Marbury v. Madison (1803), the Dred Scott decision found an act of Congress unconstitutional."

dredger, drudger: a shallow box in which meat, etc., is floured or from which, at the fireplace, flour is placed on cooking foods, e.g., "Her dredger was large enough for a whole loin."

dressed out, dressed: refers to a food animal carcass from which the head, entrails, and skin have been removed, e.g., "The steer weighed 900 lbs. before being dressed out and 575 lbs. afterwards"; "The turkey, dressed, weighed eleven pounds."

dresser: unlike now, a table upon which meat was dressed, cut or trimmed, e.g., "The dresser in the early inventory had nothing to do with 'making up' by women, even though the dressing room mentioned surely did."

dressing glass: a free standing, framed mirror, e.g., "Being poor, she had but one small dressing glass which was carried from room to room as the family needed it."

dressing table: a small table, with one or two drawers beneath and sometimes one or two small drawers at the back or sides of the top, often with a backboard, e.g., "In her bedchamber, she had a mahogany dressing table."

drill, seed drill, corn drill: as now, a device for boring holes; a manually operated device that inserted seed into a hole made by the lower end of the device, e g., "The drill was a great labor-saver in spring planting." Also see **sow.**

dripping pan: a utensil for cooking meat, with a perforated tray positioned above the bottom, through which the melted grease and oil could drip, the same saved for use later in illumination and soap making, e.g., "Hunt gained a dripping pan and several other kitchen items from the estate."

droit: (Fr.) in French law, a right, e.g., "In Louisiana and Canada, the researcher encounters droits of many sorts; droit d'accession, droit d'execution, droit de detraction, droit de suite, etc."

drop-front desk: See **fall-front desk.**

drop-leaf desk: See **fall-front desk.**

drop-leaf table: usually, a finished dining table, having two leaves that fold downward for economy of space when not in use, and often with a small drawer on one or both ends used for knives, utensils, etc., "Her Sheraton drop-leaf table was of beautiful cherry and walnut, and was made about 1840."

dropsy: a collection of water in the body; retention of water, e.g., "General Winfield Scott suffered so from dropsy that he had to be lifted upon his horse." Also see **defluxion.**

drover: sometimes, one who fattened cattle; usually, one who herded or drove cattle to market, e.g., "In the 1860s, Richard Roberts and his son were farmers and drovers."

drugster: an early druggist, e.g., "The references to him as a drugster and as an apothecary both meant the same thing."

drummer: early, a travelling salesman; later, and sometimes now, commercial agents who supply retailers, e.g., "As a drummer, he had many occasions to travel by stagecoach."

dry, dry states, dry areas: any political **subdivision** (q.v.) that prohibits the sale of alcoholic beverages, e.g., "It is dry from the north Chattanooga city limits to the south limits of Cincinnati."

dry goods: any merchandise, other than hardware, fuel, food and spices, kept by a storekeeper or merchant, e.g., "As a dry goods merchant, he stocked shoes, cloth, sewing materials and equipment, and dyes."

dry sink: a small- to medium-sized cabinet, usually with a compartment or drawers and closeable doors beneath the top, and the top divided into a work space and a shallow well, e.g., "She kept a walnut dry sink in the bedchamber."

dryfatt: a barrel, cask, or other large container used to hold and ship dry goods, especially powders, e.g., "The powdered sulphur was shipped in a dryfatt."

ducat: any of the silver or gold coins of various values issued at various times in Europe, and found in the writings of colonials, e.g. "He paid three gold ducats for the colt."

duces tecum: an early writ or court order directing that a person appear before the court and bring certain papers, documents, or writings with him, e.g., "The Sussex order books revealed several subpoenas duces tecum."

duchess: the lady of a duke, e.g., "Mrs. Simpson became the Duchess of Windsor upon her marriage to the former heir to the throne."

duck: strong, heavy, plainly woven cotton or linen material, sometimes dipped in oil, wax, or tallow in order to render it waterproof, e.g., "During the Revolution, she made duck duffel bags for her sons to carry to war."

ducking stool, dunking stool, trebucket, tumbrel: a stool to which criminals, **scolds** (q.v.) and ne'er-do-wells were tied for ducking under water as punishment, e.g., "Elizabeth Sherwood of Queen Ann County was sentenced to the dunking stool for witchcraft."

dudgeon: a small dagger, e.g., "His dudgeon and **pepperbox** (q.v.) probably revealed his need to carry small weapons in his business travels."

due bill: any written acknowledgement of a debt, often early used as money, e.g., "The entry noted that the defendant had given Parker a due bill in the amount of $6.00."

duffel: coarse, napped woolen cloth, often used to make luggage bags, e.g., "His duffel bag served both to carry clothes and as a cover at night."

duke: a title of nobility that conferred no real estate or jurisdiction, yet ranked next below the Prince of Wales in deference and allegiance owed, e.g., "The Duke of Windsor would have been the King had he not abdicated."

dulcimer: early, unlike now, a small stringed instrument played by striking the wires with small sticks, e.g., "The dulcimer of the early days was played differently from now."

dumbwaiter: in furniture, a small stand of stacked shelves that revolved independently, usually mounted on a pedestal, often placed in a parlor and holding small dishes of candies, sweetmeats, nuts etc., e.g., "When the men adjourned to the parlor, her mahogany dumbwaiter was placed there."

dun: a color; brown and black; early used to describe animals, especially horses and dogs, e.g., "The horse was dun and the mare was **brindle** (q.v.)."

dungfork: a manure fork; a large, tined fork used to scoop and move manure from a stable or barn, e.g., "His purchase of a dungfork and two 'scoops' revealed his ownership of horses or cattle, or both."

dungle fowl, dung hill fowl: See **chickens.**

Dunmore's War, Lord: See **Lord Dunmore's War.**

Dupper's Beer: a beer made by the London brewer Dupper, believed to have caused the death of more than 200 colonists in the 17th century, e.g., "George Sandys cheered the prosecution of Dupper for his poisonous beer."

duroy: thought to be corduroy, perhaps of cotton, e.g., "During the 1760s, Parham stocked and sold duroy by the yard."

duster: similar or identical to a **salt box** (q.v.), and used for salt, pepper, or other powdered or granulated table seasonings, e.g., "As a duster for cinnamon or pepper, she used her salt dishes."

Dutch auction: an auction at which a price is called out in excess of the value of the property, and then is gradually reduced until someone buys the item or property, e.g., "Dutch auctions occasionally were held in early Ohio and Pennsylvania."

Dutch cupboard: a cupboard with closeable doors and shelves above and below, so called by reason of their popularity with German settlers, sometimes imprecisely called a **pantry** (q.v.), e.g., "Her Dutch cupboard was decorated and was white."

Dutch metal, Dutch gold: a foil of copper and zinc alloy, used as a substitute for gold foil, e.g., "If the patina is, early inlays of Dutch gold are easily mistaken for true gold." Also see **gold.**

Dutch oven: unlike now, a footed, shallow iron pot with a recessed, rimmed lid, e.g., "Dutch ovens were placed in the hot coals, and when she needed more heat for the dish being prepared, hot coals were placed in the recessed top."

Dutch, Deutsch, Pennsylvania Dutch: persons of German, Austrian, and central European descent or origin, and those of the Germanic tongue, usually not including persons from Holland, Belgium, Luxembourg, Denmark, or France, e.g., "His ancestors came from Mulheim to Bucks County, and were thereafter referred to as Dutch farmers."

Dutchware: See **spatterware.**

duties: usually, fees or taxes levied upon goods moving from one country to another; sometimes, any tax or burden levied by any governmental agency, e.g., "The Virginians considered the Crown duties on tea, sugar, and wine to be without justification."

duvanto: an unknown fabric; perhaps duvetyn, a cotton, wool, or silk napped material, in twill or plain weave, e.g., "The 1761 account of William Hunt with Belsches Brothers reveals the purchase of 1/2 yard of duvanto."

dying declaration: usually, those statements concerning the manner and nature of his injuries and the parties responsible made by one who believes that death is imminent, e.g., "The court minutes revealed that Hunt was named as the perpetrator by the dying declaration of Smith."

dysentery, flux, bloody flux: severe diarrhea, often accompanied with blood; an intestinal disorder very often fatal in early times, e.g., "Despite his enormous wealth, Sir Francis Drake could not be cured of dysentery, and so, raving and delirious, he died in 1596."

dysmenorrhea: as now, pain and cramping during the menstrual period, e.g., "For severe dysmenorrhea, he administered aconite, arsenic salts, amyl nitrate, and belladonna."

dyspepsia: early, any difficulty with digestion, e.g., "He was dyspeptic, and so chewed mint and hops and took cod-liver oil regularly."

dyspnoea: early, any difficulty in breathing, e.g., "His shortness of breath was said to have been dyspnoea, but may have been angina."

E

e'toffe du pays: (Fr., usually pronounced "a-toff-dew-pay") thick, woolen, homespun cloth, typical of the French colonies, e.g., "The Cajun mother made her children's coats of e'toffe du pays."

Eagle: a ten dollar U.S. gold coin, e.g., "To the regret of many, Eagles and all other gold coins were taken out of circulation in 1935."

earbobs, eardrops: earrings, e.g., "She had cloisonne earbobs." See **bobs.**

earl: once the highest inheritable degree of nobility, now the third, ranking between a marquis and a viscount, corresponds to the French 'comte' and the German 'graf', e.g., "While the title of earl was unknown on this continent, some, like the Thomas Roberts family, could have so claimed had they remained in the Old Country."

earmark: a mark or brand, often recorded at the early clerks' offices, and placed on an ear of animals, usually sheep, thereby revealing ownership, e.g., "Fencing had not been invented, so he entered his earmark into the records of the Clerk of Courts."

earthboard: the part of the plow that peels the dirt off the blade, e.g., "His reference to making an earthboard revealed his planting activity."

earthenware: any utensil or dish made of fired clay, very common early, e.g., "The inventory revealed that she had two earthenware water jugs."

easement: a right of a person to use the land of another for some special and specific purpose, e.g., "He sold a portion of his land to Jones, but maintained a roadway easement across it."

Eastern Shore: usually, those counties of Delaware, Maryland and Virginia that border the eastern shore of Chesapeake Bay, e.g., "The Eastern shore has been so-called in the records since considerably before 1700."

ebony, ebon, eben: very hard, beautiful, naturally black wood, early brought to the colonies from South America, e.g., "They very much prized their ebony deedbox."

ecchymosis: red or black and blue inflamed splotches on the skin, e.g., "While apothecaries made up a mercurial ointment for the treatment of ecchymosis, early housewives often used a piece of raw red meat for the same purpose."

ecclesiastical councils, ecclesiastical law: judicial/advisory tribunals formerly (and still occasionally) held in New England and other jurisdictions for determining disputes usually concerning orthodoxy, etc., between clergy and between clergy and church, e.g., "His view of baptism was upheld after hearing and consideration by the ecclesiastical council."

eccoprotics: mild purges, e.g., "As eccoprotics, the physician prescribed poke root and flax-seed oil, and the housewife made **poke sallet** (q.v.)."

eclectic practice: a medical methodology often characterized by conventionally educated practitioners as 'dangerous' and 'spurious'; the practice of healing methods not accepted by the bulk of the medical profession, e.g., "His views concerning healing with electricity were considered eclectic by some, and pure quackery by most."

ecphractics, ecphracticks : early, concoctions supposed to thin the liquids - humours - of the body, e.g., "Most ecphracticks contained alcohol, some, (to the pleasure of the teetotalers) a very high percentage."

ectype: a copy, e.g., "Early court orders often required that parties be handed ectypes of writs or orders."

-ee: a suffix from the Latin; a person or persons upon whom some legal effect has been or is to be brought by another, e.g., "Having had a lien filed against him for his failure to pay, he was a lienee." (see also **-or**, a suffix.)

effects: tangible **property** (q.v.) of a personal nature other than real estate, e.g., "In addition to the other **personalty** (q.v.), his many effects, including three **weskits** (q.v.), were listed in the inventory."

effluxion (of time): the expiration of a term of years, established in a lease or land rental agreement, e.g., "The old court record spoke of the effluxion of term, meaning that the lease had expired by its terms."

eigne: (Fr.) the first born, e.g., "Louisiana records often refer to someone as the eigne who was the first born of a family."

ejectment: (writ of or action in) a legal action by which one is ordered to vacate land or premises illegally held after expiration of the term, e.g., "The tenant would not leave after the lease expired, so a writ of ejectment was sought."

elaterium: an extract of wild cucumbers that acts as a powerful purge, e.g., "He prescribed elaterium as a last resort."

elbowchair: an early term for any ordinary chair with arms that usually were padded or upholstered, e.g., "There was an elbowchair and a **settee** (q.v.) in the inventory and appraisement."

elder title: the state of having **perfected** (q.v.) ownership prior to some other person, e.g., "In the dispute between Hines and Gross, the court found Hines to have the elder title."

electric belts: belts, worn at the waist, made of fiber and containing small current-carrying wires that were plugged into a wall outlet or powered by a battery; gadgets of the late nineteenth and early twentieth centuries, said to have great curative powers, e.g., "Many were the ignorant who bought electric belts, thinking that instant cures to many ailments might thereby be had."

electuaries: a paste-like lump or mass of medicines in a vehicle such as syrup, molasses, or honey, early used for humans and animals by placing it on the teeth and gums or between the same and the cheek, e.g., "In 1660 Haddon charged 140 pounds of tobacco for two purging electuaries."

elisors: an early term for persons appointed by a court to select citizens as potential jurors, or, in some jurisdictions, to execute any writ, e.g., "The California court's writ of **venire** (q.v.) was carried out by the elisors."

elixir(s): any strong medicine; a medicine or concoction having wide application, e.g., "His elixir of fruit juice, horehound, and grain alcohol was very popular, more for the alcohol than for curative power."

ell: a common early measure of cloth, equalling one and one quarter "yards" (36" X 45"), e.g., "Virtually every account of early dry goods merchants refers to ells of this or that **stuff** (q.v.)."

elvelock: a woman's hairdo in the form of a knot of hair at the back of the head, e.g., "Elvelocks were very popular at the time of the Civil War."

Emancipation Proclamation, The emancipation: that Presidential order of Abraham Lincoln, dated July 1, 1863, that declared all persons previously held in slavery in the States of the Union to thereafter be and remain free, e.g., "Since Lincoln had no jurisdiction in the Confederacy, the Emancipation Proclamation could not be effective until the defeat of the South."

emancipation: a release from the bonds of age, contract, or servitude, e.g., "At the age of fifteen she was emancipated from her term of servitude at the age of fifteen"; "An emancipated child is one over whom all measure of parental control has been relinquished."

emancipation: See **Emancipation Proclamation.**

Ember Week, Ember Days: any week in which an Ember Day falls; ancient English holiday observed widely in the early colonies, e.g., "The Book of Common Prayer prescribed Ember Days as the Wednesday, Friday, and Sunday after the first Sunday of Lent, the day of the Feast of the Pentecost, September 14th, and December 13."

emblazoned: anything decorated or adorned with a symbol of heraldry; an enameled or inlaid surface, e.g., "The shield was emblazoned with the Parker arms"; "The jewelry box was emblazoned in red and yellow stained woods."

emblements: early crops and other growing harvestables produced by labor of the owner, e.g., "Upon one's death, his emblements passed to his administrator or executor as personalty."

embrocate: to rub an injured or diseased part of the body with lotions containing alcohol, e.g., "Dr. Drake gave him 'pink lotion' with which to embrocate the rash."

emeroids: See **hemorrhoids.**

emetic, emetick: as now and very common, early concoctions used to bring about vomiting, e.g., "The doctor consistently used ipecac as an emetic."

emigrants: those who leave one place or region intending to remain in or take up permanent residence in another, e.g., "He was among those emigrants who after 1740 left the Palatinate for the colonies."

eminent domain: the taking of private property for public use, for which the owner is compensated, e.g., "The government exercised its power of eminent domain when it took his land for a road and his cattle to feed the Revolutionary army." Also see **condemnation.**

emmenagogues: early, medications thought to induce menstrual flow or abortion, e.g., "Being unmarried and pregnant, the old women advised her to take **coal oil** (q.v.) and quinine as an emmenagogue."

empasm: any powder or substance used to rid the body of odors, e.g., "Common folks of the sixteenth century thought empasms were neither necessary nor particularly desirable."

emphysema: as now, yet not early understood, e.g., "For emphysema, Dr. Drake sometimes prescribed arsenic, cod-liver oil, and prussic acid."

empiric: a medical practitioner who acts without science or training, e.g., "He was called an empiric by the polite, and a charlatan by the other of his neighbors."

empyema: any congestion or gathering of mucus in the chest cavity, e.g., "Black snakeroot and asafoetida were popular as remedies for any empyema."

en ventre sa mere: (Lat.) early common legal expression for "in the mother's womb"; the unborn, e.g., "He **devised** (q.v.) the land to the children jointly, and included any child en ventre sa mere at his death." See **mere.**

enamel: early, unlike now, an inlay, usually in wood, e.g., "The antique **press** (q.v.) was said to have been enameled with gold and rosewood."

encomienda: a feudal grant of land from a Spanish territory, e.g., "The Mexican records concerning encomiendas are significant to Southwestern genealogists."

endite: See **indict** herein.

enfeoff, enfeoffment: See **feoff.**

engine: unlike now, any large mechanical device with parts that move to some mechanical purpose, e.g., "The engine for the mill was a turnstile."

engineer, pilot: early, unlike now, the operator of a locomotive, engine, or other heavy moving equipment; an elected office concerned with the mechanical equipment or surveys, platting, and boundaries of a county, e.g., "He was a railroad engineer"; "He was elected County Engineer."

English Case Drink: See **case drink, English.**

English lock: a type of firearm; a flintlock, e.g., "He carried an English lock of .60 caliber."

engrain: to decoratively stain the graining in wood, thereby achieving variations in coloring and shading, e.g., "The mahogany was engrained with a black stain."

enneatical days, or years: the ninth day of a disease, after which it was early thought that a change was sure to follow; every ninth year of life, signifying a change or cycle, e.g., "They anxiously awaited the enneatical day, believing that his condition would then improve."

entailment, fee tail, fee tail male, fee tail female, etc.: a common (now legally ineffective) estate in land limited to a person and his or her **issue** (q.v.); an early estate in land wherein the **descent** (q.v.) is settled and determined, and by which **grantors** (q.v.) or **devisors** (q.v.) restricted all future transfers to the lineal descendants of the **grantee** (q.v.) or **devisee,** (q.v.) e.g., "By making the 1747 deed 'to Sarah Drake and the heirs of her body', William Hines intended to entail the land."

entrements: (Fr.) small plates of food served between main dishes, e.g., "The banquet menu revealed seven entrements, including sweetbreads in cream."

entry (architectural): unlike now, in the North, a small room at the front entrance; in the South, a hallway extending from the front entrance through the house and doored at the rear, e.g., "In the South the entry sometimes was called a **dogtrot** (q.v.)."

entry: in law, a notation in a journal or record of some legal activity or decision; in land, the initial action taken in acquiring title to land that is to be settled. In the latter, an entry was followed by a warrant for survey, a plat, and a deed. A **caveat** (q.v.) could be filed by one who claimed any portion of the land within an entry, e.g., "The judge ordered that an entry be submitted detailing the agreement"; "He filed an entry for 100 acres lying along Chowan River."

enumeration: in genealogy, usually, and somewhat imprecisely, any census or numbering of people in a given area, e.g., "Since only the heads of households were named, the **Decennial Censuses** (q.v.) from 1790 through 1840 are properly called enumerations, not censuses." Also see **censuses** and **enumerator.**

enumerator: one who makes lists of people, generally for tax or census purposes; properly, one who records an enumerations i.e., a count of persons, e.g., "He was employed as an enumerator for the southern half of Cumberland County, TN.

epergne: (Fr., pronounced "a-pairn") two or more small serving dishes grouped together and mounted in a decorative metal frame, usually placed in the center of a table, e.g., "She served several **sweetmeats** (q.v.) and jellies in the silver epergne."

ephemera: unlike now, a fever that subsided in one day, e.g., "The old doctor waited until the second day to treat the fever, thinking it might be only a common ephemera."

ephemeris: a journal or day book, e.g., "He referred to his writings in the ephemeris as his 'day notes'."

epidemics: a widespread infectious disease, e.g., "Of the seventeenth and eighteenth centuries' epidemics, conspicuous were beri-beri, very early; calenture (yellow fever), 1609(?), 1624(?), 1649, 1668, 1691, 1699, 1793; dysentery and 'fluxes', 1607-08, 1618-19, 1684-86; influenza ('flu') in 1623, 1627, 1635, 1647, 1688 (perhaps the worst), 1697-99 (perhaps the worst of New England); malaria, 1657-59 and 1677-95; measles, 1693-1700, 1713;

scurvy and common diseases when seasoning was inadequate, very early; and smallpox, 1667 (perhaps the worst), 1696, 1731."

epigraph: a quotation at the beginning of a writing, intended by the writer to be thought provoking, e.g., "The epigraph was a quote from Churchill concerning the strength and will of the American people."

epilepsy: as now, but not at all understood, e.g., "Having no understanding of epilepsy, Dr. Lockhart often administered arsenic, bromides, copper, zinc and silver chloride, and even musk."

Epiphany: an ancient holiday (still observed), celebrated in the colonies on the twelfth day after Christmas (January 6th), e.g., "The Book of Common Prayer prescribed Epiphany as a day for celebrating the coming of Christ as foretold by the appearance of the Star of the East."

epistaxis: a nosebleed, e.g., "For severe epistaxis, Dr. Lockhart plugged the nares, and administered digitalis and turpentine."

epistler: an early term for one who wrote letters and correspondence for others, e.g., "He served the local folks as an epistler, however, they called him a 'scribbler'."

epitaph: a statement, quotation, or verse on a monument or headstone, usually as a memorial to the deceased, e.g., "There are some particularly moving epitaphs to be found in New England."

epitherm: any liquid medication applied to the outside of the body, e.g., "Mercurial ointments were popular epitherms of the nineteenth century."

epulotic: a medication thought to cause a wound to heal, e.g., "Powdered sassafras and 'slippery elm' bark, as used by the Indians, were widely prescribed as epulotics."

equinoxes: either of the two times each year when the sun crosses the equator, and day and night are everywhere of equal length, occurring around March 21 and September 23.

equity, courts of: cases that sought remedies unavailable at common law, where fairness or the balancing of interests was decided by church officers became known as cases 'in equity', and the church officers making such decisions as chancellors. In some states chancellors still sit, e.g., "The courts of equity provided remedies based upon fairness; often said to be beyond the 'letter of the law'"; "He sought equal use of the property in Tennessee, hence the case was in equity and heard by the chancellor."

Era of Good Feelings: that decade following the War of 1812, during which war was over, the United States began to consider itself a power to be reckoned with, the westward movement into the Great Plains and beyond was underway, ***King Cotton*** (q.v.) reigned supreme, canals were undertaken, manufacturing - albeit primitive - was everywhere, the Indians were perceived as posing problems only in the distant west, and society appeared to be opening its doors upward, e.g., "As Mrs. Haskins looked about it seemed that all of life was better; the Era of Good Feelings dominated central Pennsylvania."

error, writ of: a statement of a person appealing a decision of a lower court, setting forth the errors made by that court, e.g., "The writ of error stated that the lower court refused to permit the defendant to examine the witness."

erysipelas: any early rash of red, dark or yellow hue, sometimes accompanied by swelling, e.g., "Belladonna and aconite were widely prescribed for erysipelas."

escheat: to revert to a prior owner, usually a government, through some failure of conditions, e.g., "Without justification, he neglected to clear the land or improve the property in any other way, so it escheated to the colony."

escritoir: (Fr.) a writing box with instruments of writing accompanying it, e.g., "The inventory listed a mahogany escritoir."

escritura (sp. varies): any written instrument or document, e.g., "Early records of the Southwest reveal many references to escritura."

escutcheon: an ornament, usually of metal, surrounding a keyhole; early and now, a shield of a family; an armorial ensign, e.g., "The escutcheons of the mahogany ***armoire*** (q.v.) were of solid gold"; "The family escutcheon was inscribed on a plaque of ebony and mahogany."

esquire, squire: a title of honor and dignity; that title given those less than a knight who deserved recognition; rarely, a title given to one who could read or was well educated, e.g., "The lawyer was proud of the title esquire."

estate: at ancient law, any interest in real property; generally and in genealogy, the totality of legal proceedings of a deceased person; a valuable tract of land, usually including a large dwelling, e.g., "His estate in the land was one of fee determinable"; "Her estate was not settled until four years after her death"; "Their estate in the mountains was magnificent."

estate by the entirety (or entireties): since early a husband and wife were viewed as but one person (the man), it followed that a conveyance to them could create but one estate, neither could dispose of it without the consent of the other, and at the death of either the entire interest was vested in the survivor, e.g., "By reason of the fiction that husband and wife were one person, estates by the entirety could exist only in married couples." (See ***joint tenancy***.)

estate for years: that less-than-freehold interest in land for a fixed or determinable period of years, e.g., "When Luke leased the land to Griffith for twenty years, Griffith was said to have had an estate for years."

estreat(e), excript: an early term for an exact copy of a document or original writing, e.g., "The Surry court ordered that either the writing itself or an estreate be presented."

estrepement, writ of: an early ***common law*** (q.v.) ***action*** (q.v.) by which the remainder interest holder prevented the owner of a life estate from "wasting" or acting to the harm of the remainder holder, e.g., "The Pennsylvania court ruled that a writ of estrepement should issue against the lake proposed to be created on the land by the life tenant."

et al.: (Lat.) literally, "and others", e.g., "Genealogists should remember that ancestors may be revealed in the files of those lawsuits wherein the caption lists known relatives followed by the words et al."

et ux., et uxor: (Lat.) and wife; and husband; e.g., "The deed was to Jane Smith, et uxor, hence, even though the husband's name did not appear, the researcher knew that Jane was then married."

evensong: prayers or worship offered at sunset or in the evening, e.g., "The priest referred to their evening prayers as evensongs."

evidence: in genealogy, any writing, relic, memento, tale, or remembrance that in any way tends to establish any lineage; facts, writings and states of being offered as proof of lineage or relationship, e.g., "Even though genealogists are not bound by courtroom rules of admissibility, hearsay evidence is not thereby rendered more reliable."

evidentiary: facts that in any way tend to establish other facts; facts tending to any extent to prove some proposition or hypothesis, e.g., "The inscription on the headstone was evidentiary as to the spelling of the name of the deceased.

evil: a three-tined manure fork, e.g., "He used an evil to spread manure in his garden."

ewe: a female sheep, e.g., "The inventory listed both rams and ewes."

ewer: a bowl or container usually brought to the table for the washing of hands; large "fingerbowls"; sometimes, widemouthed pitchers, e.g., "The inventory reference to silver ewers revealed a measure of wealth at sometime."

ex facto, de facto: refers to some state of being resulting from an act that is or may be unlawful or improper, e.g., "Ownership ex facto resulted when he found and took up stray cattle that bore another's brand."

ex tempore: the passage of time; in consequence of a passage of time, e.g., "The order revealing that his leasehold had died ex tempore told the researcher that the term had expired."

ex testamento: by the action of a will; the opposite of **ab intestato** (q.v.), e.g., "The court described his ownership of the land as ex testamento, meaning that he had gained it through the will of another."

examined away: See **separate examination.**

except: in court records, to take written exception to a ruling, usually as to evidence or documents, e.g., "The record showed that upon the court reading the document to the jury, he excepted."

excepting, excepted: reserving, e.g., "Drake's conveyance of the land excepted the portion used as the family cemetery."

excise tax: a tax on goods, merchandise, or commodities being sold at retail (usually), e.g., "The excise taxes levied on rum and tobacco by the British served only to aggravate the colonials."

excommunication: censure of a church or discipline by a governing religious authority, e.g., "Excommunication was a most feared punishment in the days of deep religious convictions."

execute, execution: the signing or formalizing of a document or writing that requires such an act; those common actions taken, usually by a constable, sheriff, or a deputy of those officers, to enforce a judgment or other court order; the actions of an executor in carrying out the provisions of a will, e.g., "The contract was executed by the parties on the 5th of July, 1786"; "The sheriff having been ordered to execute on the judgment, he took into custody the slaves of the defendant"; "In executing the provisions of the will, the executor had to have several tracts of land surveyed."

executed writ: the accomplishment of the purpose of any **writ;** (q.v.) a writ or order endorsed to the effect that it has been accomplished, e.g., "The writ, carrying the endorsement 'exec.', revealed that its purpose had been accomplished by the sheriff."

executor, executrix: a person, male or female, appointed by a **testator** (q.v.) or **testatrix** (q.v.) in a will and approved by the court to carry out the terms of that will, e.g., "He was appointed executor and she executrix, and they were issued **letters testamentary** (q.v.), in the estate of John Smith, deceased."

executory: that which is yet to be done or executed; incomplete; that which depends upon the happening of some future event, e.g., "The genealogist should be aware that executory deeds and contracts often have effects similar to wills"; "An executory interest in land is created when a deed provides for a transfer of title upon death of the owner."

exemption: a freedom from some duty incumbent upon others of the same class or group, e.g., "Occasionally exemptions from tithes were granted by reason of poverty, prior military service, or disability."

exequies: burial rites, sometimes a funeral, e.g., "The exequies took place at the grave site."

exit: a notation common in court reports meaning the issuance by the court of some order or process, e.g., "The entry revealed exit fi. fa. meaning a writ of *fieri facias* (q.v.) was issued in that case."

exit certificate: an issuance of a certificate, usually by a clerk of a court or administrative official, e.g., "The Surry court noted 'exit certificate 100 ac. Clerk', meaning the Clerk of the Court had issued a certificate for 100 acres of land."

expectancy: that which is expected, but for which there is no certainty or obligation upon others, e.g., "Even though it could be changed at any time, he had an expectancy by reason of the bequest to him in his yet living father's will."

extinct: usually in genealogy, a statement that a political subdivision has been abolished, or that a claim in heraldry or nobility has been lost beyond reprieve, e.g., "The county of Franklin is now extinct"; "The earldom which might have been his is now extinct."

extinguishment of legacy: where specific property is the subject of a **devise** (q.v.) or **bequest** (q.v.) and at death of the **testator** (q.v.) the property no longer exists, e.g., "The order stated that the bequest of cattle failed by reason of extinguishment."

extract: in genealogy, a section from a document, letter, book or writing, usually taken whole and verbatim from the original. This, in contrast to an **abstract** (q.v.) which condenses the information cited, e.g., "He extracted the last four paragraphs of the Gettysburg Address for use in his class."

exudation, exsudation: a sweating or perspiring, e.g., "Causing exsudation was one of the ways to bring the 'humours' into balance."

F

f. feci: See *fieri feci*, q.v.

facias: (lat.) an order from a court or a writ to a sheriff, constable, officer of the court, or a deputy thereof, "that you do cause", e.g., "The early writs of scire facias ('cause him to know hereof') are familiar to all genealogists who have worked with courts' records"; "Fieri facias ('cause it to be made') was frequently used to order a constable or sheriff to collect the amount of a judgment from such of defendant's assets as were available."

faggot, fagot: a bundle of sticks bound together, usually for burning, e.g., "He had provided the fagots for the lamps on the outdoor walkways at the Governor's mansion."

faggot fork: a tined fork used to move or place faggots within a fireplace or receptacle, e.g., "She used the faggot fork to so place the wood as to cause an even fire."

faience: (Fr., pron. fay-e-ens) delicately decorated, French earthenware, e.g., "Brittany's bowl of faience was made in New England, even though the name would not so suggest."

Fair Use: "...relates to the extent to which copyrightable writings or materials may be used without express license...." or permission. Loews Inc., v Columbia, etc. (1955 DC CA) 131 F. Supp. 165, 175; 105 U.S.P.Q. 302; aff'd', etc., 356 U.S. 934, generally, e.g., "Her use of his writings was for classroom comparison and analysis, hence was Fair Use."

Fair-play men: an irregular tribunal brought into existence in Pennsylvania about the year 1769, e.g., "The actions and decisions of the Fair-play men were not authorized by any government."

fairy lamp: a lamp using a short squatty candle, often with 2 wicks and widely used during Victorian times before *coal oil* (q.v.) was widely available, e.g., "She had a fairy lamp made of china and one of metal."

fake: a coil of rope, e.g., "The inventory included a fake of hemp."

fall: See *mawl* and *fall, saw, and mawl*.

fall, saw, and mawl: an early expression used in granting to a tenant or lessee the privilege of freely cutting and using the timber on a tract of land, e.g., "Luke granted Griffith the right to fall, saw, and mawl the trees on the leased land."

fall-front desk, drop-front desk, drop-leaf desk: a free standing desk, usually with drawers below, and a hinged writing surface that folds upwards concealing small inside compartments and small drawers, e.g., "The walnut fall-front was the finest *desk* (q.v.) in the estate."

fall shoes: See **French fall shoes.**

falling sickness: epilepsy, e.g., "Falling sickness was not early understood, and musk was one of the medications thought efficacious."

fallow: at rest; usually, to permit a field to lie unplowed and uncultivated for some extended period or for a season; pale red or pale yellow, e.g., "He let the forty acres lay fallow for four years"; "The cloth was fallow and brown."

Family History Centers: See **Mormons.**

family name files: those alphabetical files maintained by libraries and genealogical societies that contain unbound correspondence, obituaries, research notes, sources, and miscellaneous materials having to do with a specific family or surname, e.g., "In the Family Name Files under 'Haskins' she found a short biography of the missing ancestor."

family name: See **surname.**

family tale, family tradition: a story, tale, or recollection passed down through a family for a number of years or generations, usually not written, e.g., "According to tradition, his family was descended from a brother of Sir Francis Drake."

family unit chart, family group sheet: a widely used genealogical form to record pertinent information concerning births, marriages, deaths, parents, and issue of a single husband and wife group. Quite usually a researcher maintains one family unit chart for each marriage encountered, e.g., "She kept a family group sheet for every marriage uncovered during her research."

fancy: unlike now, at various times, of the highest quality or designed to suit the most discerning taste; interestingly, if referring to a male, it also meant lover, yet a "fancy woman" was a prostitute, e.g., "To say she had a fancy gown revealed that it likely was expensive"; "He was her fancy man, and she was with him whenever possible"; "To say in public that she was a fancy woman was an insult of the highest sort."

farm: before about 1825, ground or land under lease to or being "share cropped" by another person; similarly a farmer was one who farmed leased or rented land, e.g., "One described in 1740 as a farmer probably did not own the land."

farm table, harvest table, country table: a plain, wide, longer than ordinary, often roughly finished utility table, sometimes with a single drop leaf, e.g., "She used the farm table for many purposes, and always sorted and cleaned her fruits and vegetables there."

faro: early and now, a popular gambling game played with cards, where betting is done as to the order in which cards will fall, e.g., "The early mining towns had more than their share of faro tents."

farrier: very early, one who doctored animals; early, or a blacksmith whose business was horseshoes and nails, therefor; later, one who, for hire, made horseshoes, shoed horses, and was knowledgeable in cutting and trimming horses feet, e.g., "The farrier came by once a month to check the horses' hooves."

farrow: a litter of pigs, e.g., "The inventory revealed three sows, two farrows, a boar, and ten shoats." Also see **swine.**

farthing: a British coin taken from circulation in 1961, having had a value of 1/4 of a pence (p or d) or 1/40th of a Shilling (S or s), e.g., "A farthing of 1850 had the purchasing power of about twenty cents ($0.20) in 1992."

farthingale: a hoop over which was worn a dress, petticoats, or a skirt, the same used to cause the garments to flare out; a flared or hooped dress, skirt, or petticoat, e.g., "Scarlett wore a whalebone farthingale under a green velvet dress."

fat lamp: any lamp that used animal fat or suet as fuel, e.g., "Even though her betty lamps were in fact fat lamps, she did not refer to them by that name."

fat: an early word meaning a vat, e.g., "In 1700 the word fat was still in use to describe a large kettle used for soaking or fermenting liquids."

fathom: a measure of depth equalling six feet, e.g., "In 1785 the channel in New York harbor was twelve fathoms at its greatest."

fatling: a young animal, usually a calf or steer, fed until fat enough for market, e.g., "The **husbandman** (q.v.) was anxious to take the three fatlings to market."

fealty: in feudal law, a duty owed a feudal lord, e.g., "In 1740, William Cole was to deliver 'two fatt capons' and do a day's labor as tokens of fealty to the owner of the 'Mannor of Gunnpowder'."

feasance: a deed or act; a doing of something, e.g., "Malfeasance is an act preceded by evil or unlawful intent, nonfeasance indicates a result brought about through innocent inaction, and misfeasance denotes the result that follows from an act having a different purpose and intent, e.g., "His malfeasance was evident in his breaking down the kennel door when he led his neighbors hunting dog away."

feather tick: a large, heavy cloth bag filled with feathers and down and used as a mattress; by reason of softness and warmth, feathers were the most desirable of ticking, e.g., "She had three **ticks** (q.v.), and one was a feather tick."

febrifuge: any medication thought to aid with fevers, e.g., "Eucalyptus and quinine were popular febrifuges."

Federal Courts: those courts, including the tax courts, U.S. District courts, Courts of Appeals for the Circuits, and the U.S. Supreme Court, having jurisdiction in appeals, jurisdiction in Federal crimes and Constitutional matters, and in civil matters between citizens of different states where the amount in dispute is in excess of a certain amount, e.g., "Martha's only appeal from the highest court of South Carolina was to the Federal courts, namely the U.S. Supreme Court."

Federalist Papers, The: a series of eighty-five essays by Alexander Hamilton, John Jay, and James Madison concerning the ramifications of an adoption of the Constitution, e.g., "The Federalist Papers have long been held most reliable concerning the debates and thoughts of the framers of the Constitution."

fee conditional: any estate that is restricted to certain heirs; all fees conditional are "base fees", yet the converse is not true, e.g., "Since the land was conveyed to one of his daughters with the condition that she transfer it only to her daughters, it was a fee conditional, more particularly, a fee tail female." Also see entailment.

fee determinable: an ancient legal term signifying that the transferred rights in land would be varied or extinguished upon the happening of certain events or the passage of a certain time, e.g., "The transfer of the land was in fee determinable with the condition that should she remarry, the land was automatically transferred to her eldest surviving daughter."

fee simple: (Lat., feodum simplex) an ancient legal term signifying that entire measure of ownership in land which one might own under the law in effect, e at the transfer, e.g., "He gained the land in fee simple from his father, even though he had been told that it would be **entailed** (q.v.)."

fee tail: a **conditional fee** (q.v.); also see **entailment**.

feed sack: See **tote sack**.

fellmonger: a dealer in skins and hides, e.g., "Meachum is thought to have been a fellmonger in early New York City."

felt: cloth (early, of wool) made without weaving but instead by pressing the fibers together under heat, e.g., "The felt was inexpensive and yet served the cabinetmaker well."

female trouble: as now, any of several general complaints concerning the female reproductive system, e.g., "For female trouble, the American Indians employed teas of Geranium, currants, cedar berries, milkweed, and black haw." Also see **dysmenorrhea**.

feme, feme covert, feme sole: (Fr., femme) a female, e.g., "A feme covert was a married woman and a feme sole was an unmarried, divorced, legally separated, or presently unmarried, widowed woman, or a married woman who through prenuptial agreement or other action at law could act and contract - 'be a free trader' - in her own right."

feme sole trader: in SC, PA, and several other jurisdictions, a married woman could trade with and be answerable on her own account to a merchant, e.g., "As a feme sole trader in Philadelphia she was liable for her purchases, and it was not required that her husband be named as a defendant."

fence county: a county in which a 'stock' or 'fence' law has not been adopted; a county where cattle must be fenced out, not fenced in, e.g., "Since it was permissible to let cattle run at large, early Georgia was called a fence county."

fence rows, fencerows: lines of fence and the ground in which the fence posts stood, e.g., "The fencerows always were a likely place to find small game."

fence viewers: after about 1750, persons elected in each county of many New England colonies and of PA whose duty it was to inspect all fences and see that they were kept in good repair, e.g., "If the fence viewers found fences in disrepair, that owner could not recover for trespass by the animals of others."

fender, fireplace fender: a usually decorative, low metal shield with curved ends, placed in front of a fire to prevent ashes and coals from spilling out into the room, e.g., "The fender was of highly polished brass."

feof, enfeoff, enfeoffment: possession; an ancient legal term meaning to give over or place in possession, e.g., "The term enfeoff in a deed meant that possession was being granted along with ownership."

ferae naturae: (Lat.) wild animals, e.g., "Unlike in old England, ferae naturae were free for the taking to all early colonials."

ferret, ferit, ferreting: thin, narrow, decorative cloth of silk or cotton, e.g., a narrow woolen tape used to decorate clothing, e.g., The ledger of Parham's store revealed several purchases of yards of ferit;" "She sewed ferreting around the edges of the shawl."

ferrotype: See **tintype**.

ferry, ferries: as now, a boat used to transport people, animals and goods across a body of water for pay; (verb) to move people, animals and goods across water for hire at rates usually set by the county court, e.g., "By 1750, there were 150 ferries licensed on James River"; "For his livelihood, he ferried folks across the Chickahominy at Richmond."

fetch: as now, a very common early expression meaning to bring, e.g., "He often said that a horse was worth only what it would fetch that day."

feudalism, feudal system: that economic system of England and Europe during the middle ages, where lords owned land and vassals tended them; pertaining to interests held by a superior or lord; the feudal system (introduced to England by William I) prevailed in Europe and the British Isles throughout the eleventh, twelfth, and thirteenth centuries, and only very gradually disappeared, e.g., "To the casual observer, Maryland of the 17th and early 18th centuries and the area of the Hudson River until well into the 19th century appeared near feudal in their institutions"; "The earliest colonial immigrants left behind what yet was nearly a feudal society."

fiddleback chair, fiddleback wood grain: a chair with a back built in the shape of a violin; ornate and rare graining or configuration in fine wood, e.g., "The fiddle back dining chairs had upholstered seats and were of mahogany"; "The Empire table was of fiddleback walnut and was extraordinarily beautiful."

fiduciary: one who, by his own choice, acts principally in behalf of another person and is duty-bound to act to the benefit of that person, e.g., "The duties of an administrator and executor are of a fiduciary nature; to preserve and properly handle the assets of the deceased to the benefit of the heirs."

Field bed: a four-posted, canopied bed, e.g., "The posts of a Field bed typically were not more than four feet high."

field stone, field rock: See **headstone**.

field tree: See **plow tree**.

fieri facias: See ***facias.***

fieri feci, ***f. feci***: a common return on early writs fieri facias meaning that the officer has done as directed so far as assets could be found, e.g., "The sheriff sold all the cattle he could locate and endorsed the writ 'f.feci'." See ***writs*** and ***facias.***

figure, ***figuring***: to dance, e.g., "There are many references to persons figuring waltzes, Virginia reels, and other dances." Also see ***boards.***

filius: a son, e.g., "In his order, the Louisiana judge referred to the son of the family as filius familias (of the family), meaning that the child was an unemancipated male offspring."

filly: a young, female horse (and occasionally a newborn female mule) that has lived beyond a few days and has yet to be bred, after which it would be referred to as a ***mare*** (q.v.), e.g., "The filly resembled her ***dam*** (q.v.) and was chestnut." Also see ***horse.***

fire dogs: See ***andirons.***

fire screen: a light, movable shield, usually several feet in height, and of any of many styles and materials, designed to be moved about and placed between the fire and a person sitting or sleeping in the room, thus preventing discomfort to that person, e.g., "Her two fire screens were elegant, and of brocade in walnut frames."

fire tongs: as now, long-handled iron pincers or grabs used to adjust, move, or position burning wood in a fireplace or stove, e.g., "The fire tongs always were near the fireplace in case burning wood fell out into the room."

firearms, expressions based upon: as now, e.g., "Our ancestors said 'long shot,' meaning not likely to succeed; 'hot shot,' describing one who has recently come to considerable power; 'big shot,' for an employer, boss, or supervisor; 'lock, stock, and barrel,' meaning complete; 'go off half cocked,' meaning to start before preparation is complete; 'aim high,' that is, to have lofty and difficult goals; 'set one's sights on something,' meaning to have a definite objective or goal; and 'straight as a ramrod,' meaning to have erect posture or be scrupulously honest." Also see ***shooting irons.***

fireback, ***fire plate***: a heavy metal plate placed in the back of the fireplace to prevent the masonry from crumbling, e.g., "Most unusually, the iron fireback had ornate decoration."

firelock: See ***flintlock*** and ***matchlock.***

fireplace fender: See ***fender.***

fireslice, ***fire peel***: a small, shallow shovel used to move ashes and coals, e.g., "She used the fireslice to move coals to the ***trivets***(q.v.)."

firkin, sugar firkin: a tightly lidded, handled container, made of wood early, and later of tin or other metal, and used to store granulated or lump sugar; one quarter barrel, about 8 gallons, usually of cheese, e.g.; "There were thirty firkins of cheese listed in the manifest." "Her sugar firkin was of tin""

first cousins: persons who share one or more common grandparents, e.g., "Her mother's sisters' children, were her first cousins."

fish kettle: an oblong, iron kettle used for and often shaped like a fish, e.g.,"She poached whole fish in the fish kettle."

fishmonger: a merchant or dealer in fish and seafood, e.g., "Before emigrating, Richard Roberts was a Welsh fishmonger."

fistula: a canal, opening or passage resulting from injury or disease that permits drainage to the surface, e.g., "Fistulas, especially in the abdomen, were not understood by early physicians, and but few undertook to disturb or treat them or their cause."

fitchew: See ***skunk.***

fixed, fixt, unfixed, unfixt: refers to the state of repair of metal mechanical devices, e.g., "The 1679 Judith Parker inventory lists two 'pistolls, 1 fixt, 1 unfixt'."

flagellet(e): a small flute, e.g., "Curiously, the inventory revealed a recorder, a flute, and a flagellet."

flagon: an ancient term for a large mug or flask with a narrow mouth from which alcoholic beverages - typically rum, mead, or beer - were drunk, e.g., "The earliest records of New England inns reveal drinks being served in flagons."

flail: an implement used to separate grain from husks and other chaff, e.g., "She had a hickory flail which she had used for years."

flame grain, crotch grain: the beautiful and desirable wood grain created in the crotch of a tree, e.g., "Flame grain walnut and mahogany were much prized by cabinetmakers." Also see ***burl grain.***

Flandersware: stoneware, originally from Holland and France, e.g., "Her Flandersware platters were most unusual. "

flapdragon: an early drinkers' game in which raisins were plucked from burning rum with the fingers, e.g., "Flapdragon was a popular pastime of drinkers and revelers during the long New England winter nights.

flask: early, a bottle or powder horn; later a small bottle with a lid or stopper, e.g., "The flasks used now to carry alcoholic beverages on the person derive from small, early vessels used for any liquid or finely powdered substance, such as gunpowder."

flat: as now, a shallow wooden box, usually holding ten or a dozen smaller containers for berries, small fruits, or vegetables; a flat bottomed boat used to transport freight; a superlative meaning very much so, absolutely, without doubt, total, etc., e.g., "She took two flats of berries to market to trade for other produce"; "He had a flat that he used to ferry goods to Charles City"; "Lee flat whipped Hooker at Chancellorsville"; "To a little boy holding a $10.00 bill he said, 'You flat have that money'."

flatiron, flat iron, sad iron: early, a heavy, black iron tool with a flat, polished bottom that was heated on a stove or trivet and used for smoothing or "ironing" clothes or cloth goods; later, any smoothing tool made of iron or steel, whether the heat source was self-contained or not, e.g., "She had three flatirons, each of which was used alternately while the others were heating."

flax wheel: a small, treadle-driven spinning wheel, usually used to make thread from flax (linen), e.g., "Virtually every home of the nineteenth century had at least one flaxwheel." See also *spinning wheel.*

fleam: a common pointed instrument, held in the hand, and used to bleed people and animals, e.g., "The cattle fleam and branding iron were the only farm tools that appeared in the inventory."

fleeter, fleeting dish: a shallow, handled bowl or dish used to skim cream from the surface of fresh milk, e.g., "At each milking, she used the fleeter to skim the cream from the milk."

flesh fork, fleshhook: a handled, hooked, metal fork, usually pointed or with two tines and used to remove meat from a boiling kettle or pot, e.g., "She used a flesh fork to remove the large pieces of boiled meat, which she then cut up and served."

fleshing knife: a common, curved-bladed, heavy knife used to strip the tissue refuse from the inner side of animal skins preparatory to curing, e.g., "There was a flesh knife and two large **crock jugs** (q.v.) in the inventory of Judith Parker's belongings."

flint glass: See **leaded glass**.

flintlock, snaplock: a very common, early, hand-held firearm discharged through the action of a piece of flint striking a small, rough, metal plate (steel), thereby creating a spark that ignited the gunpowder, e.g., "Before 1840, the flintlock was the most common of American firearms."

flip: a favored intoxicating drink consisting of rum and cider, beer, or ale, sweetened, and usually heavily seasoned with cinnamon and nutmeg, often served warm, e.g., "Many were the flips enjoyed in old Raleigh Tavern."

flipdog: a poker-like iron rod, heated to red heat in the fire and then thrust into drinks, especially *flips* (q.v.) for the purpose of warming them, e.g., "A large mug filled with rum, water, sugar, and butter, into which a red-hot flipdog had been thrust, became the much enjoyed **hot buttered rum** (q.v.)."

flivver: an early term meaning an old or barely operable automobile; thought by some to have derived from the words Henry Ford and livery, meaning a cheap or low quality automobile, e.g., "Winny always referred to her son's old cars as flivvers." Also see **tin lizzie.**

flock: old rags, scraps of wool, or pieces of cloth, often used to stuff ticking bags or weave into rugs, when e.g., "Being a widow, her flock rug was the best she could afford."

Florin: a coin (first silver, then copper) equalling one tenth a Pound (two shillings, or $12.00 to $15.00 in 1992), and equal to a Netherlands Gulden, e.g., "The silver florin was usually accepted as payment by colonial American merchants."

floss: unlike now, soft, shiny silk thread of wide utility, e.g., "She often used floss in her embroidery work."

flow blue: occasionally called "flowing blue"; china ware, usually ironstone, imprinted with designs of cobalt blue coloring of many shades that flowed or "bled" into the dish or bowl producing a smeared look, now highly prized, it was made after about 1830, e.g., "The flow blue **pitcher and bowl** (q.v.) kept in the master bedroom were made in Holland."

flub-dubs: extravagances; unneeded and unwarranted decorations or finery, e.g., "Lincoln referred to the pretentious White House decorations bought by Mary as purchases of flub-dubs."

flummeries: See **desserts.**

flux, bloody flux: See **dysentery.**

flyboat: a light, shallow-draft, fast sailboat, popular on inland bays and wide waterways, e.g., "On windy days, Hunt used a flyboat to ferry men to and from James City."

foal: to give birth to a horse or mule; a newborn horse or mule, male or female, e.g., "The jenny was ready to foal"; "The foal, being female, would be called a *filly* (q.v.) after but a few days and until she had matured and been bred."

folio: occasionally, any very large book; early and now, a dimension or measure of documentary material, usually of about thirty inches on a side; sometimes, pages printed on both sides, yet numbered on the first side only, e.g., "The volume was in folio and was quite unwieldy"; "The record was paginated in folio, so the researcher had to exercise care in citing it."

fontanage: a knot of ribbons on the top of the hat, e.g., "By 1800 the fontanage was no longer considered stylish."

fonzy tish: from the German "pflantzentisch" meaning plant stand; a slice of a tree, usually walnut, butternut, or cherry, cut at right angles to the trunk, highly polished on one surface, and used as a stand for plants, thus keeping their drippings off the carpets, e.g., "Her Dutch husband had sanded and polished her butternut fonzy tish until the finish was like a **looking glass** (q.v.)."

foolscap: writing paper; a size of paper, usually 13 1/2 X 17, e.g., "The writing paper of early students often was a sheet of foolscap cut into quarters and tied together with a piece of thread."

foot warmer: usually, a small box, sometimes free standing, but often made to attach to the stretchers of a work table or desk, and having a metal liner into which hot ashes or coals were placed in order that the person there working might be able to warm their feet by placing them on the box, e.g., "Bookkeepers and office workers found foot warmers a necessity by reason of the inefficiency of fireplaces."

footman: unlike now, a *trivet* (q.v.), e.g., "There were 2 footmans in the inventory."

footstool, foot stool, cricket: a low seat or stool, used for sitting or in front of a chair as a resting place for the feet, e.g., "The inventory revealed a bench and a footstool."

Forbes Road: See **roads, early.**

forced heirs: in Civil Law, any persons who a testator may not deprive of their share of the estate without formally disinheriting them, e.g., "Those researching in early jurisdictions that applied the Civil Law, such as Louisiana, should be aware of forced heirs."

forcemeat: stuffing, as in a turkey, e.g., "The forcemeat contained, in part, soft sweet sausage and oysters."

forcible entry and detainer: an action to recover possession of land when the rightful owner has been wrongfully kept from the premises, e.g., "Forcible entry and detainer was the proper action when the neighbor fenced in plaintiff's land, undertook to graze cattle on it, and refused to leave."

forcible trespass: a North Carolina action corresponding to ***forcible entry and detainer*** (q.v.) but applicable only to personal property, possession of which has been taken through force or an appearance of force, e.g., "Even though he was not really afraid of the taker, the owner of the hounds sought possession of them through an action alleging forcible trespass."

ford: a place where a river or stream may be passed on foot or (occasionally) on horseback, e.g., "Chattanooga and Atlanta still have major ways called Shallowford Road named for the early shallow fords to which the roads led."

foreign judgment: a judgment from a court in a county or state other than that in which it is being sued, e.g., "Her discovery of a foreign judgment filed in the Marion County court records by her ancestor led her to his home county."

forks: contrary to popular belief, even though seldom seen in the 17th century, three- and four-tined forks for eating were in rather common use in this country by the period of the American Revolution, e.g., "Her silver forks had three tines and were made in England." Also see ***manure fork*** and ***dung fork.***

forms: record-keeping aids necessary to the family researcher and usually available in libraries and bookstores, e.g., "He had preserved all the information on various lineage forms."

forsworn: an untrue oath where the person giving it knows of the falsity, e.g., "He was said to have forsworn in the affidavit, meaning that he knew the statement to be untrue at the time."

fortnight: fourteen days; one half a month or half the period of the moon, e.g., "Expressions using fortnight, such as 'He will be gone about a fortnight' were very common in the early days."

forts: See ***stockades.***

Forty-niners, The: those 125,000 or so prospectors and opportunists who came from all over the world to California after the discovery of gold at Sutter's Mill in January of 1848, e.g., "Tens of thousands of descendants of the Tennessee Forty-niners now live in the west."

fossil: unlike now, any mineral dug from the ground, e.g., "His reference to mica as a fossil did not mean that it was the remains of prior life."

fostered, fostered out, foster parent: an ancient Irish custom carried to the Americas and here modified to an arrangement whereby a child is given into the custody of another and in exchange for care and keeping is expected to perform the duties of a natural child; the condition of a person not of age, who, by agreement of his or her parents, was living with a family other than his or her own, and who is expected to perform services and otherwise conduct himself or herself as would any other child of the agreed family; one who carries out the duties of raising a child without legally claiming that child as his or her own, e.g., "At the age of twelve, Maggie was fostered out to the Rev. Pinney home, there to remain until she married." (See **adoption** and **apprentice.**

foulard: an early, commonly used, then usually lightweight printed silk cloth, e.g., "His cravat was of lavender foulard."

foundling: an abandoned child which the natural parents have no intention of reclaiming, e.g., "Since James was a foundling at the church door, his lineage was most difficult to ascertain."

four-plated stove, two-plated, six-plated, etc.: referred to the number of "plates" - cooking spots, 'burners' - on a wood- or coal-burning cookstove, thus revealing its size and that it was for cooking and not heating, e.g., "The Rev. Cole inventory listed a '6 plate' stove, revealing a very large cooking stove." Also see **cookstove.**

four-poster, poster bed: a bed with posts designed to hold a canopy, e.g., "The canopy frame for her four-poster had been lost for many years." Also see **pencil-post bed.**

fowling piece, birding piece: early term for a common, long-barrelled, large-bored shotgun used for bird and small game hunting, e.g., "The stock and forearm of his fowling piece were of burl walnut." Also see **shotgun** and **cap and ball.**

fox, foxed: unlike now, one material decorated with another, usually leather or cloth, the prime or better material being that which is foxed with a secondary substance, e.g., "Her best shoes were lace foxed with beaver"

foxing: yellow or brown stains that appear on old paper, e.g., "The paper showed foxing, yet was very strong."

foyer table: usually a long, rather narrow, well finished table made of better wood, sometimes of stand-up height, and used in foyers and entrance hall as a place for guests' hats and gloves, and usually maintained with a doily, lamp, and a floral arrangement, e.g., "Her foyer table was of inlaid mahogany, and always held a fresh flower arrangement."

fractional currency: **See** shin-plaster.

fraktur: originally, a German type style; early PA, a colorful, often fully handmade (sometimes partly printed), painting, usually depicting birds, flowers, decorative calligraphy and scroll work, and bearing the names of those who are the subject, e.g., "The fraktur birth certificate of his ancestor was his most prized memento."

frambisia: See **yaws.**

frankincense and myrrh: early, very valuable resins from trees grown in Ethiopia, and used in the making of incense and perfumes, e.g., "The story of the Wise Men and their frankincense and myrrh is well known to all Christians."

Franklin (State of): that State of the Union, the constitution of which was adopted at Jonesboro, TN., in 1784, that arose partially from the need of settlers to protect themselves from the Cherokees and eventually became a portion of east Tennessee, e.g., "Many descendants of the residents of Franklin now live in Texas, and left genealogical records in Tennessee."

fraternities, sororities, and societies: as now; in genealogy, a valuable source of vital records concerning ancestors, as many early Americans belonged, e.g., The Colonial Dames, Masons (F. & A.M.), Knights of Columbus (K. of C.), United Order Of African Ladies and Gentlemen (U.O.A.L.G.), Rebekah Lodge, Order of Red Men (O.R.M.), Woodmen of the World, Shrine, Order of Odd Fellows (I.O.O.F.), Moose (L.S.M.), Sons of Italy, and the Elks (B.P.O.E.), to name but a few, all kept records valuable to the researcher."

free blacks, free negroes: those negroes who were free men, whether by being granted freedom by their masters, or by becoming citizens of, or being born in, one of the non-slave states or colonies, e.g., "The early records often refer to free negroes or free blacks."

free school: an early term meaning a school supported by taxes, private sources, or churches, where no charge was assessed for the participation of a student, e.g., "She attended the first free school in the county."

free willers: See ***Redemptioners.***

free woman of color: a pre-Civil War term for any woman, other than those of the white race, who was not bound to servitude, e.g., "Being half Cherokee, she was carried on the records as a free woman of color."

Freedman's Bureau: the result of Congressional action that sought to preserve the civil rights of the Negro, required by reason of the Southern ***Black Codes*** (q.v.) and other continued efforts of the South to subjugate the Negro, e.g., "The authority of the Freedman's Bureau of 1865 was enlarged in 1866."

freedman, freedmen: early, any person previously bound to servitude, and now freed; a manumitted or freed Slave, e.g., "The formation of the Freedman's Bureau in 1865 brought consternation to the old South."

freehold, freeholder: a ***fee (q.v.), fee tail (q.v.),*** or a ***life estate*** (q.v.)in real property, or the holder of one of those estates, e.g., "While most land in the ***manor*** was leased for the life of the holder, Dimmitt was a freeholder, the owner in fee of his tract." (See also ***fee simple,*** and ***entailment.***

freeman's roll: in the early colonies, a list of ***burgesses*** and ***freemen*** maintained by the county, precinct, or town, e.g., "The early freeman's rolls are very helpful to the family historian."

French and Indian War: that armed conflict that occurred 1756-1763 between England and the American colonies on the one side, and the French and allied American Indian forces on the other, e.g., "There were very few formal discharges from military service at the time of the French and Indian War."

French fall shoes: apparently, low, better quality dress shoes, for either men or women, e.g., "Some 17th-century references speak of French fall shoes." See ***shoes.***

French influence: many words arose from our experiences with the French who settled or maintained commerce with the colonies, e.g., "Bayou, toboggan, caribou, crevasse, levee, depot, cents, dimes, chowder, beaucoup, and the many Creole dishes and names are but a few."

French polish: a fine furniture finish, consisting of shellac mixed with spirits, and applied in several coats with great care, e.g., "French polish was used on only the finest of furniture."

French Wine: in early times, any better wine, but usually from France, e.g., "The manifest revealed two bbls of French Wine from the Canary Islands."

freshet: annual or regular periods of high water in rivers and streams, e.g., "Grant knew that when the spring freshets came, the fords would not be passable."

Friars: religious orders of men; a) Franciscans, Gray Friars and Minors, b) Augustines, c) Dominicans (Black Friars), d) Carmelites (White Friars), e.g., "The records of the Orders of Friars often are helpful in research." See also ***orders of nuns***.

Friends: See ***Quakers.***

frigate: very early, a light vessel of both sails and oars; later, a light, square-rigged, sailing vessel; since mid-nineteenth century, a man o' war larger than a destroyer and smaller than a cruiser, e.g., "The frigate *Golden Eagle* was noted for its extraordinary speed."

fringe loom: a common, small loom used to make fringing, e.g., "Fringe looms often appear in early inventories." Also see ***belt loom.***

Frisian: that Germanic tongue most like English and spoken by those called Frisians from the areas bordering the Netherlands province of Friesland and the Frisian islands in the North Sea, Denmark, and Western Germany, e.g. "Of those who spoke German, the colonials most quickly came to know the meanings of the West Frisians."

frock, frockcoat: early, a tight-fitting coat for men; later, a dress or coat; today, any outer garment for a woman, e.g., "His frockcoat was of Irish linen and wool."

froe, frow: a common, large, thick-bladed tool with the handle at right angles to the blade, used to make shingles or cut wood into thin pieces, e.g., "He made the ***cedar shakes*** (q.v.) with a frow and a lot of work."

frog: a sheath hung from the belt to hold a sword or knife; a piece of heavy indented or pierced glass and used to hold buds or flower stems, e.g., "Her frog was of pink ***milk glass*** (q.v.)."

froise: (Fr., froissier) bacon or ham enclosed in a pancake, e.g., "Froises have always been a favorite in old Louisiana."

fruitery: a place for storing fruits or other such produce, e.g., "Maggie called her ***cold cellar*** (q.v.) a fruitery." Also see ***buttery.***

fuero: (Sp.) a code of laws, e.g., "References to the fuero in the early Southwest refer to codes, either civil or criminal."

Fugitive Slave Law (and Acts): those enactments of Congress (1793 and 1850) and several states having to do with and requiring the return of slaves who had unlawfully fled from their owners to "free" states, e.g., "The ***Dred Scott decision*** (q.v.) was said to have confirmed the validity of the Fugitive Slave Laws."

Fulhamware: ceramic ware, particularly popular for tankards, mugs, drinking glasses, etc., "Fulhamware mugs occasionally were listed in the inventories of affluent New Englanders."

fuller: one who cleanses (usually), thickens, or felts cloth, from which derives the surname Fuller, e.g., "Dimmitt worked as a fuller in early Maryland."

fungibles: movable, usually specifically unidentifiable, tangible personal property that may be replaced by number, weight, or measure, e.g., "His storage of wheat at the elevator called into play the law of fungibles."

furlong: ten (10) chains or forty (40) **poles** (q.v.) or **rods** (q.v.) equal one (1) furlong; there are eight furlongs in a mile, e.g., "The race was ten furlongs or 1.25 miles in length."

furnace: unlike now, any smelting installation, but usually for iron, e.g., "Catherine Furnace was to forever be associated with Lee and Stonewall Jackson."

furnishings: unlike now, one's personal items of dress or appearance, e.g.,"Among the furnishings were several items of jewelry, a hand mirror and 2 combs, and a pair of gloves."

furniture: unlike now, those furnishings customarily found in the space or with the object being considered, and necessary to make it complete and usable as designed, e.g., "The furniture of her bedstead included **curtains** (q.v.), **comforters,** a **rug** (q.v.), and a **ticking bag** (q.v.)."

fusee, fusilier: one who is armed with a firelock of **flintlock,** (q.v.) e.g., "The 16th Fusiliers, true to their name, were foot soldiers armed with English-made flintlocks."

fustian: a strong cloth made of linen or wool and cotton, e.g., "Fustian was an early favorite for better work clothes."

G

G.I. Bill: those congressional enactments that provided relief, medical attention, funds for education, and guaranteed loans to the veterans of World War II and other conflicts since then, e.g., "Since 1945, the G.I. Bill has provided educational opportunities for (and genealogical records of) millions of veterans."

gaffer: early, a term of respect; later and now, an old man of little worth or estate.

gages: plums, e.g., "For 'plums in brandy', she directed that green gages (apricots) or blue gages (plums) be cooked in water with sugar equal to 1/2 the wgt. of the fruit, to which brandy was added when the mixture was bottled." Also see **shrubs.**

gaits, horse: as now, e.g., "A walk is as now; the pace, where both legs on a side are moved forward almost simultaneously, is used in cart racing; the trot, also used in cart racing, is a rough saddle ride between a walk and a run where the diagonal legs move forward almost simultaneously; at a rack, a rapid smooth pace is gained, and the diagonal legs move together but not simultaneously; in a canter, an easy comfortable run or gallop is provided; and at gallop, the animal may be brought to its full speed, however it is exhausting for the beast."

gallop: See **gaits.**

game pouch: an early, medium-sized, usually waterproof, heavy cloth bag with a shoulder strap, the same worn while hunting and serving as a carrier for dead small game, e.g., "She had lined his game pouch with **oil cloth** (q.v.) to prevent the blood from leeching through to his clothes."

game table: early, any of many styles of wooden tables, used for playing chess, cards, or other games, often large with a rotating and folding top and made of better woods - cherry, mahogany, or walnut, e.g., "Her Empire-style game table was of cherry with a walnut top that folded and rotated."

games (of children): as now, e.g., "Among the myriad early children's games were:

whizzer or spin the button (twisted string and buttons);

king of the mountain (a contest of strength);

mumblety-peg (mumbly peg) and baseball with a knife (played with **pocket knives** (q.v.);

red rover come over (a tag-like game);

gray wooley (meaning lost);

clicking wheel (played with a wagon **tire** (q.v.) and a horseshoe);

ring around rosie (a dance of sorts);

buck (a game with the fingers);

hide and seek and tag (as now);

snake in the grass (attempting to dodge small dangers);

marbles or nubs, as now;

kick the can (tag of sorts timed by reaching a kicked can);

checks, a game played with peach seeds;

pick up sticks (moving small sticks without disturbing others)."

Also see **King's X, bowls, break the Pope's neck, pallmall.**

gangrene: death and decomposition (putrefaction) of soft tissues of the body from any number of causes, disease, trauma, loss of circulation, etc., e.g., "For gangrene of a large area, acids and maggots were used to remove the dead flesh, and, failing that, amputation was the only remedy."

gaol: a jail, e.g., "Early records frequently speak of gaoling the defendant." This spelling is still used in Britain.

gargles: as now, medications for sore and dry throats and coughs, e.g., "As gargles, among others, frontier women made teas of water lilies, sage with honey and vinegar, slippery elm, yellow root, quince seeds, mint and thyme, flaxseed, and catnip."

garlix: a fabric of unknown nature "The 1761 account of Berry Smith revealed the purchase of a 1 1/2 ells of garlix."

garret: any space under the roof and above some other room, e.g., "He kept the old **joiner's** (q.v.) tools in the garret."

Garter, Knights of the Garter, Knights of the Order of St. George: the mark of the highest order of English knighthood; a symbol reflecting that order ranking next after nobility, e.g., "The garter of the Knights of the Garter is of blue leather, and the badge is an image of St. George."

gastralgia: almost any severe stomach pain; neuralgia of the stomach, e.g., "For gastralgia, remedies such as alum, atropia, Arsenic, Bismuth, and ether were prescribed."

gastric catarrh: inflammation of the lining of the stomach, e.g., "There being little difference usually, most of the remedies for gastralgia were employed for gastric catarrh."

gastric ulcers: See **ulcers.**

gateleg table, swing-leg table: often simply "gateleg"; a popular variation, in many sizes and woods, of a **drop leaf table** (q.v.), having hinged legs on two sides that fold inward until flush with the table frame, permitting a lowering of the leaves, thus conserving space; generally the more legs, the older the table, e.g., "The cabinetmaker made gatelegs of any good wood at hand, but preferred walnut, cherry, or butternut."

gauze: similar to now, a silk or cotton cloth woven so thinly as to be nearly transparent, e.g., "Gauze, especially silk, was so expensive that any purchase of it in quantities for home use reveals a measure of wealth in that family."

Gay Nineties: the name given the decade of the 1890s, e.g., "The Gay Nineties were so called by reason of the prevailing feelings of peace and security, the invention of new conveniences including electric lights, the telephone, telegraph, and record player, rapid inexpensive transportation, dominance on the World scene, manufacturing and inexpensive products for everyday and everyone, expanding cities and employment, ever advancing education, and, perhaps most of all, the growth and relative prosperity of the middle class."

gazetteer: a publication telling of towns (existing and extinct), the locations of county seats, waterways, roads, and places of interest within a certain area, e.g., "The North Carolina Gazetteer revealed the location of Jarrett Creek."

geedunk: an early term of the military, especially the Navy and the Marine Corps, meaning candies, ice cream, confections, or other sweets available to the shipboard crew, e.g., "Every early U.S. Navy ship had its geedunk stand."

geld: money, or a compensation or value, e.g., "The word geld indicating compensation for some loss is occasionally seen in colonial records."

gelding: See **horse.**

genealogy: the study of lineage and family history through the gathering of data concerning those to whom one is related by affinity, consanguinity, or through historical interest, e.g., "He spent years doing genealogical research on the family of his daughter-in-law."

general assumpsit: See **assumpsit.**

General Land Office: See **land grants.**

general reference section: that portion of the library where works such as indices to periodicals, dictionaries, encyclopedias, reference works, maps, and gazetteers are located, e.g., "The Encyclopedia Britannica is located in the general reference section."

genesis (of counties): in genealogy, the origins or political parentage of a county, e.g., "From the county history, she learned that the genesis of Blair and Huntingdon Counties, PA, included Bedford and Cumberland County."

gentleborn: See **gentleman** and **base begotten.**

gentleman, gentlewoman: a person of affluence and gentility, or born to those of high station in the community, usually with a greater than average level of education, the so-called gentle-born, e.g., "In the 18th century, to be called a gentleman or gentlewoman was a great compliment."

Geologic Survey, U.S.; U.S.G.S: to genealogists, that government agency that creates and supplies maps of many areas of the U.S., e.g., "The U.S.G.S. maps (topos, **quadrangles,** q.v.) are invaluable in gaining knowledge of places where ancestors lived."

German influence: many words arose from our German ancestry, e.g., "Hex, sauerkraut, bummer, check, delicatessen, ecology, hoodlum, kindergarten, nix, phooey, scram, spiel, and frankfurters are but a few examples."

get a livelyhood: to earn a living, e.g., "The mother pleaded that her son should not be indentured as he could get a livelyhood."

gig: a light, two-wheeled carriage pulled by one horse; a small, pointed, long-handled, 2- or 3-tined spear used to catch frogs, fish, and small animals, e.g. "As now we are eager to have our first car, sons of wealthy early families looked forward to their first gig"; "They went frog gigging." Also see **chaise.**

giggs, jigs: See **dances.**

gill: a measure of liquid, often whiskey or brandy, equal to one half cup, e.g., "He told the **barkeep** (q.v.) he would have a gill of Scotch whiskey."

gin men, ginmen: employees of a coal mine who do general labor about the operations, e.g., "Gin men appear in early Kentucky and Ohio records."

ginseng: as now, a root supposed to have medicinal value, e.g., "He made up tonics of ginseng and other plants."

girth, girt: a strap attached to a saddle that goes under the belly of a horse to hold the saddle in place, e.g., "The girth is too tight."

Gists Road: See **roads, early.**

give out: used in any tense, to be exhausted, usually temporarily, e.g.,

"When told to pick another four bushels, he declared that he was give out"; "My legs give out on me."

given name: those names other than surnames given to children, e.g., "Their given names were Biblical; Joshua, Daniel, Absolom, Rebecca, and Ruth."

glaize, glaise, glaze: to put glass in a frame, e.g., "He was ordered to glaize the courthouse windows."

glebe, glebe land: land owned by the church, the income from which goes to the church, e.g., "The National Genealogical Society owns real estate that originally was glebe land."

gleet: See **gonorrhea.**

glyster: See **clyster.**

go without day: refers to a dismissal by a court of a party or his claim, e.g., "After his filing of a frivolous claim, the court ordered that Jones go without day, meaning without further day (time) in court."

Godparent, Godfather, Godmother: a person, very often unrelated, who has pledged himself or herself (usually with religious overtones, yet without financial responsibility) to the care, well-being, and upbringing of a child, especially in the event of death or misfortune of the parents; considered an honor to both the child and the Godparent, e.g., "His father's life-long friend was asked to be his Godfather."

goin' jesse, a-goin jesse: source unknown; a superlative, e.g., "The old letter mentioned that the grist mill really was a goin' jesse."

goiter, goitre: as now, an enlargement of the thyroid gland, e.g., "By 1885, goiter was being treated with iodides, particularly of potassium and mercury."

goloeshoes: See **shoes.**

gonorrhea, gleet, clap: a venereal disease; however gleet sometimes also meant any seeping wound, e.g., "The social disease gleet often was treated with cod-liver oil or turpentine, all to no effect." Also see **syphilis.**

Good Queen Bess: Elizabeth I, e.g., "Because of widespread feelings of security and pride during her reign, Elizabeth I was often referred to as Good Queen Bess, even long after her death."

goods: a common term referring to personal property, excluding animals and intangible assets, often used to refer to stock in trade or merchandise, especially cloth or clothing, e.g., "The goods named included articles of clothing, shoes, and fabric."

goodwife:

goosewing: See **broadaxe.**

gorget: as now, a decorative large pendant, often of some symbolism or religious meaning, e.g., "She wore a small Indian gorget that her son had found."

gout: a painful inflammation and swelling of the joints, often in the feet (the big toe particularly), hands, and ankles, caused by excessive uric acid in the system, e.g., "Gout, as with so many other ailments, was not understood, and often was treated with black snakeroot."

Grand Army of the Republic, G.A.R.: the counterpart of the **United Confederate Veterans** (q.v.); a fraternal organization of Union Veterans of the Civil War, including those who served in the Navy, it was a powerful political force in the late 19th century, e.g., "If one hoped to be elected to office in the 1880s, he sought the aid of the G.A.R."

grand aunt, grand uncle: synonymous with "great aunt" or "great uncle"; a sister or brother of one's grandparent, e.g., "Her grand aunt, Jane, was a sister of her maternal grandfather." See **great aunt and great uncle.**

grand jury: See **jury.**

grandparent: a parent of a parent of the subject person, e.g., "His mother's mother was his favorite grandparent."

Grange, Grangers: a 19th and 20th century society of people engaged in farming; very early, a grange was a farm having all the buildings and conveniences needed for husbandry, e.g., "The organization and its members known as the 'Grange' and 'Grangers' arose from the need of farmers to organize much as a union, in order that their collective bargaining powers be put to use."

granny woman: apparently, a **midwife** (q.v.) with whom one was well acquainted, e.g., "She wrote that when her time was near, he sent for the granny woman."

grant (of land): often imprecisely called a **patent** (q.v.); usually, a transfer of title to land by government, through which settlement was brought about, in consideration, variously, of a minimal measure of improvement, or the payment of money, or both, e.g., "He was granted 160 acres by the Crown, and was required only to construct a small habitation and commence cultivation of a small part of the tract."

grantee: one to whom something is transferred by deed, quite usually land, e.g., "The deed for 100 acres named as grantees both Robert and his wife." Also see **grantor.**

granting clause: that wording in a deed that describes or names the parties who thereby are gaining ownership of (usually) land, e.g., "The granting clause named John, Mary, and Henry Hudson as the **grantees** (q.v.) of the land."

grantor indexes, grantee indexes: indexes to deeds compiled alphabetically in the surnames of the sellers (grantors), and in the names of buyers or transferees (grantees), e.g., "He found that grantee indices served the same purposes as did reverse indices in other states." See also **direct and reverse indexes.**

grantor: a person or persons transferring or conveying land usually to another, generally by deed, e.g., "The grantor in the deed was his father-in-law." Also see **grantee.**

grass widow: early, a woman whose husband has been gone for a long period or has abandoned her; 20th century, sometimes a divorcee, e.g., "Since he had boarded a boat going down Tar River and never again was heard of, she was called a grass widow."

Grasshopper Plague, the Great: See **Plague of 1874.**

grate: as now, a frame or iron rack to hold burning wood or coal, perforated so as to allow ashes to fall through to the floor of the fireplace, e.g., "Every summer the **blacksmith** (q.v.) would make up several grates for sale later."

grave marker: See **headstone.**

grave rock: See **headstone.**

graver, scauper: any of several shapes of tools used by the engraver or **chaser** (q.v.), e.g., "The inventory listed three gravers, suggesting his work as an engraver."

grays: a term used to refer to a team of two or more gray horses, e.g., "He used only his grays on the **pleasure wagon** (q.v.)."

grease and grits: a mixture of hot pork fat, bacon, or salt pork and **hominy grits** (q.v.); an early staple among Southern poor, e.g., "To many early Southern children, grease and grits often was all they could expect to eat for days on end." Also see **mush.**

great aunt or uncle, grand aunt or uncle: a sister or brother of one's grandparent; the relationship of one to the brothers and sisters of any ancestor are determined by taking the number of greats in the title of the ancestor and adding one (1) more great before the word "aunt" or "uncle", e.g., "The sisters of his great-great grandmother (two greats) were his triple-great aunts (three greats)."

great grandparent: any ancestor prior to one's grandparents; a grandparent of a parent of the subject person; each additional "great" designates an additional past generation, e.g., "His grandfather's great grandmother was the most interesting of his great-great-great grandparents."

Great Law: that Pennsylvania law of 1682 by which corn fields were to be fenced to five feet in height; unlike now, cattle had to be fenced out, not fenced in, e.g., "If one had complied with the Great Law, he could recover damages from an owner of any animals or cattle that trespassed on the land."

great men: leaders or those highly respected by their own people, e.g., "In Sept. of 1686, the court ordered 'four great men of the Nottoway tribe' to appear and answer for the killing of Mr. Jordan's cattle by Indians."

great pox: See **syphilis.**

great wheel: See **spinning wheel.**

greatcoat, great coat: a large, heavy coat designed to be worn over other clothes in extreme weather, e.g., "The children liked to play by wearing his old greatcoat."

Green Mountain Boys: that small force recruited by Ethan Allen from the area of Castleton, VT (in the Green Mts.), that captured Fort Ticonderoga and Crown Point on 10 and 12 May, 1775, e.g., "Dan Brown and Stephan Sherwood were proud of their service with the Green Mountain Boys. "

Gregorian calendar: See **Julian calendar.**

Gregorian period: those years of the Gregorian calendar, e.g., "The Gregorian period or epoch began in 1582."

grey wooley: See **games (of children).**

griddle: word unknown in 18th-century England, apparently a grill or perforated iron cooking surface, "He wrote that he had griddled the lamb."

gridiron: unlike now, a large rack upon which to place pans, skillets, etc. while cooking, usually having iron rods both front to back and left to right, e.g., "The **blacksmith** (q.v.)charged him 2 **Shillings** (q.v.) to make a new gridiron."

griff: a word of early Louisiana meaning the offspring of a negro and a mulatto, e.g., "He wrote that the woman was 'too light to be a negro, and too dark to be a mulatto, hence (she) must be a griff.'"

grippes, grippe, gripes: cramps in the stomach, abdomen, or bowels, usually the last named; sometimes labor pains; occasionally severe menstrual cramps, e.g., "In the seventeenth century it was thought that passing clouds might sometimes intensify the grippes of labor."

grist mill, mill: a mill, powered early by water or animals, designed to grind various cereal grains into flour or meal, usually for hire, e.g., "He took the buckwheat, corn, and wheat to the grist mill for grinding."

grits: finely ground **hominy** (q.v.), usually served either as cereal with milk and a sweetener, or with butter as a side dish with eggs and meat, e.g., "A winter breakfast in old North Carolina quite usually included grits."

grocery up: to supply the family with staples and food sufficient for several days or weeks, e.g., "They went to town every Saturday and socialized, bought sewing materials, and groceried up."

grog: an inexpensive drink of rum diluted with water, e.g., "He could only afford an occasional grog."

grubbing hoe: a heavy hoe used to break ground, e.g., "Grubbing hoe work was too heavy for her, so her son opened the garden every spring."

grunts: See **desserts, early.**

guard, national guard: See **militia.**

guardian ad litem: a guardian by authority of the law, statute, or court, of an **infant** (q.v.) or other person legally incompetent to transact his own business or maintain his own well-being; guardians ad litem are required to prosecute in behalf of the protected or defend them from others, e.g., "When Jones sued the heirs, the court appointed guardians ad litem for those who were not yet of age."

guardian: a person (judicially or by agreement) who is charged with the care and responsibility of the person, or property, or both, of another, e.g., "He was appointed guardian of his 90-year-old mother"; "Being over fourteen years old, he selected, and the court approved of his uncle as guardian"; "A **testamentary guardian** (q.v.) is one appointed by a provision of a will."

Guinea: a gold coin of Britain, having a value of about a **Pound (£)** (q.v.) and minted from the 1660s until well into the 19th century, e.g., "The Guinea was very common in the American colonies."

gun lock: See **lock.**

gunny sack, gunny: a burlap sack; a heavy sack or bag, often used to carry feed or grain and made of jute, e.g., "Very poor children often had clothes made from old gunny sacks." Also see **tote sack.**

gunsmith: usually one who makes or repairs hand-held firearms, e.g., "The **long rifle** (q.v.) was the crowning achievement of the early Kentucky gunsmiths."

gussied up: slightly overdressed, usually used in referring to a young woman, e.g., "She gussied up before he arrived."

gust: early, any hurricane, tornado, or very heavy storm; later and now, a moderately strong wind of short duration, e.g., "Those Tidewater settlers who survived the immense and devastating hurricane of 1667 usually referred to it as 'The Great Gust.'"

H

habendum clause: the clause or wording in a deed that describes the nature of the interest conveyed, e.g., "The habendum clause provided 'should the **grantee** (q.v.) die without **issue** (q.v.), then, the land shall revert equally to all other grandchildren of the **grantor** (q.v.) then living'."

habeus corpus, writ of: any of a number of ancient **writs** (q.v.) directing a sheriff or other officer of government to bring a person forth for hearing or trial, e.g., "Often, one of the early acts of a President in wartime is to suspend the rights of aliens to writs of habeus corpus."

hack, hack lines: early, horses kept for hire; later, a business having for hire horses and wagons for pleasure or work, e.g., "A driver for Peoples Hack Line took Bill and Ida to the train." Also see **livery.**

hair picture: a framed depiction of a person, design, or scene made of woven human hair, very popular during Victorian times, especially as mementoes from a woman to her lover; the craft is known to have been practiced even before 1700, e.g., "As a birthday gift to her fiancee, she made a tiny hair picture of her silhouette."

haircloth: any cloth into which hair has been woven, usually cotton and horse hair, e.g., "The chair was of haircloth." Also see **horsehair upholstery.**

half boots: See **shoes.**

half chest: See **chest.**

half Eagle: a five-dollar U.S. gold coin, e.g., "A Half Eagle was about two days' pay for a common laborer of 1890."

half section: See **section.**

half table: See **console table.**

Half-Crown: a common British coin worth 2S,6p, e.g., "A Half-Crown would pay a laborer for a full day of work in 1825."

hall: unlike now, the living section (main room and kitchen) of a one-room early home, e.g., "The hall mentioned in the 1680 inventory meant the living quarters of the small house."

hall tree: unlike now, a very high-backed, armed, foyer or hall chair, without upholstery, and with a mirror mounted in the back at chin level, with coat and often an umbrella rack in either side, and sometimes a compartment beneath the raisable seat, e.g., "The mahogany hall tree was of the Empire Style and was beautiful."

hame, hames: part of the harnessing of horses, mules, and other draft animals; the usually wooden, curved, upright struts attached to the collars and to which **traces** (q.v.) are attached, e.g., "The hames seen on many early draft horses were polished and decorated with brass buttons."

hammock chair, swing chair: a swinging chair for adults, having arms, back, and a foot rest, and usually hung from a rafter or a tree, e.g., "She very much enjoyed the hammock chair on hot summer evenings."

hammock: as now, a cloth or web bed, designed to be hung between posts (or trees) and rolled up when not in use, e.g., "In addition to her beds, the 1725 inventory listed two hammocks."

hand irons: See **dog irons.**

hand: usually, a paid laborer or farm worker, a hired hand is one who assists in physical labor in exchange for compensation; a measure equaling four (4) inches,e.g., "The early censuses often revealed the presence of hands within the household." "In the U.S., the height of horses is always measured in hands; a fourteen-hand horse being a medium size animal."

handgun: See **revolver** and **derringer.**

harness, harnessing, traces: refers to the total equipment by which a horse (or other animal) is equipped to pull a load, e.g., "Typically, a complete harness could consist of the crown piece, front, blinkers, cheek strap, noseband, bit, sidecheek, throatlatch, reins, hames, collars, martingale, hame tug, bellyband, breeching, crupper, hipstraps, and terret."

harnessmaker: one who made harnessing; one having knowledge of leather, metal fittings, and the needs of those who used animals to pull vehicles, e.g., "The local harnessmaker replaced the leather sleighbell straps."

harpsichord: early, a common keyboard instrument, the strings being mechanically plucked, e.g., "The Mason harpsichord may yet be seen in their ancestral home." Also see **spinet.**

harrow: an implement for smoothing soil preparatory to planting, having either several tines (early) or discs mounted side by side, e.g., "The old harrow was designed to be used with either horses or a tractor."

Hartshorn, Hartshorn cookies: ammonium chloride, used by **Pennsylvania Dutch** (q.v.) and German women as a seasoning when making cookies called springerles, e.g., "The reason for using Hartshorn is now lost." Also see **springerles.**

harvest mite: See **chigger.**

harvest table: a long, narrow table, usually without finish, and sometimes with a drop leaf on one side, used to prepare fruits and vegetables for canning or preserving, e.g., "The old harvest table was made of but two boards and was very valuable as an antique."

hat box: See **bonnet box.**

hat pin: a necessity in the days when women regularly wore hats, often beaded and, for the rich, jewelled or of silver or gold, e.g., "She had nearly as many hat pins as she had hats."

hatchet: a very common, short-handled, sharp-edged tool of many uses, including trimming timber, chopping brush and small trees, and killing poultry and small animals, e.g., "His hatchet always was at hand, especially when *fencerows* (q.v.) had to be cleared."

hautboy: an early word for oboe; a musical instrument, e.g., "In 1679, Judith Parker owned two flutes, a recorder, and a hautboy."

having the stone: See **stone.**

hawker: a peddler, a travelling salesman who carries goods with him for sale, e.g., "The early newspapers often speak of hawkers."

hay fever: as now, an allergy, e.g., "Hay fever, like all allergies, was not understood, and often was treated with quinine or by the inhalation of carbolic acid."

hayfork: See **pitchfork.**

haying time: that late summer period when hay was cut, dried, baled or stacked and prepared for winter, e.g., "At haying time, every able-bodied man and boy was put to the task of 'making hay'."

head of household: that person who is or appears to be in control and charge of the other members of a family unit; usually, an owner, lessee, or tenant of property, if he or she also resides there; early, usually the father/husband or grown son, and if that member was dead or gone, then the mother or a *femme sole* (q.v.), e.g., "Her husband having been dead and her sons not grown, Great Aunt Jane appeared as the head of household in the 1880 census."

head rock: See **headstone.**

head tax: a poll tax; a tax levied on all persons of a certain age and class, and having no requirement or qualification except one's presence within that class, e.g., "The head tax of 1684 was deeply resented by the poor."

headaches: as now, e.g., "In the early days headaches were viewed as an ailment rather than a symptom, hence were treated with everything from strong coffee to arsenic."

headrights: those rights and privileges, often including grants of land, partial relief from certain taxes, and bounties paid by governments, afforded those who paid for or otherwise provided transportation for emigrants to the colonies, e.g., "As the owner of 16 headrights, Huntt was eligible for 800 acres of Virginia land." Also see **land grants.**

headstone, field stone, field rock, head rock, grave marker, tombstone, or monument: a marker designating the place of interment of one or more individuals, usually inscribed; sometimes crudely made from native stone and without inscription, or with initials only, e.g., "At his gravesite, she found only a rough field stone bearing his initials"; "Since the headstone was nearly illegible, he used paper and chalk to make a rubbing of it."

hearsay: from hear and say; statements setting forth or repeating prior words of a third person not now present or available for questioning, such words being offered as proof of the matter stated by that third person, e.g., "Even though John told Mother that Jane took the family dishes, Mother can not now repeat those hearsay statements in court to show who has the dishes because John is dead, and he may have been mistaken, joking, exaggerating, or lying."

heart disease: as now, vastly differing symptoms and pathologies, e.g., "As stimulants for heart disease, the Cherokees made a holly tea, the Dakotas and Winnebagos administered horsemint, the Delawares prescribed Virginia pokeweed, and the Pawnees thought Morning glory was the best cure."

hearth: as now, the stone, brick, or masonry floor of a fireplace, including that portion extending out from the fire, e.g., "Most of the early cooking was done at or on the hearth."

hectic fever: phthisis; a wasting disease of the lungs that probably often was emphysema, e.g., "Hectic fever was treated with calcium phosphate, quinine, and various tonics, none of which helped very much."

heifer, heffer: a cow that has not been bred, usually under 3 years old, e.g., "The inventory listed 3 cows and 2 heifers."

heir: one who inherits property, real or personal, by virtue of the death of another, e.g., "He was an equal heir with his sister." Also see **devise** and **bequeath.**

heirloom: any artifact, memento, or writing having value by reason of its family or lineage related origins, e.g., "Paul's most treasured heirloom was his grandfather's pocket watch."

heirs and assigns: a common legal expression in deeds, wills, and instruments of transfer that confirmed that the asset is being transferred without restriction to further transfer by the recipient and to whomever he designates or whomever should come after him at his death, e.g., "In early times, if a deed was made 'to John Smith', instead of 'to John Smith and his heirs and assigns', at John's death the title would have reverted to the **grantor** (q.v.)."

heirs of the body: lineal descendants only; natural offspring; an ancient phrase signaling an **entailment** (q.v.), e.g., "Hines' bequest was designated to Sarah 'and the heirs of her body', hence his son-in-law received nothing"; "The conveyance was unlawful and held to be in **fee simple** (q.v.) since 'to Sarah and the heirs of her body' created a **fee tail** (q.v.)."

hematuria, haematuria: blood in the urine from any cause, e.g., "Not realizing it was but a symptom, for hematuria the old doctor administered potassium citrate, turpentine, ergot, and lead acetate."

hemoptysis, haemoptysis: any expectoration of blood, e.g., "Not recognizing it as but a symptom of another problem, early physicians often prescribed ipecac or lead acetate for hemoptysis."

hemorrhoids, emero(i)ds: as now, e.g., "The doctor concocted a salve for emeroids."

hepatic diseases, hepathic diseases: pertaining to liver and liver functions, e.g., "Hepathic diseases often were treated with tonics, ammonium chloride or iodide, ipecac or rhubarb."

heraldry: the discipline of settling the rights of persons and families to bear arms, of tracing genealogies, determining of precedence, and setting forth or recording honors, e.g., "The business of heraldry is the peculiar province of the **Heralds' College** (q.v.)."

Heralds' College: an English corporation by royal authority, est. 1483, engaged in setting forth **heraldry** (q.v.), e.g., "Questions of one's rights to particular armorial bearings may be decided by the Heralds' College."

hereditament: any right, asset, or thing connected or associated with land that may be inherited, usually not including buildings, e.g., "Since the deed included all hereditaments, John was confident that he owned the flag pole, water well pump, and the fencing and posts."

hereinafter, hereinbefore: legal jargon used to refer to a term or provision within the same document, e.g., "...being the tract hereinafter described" or "...being the persons hereinbefore mentioned."

herpes: unlike now, any spreading, inflammatory condition of the skin or mucous membranes, e.g., "In early days, herpes often was treated with silver oxide, belladonna taken internally, calomel ointment, or electricity!"

Hessians: usually, those mercenaries from Hesse, Germany, who fought with the British in the American Revolution, many of whom defected, e.g., "While more than 900 Hessians were captured at Trenton, Washington suffered but 5 casualties."

hiccoughs: See **hiccups.**

hiccups, hiccoughs: as now, e.g., "Myriad cures were prescribed for the hiccoughs, including camphor and chloroform."

High Sheriff, high sheriff: See **sheriff.**

high-tail: See **skedaddle.**

high wheel cycle, high wheel bicycle, wheel: an early bicycle with a very large front and much smaller rear wheel, so designed to ride over the rough roads of the early years, e.g., "Billy rode his high wheel cycle on a tightrope."

highboy: a popular, early chest of drawers on 8- to 12-inch legs, usually with 3 to 5 drawers, and occasionally with one or two doored compartments below the drawers, "The highboy listed in the estate was of bird's eye maple and was of the Queen Anne period."

hind: a male deer, particularly the English Red deer, e.g., "Drake's ship Golden Hind was named for the fleet and powerful Red deer hind."

hip flask: as now, a small-mouthed, thin, lidded, glass or metal container for spirituous liquors, carried on the person, usually under the coat and hidden from view, e.g., "Many early hip flasks were of blown, colored glass."

hitch, hitched: refers to a team of horses in place and the harnessing; refers to the fact that animals are in harness, e.g., "His hitch was well groomed and powerful"; "They are hitched and ready.".

hither, thither, and yon: See **yonder.**

hoarseness: as now, e.g., "Hoarseness often was treated with horseradish, borax, sulphurous acid spray, or tannin."

hobble, hopple: a tie between the legs of a horse or mule to control the length, and so the speed, of its gait, e.g. "He always hobbled the horse to prevent it from **cantering** (q.v.)."

hobby horse: a stick with a depiction of a horse's head mounted on one end, the same straddled by children who then ran pretending to be riding a horse, e.g., "Every little boy of the 17th, 18th and 19th century rode a hobby horse at one time or another." Also see **shoo fly rocker.**

hobnail glass: glassware having small, round, smooth bumps on the surface, e.g., "Her favorite candy dish was of hobnail **milk glass** (q.v.)."

hock, hockheimer: usually, any white wine, originally a Rhine wine, e.g., "The Pennsylvania Dutch often spoke of a 'glass of hock'."

Hock-day, Heck Day: the second Tuesday after Easter week, e.g., "Such ancient holidays as Hock-day, Hock-tide, etc., were abandoned by the American Colonials."

hoecake: a small, early cake made of corn meal and water, unknown in England even by 1800, e.g., "While it is said that hoecakes were so named because they were baked on a hot hoe, most historians do not believe it."

hog cholera: See **cholera.**

Hogmanay: the last day of the Scottish year, now December 31, but formerly March 24; small cookies made for the Hogmanay holiday, e.g., "Many early Scots settlers celebrated Hogmanay by permitting their children to go door to door for treats"; "Hogmanay cookies were sweet, light, short cookies made for the holiday."

hogshead: an early measure of volume equalling 63 gallons, a barrel used most frequently for the shipment of tobacco, e.g., "He transported three hogsheads of tobacco on the ship *Charming Nancy*."

hold one harmless, hold harmless: to guarantee that if another suffered monetary damage, that person would be compensated equal to the loss, e.g., "It was common practice to require the father of a bastard child to hold the parish harmless from the expense of keeping that child."

Holland, influence of: many words arose from our Dutch ancestry and their food, e.g., "Waffle, coleslaw, cookie, landscape, caboose, sleigh, snooping, Yankee, and poppycock (dung) are but a few."

holland, chect holland: a fine linen cloth made in Holland, e.g., "Early merchants' inventories almost always reveal a stock of holland."

Holland china: See **delftware.**

Hollanders: See **Dutch.**

hollow shave: See **shave.**

holographic will, olographic testament: a document intended by the deceased to be his or her will, hand written, signed, and kept by the deceased in such a fashion or place that its importance is apparent, e.g., "The handwritten document was submitted, **parity of hands** (q.v.) was accomplished, the evidence revealed that he intended the writing to be his will, and the court admitted it as his holographic will."

home place: one's principal residence; the word is nearly synonymous with **domicile** (q.v.), e.g., "She owned several tracts of land, but she considered the one on Snake Creek to be her home place."

homeopathic medicine: that frequently encountered early practice in which cures were undertaken by prescribing herbs and drugs thought to create the same condition as that from which the patient was suffering, e.g., "Homeopathic physicians fell into wide disrepute early in the twentieth century."

homespun: a plain cloth made of yarn spun in the home, e.g., "Very plain homespun clothing was the mark of the early rural working family."

Homestead Acts: the several legislative acts of Federal and states' governments by which land was granted in exchange for settlement and (or) improvement thereon, e.g., "He built a cabin and undertook to clear the land that he had gained under the Homestead Act." Also see **seating.**

hominy, hominy grits: a common food, especially in the South; corn stripped of the hull by lye, and served either whole kernel or ground as hominy grits, e.g., "Fried hominy was a favorite food when served with ham or bacon."

homolgate: in Civil law, meaning to approve, e.g., "Early Louisiana records occasionally speak of a court homolgating an agreement."

hooch: **See** corn whiskey.

hood boy: See **hautboy.**

hooker: a prostitute, e.g., "The word 'hooker' was used to describe a paid whore before General Hooker was even born."

hooping cough: See **whooping cough.**

Hoosier cabinet: See **pantry.**

hornbook: an early teaching device for children; usually, the alphabet, numbers and tens of numbers, and simple fractions were printed on a board, over which a very thin piece of horn (later celluloid) was placed to protect the printing, e.g., "Hornbooks now are very rarely seen outside museums."

horse: now, any adult of the equine family; early, the word referred only to a male equine, including mules; a colt was a young male, a gelding was a neutered horse; a ridgling was a horse with one testicle removed, a stallion was a horse not neutered and used for breeding; a female, if bred once or more, was a mare, a filly was a young, unbred female, and a foal was a newborn of either sex, e.g., "She had a mare with a foal at her side, a horse, and a young colt."

horse collar: See **collar.**

horse hair upholstery or cloth: a popular, durable fabric used for upholstering from the earliest times until the early 20th century, it was made from woven horses tail and mane hair and usually dyed black, e.g., "She had a **settee** (q.v.) and two **side chairs** (q.v.) upholstered in horse hair."

horse harness: See **harness.**

horse pistol: any large handgun, originally referred to handguns carried in a saddle holster, e.g., "He referred to his old '.44' as a horse pistol."

horse tree, field tree, plow tree: that large old tree left standing in the middle of the field upon clearing, used to provide shade and an occasional resting place for horses (and men) being worked in the hot summer sun, e.g., "Many of the old oak plow trees yet stand in Ohio."

horsecars: See **streetcars.**

horses, famous: as now, e.g., "A listing of famous horses of American history surely would include Johnson's Messenger, Cobb's Terpsichor, Andrew Jackson's Truxton, Endecott's Bill, Grant's Cincinnati, Jeb Stuart's Highfly, Sheridan's Rienzi, Lee's Traveller, Stonewall Jackson's Old Sorrel, Keogh's Comanche, and Man O' War."

horseshoe box: a small, usually **primitive** (q.v.) wooden box designed to hold 1 or 2 pairs of horseshoes to be carried to **horseshoe games** (q.v.), e.g., "The family still has Bill Midlam's horseshoe box."

horseshoes, horseshoe game: a game, usually played by men and boys, in which the iron shoes of horses are thrown at standing iron posts with the intention of catching the posts with the open end of the shoes, e.g., "Virtually every early picnic of rural families included men playing horseshoes."

hosepipe: early, any flexible, rubber tubing used to move liquids; our present garden hose, e.g., "The general store stocked hosepipe on a roll, and cut off the length desired by the customer."

hot buttered rum: an early and highly favored drink, especially in cold weather, consisting of a mugged mixture of rum, water, butter, and sugar, the drink then heated by plunging a red hot **flipdog** (q.v.) into the mug, e.g., "Many was the cold night visitor to early New England inns who were refreshed by a warm fire, friendly **barkeeps** (q.v.), **flips** (q.v.), and hot buttered rum."

hour glass, sand glass: as now, a device to measure the passage of time, e.g., "The inventory revealed a 'large sand glass'."

house girl: usually a young slave woman assigned household tasks; early, perhaps a young indentured servant similarly engaged, e.g., "Some early comments concerning house girls seem to refer to young, indentured white women."

hue and cry, hues and cryes (to put out or call out): a message shouted to anyone within hearing that a felon was fleeing, and all who heard were required to take up the chase, e.g., "Upon being asked how the criminal had escaped, the Sheriff related that the man was young, was 'fleet afoot', and that he had 'put out hues and cryes all the while'."

humours: early, the four elemental bodily fluids, i.e., blood, phlegm, black bile, or yellow bile, e.g., "It was thought that imbalance of the humours was the cause of most disease." Also see **bleeding.**

hundred: a subdivision of a shire, governed by a constable and with its own court; a term occasionally appearing in American records, e.g., "In large part, hundreds no longer were significant in governmental affairs after our **town** (q.v.) and county governments were established."

hundredweight, cwt.: a hundredweight; one hundred and twelve pounds, e.g., "The inventory revealed three cwt. of bronze."

Hungarian water: a **cologne** (q.v.) or incense, e.g., "Her recipe for Hungarian water was one pint spirits of wine (alcohol), 1 oz. rosemary, and

2 drachms **ambergris** (q.v.)."

huntboard: a sideboard on tall legs; a table used to serve refreshments during and after a hunt, reachable from horseback, consisting of a rather narrow, long top surface (the "board"), on tall legs, and usually having a dooreddoored compartment beneath the top, e.g., "Her huntboard was of finely finished tulipwood, and had cherry inlays in the board." Also see **sideboard** and **butler's sideboard.**

hunting pouch: See **shot pouch.**

husbandman: very early, one who bred and raised livestock; later, any farmer who kept animals, e.g., "Since the 1660 record reveals that he worked as a husbandman, he likely bred and raised cattle."

hutch: formerly, see **hutch chair**, recently, a cabinet with legs, usually tall, often with glassed doors above and exposed shelves, and drawers or doored compartments below, e.g., "She used her hutch as a linen storage and curio cabinet."

hutch chair, hutch table: a chair and table combined, where the table top is hinged so as to raise to the perpendicular and provide a back for the chair thereby revealed, e.g., "Her hutch chair saved much space."

hydrocele: a collection of fluid within the scrotum, at times accompanied with a tumorous growth, e.g., "Excision, electric puncture, and injection of iodine all were thought helpful for the hydrocele."

hydromel: See **mead.**

hypotheque: a **Civil Law** (q.v.) **mortgage,** (q.v.) "Early Louisiana records occasionally refer to an hypotheque, meaning the same as mortgage."

hydrothorax: as now, a distended belly; an accumulation of fluid in the abdominal cavity, e.g., "Hydrothorax was treated by a near fluidless diet, iodine injections, or by the often fatal act of puncturing the belly to bring about drainage."

hypochondria: as now, e.g., "For hypochondria, asafoetida (sp. varies), caffeine, and opium were administered."

hysteria: any "fits" or baseless fears, screaming, crying out, or unusual conduct thought to emanate from the mind, e.g., "Hysteria, not being understood, often was treated with cold compresses to the extremities, asafoetida, musk, quinine, vaporous oils, and alcoholic cordials."

I

ice box: before refrigeration, a usually cork insulated, metal lined, large chest, usually made of oak, and with a compartment in the top designed to hold blocks of ice weighing 50 to 100 lbs. and occasionally more, with one or two additional doors opening to shelves or compartments used to store perishable foods, e.g., "The 'ice man' delivered on Tuesdays and Fridays, and placed the ice purchased directly into the ice box."

icterus: See **jaundice.**

Ides, ides: the 15th day of March, May, June, and October, and the 13th day of the other months, e.g., "Early judges occasionally referred to future court or hearing days as commencing on the Ides of May, or some other month."

illiterate: in genealogy, a person unable to read or write sufficiently to correspond with others, e.g., "While able to take care of his daily business, he was illiterate."

immigrant: one who comes to a nation with an intention to remain, e.g., "He was one of the many German immigrants who came to America after 1709."

immigrations: some significant immigrations of other than those from England were 1624 - 1664, the Dutch and Walloons; 1637 - 1655, Swedish; 1683 - 1685, Palatines and Rhinelanders; 1685, French Huguenots; 1689, Scottish; 1710, Palatines; 1714 - 1725, Scotch-Irish; 1725 - 1775, Germans and Swiss; 1735 - 1755, Moravians; 1827 - 1830, the great German and Irish movements; 1843 - 1885, Scandinavian; 1854 - 1870, Chinese (often railroad workers); 1885 - 1914, eastern and southern Europeans, Russians, Poles, Estonians, Latvians, Lithuanians, and Greeks.

imparlance: an extension or granting of time for a party to a lawsuit to further plead his or her cause, e.g., "Notation in a lawsuit of an imparlance should alert the researcher that a record of the case may also appear in the succeeding term of court."

impetigo: as now, a contagious skin disease, often accompanied by sores on the face, feet, and legs, particularly among children, e.g., "Impetigo was treated with lead acetate, zinc oxide lotion, and quinine."

impotence: as now, e.g., "Impotence - a 'secret ailment' - was treated with gold chloride, lead arsenate, and (later) with electric shock."

impressment: the ancient English government privilege of forcing persons or equipment into the service (usually, the navy) in time of war, e.g., "The impressment of merchant seamen into the Royal Navy very much aroused and angered the colonials."

imprimis, imps.: in the first place; first of all; a legal term meaning the first of those listed, e.g., "The appraisal mentioned the kettle imps., referring to the first of several kettles and containers mentioned in the inventory."

in contemplation of death, contemplation of death: an expectation that death will surely follow by reason of some obvious sickness, injury, or impending danger, e.g., "The transfer of the land to his sons was in contemplation of death, hence was said to be a **testamentary disposition** (q.v.)."

in diem, i.d.: for one day, e.g., "Some early records refer to an **imparlance** (q.v.) in diem."

in esse: literally, in being; in wills and agreements, an unborn child; occasionally, **in ventre sa mere** (q.v.) is substituted, e.g., "He left the land equally to his two children and his child in esse." Also see **in posse.**

in gremio legis: protected by law, e.g., "Early Massachusetts records occasionally refer to livestock being in gremio legis until ownership is established."

in loco parentis: in the place of a parents; acting as a parent, e.g., "Early records often refer to children in loco parentis, meaning they assumed the duties and responsibilities of a parent to their usually younger siblings."

in mora: a borrower, usually of property, who has failed to return it, e.g., "Louisiana records sometimes refer to a person in mora."

in perpetuam rei memoriam: literally, in perpetual memory of the matter; referred to depositions taken to preserve a record of testimony, e.g., "He was asked to take Jones' testimony in perpetuam rei memoriam."

in personam, in rem: a legal action against a person; a legal action by virtue of or against some property, e.g., "If a record refers to a sheriff serving a writ in personam, that sheriff found the person, but if the service was in rem, the researcher knows that the party sued may not have been in that county, but some property of his was."

in posse: unborn, a living fetus, e.g., "A child before birth is in posse, and after birth is **in esse** (q.v.)."

in rem: See **in personam.**

in the bed: "in bed"; at rest or asleep on a bed; derives from the need to physically get into the early canopied and curtained beds, e.g., "Even now, references to a person being in the bed are common across the South."

in the room of: in place of; instead of, e.g., "The 1780 North Carolina roadwork record listed Nathaniel Drake as in the room of another man."

in-law: early, those who were related through affinity, adoption, or any other legal action that resulted in one being considered a part of the family unit; presently, those who are related through marriage only, e.g., "The boy spoken of in the record as his son-in-law was, in fact, an adopted child"; "Jane's husband is Jack's only in-law yet living."

incense burner: See **censer.**

inch: early, a measure of length equal to three (3) grains of barley laid end to end; one twelfth part of a foot, e.g., "An inch was described by Shakespeare as 'a nice point of time', and still in Johnson's time as three grains of barley."

inchoate rights: any interest in real estate which has not yet been realized or vested in the owner; in genealogy, usually those rights of a wife during her husband's life that may ripen into dower rights at his death, e.g., "Their land having been in her husband's name, when he died her inchoate rights ripened into a one-third interest in the income from that land." Also see **dower.**

incontinence: as now, e.g., "Belledonna, bromides, and ergot all were administered for urinary incontinence, to no avail."

incontinent: early, unlike now, unchaste or self-indulgent, e.g., "His early reference to her incontinence had nothing to do with bodily functions."

incorporeal property: See **corporeal property.**

increase: usually referred to after-born animals or slaves, e.g., "The will provided that Sarah inherited the slaves Jammy and Sal and their increase."

incunabula: very early (1450 to 1500) books printed with movable type, e.g., "In addition to the Library of Congress, the Pierpont Morgan Library of New York City and the Huntington Library of San Marino, CA, have substantial collections of German incunabula."

indenture: early, a covenant or agreement, so named because the counterparts were indented or were cut in an unusual pattern in order to prevent alteration; early, a document stating a debt in time and (or) service owed by one person to another, quite usually executed where transportation or training was to be exchanged for labor and time; recently, a deed or agreement, e.g., "His obligation to serve Captain Smith for four years was set forth in the indenture."

indentured servant: one who entered upon an agreement by the terms of which he or she exchanged time and labor for land, transportation, or training, e.g., "In exchange for being transported to the Virginia Colony, she had agreed to serve seven years as an indentured servant."

indexes, indices: plural forms of "index" e.g., "The indexes were contained in four volumes."

India rubbers: See **shoes.**

Indians, American, influence of: many words arose from our experiences with the native Americans, including the Eskimos, e.g., "Pemmican, wigwam, hickory, pecan, chipmunk, moose, terrapin, hominy, totem, papoose, moccasin, tomahawk, raccoon, opossum, skunk (segankem), squash (askutasquash), smoke a peace pipe, Indian summer, Indian file, play possum, bury the hatchet, war path, igloo and kayak are but a few of such words."

Indian Title: those rights to land said to result from treaties between the white settlers and the American Indians; an unwritten legal presumption that the Indians had rights in land by virtue of their ages-old occupancy or use thereof, e.g., "The Indian Title to the land north of 'Boundary Road' resulted from the Greenville Treaty"; "The earliest settlers of Cumberland County believed that the Indian Title had been extinguished by the French and Indian War."

Indian wars: refers to the many military conflicts with the American Indians that took place during the last half of the nineteenth century, generally in the western states and territories, e.g., "Before leaving for the Indian Wars, he made a deed conditioned upon his return from there."

indices; See **indexes.**

indict, endite: a written accusation addressed to a court by a grand jury that one has acted or failed to act in such a way as to violate the law, e.g., "The notation in the old papers that he had been endited revealed that the grand jury had determined that he should be tried."

indigo: a plant originally cultivated in the Southern colonies, and from which blue dye was made, e.g., "The indigo trade was thought to be a future mainstay of the Virginia colony."

indulgence: a remission of punishment for sins, e.g., "The sale of indulgences caused many differences among early Catholic clergy."

infant: a child through the seventh year; at law, one under twenty-one years, e.g., "As now, a person was in natural infancy until the eighth birthday, and was a minor - a legal infant - until 'one and twenty'."

infantia: in Civil Law, one under seven years, e.g., "The researcher of Louisiana should not confuse infantia with **infant** (q.v.), the former meaning under 7, the latter, usually, under 21."

inficiato: in Civil Law, a denial of a debt or obligation, e.g., "As to the money owing, the old parish record showed him to be inficiato."

ingross, ingrossing: the making of a perfect copy of a draft or other complete preliminary draft, e.g., "The clerk of the **land office** (q.v.) was ordered to ingross the grant to be made to Hughes."

injunction: usually, an order by a court prohibiting some action; occasionally, an order by a court that some action be taken, e.g., "The file revealed that he was enjoined from being anywhere near her house"; "The 1704 injunction required that he fence out the neighbor's cattle."

inkhorn, ink bottle, ink vial: a small container, often carried on the person, originally made of the closed end of a small horn, and used to hold liquid ink, e.g., "His inkhorn was made of the tip of a goat horn with a cork stopper."

inlot: a lot or parcel of land lying within a village or municipality, e.g., "He owned Inlot 6 and also **Outlot** (q.v.) 8 that adjoined it."

inmate: unlike now, one who dwells in the house of another, often for pay; a prostitute who frequently enters a house of prostitution in order to engage in her trade, e.g., "The tax records revealing that he was an inmate in Martin's house had nothing to do with crime."

inn: early and now, a facility offering food, drink, and rest for overnight, e.g., "The inn at Salisbury was there before 1790." See also **ordinary, tavern,** and **pub.**

innocent woman: one who has never had illicit intercourse with a man, e.g., "The term innocent woman was not synonymous with virgin, since one could be a widow and yet be innocent."

inoficiocidad: anything done contrary to a duty or obligation, whether in nature or assumed, e.g., "Early records of Texas and Florida sometimes speak of one being inoficiocidad as to contractual obligations or taxes."

insinuacion: presentation of a legal document to a judge or magistrate with the intention of gaining his approval sanction, e.g., "In very early Texas and Florida records occasionally one will be said to have gained insinuacion of a contract."

insinuation: in Civil Law, the presentation for recording of a document evidencing a gift, e.g., "Unlike **insinuacion** (q.v.) in Texas, insinuation in Louisiana means to record."

insomnia: as now, "Alcohol, belladonna, opiates, and phosphorus all were prescribed for insomnia."

instant, inst.: the term used to reveal that a writing was being done during the same month as some prior writing, e.g., "When responding on March 25th to a letter written to you on March 10, it is appropriate to write, 'I received your note of the 10th instant'." Also see **ultimo.**

instanter: immediately, at once, e.g., "Many early records tell of courts ordering subjects to perform some act instanter."

institor: a clerk in a store, e.g., "Occasionally, in Louisiana court records, genealogists will find persons being referred to institors for this or that person."

instrument: as now; a formal document of any kind, e.g., "The instrument of transfer was a deed."

intended wife: an engaged or betrothed woman, e.g., "Many early records reveal matters concerning intended wives."

inter alia: among other things, e.g., "The court said he had complained of a trespass inter alia, meaning that he also complained of other matters."

inter vivos: from one to another, where both are living, e.g., "The entry revealing an inter vivos gift revealed that both parties were at that date alive."

interdiction, interdit: in Louisiana, a suit seeking a **curator** (q.v.) of one who is no longer capable of caring for his affairs and property, e.g., "The order stating that Ebert was interdit meant that their had been a case seeking interdiction and that it had succeeded."

intestato: See **intestate.**

intent to be naturalized: See **naturalization.**

inter-library loan: that service provided by most libraries, by which, through loan, materials in one library are made available to the patrons of another, e.g., "While the local library was small, through the inter-library loan service, she could gain use of the genealogical materials of the huge metropolitan library."

intercourse: See **cover.**

intertrigo: an early medical term, the meaning now unknown, e.g., "Zinc oxide, calcium carbonate, glycerate of tannin, and bismuth were administered for intertrigo."

intestate, intestacy: one who dies without a valid will, e.g., "She left no will, so it was said that she died intestate, and an **administrator** was appointed."

intestate succession: gaining ownership or rights in property by reason of the effect of laws concerning assets of those who die without a will, e.g., "His father having died **intestate** (q.v.), he and his siblings took the property by intestate succession."

introduction: that writing at the beginning of a literary work that states the parameters of the work and the approach of the author to the subject matter. It often reveals what periods or persons are not included, e.g., "The Introduction related that the material was set forth by family units in chronological order, commencing with an immigrant ancestor who was born in 1704."

intussusception: a term of varying meanings, usually an intestinal restriction or blockage, e.g., "Belladonna, effervescent enema, tobacco enema, and 'irrigation of the bowels' were given for an intussusception."

invalid's chair: a high-backed, sturdy, armed potty chair for the elderly or infirm, e.g., "A better quality invalid's chair could be purchased in 1890 for about the same sum as a pair of high quality ladies shoes."

inventory: an itemization of a group of assets; in genealogy, usually that list of the personal property owned by a person at the moment of death, e.g., "His inventory included two slaves and his father's watch." Also see **appraisal.**

Irish influence: many words arose from our Irish ancestry, e.g., "Shenanigan, buddy (bodach), shebang, shanty, and biddy are but a few."

Irish whiskey, Irish: a barley-based whiskey from Ireland, e.g., "Irish became a favorite here after the **Potato Famine** (q.v.) immigrations of the mid-19th century."

iritis: as now, any inflammation of the iris of the eye, e.g., "Incredibly, Dr. Lockhart administered blisters behind the ears, leeches, and occasionally mercuric arsenate in advanced iritis."

iron (to), irons, smoothers: the expression "to iron" was unknown early, and only in the 20th century have we "ironed" clothes; throughout history, we have "smoothed" cloth with "clothes smoothers" made of iron (usually) or brass, e.g., "The 'smoothers' of the 18th and 19th centuries are the irons of the 20th"; " Her smoothing irons included a **sad iron** (q.v.), a **flat iron** (q.v.) and a **polishing iron** (q.v.)."

ironmonger: one who sold or dealt in hardware, iron, and metal products; one who ran an **iron furnace** (q.v.), e.g., "He was an ironmonger in early Shenandoah County"; "The ironmonger and owner at Catherine Furnace had no idea that it would be remembered so long as men speak of war."

ironstone: originally, better white pottery from England; later, any heavy, white pottery or dishware, e.g., "She was proud of her grandmother's ironstone pottery."

isinglass: usually, the crystalline, near transparent form of the mineral mica, used to cover the viewing aperture in a stove, e.g., "**Pot-bellies** (q.v.) with isinglass were familiar to all of the period 1765 - 1935."

issue: in genealogy, children or sometimes descendents of a specific person, e.g., "The issue of John and Mary all had red hair and brown eyes."

Italian influence: many words arose from our Italian ancestry and their food, e.g., "Pizza, spaghetti, lasagne, espresso, parmesan, macaroni, and broccoli are but a few."

item: a term often found in wills, especially early, that separated devises, bequests, or paragraphs, e.g., "The third, fourth, and fifth items of the will were bequests to his daughters."

iule: yule, Christmas, e.g., "Occasionally one finds the word iule in very early Virginia records."

iulebs: a medication now unknown; juleps ?; shown at York County, VA, Records, Vol. 3, p. 66

J

jack: now, a flask; early, a small, often decorated container, carried about on the person and containing alcoholic beverages, e.g. "A Surry

County inventory listed a 'jack and yt with silver', meaning a pocket flask **chased** (q.v.) with silver."

jack knife, jackknife: a large utility knife with one or more, usually three, folding blades intended to be carried on the person, e.g., "Most men of the 19th century carried a jack knife." Also see **pen knife.**

jackboots: See **shoes.**

jag: a small, usually unmeasured quantity of firewood, considerably less than a **rick,** (q.v.) e.g., "He asked the neighbor if he might borrow a little jag of wood."

jailing for debt: See **debtors' prisons.**

jake: an intoxicating liquor made by mixing Jamaica ginger with other intoxicants such as wine or cider, e.g., "Early Oklahoma reports sometimes refer to barrels or bottles of jake."

jam cupboard: See **jelly cupboard.**

Jamaica spirits: See **rum.**

Jamestown colony: the first (May 24, 1607) successful English settlement on the American continent; consisted of 105 men, 73 of whom died in the first 7 months, and succeeded in no small part because of the arrival of supply ships (Jan., and April, 1608), the efforts of the famous Capt. John Smith, and by their undertaking to raise crops for sustenance, e.g., "The 1609 charter of the Jamestown colony granted it land 400 miles wide, from 'sea to sea'."

japanned: finely lacquered and finished wood, usually black, and originally from the Orient, e.g., "Her japanned jewelry box was beautiful."

jardinier: a large porcelain vase or pot for plants or flowers.

jardiniere stand: usually, an ornate, low, wooden flower or plant stand, often placed in a parlor or hall, e.g., "The affluent of Pennsylvania had jardinier stands; the poor had **fonzy tishes** (q.v.)."

jaundice, icterus: a condition brought about by excessive bile in the system and characterized by a yellow color in the skin and whites of the eyes, e.g., "In early times, arsenic, ammonium chloride, iodine, nitro-muriatic acid, and rhubarb were administered for jaundice."

jelly: unlike now, referred to flavored, usually clear, gelatin made from hog's feet, or the amber colored jelly resulting from cooking down sheeps' feet, e.g., "She made the best jelly by adding sugar, cinnamon, mace, lemon juice, and white wine sugar to the gelatin resulting from boiling down hogs' feet."

jelly cupboard: a short-legged cabinet, with doored compartments of 3 or 4 shelves, used for storing canned foods, jellies, preserves, etc., e.g., "As were most in the North, her jelly cupboard was made of poplar."

Jenkins Ear, War of: 1739 - 1742; that conflict between Spain and Great Britain, the result of which in the American colonies was the British siege of and retreat from St. Augustine in May, June, and July of 1740, e.g., "Unfortunately, the records of the battles at St. Augustine during the War of Jenkins Ear yield little of value to the genealogist."

jenny: a female donkey, e.g., "He had a jenny for the children's **cart** (q.v.)."

jerkin: a doublet-like, tight-fitting, sleeveless garment, often made of leather or other heavy material, e.g., "Many drawings of 17th-century colonial men depict them wearing **doublets** (q.v.) or jerkins."

jesse: a large chandelier, usually hung in a great hall, church, or meeting house, e.g., "The parish record referred to a silver candle jesse."

jewels: as medicines; gemstones early were thought to have value as remedies and tonics, e.g., "It was believed that tinctures of jewels such as coral and pearls were good tonics, ground emeralds controlled passions, ingested diamonds brought courage, rubies removed idle fancies, and amethysts prevented drunkenness and excess sleeping."

jigger: See **shave.**

jigs, giggs: See **dances.**

Jim Crow laws and institutions: after a black-faced minstrel of the antebellum South, the expression "jim crow" came to be a label somewhere in derision between the belittling "colored" or "darkey" and the epithet "nigger," e.g., "To list but a few, there were jim crow sections on streetcars, jim crow drinking fountains, jim crow rest rooms, and jim crow benches in the park."

jitney: a vehicle, other than animal-powered and not on tracks, operating on a more or less repetitive schedule, and used to move people, e.g., "Newspapers of the early 20th century often refer to a gasoline jitney."

joe: See **Dobra.**

jog, jogger: unlike now, a push, or one who pushes dully and slowly; a light shake or jerk, e.g., "His reference to the man who jogged the load had nothing to do with running in an effort to improve health."

johnny cakes: probably derived from journey cakes; small, hard crusted loaves of bread or large biscuits provided as refreshment to those about to travel some distance, e.g., "He put the johnny cakes in his **pocket** (q.v.)."

joiner: one who makes a livelihood by knowing of and joining wood by glue, different joints, etc; a now nearly forgotten trade, once very important to the cabinet and furniture makers, requiring knowledge of characteristics of expansion, contraction, warping, etc., in various woods, e.g., "He was known widely for his near perfect joining."

joint tenancy: a legal term describing joint ownership where the interests were acquired by the same instrument and are in all ways identical, e.g., "The deed transferred the property 'to Jane and her daughters, jointly', and so created a joint tenancy."

jointist: See **bootlegger.**

jointure: referred to the gaining of an estate for life by a widow as a result of the death of her husband, e.g., "The court spoke of the jointure of the **relict** (q.v.), revealing to the researcher that she had gained assets or income as a result of her husband's death."

journals, journal entries: See **minutes, minute books.**

journey: a day's travel, e.g., "From the French jour meaning a day, we have journal for day book, tout jour for forever, and journeyman meaning one who works by the day."

journey cakes: See **johnny cakes.**

jowler: a hunting dog, e.g., "The inventory reference to a 'jowler **slut** (q.v.) and three dogs' revealed the presence of four hunting dogs, three of which were male."

judex: a judge, e.g., "Civil law systems such as Louisiana often refer to a judge as judex."

judges' minutes: See **minutes, minute books** and **courts orders.**

judgment by his peers: early, a trial by twelve, now six or some other number, of jurors, e.g., "The order revealing that it was the judgment of his peers that he pay money simply meant that a jury so decided."

jujubs, jujubes: small plums, e.g., "She mentioned making wine from jujubs."

julap, julep: unlike now, water, usually sweetened with **sorghum** (q.v.) honey, maple or cane sugar, and used as the vehicle for medicine, e.g., "She ground the herbs to a fine powder and made a julap for the children.

Julian calendar: that calendar authorized by Julius Caesar in 46 B.C. that was shown (in 732) by Bede to be 11 minutes, 14 seconds long, thereby gaining a day about every 128 years, the same abandoned in favor of Pope Gregory's (Gregorian) calendar by the western nations commencing with France in 1582 and ending with the British Empire and the American colonies in 1752, e.g., "In abandoning the Julian calendar, the day following 2 September, 1752, became September 14, 1752, and March 25 was replaced by January 1 as the first day of the new year.

jumbals: See **desserts, early.**

Junior: See **Senior and Junior.**

jurat: literally, "it was proven"; early, a magistrate; that subscribing witness who swore to or affirmed the validity of any writing; often mistakenly read as "Junior", e.g., "The jurat was his brother."

jury: a group of people (in early times, men only) sworn to ascertain the truth upon such evidence as is presented to them concerning some matters of fact; juries varied in number from six to twenty-four persons, e.g., "Twenty-four was the number of persons seated for a grand jury"; "The petit jury consisted of twelve men, all said to be 'tried and true'." See also **venire.**

jury of matrons: See **matrons, jury of.**

jus: a right under the Civil Law, as in Louisiana, e.g., "Early reports often speak of rights such as jus legitum, jus disponendi or jus futurum, meaning a legal right, right to dispose of some property, or a future right."

jus ad rem: a contractual right to some personal property, e.g., "The Louisiana court order revealed that the question concerned Ebert's jus ad rem."

jus deliberandi: right to examine property before accepting it as one's share of some inheritance, e.g., " Before accepting the horse as his share of the Louisiana estate, he exercised his jus deliberandi."

justice of the peace: an elected officer (appointed in some jurisdictions) to maintain the peace in the county, and qualified to administer oaths and perform marriages; a judicial officer having quite limited authority, only as to only minor crimes, misdemeanors, and matters of the peace; early, an officer of considerable importance before modern transportation facilitated trips about the county by a sheriff or his deputies, e.g., "As a justice of the peace in 1835, Cole was highly respected."

K

kay: See ***key.***

kas: a word of Holland and Pennsylvania Dutch, meaning a painted ***wardrobe*** (q.v.), e.g., "Her Dutch kas had two drawers in the bottom and was very ornately painted."

keck: to vomit, e.g., "She sought to make the child keck by putting her finger down his throat."

keelboat: usually, a large, shallow-draft, flat-bottomed river boat, e.g., "Keelboats were common on the river at Plattsmouth."

kelderkin: a small barrel, e.g., "The inventory of the old Hollander listed three kelderkins."

Kentucky rifle, long rifle, Pennsylvania rifle: a long, rifled barrelled, flintlock musket developed simultaneously in Pennsylvania and Kentucky, noted for accuracy, and carried by many pioneers, hunters (***long hunters,*** q.v.), and fighters, e.g., "Daniel Boone's favorite Kentucky or long rifle has been lost over the years." Also see ***flintlock,*** and ***musket.***

kerosene: See ***coal oil.***

kersey: a heavy wool or wool and cotton fabric used for outer coats, e.g., "She needed 4 ***ells*** (q.v.) of kersey to make winter coats for the family."

ketch: a small sailing ship with 2 masts, the forward being the larger of the two, e.g., "Many ketches operated between the colonial South and the Caribbean Islands."

key, quay, kay: a wharf, or point of loading and unloading of ships and boats, e.g., "John Cotton had an early trading post at South Quay."

kibble: early, a large metal bucket used to lift ore and debris from mines; later, occasionally a metal bucket used in a water well, e.g., "The old Welsh miner found it humorous that the well bucket was called a kibble."

Kidd, Capt.: See ***pirates.***

kidney disease: as now, but not understood early, e.g., "For what were then thought to be kidney diseases, spinal ice bags, eucalyptus, and pipsissewa were administered."

killing time: that time of the year, usually autumn, when swine and cattle were slaughtered and the meat prepared or preserved for the winter, e.g., "They made

two hundred pounds of sausage and smoked 14 hams at killing time."

kilometer: See **meter.**

kindly: early, and now, especially in the Appalachian Mts., and distinct from the more common usage, a friendly request that something be done after a fashion or in a manner somewhat less exacting than that usually expected, e.g., "He told her that if he would kindly repair the upholstered chair, he would be much **obliged** (q.v.)."

kin, kinship: a loosely defined term referring to any and all of one's relations, whether by affinity, consanguinity, or by law, e.g., "As to her, his kinship was that of cousin."

kings and queens, reign of: See **regnal years.**

King's Attorney: a prosecutor or attorney representing the government, colony, or county, e.g., "As do our District Attorneys, The King's attorney or his assistant prosecuted most of the criminal cases."

King's English: usually, the "proper" English spoken by the upper class and the educated, as opposed to **cockney** (q.v.), Scottish, Irish, and other dialects, e.g., "In speaking, he was said to 'murder the King's English'."

King's X: a very ancient expression by which children declare themselves temporarily exempt from game rules, e.g., "When her mother called her from the game briefly, she shouted King's X, thereby invoking the ancient authority of the King as witnessed by his mark, and so preserving her status in the game." Also see **games.**

kippacks: shoes homemade by the poor or rural settlers and fashioned of three pieces of leather, one upper, one for the sole, and one for the heel. See **shoes.**

kitchen garden: that small garden kept by a housewife in which were planted medicinal herbs and plants, spices, vegetables, and fruits to be used by the family, and not for barter or trade, e.g., "She was proud of her kitchen garden and tended it daily."

kitchen table: a medium sized, sturdy, drawered table, often with one of more bins mounted below the drawers, e.g., "The kitchen table served as her work area for kitchen chores."

Klondike gold rush, Klondike: that rush of gold prospectors and speculators to the area on the Alaska border near Dawson, Canada, that took place beginning in August, 1896, e.g., "The Klondike yielded an estimated $175,000,000.00 in gold."

knee buckle: buckles used to tie **breeches** (q.v.) below the knee, e.g., "He had a pair of **Dutch gold** (q.v.) knee buckles."

kneehole desk: a table with a flat top used as a writing and work surface, having adequate space in the center beneath the top to place a chair, and having 1 to 3 drawers or doored compartments on each side of the opening, e.g., "His kneehole desk was of solid mahogany."

knight: that rank of honor next below a **baronet** (q.v.); since mediaeval times, a person who has been accorded that non-hereditary dignity by a sovereign, e.g., "Among the many famous knights were Francis Drake, knighted by Elizabeth I, and Winston Churchill, so honored by Elizabeth II."

Knights of the Garter: See **Garter.**

Knights of the Order of St. George: See **Garter.**

knock down: the accomplishment of a sale at auction, e.g., "The carriage was knocked down to Mrs. Haskins."

knot: See **nautical mile.**

Korean Conflict, Korean War: the conflict between North Korea (and allied Communist China forces) and the United States that took place between 1950 and 1953, e.g., "Public Law 550 provided the **G.I. Bill** (q.v.) for veterans of the Korean War."

kraut cutter: See **cabbage plane.**

Ku Klux Klan: that secret organization formed during the post-Civil War years, having as its purpose the subversion of the newly acquired rights of blacks, e.g., "After 1867, the Ku Klux Klan and its Ku Kluxers or Knights was responsible for all manner of lawlessness and violence."

L

lac: a resin from insects, the base for shellac, the fine, common wood finish, e.g., "Few were the furniture makers who did not know of orange, brown, and white lac."

lacquer: that finish found on most furniture of the 20th century, e.g., "Average quality furniture of the period 1910 to 1980 almost always is finished in lacquer."

lactation, lactate: the secretion or production of milk by a female animal, e.g., "For excessive lactation in women, Dr. Drake administered quinine, belladonna, and camphorated oil."

lacus: See **alloy.**

ladderback chair, ladder-back: any of the several styles of chairs having horizontal slats in the back mounted so as to appear like a ladder; if not a reproduction, the more slats, the earlier the chair, e.g., "Her ladderback had nicely turned posts holding four slats, and she suspected it was of the 18th century."

ladies hat box: See **bonnet box.**

ladies saddle: See **side saddle.**

Lady Day: the feast of the annunciation of the Virgin Mary; usually March 25th. Anciently, that date upon which many land rents for the growing season following were due, but it was observed on August 15th in early Ireland, e.g., "Lady Day was often celebrated in the early colonies.""As land rent, Owen Griffith was to 'pay 10S on Lady Day next'."

lamb: a sheep, male or female, under one year old, e.g., "The inventory revealed a ewe, 2 rams and 4 lambs."

lamp oil: See **coal oil.**

lamps: any illuminating device, including those that contained candles, e.g., "He had whale oil, coal oil, and candle lamps in his collection." Also see **betty lamp.**

lana: in Civil Law, wool, e.g., The old Louisiana reports sometimes refer to lana cloth or **stuff** (q.v.)."

lancet, lance: a small pointed instrument used to open boils, blisters, and in **bleeding** (q.v.), e.g., "Old Ben had a lancet that had belonged to his grandfather."

land certificate: See **land grants.**

land descriptions: See **metes and bounds,** and **courses and distances.**

land grants, land certificates, land warrants, general land office: a grant from the public; usually used synonymously with land patent; that document or the act by which government conveys an interest in public lands to an individual, corporation, or institution; usually a transfer of government land that had not previously been titled to anyone, or, if previously titled, had reverted to, or been purchased by government, e.g., "His land grant was for 200 acres that had reverted to the colony when the prior grantee had died without known heirs." Also see **certificate land.**

land patents: See **land grants** and **patents.**

land warrant: See **land grants.**

landau: a 4-wheeled carriage of the wealthy, with a top divided so that the back and front halves could be opened or closed independently, e.g., "The gold decorated landau of Marshall Field was well known in old Chicago."

landmark: early, a monument establishing a boundary between two tracts of land, e.g., "It was illegal to remove early landmarks."

landholder: generally now, synonymous with **freeholder** (q.v.); one who owns or holds land for himself or in trust for another, e.g., "He purchased the tract in **fee simple,** (q.v.) and so became one of the forty landholders owning more than 300 acres within the county."

lap robe: a large, heavy blanket for use in a carriage or sleigh, often of animal fur, e.g., "Dr. Drake had a bearskin lap robe."

lappage: an overlapping of boundaries of real property, e.g., "The court determined that the lappage of their grants amounted to two **rods** (q.v.) along the west boundary."

larboard: synonym for **starboard** (q.v.).

larder: a pantry; a place where food was kept or stored prior to cooking, e.g., "She kept the canned fruits and vegetables on shelves in the larder."

Larkin desk: an early 20th-century cabinet known for quality and usually of oak, with a fall-front writing surface revealing small compartments within, a doored curio or book compartment above the fall front, and a paned, doored area containing book shelves, usually on the left, "While the desk perhaps is best known, Larkin made other items of furniture as well."

lascivious: as now, e.g., "The old Connecticut court branded indecent sexual acts by one against the will of another as lascivious carriage."

latch: usually referred to the wooden latch bar inside the door, the same lifted by a string or a handle, e.g., "The wooden beam used as a latch on the heavy door rendered the house quite safe from burglars and others not wanted." Also see **latch string.**

latch string: that small rope or heavy string that extended through a hole to the outside a door, and when pulled upon lifted the latch bar inside, e.g., "The expression 'the latch string is always out for you' meant that the person was always welcome at that home." Also see **latch.**

late, late of, of late: one who has died or, occasionally, has departed a county or area, usually in the not distant past, e.g., "The deed revealed that he had received the land from his late father"; "The deed was from John Martin, late of Surry County."

laundry bat: See **bat.**

laundry stove: usually a small, low, wood or coal burning stove with a flat-topped heating surface and no oven or other compartment, designed for use in the laundry room to heat water and soaps, and boil dyes, bleaches, clothes, etc., e.g., "Only the affluent had laundry stoves or, for that matter, laundry rooms."

laurels: gold coins minted in England in 1619, e.g., "Reports of the early colonies occasionally refer to laurels, meaning money."

lavender water: a cologne or incense, e.g., "Her recipe for lavender water was 2 cups spirits of wine (alcohol), 1 oz. concentrated lavender oil, 2 **drachms** (q.v.) **ambergris** (q.v.)."

laver: early, any bowl used for washing; later, the font or water of baptism, e.g., "The porcelain laver revealed by the inventory doubtless was a washing bowl used with a pitcher."

law court of appeals: See **appeals, courts of.**

lawn: a sheer cloth made usually of linen, or sometimes very fine cotton, e.g., "The ledger of William Parham's store revealed sales of yards of expensive lawn."

lay: a share of the catch on whaling and fishing boats, e.g., "It was said that Bates' lay of the whaling venture was 8%."

layd to, laid to (another): apparently, to name the father of a bastard child, e.g., "The court record stated that 'she layd a bastard child to Carpinder....'"

lay out, lay by: to fail to appear as directed, usually for work; to stand idly by while another does your share of assigned work, e.g., "When the man did not appear at 7:00, the boss said 'I suppose he has laid out once again'"; "Jones was known to lay by while the others worked."

leach, lye barrel: a wooden container or barrel in which ashes and water were placed to make lye, e.g., "He had a tap in the bottom of the leach, from which she drew off lye to make soap."

leaded glass, lead glass, flint glass: heavy, brilliant, extremely clear glass containing lead oxide and used in the best of glassware, e.g., "The cut, leaded glass bowl was exquisite." Also see **crystal.**

leaders, lead horses: that horse or horses placed in front in a multi-horse team, particularly aware of slight commands and well trained to commence movement when so ordered, e.g., "The leaders in old Lew's team of six were a pair of beautiful, near-white Belgians."

Leaghorn hat, leghorn hat: a high quality straw hat with a soft brim, e.g., "The 1761 account of Berry Smith revealed the purchase of a Leaghorn Hat."

league, leuca: a measure of distance, varying but usually 18,225 ft., about 3 1/2 miles; in Spanish law, a league was 2.63 statute miles; in French law 1,500 paces; in early English law, 1,000 paces, e.g., "The distance the English ship travelled was stated in nautical miles, three of which equaled a league"; "In researching early Texas land grants, the researcher should remember that a square league was 4,428 acres, or a bit less than seven sq. miles."

lease: a possessory right in land; a relationship between a *freeholder* (q.v.) and a **tenant** (q.v.) by which the tenant pays something of value for possession and specific use of land for a period of time, e.g., "His lease was of fifty acres for twenty years at 500 pounds of tobacco per year." Also see **lessee,** and **lessor.**

lease and release: an ancient method of conveyancing by which a lease was entered upon and the following day a release of **seisen** (q.v.) was given over, the legal result being a **conveyance** (q.v.) in *fee simple* (q.v.), e.g., "The researcher must carefully examine all very early 'leases', as they may be a part of a conveyance sale by lease and release." Also see **lease.**

Leather Sealers: early elected officials in Pennsylvania whose duty it was to examine and approve the making and tanning of leather and goods of leather, e.g., "Leather Sealers were well known to early Philadelphia."

leatherdresser: the calling of one who cured and prepared hides for use as leather, e.g., "The leatherdresser supplied the raw materials for the **harnessmaker** (q.v.)."

lega: See **alloy.**

legacy: a transfer of personal property by will or by order of a court in a proceedings involving an estate, e.g., "As his legacy, he received $6,000.00 and some corporate shares."

lemner: very early, one who drew or painted **pictures** (q.v.) for hire, e.g., "The 17th-century description of the man as a lemner referred to his calling."

lessee: one who, in exchange for payment or other thing or act considered of value, has specific possessory rights in the use and benefits of land without it owning the same, e.g., "He was the lessee of one hundred acres for thirty years."

lessor: one who gives over to another rights of use and possession in land for a certain term, in exchange for something considered of value, e.g., "The lessor provided that the lessee might use such timber as was needed to build a house."

letter of attorney: See **power of attorney.**

letters of administration: the documents confirming that a person has been vested by a court with authority to control and direct actions having to do usually with the **intestate** (q.v.) estate of another; the court entry by which one is named **administrator** (q.v.) or **administratrix** (q.v.), e.g.,

"Her letters of administration also were filed in the adjoining county, since the decedent owned property there." Also see **bond**.

letters patent: See **patent**.

letters testamentary: those documents confirming that, pursuant to a will, a person has been vested with the authority to control and direct actions having to do with an estate where the decedent died **testate** (q.v.); a court order or entry by which one is confirmed as **executor** (q.v.) or **executrix** (q.v.), e.g., "Having qualified as executrix of the will of her husband, Mary was issued letters testamentary empowering her to execute the will." Also see **letters of administration**.

leuca: **See** league.

levy: in genealogy, to levy a tax means to impose it, e.g., "The colony levied a tax of 1 shilling on each horse used in farming, the same payable to the circuit court of each year."

lex loci: the law of the place, e.g., "The researcher often encounters the expression lex loci when a court spoke of the law of some other state where a contract had been entered upon."

lex scripta: written or codified law, as opposed to common law, e.g., "The Surry court stated that lex scripta had superseded the common law."

liability: an obligation, debt, or duty owed to or in favor of another person, firm, corporation, or government, e.g., "Among the liabilities of the estate was the charge by the undertaker."

liber: unlike now, open and accessible, also the state of a freeman, e.g., "The judge's use of the word liber in speaking of his indentured servitude had nothing to do with books."

liber niger: the title of a book of accounts of Edward IV, wherein were listed his musicians and entertainers, household expenditures, etc., e.g., "From the Liber Niger Domus Regis we derive the expression 'putting her in his black book'."

library (-ies): most have collections dedicated to family history and genealogy; the 3 largest in the U.S. are the Mormon Library in Salt Lake City, the Allen County Public Library, and the New York Public Library, e.g., "He often went to Fort Wayne, to work with the genealogy collection of the Allen County Library.

library table: a sturdily built, medium to large table, often of a height sufficient to work standing up, and usually having a drawer and open book shelves on both ends below the writing and work surface, e.g., "Their library table was of inlaid walnut."

lichen: early, any skin disease with eruptions or having a scaly or lichen-like appearance, e.g., "Dr. Lockhart used alkalies, arsenic, cyanide ointment, and mercurial ointments for the lichen."

licenciado: an attorney or advocate, e.g., "Early Texas reports and writings speak of licenciados, usually meaning lawyers."

licitacion: to sell at **auction**.

lien: when one fails to pay for services or goods, the supplier usually has a lien right enforceable against those assets to which his supply or effort contributed or improved; a lien usually must be in writing and recorded, e.g., "Lien records often reveal the occupations and whereabouts of ancestors."

life estate: a possessory interest in land, once a part of **dower** (q.v.); a **freehold estate** (q.v.) for the remainder of the life of the person owning it, that could not be mortgaged or encumbered to an extent greater than the interest, and could only be conveyed away through the joinder of the remaining interests - the 'reversion', e.g., "Her life estate was provided for in her husband's will, and the land became the property of their son at her death." Also see **remainder.**

life interest: See **life estate.**

life tenant: See **life estate.**

light: unlike now, a window or a hole cut in a wall in order that light might be admitted, e.g., "When the 17th-century Isle of Wight County court spoke of the burglar entering through the light, he was not speaking of illumination."

light wood: fine, dry kindling, e.g., "He filled the basket with light wood for her to have near the stove while he was gone."

lighter: a small vessel used to transport goods to and from a larger ship anchored offshore, e.g., "Because the large ship drew too much water to dock at most places in Chowan River, lighters were used to load the tobacco and offload the wine and cloth."

limoges, limogia: paint; a French city, fine painted porcelain named for the French city of the same name, e.g., "The inventory of painted porcelain included some very early limoges."

line bees, lining bees: a skill possessed by few, it was the ability to watch a honeybee in flight and thereby locate the bee or honey tree, e.g., "Cane sugar being scarce and expensive, his skill at lining bees was appreciated by all the neighbors."

lineage: usually, the sum total or entirety of one's ancestry through a particular person or ancestor, e.g., "His Roberts lineage was most interesting."

lineal: in line of direct ascent or descent; relationship of parent to child through one or more generations, e.g., "He was lineally descended from Miles Standish."

linen draper: a merchant of linen, e.g., "John Griffin was an early linen draper of Cheapside, London."

linsey-woolsey, crazy quilt: usually, a quilt made of patches of different colored wool cloth, and stuffed with wool for warmth; occasionally, a heavy, homemade, linen and woolen coat, especially for men and boys, and often of quilt appearance, e.g., "She kept all the woolen and linen scraps for use in quilts and linsey-woolsey coats."

liquor shop: a place or business where intoxicating liquors are sold, e.g., "The Court referred to the business as a liquor shop, thereby revealing that liquor was sold but not consumed on the premises."

liquors: alcoholic beverages, e.g., "Spirituous liquors are those distilled and made from other than berries and fruit, malt liquors are beer, stouts, porter, and ales, and vinous liquors are made by the fermentation of fruit or fruit juices, usually grapes."

listed for foot, listed for horse: an indication that the person named, either through personal capacity or financial standing, was in a position to supply to the commonwealth or militia a man to do duty as a foot soldier, or able to supply a man and a horse for cavalry duty, e.g., "William Hunt was listed for horse, and James Griffen for foot."

listed for horse: See **listed for foot.**

literary property: writings or compositions protectable by law, e.g., "The Constitution provides specific rights to protection in literary property."

liter: a unit of measure of volume, equalling about 2.1 pints, e.g., "His *flagon* (q.v.) of 1/2 liter held a drink of about a pint, or two cups."

litigation: the submission of disputes for settlement by a court or other tribunal or adjudicating panel, e.g., "The litigation was heard in the circuit court of Sussex County, VA."

litigious right: a right that may not be exercised except through a lawsuit, e.g., "Old Louisiana reports sometimes refer to litigious rights."

live-ins: persons residing in a household other than that of their immediate family; unlike boarders, live-ins usually felt like and were considered as members of the family, e.g., "The census revealed his friend John to be one of the live-ins." Also see **board, etc.**

liveried: a uniform in a particular color or design, often with emblems, arms, etc., supplied by one of high station to his employees, e.g., "His liveried drivers were known to all of Savannah."

livery of seisen: the **common law** (q.v.) ceremony by which possession was delivered over to a purchaser, e.g., "In livery of seisen, the parties went to the land, and the seller handed a twig, piece of dirt, or other symbol of possession to the buyer."

livery, livery stable: the business of publicly renting out wheeled vehicles and (or) horses; an establishment for the rental of, and care and keeping of horses for hire, e.g., "Turner operated a livery stable at Salisbury for more than forty-five years."

loaf sugar: cakes or loaves of sugar, usually weighing 5, 7, or 9 pounds; the form in which sugar was sold before granulated sugar and cardboard packaging were available, e.g., "The price of loaf sugar in Sussex, VA, in 1760 was equal to $15.00 per pound in 1992 money"; "Sarah bought loaf sugar, and grated or cut it as needed." Also see **sugar grater.**

locatio: letting for hire, e.g., "The old Louisiana reports sometimes refer to a wagon, hack, or carriage locatio, meaning those vehicles at or for hire."

lock: the mechanism of a firearm by which a propellant is contained and ignited for firing, e.g., "The expression 'lock, stock, and barrel', meaning complete or entire, arose from the fact that those were the three components of a complete hand-held firearm."

lockjaw: See **tetanus.**

Locust plague of 1874: See **Plague of 1874.**

lodeman, loadman: a calling; a pilot of a boat or ship who brings the vessel to wharf after others have brought it to that immediate area, e.g., "The lodeman found work in the harbor at Savannah."

Logan's Elm: that giant elm tree south and east of Columbus, OH, destroyed by the Elm blight in the 1960s, under which Chief Logan was said to have spoken his famous words concerning his loss of land, home, and all family at the hands of the early settlers, while he sought only peace, e.g., "After it died, Logan's Elm was cut into pieces and sold as souvenirs."

logcats: a now unknown game, probably played with dice, e.g., "As had Shakespeare, some early 17th-century writers referred to logcats."

loggerheads: small, iron or steel, removable catches that connected the collars and **hames** to the **traces**, and so transferred the power of a draft animal to the load; occasionally, the post at the rear of a whaleboat around which the harpoon line was wound, e.g., "The expression 'at loggerheads', meaning a meeting of diametrically opposed beliefs, arose from the fact that a loggerhead is that precise point at which the power of a draft animal meets the full resistance of the load."

long hunters: See **Kentucky rifle.**

long johns: See **drawers.**

long rifle: See **Kentucky rifle.**

long ton, short ton: 2240 lbs, as distinguished from a short ton of 2000 lbs., e.g., "Their conflict was over whether the order for a ton of lead meant a long or a short ton."

looking glass: a mirror, e.g., "The 1679 inventory revealed the presence of a large looking glass."

Lord Dunmore's War: named for VA Governor John Murray, Lord Dunmore, who, in 1774, in order to gain control of the then Northwest, seized western PA, thereby bringing on conflict with the Ottawas and the Shawnee under Chief Cornstalk, it was ended with the defeat of the Indians at the Battle of Point Pleasant, WV, on Oct. 10, 1774, e.g., "The Treaty of Camp Charlotte was one of the results of Lord Dunmore's War."

losset: See **trencher.**

lot: unlike now, one or a group of items, e.g., "He sold two lots of assorted **ironstone** (q.v.)."

louage: in Civil Law, a contract for hiring or letting, e.g., "The Louisiana reports sometimes refer to louage contracts."

lounge: an upholstered, long couch with a back and an elevated end designed as a head rest, e.g., "The lounge was Victorian and was of tufted wool and walnut." Also see **couch.**

love seat, courting chair: an upholstered chair for two people, popular during the Victorian era and afterwards, sometimes so designed that those seated were side by side and facing in opposite directions, e.g., "Their love seat was of walnut with a brocaded upholstery."

lowboy: any of many shapes and styles of small, low, short-legged chests, having one or two drawers beneath a flat-topped surface, and often with a mirror mounted above, e.g., "She considered her Victorian lowboy to be her best piece of furniture."

Loyalists: those whose political allegiance remained with the British during the American Revolution, e.g., "At the close of the Revolution, many Loyalists fled to Canada out of fear of retribution by their neighbors."

loyalty oaths: those oaths of allegiance required to be taken from time to time by early colonists variously to the Crown or to individual colonies, e.g., "Many times during the unrest of the 1760s the residents of Sussex county were required to swear loyalty oaths to King George."

lug: unlike now, a measure of land (pole, perch, 16 1/2 feet); to the ery early Scotch-Irish, sometimes an ear, e.g., "The very early Scottish immigrant's reference to his field being 10 lugs long revealed its length as about 165 feet."

lumbago: often sciatica; as now, chronic pain in the upper legs and lower back,e.g., "For lumbago, it was common to be treated with electricity, morphine, pitch plasters, or potassium iodide."

lumber: as now; early, sometimes standing trees suitable to being cut into lumber, e.g., "His reference to 'three acres of lumber' revealed that the trees had not yet been cut."

luminary emanations: luminescence of either animals or humans, thought to be a wondrous event found in the New World, e.g., "Susanna, the wife of Major Nicholas Sewell, was said to give off luminary emanations - sparks and noises 'like unto bay leaves in a fire'."

luncheon: unlike now, that quantity of food that could be held in one hand, e.g., "His reference to a luncheon in his pack meant that he taken a small snack with him."

luster, lustre: a decorated or elaborate small to medium sized fixture for illumination, often a small chandelier or candle holder, e.g., "The 1814 inventory listed a brass luster, and 'yt with pendnt'."

lusty: occasionally, pregnancy, especially advanced, e.g., "Shad said his wife was lusty, and her time was near."

lye barrel: See **leach.**

lynx: See **wildcat.**

M

mackinaw, makinhaw: as now, a heavy woolen coat for utility wear, e.g., "The inventory of his clothes revealed a new coat and an 'old makinhaw'."

madam: early, a compliment and means of addressing ladies, e.g., "The word Madam was reserved for ladies, and was not used in addressing women of low station."

maiden: a young adult woman, not necessarily a virgin, at least in criminal law, e.g., "Her indictment in Vermont for adulterous conduct referred to her as a maiden."

mail: early, a postman's bag or satchel, and not the contents or correspondence therein, e.g., "It is from the early meaning of the word mail that we derived mailman."

mainsworn, malesworn, malsworn: See *forsworn.*

maize: See **corn.**

major annus: leap year, 366 days, e.g., "The statement that the bull was born the last major annus, meant during the preceding leap year."

majority: See **of age.**

make hay: See **haying time.**

mala fides: See **bona fides.**

Malaga, Malaga wine (Mallego, Malligo): a strong, sweet wine, originally from the province of Andalusia in southern Spain, e.g., "It was to be expected that early southern colonials would develop a taste for Malaga."

Mallego, Malligo wine: See **Malaga wine.**

mallet: a hammer made of wood or leather, used to strike any tool with a wooden or soft handle, e.g., "The cabinetmaker had several sizes of mallets."

malt liquor: See **liquors.**

malt: any grain, soaked or cooked in water, then fermented, then dried, e.g., "The use of malt in making beer is of very ancient origin."

mammy bench: a short settee, occasionally on rockers, and usually with a small removable fence extending across one half the front to prevent an infant from rolling off, upon which one might sit while tending the child, e.g., "The primitive hickory and maple mammy bench was her most prized heirloom." Also see **settee.**

man o' war: a large ship of war, after 1700 usually owned or under the control of a government and having cannon and armament, e.g., "The men o'war operating on the **Spanish Main** (q.v.), often called at Jamestown."

mandamus, writ of: an ancient and still used extraordinary writ by which a court orders a non-judicial officer of government to do or forbear from doing some act, e.g., "In 1867 a writ of mandamus issued against a sheriff to prevent the unlawful arrest of a black judge."

mandilion: a cheaply made, sleeveless, thigh-length, cloaklike garment with slits down each side, often worn by servants during early colonial times, e.g, "Because they were inexpensively made and received heavy wear, but few mandilions appear in inventories."

mangle: a device to "press" or **smooth** (q.v.) cloth, usually with two plates that closed together, but sometimes with rollers, e.g., "Nearly all better early homes had mangles."

mania: a form of mental imbalance characterized by extreme agitation or violence, often with delusions, e.g., "In 1876, Susan's treatment for mania included doses of morphine and bromides, and applications of cold to the extremities."

Manifest Destiny: that phrase, apparently first stated in 1845, reflecting the American view that it was our "God-given" and unavoidable destiny to settle the continent, the Indians, Spanish, Russians and other claimants notwithstanding, e.g., "The cry of those who would annex Texas and be rid of 'foreign' interference in Oregon was 'It is our Manifest Destiny'."

manikin, mannikin: unlike our "mannequin", a small man, e.g., "The old Hollander's reference to Peter Schmidt as a manikin revealed Schmidt's stature."

manor, mannor: settlements of early NY and MD resembling feudal grants, and usually requiring a nominal annual **quit-rent** (q.v.); a house and the land upon which it was situated, largely eliminated except as a label for large private landholdings; occasionally used to distinguish the **home place** (q.v.) from other residential properties owned by same person, e.g., "Cole and Dimmit leased and farmed land within the Maryland Mannor of Gunnpowder before 1740."

mantelet: a light, usually small woman's cloak, e.g., "The inventory reference to a silk and linen mantelet provided the researcher with a clue to the relative wealth of the family."

mantle, mantua: usually, a negligee or strapless light gown, e.g., "One of her mantles was of the finest yellow silk."

manure cart, muck cart: a two- or four-wheeled cart or wagon upon which manure to be used as fertilizer was loaded for hauling, e.g., "The task of loading and unloading the muck cart was dreaded by all."

manure fork: See **dung fork.**

maple syrup, maple sugar, etc.: as now, e.g., "In early times the poor of the Northern colonies had only honey and maple syrup as sweeteners." Also see **sugar house.**

marble-top tables: little-known before Victorian times, but very common during the last half of the 19th and early 20th centuries, made in many styles and shapes, e.g., "The 1887 inventory of her estate revealed two marble-tops, both **parlor tables** (q.v.)."

marca, mark: German or English money, early equal to about £0.65, e.g., "Early immigrants occasionally used marcas in their purchases, thereby revealing their German contacts or origin."

mare: See **horse.**

Martinmas: November 11; an ancient holiday celebrating St. Martin of Tours, e.g., "Martinmas terms of court are occasionally found in early Louisiana."

Maritime Provinces: the Canadian provinces of Nova Scotia, New Brunswick, and Prince Edward Island, e.g., "The Acadians were those of French extraction who lived in the Maritime Provinces, particularly Nova Scotia." Also see **Cajuns.**

mark: a symbol intended to substitute for a signature, usually used by those who were illiterate or physically unable to sign their names; in husbandry, that mark - brand - on animals revealing ownership by a certain person, e.g., "His mark - O - appeared on his will and all of his deeds"; "His brand or cattle mark - OG - was duly recorded." See also **marca.**

market wagon: See **pleasure wagon.**

marksman: unlike now, one who could not write and, instead, made a mark on documents and legal instruments, e.g., "The court's reference to Hines as a marksman had nothing to do with his shooting skills."

marlin spike, marline: a common hand tool used in splicing rope, e.g., "Almost all early farmers had a marlin spike."

marriage, age of consent to: See **of age.**

marriage bonds: the first step in marrying by license of government; pledges of security proving the intent to marry (not the actual marriage) and usually required by early law, revealed names of the bride and groom, date of the bond, name of bondsman and witnesses, and insured that there were no impediments to the marriage, e.g., "Their marriage bond was recorded in 1755, was in the amount of L500, and was recorded, even though the license was not."

marriage certificate: a document completed by a minister or other person empowered to perform marriages that signifies that a marriage ceremony was accomplished, e.g., "Their marriage certificate was signed two days after the date of the license."

marrow scoop: from early times well into the 20th century bone marrow commonly was picked and eaten at meals, and a small narrow spoon-like eating utensil was required to remove it from the bones, e.g., "Along with her other Sterling, she had a marrow scoop."

Mason-Dixon Line, Mason and Dixon's Line: latitude 39 degrees, 43', 26"; that boundary line growing out of the dispute between Lord Baltimore and William Penn concerning their respective proprietorships - Pennsylvania and Maryland; ultimately, south of the line and the Ohio River, slavery was institutionalized, e.g., "By the 1850s, those living north of the Mason-Dixon Line were being called Yankees."

Massachusetts Bay Colony: that name given the early Massachusetts settlements (c. 1624 - 1629), particularly the colonies of the Dorchester Co., New England Co., and Massachusetts Bay Co., e.g., "John Endecott was governor of the Massachusetts Bay Colony from 1628 until mid 1630."

mastiff, bandog: a very large dog, frequently used for protection by families of affluence, e.g., "References to mastiffs being bred for guard purposes probably may be found as early as the 14th century."

matchlock: a design of **lock** (q.v.) in use before and contemporaneously with the earliest **flintlocks** (q.v.), whereby the trigger mechanism moved a previously ignited fire source to and against the powder used to ignite the main charge and so propel the projectile from the barrel, e.g., "The matchlock was notorious for failing to fire when moisture was present." Also see **flintlock.**

maternal lineage, maternal ancestry: those ancestors to whom the subject is related through his or her mother, as opposed to **paternal lineage** (q.v.) that relates to the father, e.g., "Proof of the ancestry of her mother's great grandmother was the most difficult of her maternal lineage."

matertera magna: See **matertera.**

matertera major: See **matertera.**

matertera maxima: See **matertera.**

matertera: a mother's sister; an aunt, e.g., "The old Louisiana reports sometimes refer to matertera, matertera magna for great aunt, matertera major for great-great aunt (sister of great grandmother), matertera maxima meaning triple-great aunt."

mate: that officer subordinate only to the captain of a merchant vessel, e.g., "The passenger list of the *Elizabeth* referred to Bates as the mate."

matrix: unlike now, that edition of a document from which all copies must be made, e.g., "The Texas court found that the copy was not from the matrix, and was invalid."

matron: a married woman, usually elderly, e.g., "The reference to Judith Parker as a proper matron revealed her middle to elder years."

matrons, jury of: twelve women impanelled as a jury to determine the pregnancy of a woman sentenced to death or long incarceration, e.g., "Before executing the sentence of hanging, the sheriff was ordered to convene a jury of matrons to determine whether or not Rebecca Hutchison was pregnant."

mattock: as now, a heavy, long-handled tool pointed on one side and with a transverse blade on the other side of the head, used to break hard ground, cement, etc., "Every farm home had a mattock." Also see **pick axe.**

maul, mawl: a very large hammer, used to drive wedges, pilings, or to split logs; to split logs into rails, e.g., "Luke permitted Griffith to 'fall, saw, and mawl' the timber on the land"; "Lincoln spoke of mauling rails in old Illinois."

Mc- or Mac-, as a prefix: an early Irish (and sometimes Scottish) prefix meaning "son of," e.g., "The McKenzie - MacKenzie - clan was and is found on the northeast coast of Ireland." Also see **O'-, ap -,** and **van - .**

McGuffey Readers: of the many textbooks, McGuffey Readers represent those few that are well known today; printed after 1836, they appear in many estate inventories, e.g., "Her great grandmother's Third McGuffey Reader was printed in 1837."

mead, hydromel: a strong, ancient intoxicating drink made with fermented honey, e.g., "Mead and hydromel made of honey have been known in England and the Scandinavian countries since at least Saxon times." Also see **metheglin.**

meander, meanders, meanderings: the lateral or wandering movements of a stream or river, e.g., "The deed stated that the east line of the Drake property followed the meanderings of Moccasin Branch."

measles, rubella: red spots turning into red blotches over the body, usually commencing at the forehead and temples; early, often fatal, e.g., " During the epidemic of 1772, measles often were treated with a mustard bath, Dover's powder, purges, phosphorus, quinine, fat rubbed over the skin, and tea made of wild cherry bark."

mediocre, mediocrity: unlike now, moderation, temperance in conduct, moderate degree, e.g., "Her reference to his activities as mediocre reflected moderation, and did not refer to quality."

meeting, meeting house: early expressions meaning a facility used by the local citizenry for meetings, religious services, and local governmental activities, e.g., The old meeting house was located not far north and west of the home of A. J. Drake."

meeting clothes, Sunday go to meeting clothes: an expression of the poor; one's best apparel, worn only for church and special occasions, e.g., "Upon return from the wedding, the children were told to remove their meeting clothes."

melancholia: as now, extreme depression, early thought to be a distinct mental disorder, e.g., "For melancholia, he administered arsenic, compounds of gold, camphor, musk, or morphine."

Melungeons: those people of the North Carolina Appalachians believed to be of mixed negro, Caucasian, and Indian blood, e.g., "Many of the dark-skinned Melungeons carry surnames well known in **Tidewater Virginia (q.v.).**"

memento: a relic or historical artifact having particular significance to one's lineage, e.g., "Her most treasured memento was her grandmother's wedding gown."

memoirs: one's memories, usually written, e.g., "Grant's memoirs concerned much of his life as a soldier."

meningitis: as now, inflammation of the meninges (coverings of the nerves), e.g., "Meningitis was not understood and was treated, to no avail, with potassium iodide, morphine, ice, and aconite." Also see **spinal meningitis.**

menorrhagia: as now, excessive menstrual discharge, e.g., For menorrhagia, he prescribed salts of arsenic, ipecac, iron compounds, and quinine."

mens rea: guilty knowledge, wrongful purpose, e.g., "In criminal cases, early courts frequently speak of the existence or absence of mens rea."

mente captus: a degree of insanity, e.g., "An early Louisiana court spoke of mente captus, meaning habitual insanity."

mercer: a cloth merchant, usually of silk, e.g., "Drake was a mercer of Chester, Somerset."

mere: mother, e.g., "The common old expression en ventre sa mere meant in the mother's womb."

merchantman: a ship used in commerce, usually unarmed, e.g., "Many early merchantmen carried servants and slaves in addition to cargo."

merino: wool of very fine quality, e.g., "A listing in an inventory of apparel made of merino reveals affluence."

mestizo: a person of mixed blood, e.g., "Early Texas reports speak of mestizos." Also see **octaroons**

meter, metre: 39.37 inches, e.g., "Though adopted in France in 1795, the metric system with its meters, kilometers, etc., never became popular in the U.S."

messuage: a dwelling house; sometimes a dwelling and the attendant buildings, e.g., "Most early deeds and many early court records speak of the land 'and the messuages thereupon'."

metes and bounds: land boundaries; objects or monuments, as opposed to **courses and distances** (q.v.), e.g., "Described in metes and bounds, the boundary was from an ash in the creek bank to a pile of stones in Flemings line, thence to the oak post in the old road, to the west line of Drake, and, finally, back to the place of beginning."

metheglin: an intoxicating drink made of fermented honey, similar to **mead** (q.v.), e.g., "Metheglin was well known in Wales even before the 15th century."

metritis: any inflammation of the uterus, e.g., For the little understood metritis, Dr. Lockhart administered various **blisters** (q.v.), iodoform to the cervix, and compounds of gold."

Mexican War: that armed conflict during 1847-1848 between Mexico and the United States, e.g., "Findlay was in the 39th U.S. Infantry in the Mexican War."

mezzotint, mezzotint pictures: an early means of creating a **picture** (q.v.) by smoothing and polishing along design lines drawn onto a rough, usually copper surface, e.g., "Mezzotint pictures were appearing in inventories as early as 1820." Also see **tintype,** and **ambrotype.**

Michaelmas: early, a common holiday dedicated to the Archangel and celebrated on September 29, e.g., "Since it was written that he died at the beginning of the 'Michaelmas term' of court, she knew the death took place very near October 1."

microfiche, microfilm: a space-saving method of storing copies of original documents, books, etc.; with microfilm - the older of the two processes - each page is photographed on rolled film with one page of the original document in each frame; in microfiche, a number of pages are reduced in size and placed on a single sheet of film, e.g., "She checked out the microfilm of local newspapers, and a microfiche of the book."

middlings: center cuts of meat, especially loins or bacon, e.g., "Because they were more meaty, she insisted on middlings when buying pork chops."

Midsummer-day: summer solstice, e.g., "June 21 - Midsummer-day - was a day upon which many early contracts and land transactions required a quarterly payment, and also was the day upon which some early English colonials celebrated the Feast of St. John the Baptist."

midwife: an ancient occupation; a woman who assists women in childbirth, often for pay, e.g., "There being no physicians in the mountains, many women employed midwives to assist in their delivery." Also see **granny woman.**

migrants: See **immigrations and immigrants.**

mile: 1760 yards, 5280 feet, "There are 40 poles in a furlong and 8 furlongs in a mile." Also see **nautical mile.**

military age: that age at which one is liable to conscription for military service - the **draft** (q.v.); usually, over seventeen or eighteen and less than forty years of age, but volunteers of fewer and greater ages have been common in all wars, e.g., "He was eighteen, hence was of military age."

military units: See *armies, organization of.*

militia: the basis for the state and National Guard units of today; an armed body of citizens, organized by a state or a colony, and (as opposed to a standing army) active only in cases of civil disobedience, local emergency, or danger to the public good, e.g., "The local militia was 'called up' to fend off the Indian threat."

milk fever: early, a disease thought to be caused by lactation, and only later discovered to be an infection, e.g., "Young mothers feared the often fatal milk fever that frequently occurred shortly after the birth of a child."

milk glass: common early opaque glassware, having a milky, pale white appearance, e.g., "She enjoyed her **hobnail** (q.v.) milkglass."

milk leg: swelling and loss of circulation causing the legs to appear white due to constriction of the large veins, e.g., "Milk leg, not being understood, was treated with tonics, turpentine blisters, and even opium."

milk paint: an early coating made with skim milk and a pigment, usually berries or stains, e.g., "Milk paint, especially in blues and reds, was very commonly used to finish **primitive furniture** (q.v.)."

milk sickness: a dreaded, often fatal, and mysterious disease, particularly of the Mississippi Valley, e.g., "It is believed that the devastating milk sickness was spread to man by cattle that had eaten snakeroot."

milk skimmer: See **skimmer.**

milking stool: a short, usually three-legged stool used for sitting while milking a cow, e.g., "The old milking stool had been around since his grandfather's time."

milksop, milktoast: a mild, effeminate man, e.g., "Her reference to her husband as a milksop was a grave insult."

milktoast: See **milksop.**

mill: See **grist mill.**

milled dollar, piece of eight, dollar, peso: early, a Spanish coin called a "Real" physically cut into eight pieces, hence a "piece of eight"; later, a peso or silver coin equal in value to 1/8 Real, e.g., "Seventeenth-century trade records have many references to milled dollars and pieces of eight."

millwright: one who designs and constructs mills and the machinery for the same, e.g., "If they were to have flour for all, they had to induce millwrights to come to the frontier communities."

Minute Men: the name given that group of American Patriots, particularly of the Massachusetts militia, who could be called out for immediate service should the colony be threatened by the British, e.g., "Genealogists have identified many, if not most, of the Minute Men." Also see **Green Mountain Boys.**

minutes, minute books, orders, order books, judges' minutes, journals, journal entries: early, the minutes were the written records of the happenings that took place in a courtroom, and usually were made by clerks of that court and preserved in minute books; later, the proceedings in any case, no matter where or when it occurred, e.g., "Unlike the old minute book entries, it now is said that courts speak only through their journals, and journal entries are often the only record of decisions."

miscegenation: a living together as man and wife by persons of different races, particularly white and negro, e.g., "The Virginia Black Code of 1705 forbade miscegenation, and severely restricted movement about the colony by negroes."

Mission Church, Old: See **Old Mission Church.**

Missouri Compromise: 1820, the name given the much debated actions of Congress by which Maine entered the Union as a "free state", Missouri came in as a slave state, and all other Louisiana Purchase territory lying north of 36 degrees, 30 minutes, was to be "free", e.g., "After the Missouri Compromise, Missouri sought to exclude **mulattoes** (q.v.) and **free blacks** (q.v.), causing the debates of the so-called 2nd Missouri Compromise."

mistery, mystery: a trade or calling, e.g., "Early, the word mistery was common, but later it was spelled mystery, from whence came the expression '...teach him the art and mystery of...'. See **art and mystery.**

mittens: early, any coarse heavy glove, with or without fingers; sometimes, gauntlets that did not cover the fingers or thumb, e.g., "The mittens she was said to have crocheted for the children may have had fingers."

moiety: (from French moien - middle) an equal part; one of two equal parts; one-half, e.g., "There being but one other child, he claimed a moiety of the property."

moldboard, mouldboard: that part of a plow behind the blade that turns the earth over, e.g., "In early times, a plow consisted of a wooden moldboard with a replaceable plow point."

money changers: an ancient and Biblical term, meaning one who converts the currency of one nation into that of another, e.g., "The Biblical reference to money changers in the Tabernacle is well known."

money scales: small accurate scales or balances used to weigh precious metals and sometimes gemstones, e.g., "The 1731 inventory of the merchant revealed a money scale."

monogamy: restrained to a single wife, e.g., "The word monogamy is the opposite of bigamy and polygamy."

monstrum: a box wherein relics are kept, often of a religious nature, e.g., "The early 17th-century inventory revealed an ebony and silver monstrum."

monument: See **headstone.**

moonshine: See **corn whiskey.**

Mormons, The Church of Jesus Christ of Latter Day Saints, LDS: in genealogy, noted for their superb library in Salt Lake City, and for their "Family History Centers" throughout the World, e.g., "She spent many hours both at the LDS Library and at the Mormon Family Center." Also see **Family History Centers.**

morning dress, morning clothes: early and interestingly, the casual, daytime house wear of a woman or the very formal daytime dress of a gentleman, e.g., "His morning clothes consisted of a cutaway coat, fancy **waist-**

coat (q.v.), and gray striped pants."

mortality tables, mortuary tables: statistics, based upon averages, by which one's life expectancy is estimated, e.g., "Our mortality tables differ widely from those of the early days largely by reason of the decreased death rate of children."

mortar and pestle: a common small, usually ceramic or earthen bowl (mortar) with a handled, hard, grinding head (pestle), for grinding spices and medicines, e.g., "She ground medicinal plants with her mortar and pestle."

mortgage deed of trust: See **trust deed** and **mortgage deed.**

mortgage deed, mortgage, purchase money mortgage: a formal, signed, and acknowledged document by which a borrower (mortgagor) conveys legal title to his or her property to a lender (mortgagee) as security for a loan of money or other thing of value; when the mortgagor (borrower) has paid the debt as agreed, the mortgagee (lender) transfers the title back by **release** (q.v.); similar to a deed of trust, except that in trust deeds the title is transferred to a third party approved by both the lender and the borrower, who releases the title back to the mortgagor upon being informed that the debt has been paid as agreed, e.g., "As security for his loan, the land was transferred to the bank by a mortgage deed." Also see **trust deed.**

mortgagee: See **mortgage deed.**

mortgagor: See **mortgage deed.**

mortis causa: by reason of a death, or in anticipation of death, e.g., "The common early expression donation mortis causa means a gift by reason of an anticipated death."

mortuary tables: See **mortality tables.**

mortuary: unlike now, a bequest to the parish church, often in payment of previous tithes not paid or to ease the conscience of the donor, e.g., "The Newport parish reference to the payment of S6 for mortuary had nothing to do with a funeral home."

mother hubbard: a straight, loose, full length, sleeved dress worn during pregnancy, often modestly adorned or decorated, e.g., "Her mother hubbards concealed her pregnancy until the final days." Also see **chemise.**

motorman: as now with subways, one whose occupation was driving a **streetcar** (q.v.), e.g., "Early New York motormen usually worked twelve hour shifts."

mouldboard: See **moldboard.**

mountebank: a term of derision; usually a physician who publicly, as at a courthouse, proclaimed the efficacy of his concoctions and medicines, e.g., "Mountebanks were often spoken of in the same vein as were keepers of brothels."

mourning cards: those usually rather heavy paper memorials to the dead, given at funerals and **wakes** (q.v.), they often were nicely printed on black backgrounds, stated the name of the deceased, date of death, age, and often a poem or saying thought appropriate, e.g., "The 1892 mourning cards for Mrs. Martha Midlam were black with her name in gold leaf."

mourning coat, mourning cloak: a black wrap worn at funerals and wakes, e.g., "Mourning coats appear in 19th century inventories of affluent people."

mourning jewelry, mourning gifts: often bore the name or initial of the deceased, the date of death, and sometimes the age of the dead person, such rings, bracelets, pins, gloves, scarves, and pendants were given to mourners as remembrances of the deceased, e.g., "She had mourning rings and gloves from the funerals of ancestors."

moustache cup: a large, handled cup for warm drinks, and having a perforated half cover molded across the top, thereby facilitating drinking without wetting one's moustache, e.g., "Wealthy men often had several moustache cups."

moxa, moxas: dried wormwood leaves and stems, placed on areas of the skin that itched or were erupted, and then ignited, e.g., "Acting as counter irritants, moxas were thought to have great curative value."

Mr. and Mrs.: titles; in early times, used only when referring to those who held public office or who had gained wealth or the respect and admiration of the community; usually used to refer only to those above the status of yeoman, e.g., "As a **Burgess** (q.v.), he was addressed as Mr. Hunt, even though he was but a **wheelwright** (q.v.)."

much oblige, much obliged: a common early expression meaning thank you, e.g., "Evan consistently showed his gratitude for any favor by saying simply 'much oblige'."

muck cart: See **manure cart.**

muffineer, muffinier: a small glass container, often of better glass, having a perforated lid and used to sprinkle sugar or other decoration on cakes, muffins, toasted breads, etc., e.g., "Diane's muffinier was of milkglass and was kept full of maple sugar."

mulatto, mulattoe: early, a person with one white and one Negro parent; later, any person of mixed black and white ancestry, e.g., "Even though she was but one-quarter black - a quaterone-, she was spoken of as a mulatto."

mule: a work animal, half **horse** (q.v.) and half donkey, usually bred for size and strength and almost always unable to reproduce, e.g., "He had a horse for riding, and three mules to do the farm work."

mule chest: usually a combination blanket and two-drawered chest on short legs, and having a hinged top that opened upward, e.g., "The mule chest dated to 1840 and was of pine."

muller: usually, a stone, metal, or glass pestle used with bowls and other hollowed containers to crush or grind sugar, spices, medicines, dyes, etc., e.g., "The expression 'mull it over' arose from the frequent early use of mullers." Also see **mortar and pestlee.**

mumps: as now, e.g., "For the mumps, the old doctor often administered leeches, and induced almost constant action of bowels."

muniments: documents concerning or proving title, usually to land or an inheritance, e.g., "The many early comments conecerning delivery of muniments arose because recording was not yet common here and was unknown in England."

mush, corn meal mush: a common, early, predominantly Northern food made by cooking corn meal in hot water until it thickens, and serving the mixture as a cereal or fried, with honey, molasses (**sorghum**, q.v.), or maple syrup, e.g., "Will Midlam said that being poor meant you ate a lot of mush."

musket: a smooth-bored, large-caliber, hand-held firearm first seen in the 16th century, and made obsolete by the rifled-barrel arms of the late 18th century, e.g., "The appearance of the rifled barrel caused muskets to fall out of favor." Also see **long rifle** and **cap and ball.**

mussuck: an early word meaning low, damp, untillable land; a small swamp or bog, e.g., "Early Virginia land records occasionally refer to land bordering a mussuck."

mustizo: an 18th-century South Carolina term for a person if Indian and negro parentage, e.g., "The term mustizo likely arose by reason of the similar term **mestizo** (q.v.)."

muzzle loader: an early firearm loaded by inserting a measured charge of powder and a projectile (**ball**, q.v.), made tight with a small piece of cloth (wadding) through the muzzle end of the barrel, e.g., "With the advent of pre-loaded cartridges, the ,muzzle loaders were doomed."

myelitis: early, any inflammation of the spinal cord, e.g., "For myelitis, he thought electricity, belladonna, and strychnine could be helpful."

myrrh: See *frankincense and myrrh.*

N

naif, neife, nativus, villein: one born a slave or a **bond woman** (q.v.), e.g., The old Louisiana and Texas reports sometimes refer to naifs, meaning slaves."

napkin: often, unlike now, a handkerchief or child's diaper, e.g., "The napkins in the inventory meant handkerchiefs, and the **diaper** (q.v.) there listed probably was a floral-patterned cloth."

Napoleon chair: an armed, backless, wooden chair without upholstery, common at the turn of the 20th century, e.g., "He bought a Napoleon chair from Montgomery and Wards for the price of a good pair of shoes."

nappery: tablecloths, table linen, e.g., "The nappery in the Mason inventory was Irish linen."

Nat Turner Insurrection: that Southampton Co., Virginia, slave revolt of 13 to 23 August, 1831, wherein 57 white men, women, and children were killed, after which a manhunt was organized and perhaps 100 negroes were killed, and subsequent to which Nat Turner and 19 of his followers were tried and executed, e.g., "Gary's grandmother played in the old tree trunk where Turner had hidden after the Nat Turner Insurrection."

NATF- forms: government printed forms designated NATF-80, NATF-81, NATF-82, etc., the same required to gain information held by the U.S. government concerning veterans, immigrants, censuses, and vital statistics; available from the Archives, genealogical bookstores, and libraries, e.g., "By sending her NATF- 80, she located the Revolutionary military records of her ancestor."

national guard: See **militia.**

nativity: the place of birth, e.g., "Salisbury North Carolina was her place of nativity."

naturalization: the action by which the government of one country grants citizenship to a citizen of another, e.g., "The Welshman, Richard Roberts, was naturalized in Ohio in 1844."

nautical mile, knot: 6,080 feet, e.g., "A nautical mile (knot) is about 1.15 statute miles of 5,280 ft."

navis bona: a sound ship, e.g., "Early New England court records occasionally refer to a vessel navis bona."

ne exeat: may not leave, e.g., "When the court has ordered a person to not leave the jurisdiction, early Georgia reports labelled it a writ ne exeat."

ne unques accouple: never married, e.g., "The old Louisiana reports sometimes refer to a person ne unques accouple en loiall matromonie, meaning never joined in legal marriage."

neat cattle, neat: livestock, but not including horses, sheep, goats, and swine; in the Western States the word 'neat' was dropped, otherwise the meaning was the same; any unadulterated, alcoholic drink consumed at room temperature, usually whiskey, e.g., "Broad Cole was taxed for four head of neat cattle"; "He preferred his Scotch neat."

necessary, a: See **privy.**

neckcloth: See **cravat.**

necropsy: an autopsy, e.g., "Early references to necropsy simply mean an autopsy."

nepos, neptis: grandson and granddaughter, occasionally the 'great' of those relationships, e.g., "Old court records occasionally speak of nepos and neptis, when referring to grandchildren in an impersonal or theoretical context."

nest egg: early, the single egg left in a chicken nest, thereby inducing the hen to lay more eggs, e.g., "The expression 'my nest egg' derives from the increase likely through leaving an egg in the nest."

New Amsterdam: See **New Netherlands.**

New France: the name given those territories early claimed by France, including portions of modern Canada and the central United States, e.g., "Until Jefferson's purchase in 1803, the land that now is Iowa was a part of New France."

New Netherlands: that series of settlements by Hollanders and Swedes in Manhattan and along the Hudson and Delaware Rivers (the capital at New Amsterdam), the territory of which was assumed and claimed by

England c1669, e.g., "To the pleasure of the genealogists, many records remain of the activities of the New Netherlands settlers."

New Spain: the Spanish colonies in the New World (western hemisphere), e.g., "Because of the heat, southern Florida was considered one of the least valuable colonies in New Spain."

New Sweden: See **New Netherlands.**

New World influence: many new words arose from our experiences with the unfamiliar conditions encountered in the American colonies, e.g., "Backwoodsman, bobsled, bullfrog, eggplant, garter snake, groundhog, popcorn, prairie, squatter, and sweet potato, are but a few."

New Year's Day: January 1, but March 25th in the Americas until 1752, e.g., "Jan. 1, 1752 was declared New Year's Day, and thus ended the 'old calendar'."

Newgate Prison: that incredibly deplorable London prison, e.g., "Many was the Newgate prisoner who sought transportation and servitude rather than remain there."

next friend: one who, though not a legal guardian, is authorized to act in behalf of an **infant** (q.v.), a married woman (early), a mental incompetent, or other person suffering a legal disability, e.g., "In 1678, when the estate was sued for a debt of her deceased husband, she was required to have a next friend appear with her in court."

Nez Perce War: the name given those conflicts of Oct. 1877 in the Pacific Northwest in which the U.S. cavalry and settlers fought the Nez Perce Indians under Chief Joseph, the latter defeated, e.g., "The Nez Perce War resulted in the Indians being placed on a reservation."

nib: the point of a quill and later steel pen; that portion of a quill pen that was dipped in ink and pressed against paper for writing, e.g., "Quill nibs were cut with a **penknife** (q.v.), and contained a slit from the point upwards and a small hole at the upper end of the slit."

night: at common law, that period between sunset and sunrise during which there was insufficient light to discern a man's face, e.g., "Before standard times were adopted and clocks became common, the old common law definition of night served quite well, and after that, night became 30 minutes after sunset until 30 minutes before sunrise."

nicknames: those abbreviations and variations of given names used to address another, e.g., "Even though her given name was Veronica, since it sounded like Fronica, her nickname was Franny."

night chair: See **closestool.**

night sweats: early thought to be an ailment and not a symptom, e.g., "For night sweats, he prescribed red wine and honey."

nil dicit: a legal claim sustained against one who failed to plead or answer a significant portion of a complaint, or after doing so abandoned or otherwise did not go forth with his defense, e.g., "Judgements were called nil dicit where the defendant left the jurisdiction after being served with summons, thereby revealing to the researcher that the person may have migrated at that time."

ninny: a person of little intellect, a simpleton, e.g., "In jest, their aunt addressed the children as ninnies."

nisei: a person of Japanese parentage born in the United States, e.g., "Many of the Japanese now living in California are nisei."

nisi prius: a general term meaning any court, no matter how otherwise named (common pleas, quarter sessions, etc.) where issues are tried before juries and a single judge, e.g., "Even though the court was called Common Pleas Court, in fact it was a court of nisi prius."

nit: a louse or flea egg, the same combed from the hair of our ancestors, e.g., "To call one a nit wit meant that he was of very little intellect."

nitre, niter, saltpeter: potassium or sodium nitrate from which were made gun powder and dynamite, e.g., "The appearance of nitre in the inventory likely revealed the need to make explosives."

noblemen, nobility: peerage (q.v.); except as visitors and occasional residents, none were recognized in the United States; usually, those who were entitled to bear arms, including dukes, marquises, earls, viscounts, and barons, e.g., "As an earl, he was of nobility and enjoyed the benefits of that station." Also see **heraldry.**

nodes: usually, swollen lymph glands not understood early, e.g., "For nodes, then thought similar to **goiters** (q.v.), potassium iodide and mercuric oleate applied locally were said to be helpful."

noggin: a large wooden mug or pitcher for beer, ale, etc.; slang for one's head, e.g., "He had his favorite noggin, and no one else used it"; "He got hit in the noggin."

nolens volens, no. vo.: whether he consents or not, whether willing or unwilling; a frequent court notation to a sheriff or other officer meaning that such officer is to serve the order or take the prescribed action whether the person being served or taken consents or not, e.g., "The writ ordering the sheriff to take the hogs into custody was endorsed nolens volens by the circuit court."

non compos mentis: not sound of mind, e.g., "The common expression non compos mentis was often used in courts' findings to explain criminal or other misconduct."

non est inventus, nonestinventus: meaning not found, or not found within the jurisdiction of the court; this expression usually accompanied the return of a Sheriff when the person sought was dead, e.g., "The court noted that Parker was non est inventus, and that the writ had been served on the representative of the estate instead."

non obstante: notwithstanding, e.g., "Early courts frequently spoke of rendering a decision non obstante veredicto (n.o.v.), meaning notwithstanding the verdict of the jury."

nonsuit: dismissal of a law suit at the order of a court, a finding that the claim filed is not valid, legal, or appropriate, e.g., "The order of nonsuit found in the records revealed that the claim was considered ill-founded."

noodling: hunting for turtles or small animals by putting ones hands into the den or hole and grasping the animal, e.g., "Every spring, Howard would go noodling for turtles."

Northwest Territory: that area of the present United States north and west of the Ohio River and Pennsylvania; it became Ohio, Indiana, Illinois, Michigan, Wisconsin and Minnesota, and was first governed by the **Ordinance of 1787** (q.v.), e.g., "In 1788, the Fridley family settled in the Northwest Territory near Marietta, which area later became part of Ohio."

nosegay: a small bunch, bouquet, or ball of aromatic materials, carried or worn on the person, originally intended to be sniffed and so counteract the noxious odors of cities, e.g., "The stench of sewage, dead animals, and horse droppings virtually required the ladies of old Boston to carry a nosegay." Also see **pomander.**

nostrums: later called **patent medicines** (q.v.); early concoctions touted as cures for many ailments, e.g., "Among the nostrums of the early years were Daffy's Elixir, Drake's Bitters, Dutch Drops, Gascoins Powder, Goddards's Drops, Scot's Pills, Seignettes Salts, Venice Treacle, and a host of others"

Notary Public, Notary: one who is authorized to administer oaths as to the truth of facts contained in deeds, affidavits, depositions, and other writings, "Mrs. Haskins was commissioned a Notary Public by the state."

novus homo: a new man, "Early courts often referred to pardoned criminals as novus homo."

nozzle: variously, a tea, coffee, or chocolate pot spout, or the socket for a candle in a chandelier, sconce, or candleholder, e.g., "She broke a nozzle on her crystal **sconce** (q.v.)."

nubilis: one who may legally be married, e.g., "Early Louisiana and Texas reports occasionally refer to a person, usually a woman, as nubilis, marriageable."

nulla bona: no goods, absence of assets, e.g., "A common early endorsement by a sheriff on a writ of attachment was nulla bona, meaning he had found no assets of the defendant."

nullius filius: son of no one; a bastard, e.g., "Even though now a bastard is considered a child of its mother, early records occasionally speak of a man as nullius filius."

nunc pro tunc: now for then, e.g., "Even though by the contract he should have finished the work earlier, the Essex court ruled that he might 'do it nunc pro tunc, and be so paid'."

nuncupative will: (Lat., to solemnly declare) an oral will; to create a valid nuncupative will, the testator must: a) be aware that death is imminent, b) with that awareness and before witnesses, make statements declaring his intentions concerning the disposition of his personal property, c) die, d) whereupon and within a reasonable time, the last wishes must be reduced to writing, e.g., "On the frontier and in sparsely settled areas where death often came quickly, nuncupative wills were frequent."

Nuns, school records kept by: See **Orders of Nuns.**

nursery chair: a small child's chair designed to be a potty chair and having a raisable play surface similar to that of a high chair, e.g., "The old nursery chair had served all of Maggie's nine children."

nurus: a daughter-in-law; a son's wife, e.g., "As an example, an early Texas or Louisiana report might speak of Jane Doe, nurus Henry Smith."

nutmeg graters, nutmeggers, cinnamon graters, spice graters: small hand-held utensils used to grate cinnamon, nutmeg, pepper, and other spices, usually home made of a small piece of grooved wood with perforated tin rounded up over the groove and nailed to the wood, the spice then rubbed against the perforated surface to grate it, e.g., "Anne's husband had punched her name into the back of her little nutmeg grater."

nymphomania: early, thought to be a disease, e.g., "For nymphomania, camphor and bromides were administered."

O

O'-, a prefix: a Scottish prefix, early meaning "son of," e.g., "In very early Scotland, the name O'Connor meant son of Connor." Also see **ap-, Mc-,** and **van-.**

oarsman: in colonial times, one who for hire provided transportation or movement of goods for others by rowing or otherwise propelling small boats, e.g., "The oarsman Hunt transported the **Burgesses** (q.v.) across James River."

oat sieve: a wooden-framed sieve, ten to twenty inches in diameter, used to separate chaff and debris from oats and other whole grains to be used in cooking, e.g., "Whenever oatmeal was to be made for the children, she got out the oat sieve."

oath, oaths: deeds and wills usually proven by the oaths of subscribing witnesses; a sworn statement that the person would comply with some requirement, or that he or she was telling the truth concerning some matter of legal importance, usually made in the name of God, e.g., "They took oaths that each would uphold the laws of King George III." Also see **loyalty oaths.**

oaths of loyalty: See **oath,** and **loyalty oaths.**

obit sine prole, o.s.p.: died without children, e.g., "Early probate proceedings often refer to a person obit sine prole, i.e., he died without issue."

obituary: a memoriam to one who has recently died, usually in a newspaper and containing dates, accomplishments, and names of family members, e.g., "She learned the names of the sons from the obituary."

obstetric: early, a midwife; pertaining to midwifery, e.g., "The parish reference to a payment for obstetric usually meant that a midwife was paid for her services."

ocasion: an accident, e.g., "Early Texas and California records refer to events as ocasion - Spanish for accident."

octaroon: early, a person of one-eighth negro blood, i.e., one black and seven white great grandparents, e.g., "In some states, as late as 1880 an octaroon was considered a negro for voting purposes."

octrol: a duty or tax on goods, e.g., "Some early Louisiana reports refer to sums paid as duties on whiskey as octrol."

of age, of majority: the age at which one became an adult, i.e., presumed able and entitled to manage his or her own affairs, and enjoy the civic privileges and rights afforded by his or her government; now, the achievement of eighteen or twenty-one years; early, 14 for males and 12 for females as common law age of consent to marriage; e.g., "Being twenty one, he was of age." Also see **emancipation.**

of counsel: an attorney employed in the case at hand, e.g., "The expression 'of counsel' appears with great frequency in early **loose papers** (q.v.)."

officers (army): See **armies, organization of.**

offspring: synonymous with natural children or issue, e.g., "In early times the word 'offspring' was more commonly used than was 'issue'."

Ohio Company: an organization of speculators and entrepreneurs who in 1747 undertook to gain a million acres, more or less, on both sides of the Ohio River in what was to be called the Northwest Territory, and further sought to make settlement possible there by dealing with the Indian claims, all to the irritation of the French who then claimed the area, e.g., "The activities of the Ohio Company in part led to a building by the French of fortifications on the Allegheny and the Ohio Rivers, and ultimately to the French and Indian War." Also see **French and Indian War** and **Northwest Territory.**

Ohio Country: the **Northwest Territory** (q.v.) subject to the **Ordinance of 1787** (q.v.) and subsequent provisions; that indeterminate area north and west of the Ohio River, including present-day Ohio, Indiana, Illinois, and parts of Michigan, Minnesota, and Wisconsin; any of the formerly French territories north and west of the Ohio River, e.g., "Little did the colonial Virginians know that what to them was the vast wild Ohio Country would one day be an economic giant." Also see **New France.**

oil cloth: a common, heavy, utility fabric, made waterproof by soaking absorbent cloth such as cotton or linen in oil, grease, or paint, e.g., "In the 19th century, the poor often covered their windows with oil cloth."

oil lamps: usually, lamps that came on the American scene after about 1860, a great improvement over candles and **betty lamps** (q.v.), they were in virtually every home by the middle of the 1880s; having adjustable wicks, usually chimneyed, of many designs and degree of decoration, some with reflectors, and burning whale oil or kerosene ("coal oil"), e.g., "She had eight oil lamps, including two small **night lamps** (q.v.)."

oil torch: a lamp for outdoor use, consisting of a metal oil reservoir of 4 to 6 quarts mounted above an open burner, the whole suspended from a post or outside wall, e.g., "Oil torches were common in the 1890s, and cost the equivalent of a pair of better ladies' shoes."

ointment pot: a small, lidded, glass jar used for home made salves, lotions, etc., e.g., "She always saved old **salve tins** (q.v.) and small jars in order that she not have to buy ointment pots when she made lotions."

Oklahoma Land Rush: the name given the opening of Oklahoma lands for settlement, e.g., "By nightfall of April 22, 1884 - the day of the Oklahoma Land Rush - Oklahoma City had a population of 10,000, and almost 2 million acres had been claimed."

old field schools: referred to early schooling or classes held in cleared fields lying fallow that were central to the settlements, e.g., "It is thought that an old field school was held every summer on an old tobacco field near the Drake plantation east of present day Courtland, VA."

Old Goody: a common, jestful reference to St. Nicholas or Santa Claus, e.g., "She wrote that she hoped Old Goody would soon arrive."

Old Mission Church: that structure at Upper Sandusky, OH, that was the home of Reverend Finlay's (a Negro) mission to the Wyandot Indians. Commenced in 1819, the mission ended upon the Wyandots being ordered to remove to Oklahoma, e.g., "Services are held at the restored Old Mission Church on each summer Sunday morning."

old style, old series, O.S.: as now, e.g., "Early courts referred to dates set forth by the Julian Calendar as old style or old series."

oleo, oleomargarine: margarine; a product of the early 20th century costing much less than butter, e.g., "Early oleo was colored yellow to imitate butter; later oleomargarine came with a small packet of yellow coloring to be mixed with it to achieve the same effect."

olographic testament: See **holographic will.**

ome bueno: literally, a good man; usually, a substantial or affluent person, usually a man, e.g., "Early Southwest writings often refer to persons of standing as ome bueno."

on ball, on ball.: against a debt or balance owed, e.g., "The court ordered that he be paid '52 monthly on ball'."

on the other side: on the opposite page, e.g., "Many court records refer to matters set forth on the other side."

once removed: See **cousins, once removed.**

opetide: the period between Epiphany and Ash Wednesday, e.g., "In early times it was thought that the ideal period for weddings was during opetide."

-or, a suffix: from the Latin, that person who causes or brings about some legal effect upon another person, e.g., "Having filed the lien to secure his money, he was acting as lienor." Also see **mortgage, testator, grantor,** and **-ee, a suffix.**

Orangemen: a secret society of Irishmen having as their purpose the perpetuation of the Protestant views of William of Orange, e.g., "The Orangemen were organized in 1795 and have been active even to now."

Order of the Cincinnati: an association of officers of the Revolution and their descendents, e.g., The Order of the Cincinnati was named for Cincinnatus, a Roman general and statesman."

orders of nuns, Religious Institutes of Catholic Women: those disciplines and orders of women who have dedicated their lives to the Catholic Church and its service, a few of which would be the Benedictine, Carmelite,

Dominican, Franciscan, Servite, and Xavier Sisters, Sisters of Charity, of the Immaculate Heart, and of Mercy, School Sisters of Notre Dame, Sisters of Our Lady of Charity, Sisters of Providence, and Order of St. Clare, e.g., "Most researchers overlook the vast records kept by Orders of Nuns concerning schooling and care of children, Catholic and otherwise, which records may be located through many sources, including local parish priests."

orders, order books: See **minutes, etc.**

Ordinance of 1787: those Congressional acts for the encouragement of development in the **Northwest Territory** (q.v.); provided for religious and legal freedom, opportunities for education, abolishment of slavery, and division into smaller states, e.g., "The Ordinance of 1787 was the first law of the United States intended to legislate activity in the territory."

ordinary: a tavern and restaurant, open to the general public and having no overnight accommodations; a place of eating and drinking, the rates of which were usually set by the county court and sometimes by the legislature, e.g., "By 1730, Peter Keiter had been licensed to operate an ordinary on the Skippack Road." Also see **roadhouse, inn, pub,** and **tavern.**

Oregon Trail: the well known trail from Independence, Missouri, to Astoria, Oregon, where the Columbia River empties into Pacific Ocean; early, the principal route for Oregon and northwest bound settlers, e.g., "The ancestors of many Oregonians and Washingtonians came across the Oregon Trail from Ohio, Kentucky, and Missouri."

organization of armies: See **armies, organization of.**

orgeat: a party punch, e.g., "Her favorite orgeat contained milk, cinnamon, rosemary, and sugar."

original sources: in genealogy, research materials that exist as originally written or preserved, as distinguished from those that have been copied, reproduced, or modified in some way, e.g., "Among the original of her pension papers was a document bearing her handwritten signature." Also see **primary sources.**

ornaments, trophies: those decorations and accoutrements supplied to a soldier or cavalryman designating unit, sponsor, etc., e.g., "The court of 1687 received an offer from Effingham to supply the county 'with Trumpetts, Drumes, colours, and ornaments'."

orphan: early, one whose father was dead, yet whose mother might yet be alive; now, one whose natural father and mother are dead and no action yet has been taken by agreement or by the court to appoint substitutes therefor, e.g., "The courts appointed guardians for orphans under fourteen, however orphans of fourteen years or more could choose their own, subject to disapproval by a court."

O.S.: See **old style.**

osnaburg, oznaburg: a common, coarse linen cloth, used widely for work clothes and utility purposes, e.g., "Virtually every drygoods merchant and general store of the 18th century listed osnaburg in their inventory."

ottoman: early, an upholstered divan or sofa; later and now, a padded, upholstered footstool, e.g., "Since the inventory revealed no other furniture for sitting, the ottoman listed probably was what we call a sofa."

ounce: 1/12 of a lb. Troy; 1/16 of a lb. avoirdupois, e.g., "Early measures of gold and silver smiths usually were set forth in Troy ounces."

ouster le mer: See **beyond sea.**

outage: an early Maryland tax levied on quantities of tobacco, e.g., "Early taxes on tobacco exports by the state of Maryland were referred to as outage."

outcry, auction: early, a sale on the courthouse steps, held by shouting an offer to sell to all who might accept that offer and buy; now, a public sale by auction held at a place determined by the owners or a court, e.g., "Many records remain of sales by outcry."

outlot: land lying close outside the bounds of that political subdivision, yet under the control of a city or municipality, e.g., "Outlot 8 of the village of Arlington belonged to Dr. Drake."

outhouse: early, any building used in daily life that was separate and distinct from the main dwelling of the property; now, a **privy** (q.v.), e.g., "The outhouse mentioned in the estate was a summer kitchen"; "At Halloween Paul and Evan always enjoyed tipping over outhouses."

oven rake, fire rake, stove rake, rake: a light, long-handled, metal, hoe-shaped utensil used to pull ashes from a stove or coals from a fireplace for use under **trivets** (q.v.), e.g., "Every household had an oven rake."

over sea: See **beyond sea.**

overseer: as now, one who superintended a large farm or plantation, usually with slaves, e.g., "The overseer was hired for the forthcoming growing season."

overseers of the poor: persons provided with government funds and charged with the duty of caring for the needs of the poor, e.g., "John Martin was an early Pennsylvania overseer of the poor."

overshoes: See **shoes.**

oxymel: a mixture of vinegar and honey, thought to have medicinal value in stomach ailments, e.g., "Oxymel was administered when the old doctor thought the stomach was not acidic enough."

oyer and terminer (courts of): literally, hear and determine, an ancient term for courts having jurisdiction in criminal matters; early, and in Delaware and Pennsylvania, the criminal branch of the lowest court of general jurisdiction, e.g., "Many states still call their highest courts of criminal jurisdiction courts of oyer and terminer"; "In 1807, his assault and battery charge was tried in the court of oyer and terminer."

ozaena: apparently meaning forgotten; a malady of the 18th and 19th centuries for which creosote or bromide inhalants, carbolic acid, and potassium permanganate were variously prescribed.

oznaburg: See **osnaburg.**

P

pace, pacers: See **gaits.**

pack of wool: 240 lbs., a horseload, e.g., "Early records sometimes speak of packs of wool when referring to the weight of that commodity."

packets: any ship or large boat that carried passengers, mail, or goods on a regular schedule, e.g., "During and after the **California Gold Rush** (q.v.), it was common to speak of making a trip to there on a packet."

pactio, pactum: bargaining, an agreement, e.g., "Many early records of Louisiana and Texas refer to pactum and the pactio that led up to it."

paddock: unlike now, a large toad or bull frog, e.g., "Her reference to the paddocks at the rear of the barn referred to the toads that lived there."

paint: a common reference to a pinto (or painted) horse, e.g., "The stranger rode a young paint."

painter: early, a panther or cougar (mountain lion), e.g., "The records of early Ohio reveal frequent encounters with painters."

palfrey: a small horse, usually thought appropriate for use by children and women, e.g., "Her reference to the bay palfrey meant a small, medium brown, riding horse."

pallet: as now; occasionally a small bed frame or bedstead (q.v.), e.g.,"They had two pallets for use when children visited overnight."

pallmall: a popular 16th- and 17th-century game in which the players attempt to hit a wooden ball through an iron ring at the other end of a lane of play similar to a bowling lane, e.g., "Drake and his contemporaries frequently played pallmall and **bowls** (q.v.).

Panic: referred to market or financial crises, if national or affecting a large area of the country, e.g., "The Panics of 1819, 1837, 1857, 1873, 1893, 1907, and 1929 are the best known of the American financial crises." Also see **Roaring Twenties.**

pantofles: See **shoes.**

pantry, hoosier cupboard: early, a room in which provisions were stored; later, a doored cabinet with a flour bin and a shelf above, a drawer with metal bread bin and hinged doors concealing shelves below, and a retractable, often porcelain, work surface between, e.g., "Her pantry was but a small **primitive** (q.v.) cabinet with a bread board for a work space."

papist, popery: a word of reproach for a Catholic; Roman Catholicism, e.g., "It was said that many New Englanders hated all papists"; "Those merely believing in and adhering to the tenets of popery were not called papists except in reproach."

parakeets: See **Carolina Parakeets.**

paraphernalia, parapherna: unlike now, property belonging to a married woman other than her **dowry** (q.v.), e.g., "Among her paraphernalia was a beautiful bay mare."

parcel: a small group of animals, e.g., "He bought a parcel of sows."

paregoric: as now, a mixture of camphor and opium dissolved in alcohol, e.g., "Paregoric was widely used as a cure for diarrhea in children."

parish: an ecclesiastical district, having its own church or churches, and pastors, priests, or ministers, e.g., "The parishes of early times had much greater influence on the lives, conduct, and property of the parishioners." Also see **processioning.**

parity of hands: a comparison of handwriting for authentication of a document where there are no witnesses summonable or available to the court; a doctrine used by genealogists to show identity of signators of documents, e.g., "Since there was no one yet living who witnessed his signing of the will, a determination by parity of hands was ordered."

parlor stove: a small, usually somewhat ornate, iron heating stove, often situated offsetting one of the outside walls, having limited fuel capacity, and fired only when guests were expected, e.g., "The parlor stove was lit several hours before her guests were to arrive."

parlor table, center table: any of many styles and designs, from simple to very ornate, small to medium-sized tables, often square with an open shelf serving as a stretcher, placed about a parlor or room, quite usually beside a chair, and used for placement of a lamp, perhaps a photo or ink drawing, and a book or two, e.g., "She had two **wingback chairs** (q.v.) and a parlor table." Also see **tea table.**

parlor, sitting room: the room where important guests were entertained, e.g., "The parlor contained her best furniture, carpet, and lamps, and went undisturbed until special guests came."

parson: early, a high honor and distinguished title; now, any preacher, usually of little education or learning, e.g., "In the early colonies, the term parson was bestowed only upon those ministers or preachers of high regard."

parsonage: early, a portion of the tithes, church lands, and offerings set aside for the minister; now, the house or dwelling owned by the church and occupied by the minister, e.g., "His parsonage included the house and 4% of the tithes and offerings received from the parishioners."

partition: a wall; a legal action by which assets, usually real property, are divided; commonly, a division of the assets of a decedent among heirs, e.g., "The will mentioned that a partition was to be built through a bed chamber, meaning that the room was to be divided by a wall"; "Since the land was left to the widow and several children, a partition of the real estate was sought."

partition, deed of: a conveyance by which co-owners divide land they own into smaller tracts; a deed resulting from the action of a court ordering the partition or separation of the interests of the parties or co-owners of any property, e.g., "All having interests by reason of the death of their father **intestate** (q.v.), the children executed a deed of partition dividing the land into a smaller farm for each." Also see **partition.**

partner's desk: a very large, sturdy, flat desk, having knee holes and drawers on both sides of the writing and work surface, and designed for two people to work facing each other, e.g., "The old Mount Airy lawyers had used the oak partner's desk for fifty years."

passage money: sums paid for transportation across the sea, e.g., "Early records show debts for passage money."

passenger lists: those listings of people who were transported, usually across the Atlantic Ocean, from certain places or on certain ships, e.g., "The name Johann Knertzer was found in the passenger lists of the ships departing Bremerhaven in 1728."

Passenger Pigeons: See **_pigeons._**

Passion Week: the week preceding Easter, e.g., "While the term Passion Week was more common in old England, it occasionally is found in early colonial records."

patacoon: a Spanish coin of the 18th century, apparently having a value of about 4S,8p, e.g., "It was not extraordinary that the early 18th-century merchant showed receipt of three patacoons."

patent medicine: so-called, since in the 19th and early 20th centuries patents might be had upon concoctions or nostrums without regard to their merits or medicinal value; any of the myriad concoctions said to have medicinal value, and consisting mostly of alcohol, bitters, plant or tar extracts, flavoring, and sweeteners, e.g., "Drake's Bitters was a very well known patent medicine of the late 19th century."

patents, letters patent: a conveyance of land from a government, either previously untitled or in which a prior title has been extinguished, e.g., "He received forty acres by deed from Smith and one hundred acres by patent from the colony."

paternal lineage: (or ancestry) those ancestors to whom one is related through his or her father, as distinguished from **_maternal lineage_** (q.v.) that relates to the mother, e.g., "Learning of the ancestry of her father's great grandmother was the most difficult of her paternal lineage."

patroon: proprietors of early Dutch New York and New Jersey manors, e.g., "The patroons often left detailed records of their tenants and lessees."

patruus, patruus magnus, patruus major, patruus maximus: father's brother, great uncle on father's side, great-great uncle on father's side, triple-great uncle on father's side.

patten: a separate thick sole attachable to shoes of women, thus elevating the shoe above water and mud, e.g., "She had several pairs of pattens for use on rainy days."

patties, patty: little pies, cakes, or sweet pastries, e.g., "The rhyme 'Patty cake, patty cake, baker's man...', for centuries used to entertain children, derives from the little pastries called patties."

patty pan: a pan for baking **_patties_** (q.v.), e.g., "There were 2 patty pans in the inventory."

pauper schools: established in Maryland as early as 1723; along with apprenticeships, they provided educational opportunities for early Southern poor, e.g., "While children of the rich were tutored or attended private schools, the poor often had to wait for pauper schools."

Paxton Boys: those farmers and frontier settlers from the area of present day Lancaster and Dauphin counties, Pennsylvania, who, in 1764, in reaction to the failure of the assembly to protect them during Pontiac's Rebellion, murdered peaceful Conestoga Indians without justification, and marched on Philadelphia for the purpose of killing those Indians who had fled there for protection, e.g., "The histories of Dauphin and Lancaster counties can lead the genealogist to the Paxton Boys."

pays, pais, per pais: See **country.**

pear cider: See **perry.**

peck: 2 gallons dry measure, e.g., "He had a peck basket."

pectoral, pectoral cross, pectoral pendant: items of decoration or jewelry worn on the chest, e.g., "Her pectoral cross was silver."

pedigree charts: those genealogical forms used to depict one's ancestry over several generations, e.g., "The five-generation pedigree chart is one of the most commonly used forms."

pedigree: one's lineage; the line of ancestry through which one descends; a chart, account, register, or drawing of ancestry, e.g., "His pedigree included Henry VI."

peel, slice, fire slice: a thin, flat, round or oblong, handled cooking utensil used to move bread, etc., about, to, and from a hot oven, e.g., "Peels often listed in early estate inventories." Also see **pey peel.**

peerage, peeress, peer: In England, Wales, Scotland, and Ireland, refers to the five (5) degrees of nobility, e.g., "The peerage - degrees of nobility - were and are (in descending order) duke and duchess, marquis and marquise, earl (very early, called count) and countess, viscount and viscountess, and baron and baroness"; "A woman might be a peeress either in her own right or by reason of marriage to a peer." Also see **peers, baronage,** and **heraldry.**

peers: originally, the nobility; now more commonly, one's equals, e.g., "A trial by one's peers means by a jury of citizens, one's countrymen." Also see **country.**

pellagra: See **blacktongue.**

Pembroke table: a small, usually well made table with short drop leaves forming a square top, e.g., "Pembroke tables were highly favored because of the space saved when not in use." Also see **drop-leaf table.**

pence (d early, or p presently): a British denomination of money used as a standard in colonial America and for many years thereafter in several of the states; early, there were twelve and now but ten pence in a shilling (**S** or **s,** q.v.), e.g., "Tobacco had an established value of two pence (2d) per pound during most of the late 17th century."

pencil post bed: a canopied bed with graceful, thin, narrow, and often gently tapered posts, e.g., "Her only really fine antique was the pencil post bed of her great grandmother."

penknife, pen knife: now, any small knife carried in the pocket; early, so called since the same were usually used to make writing pens by splitting goose quills, e.g., "Since the 1753 inventory revealed the presence of a penknife, perhaps someone in the family could write."

Pennsylvania Dutch ware: See **spatterware.**

Pennsylvania Dutch: See **Dutch.**

Pennsylvania rifle: See **long rifle.**

penny: See **pence.**

pension records: those documents and data having to do with the military movements, activities, and pensions of veterans, and their statements relating to such activities and stipends, e.g., "The proof of her ancestor's combat service was revealed in his pension records."

peonage, peons: bondage for debt; being ordered to serve a creditor nearly as a slave until the labor was thought to have equalled the obligation; it continued in the South until post-Civil War, e.g., "The records of Alabama, Florida, and Georgia reveal many instances of peonage, that should be examined by genealogists." Also see **debtors' prisons.**

peonia: a plot of land 50' X 100', formerly the reward to a Spanish soldier for service, e.g., "Early California records occasionally refer to a peonia of land, thus providing a clue to the service of the original owner."

pepperbox: a small, common, early pistol or handgun wherein an elongated cylinder served as chamber and barrel, capable of shooting five to nine shots without reloading, e.g., "As a lady of the night, she carried a pepperbox in her muff."

peppercorn: a single pepper seed, e.g., "Black pepper was purchased in the form of peppercorns in bulk, and then ground as needed by the housewife."

per stirpes: (Lat., by the stalk of) where one inherits that property, real or personal, that an ancestor would have inherited had that ancestor survived the benefactor, e.g., "Since the fourth son was dead, the devise to him went to his two sons, per stirpes."

perca: See **perch.**

perch, perca, square perch: a unit of measure, 16 1/2 feet; a pole; a rod, e.g., "In 1827, Carner sold 66 square perches of his land."

Percheron: a breed of powerful, heavy draft horses, originally bred in France, usually black or dark gray, e.g., "He had a team of beautiful black Percherons." Also see **draft horses.**

perfumer, perfumier: the occupation of mixing, bottling, and selling perfumes, e.g., "Mr. In den Hoffen is thought to have been an early Philadelphia perfumier."

periapt: See **amulet.**

periodicals: any publications issued at regular intervals; in genealogy, those publications concerned with matters of interest to researchers or concerning particular families, or areas, or both, e.g., "The periodicals maintained by the library included *1880 Hotel Newsletter*, Mrs. Linn's *Rowan County Register*, and the *Parker Register*."

peritonitis: as now, any infection of the peritoneum, e.g., "Before modern drugs, peritonitis almost always was fatal."

periwigs: as now, a wig, e.g., "In colonial times virtually all ladies and gentlemen owned and wore periwigs."

perpetuities (rule against): that provision of law, dating to Henry VIII, that limits restrictions upon the right to convey title to real estate; generally, one may not restrict transfers of title to real estate beyond a life (or lives) in being at the time of the conveyance, plus twenty one additional years, e.g., "His deed 'for so long as St. Peter's Church shall stand' and then to his son's descendents violated the rule against perpetuities."

perquisites: anything gained through work or purchased with personal sums, e.g., "Perquisites mentioned in court reports almost never include property gained through inheritance or purchased with inherited sums."

personero: attorney, e.g., "Many records of early California, New Mexico, and Texas refer to personero, meaning the attorneys in the matter."

perry: pear cider or liquor made from pears, e.g., "Perry, once very popular and easily made, was seldom seen after 1900."

personalty: all property other than real estate, and including money, e.g., "North Carolina treated slaves as personalty, however Virginia often dealt with them as though they were real estate." See **assets,**

Peruvian bark: See **cinchona.**

pesa: 256 lbs., e.g., "Early shipping and commerce records of the Spanish-speaking states often refer to pesas of raw materials."

petit: small, minor; in law, the designation of a jury convened for hearing and determining facts, in open court, e.g., "Of the common juries, there are petit juries and grand juries."

petit four, petit fours, petits fours: small, frosted or sugared cakes, early usually taken with tea, e.g., "Her reference to tea and petit fours revealed that she likely was above the **common** (q.v.) folks in manners and background."

petticoat: early and occasionally, a **waistcoat** (q.v.); usually a decorated underskirt for a woman, e.g., "Sometimes she wore several petticoats, each intended to be slightly visible when she danced and turned."

pettifogger: a lawyer who engages in less than honorable legal activity, or who undertakes petty claims of questionable validity, e.g., "In the days when those of the legal profession were considered people of high honor and station, being branded a pettifogger was a gross insult."

pettitoes: hogs' feet pickled or otherwise prepared for eating; the feet of children, e.g., "Johnson's definition of pettitoes quotes Shakespeare as 'feet in contempt'."

pew: unlike now, an enclosed seat or group of seats in a church, usually restricted to men of affluence who contributed substantially to that church, e.g., "The Washington family had a pew of eight seats."

pewter cupboard: any open shelved cupboard, e.g., "Having no china cabinet, the pewter cupboard was used to store her dinnerware."

pewter, pewterware: early, a metal considered more desirable for eating utensils than all others except platinum, gold and silver; gold and silver, having always been expensive, pewter - a mixture of tin and lead (and sometimes copper) - was long a substitute; made here before 1650, and common by 1675, virtually every estate of any size listed items of pewter, e.g., "Seventeenth-century inventories reveal many pewter plates."

pewterer: a smith of pewter; one who worked pewter, e.g., "Richard Parker was one of the earliest of the Virginia pewterers."

pey peel, pey slice: while *peels* (q.v.) and slices are familiar, "pey" peels are now unknown; may have referred to a greased peel, e.g., "The 1679 Surry county inventory of Judith Parker (copied herein) listed a pey peel."

phaeton: a better made, light, four-wheeled carriage, with a top that often was removable, e.g., "A phaeton that belonged to Andrew Jackson is on display at his home near Nashville."

Philadelphia Wagon Road: See *Wagon Road, Great.*

phlebitis: as now, e.g., "Early, phlebitis was not understood, and often was treated with *blisters* (q.v.)."

phlebotomy, phlebotomist: one who was knowledgeable in the methods of *bleeding* (q.v.) or *cupping* (q.v.), e.g., "The barber also served as the village phlebotomist."

Phoebe lamps: See *betty lamp.*

phonetic: the spelling of words through the sound of the same, rather than through custom or rules of language, e.g., "Her phonetic spelling of the German "Koerner" was C-a-r-n-e-r."

phthisis: See *tuberculosis.*

physician: those who through the use of medicines, herbs, and concoctions sought to cure illnesses; early, clearly distinguished from surgeons (*chirurgeons*, q.v.), e.g., "As a physician, he utilized many of the herbs used by the Indians."

pick, pick-axe: as now, a heavy, handled tool pointed on both ends of the head, and used to break hard ground, cement, etc., "Many inventories reveal the presence of a pick or pick-axe." Also see *mattock.*

picture: early, any depiction of a person or scene, including paintings, etchings, prints, photos, charcoal sketches, etc., e.g., "The pictures appearing in very early inventories were usually silhouettes or oil paintings."

piecrust table: any of several popular styles of small tables, including *tilt-tops* (q.v.) that have a scalloped edge (like a pie crust) on the top surface, e.g., "Her pie crust tea table was *burl* (q.v.) walnut."

pie safe: a small pantry; a short legged, doored cabinet, usually with 3 or 4 shelves, and with one or two drawers, circulation of air being achieved through perforated tin or sheet metal in the panels of the side or door, or both, e.g., "Her pie safe, as were most in the South, was made of pine."

piece of eight: See *milled dollar.*

pigeons: unlike now, meant Passenger Pigeons (now extinct) or doves, e.g., "The pigeons once seen, killed, and eaten by the millions were almost gone by 1880, and were extinct by 1918."

pigeon holes, cubby holes, cubbies: small compartments without doors, typically found in desks, e.g., "The *rolltop desk* (q.v.) had a small drawer and eight pigeon holes inside the *tambour.*

piggin: a pail, usually with a handle, e.g., "In 1820, he wrote of a water piggin."

pigs: See **swine.**

pike: See **turnpike.**

Pilgrims: See **Massachusetts Bay Colony.**

pillion, pilion: a thin seat cushion, attached to the rear of a saddle and used by women riding behind a man, e.g., "She often went with him on short trips, riding on a pillion."

pillory: See **stocks and pillories.**

pilot: a locomotive **engineer** (q.v.).

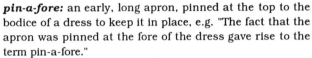

pin-a-fore: an early, long apron, pinned at the top to the bodice of a dress to keep it in place, e.g. "The fact that the apron was pinned at the fore of the dress gave rise to the term pin-a-fore."

pin-money: the allowance to a wife for her clothes and small necessities, e.g., "The term pin-money derives from the necessity that early wives buy **stuff** (q.v.), thread, buttons, pins, and needles in order that clothes might be made."

pincer mold: See **bullet mold.**

pinch: a small amount of seasoning; that amount of **snuff** (q.v.) placed between the teeth and lip or cheek, e.g., "All cooks know what a pinch is"; "To one who dips snuff, a pinch is that quantity he regularly uses."

pinch box: See **snuff box.**

Pinchbeck gold: said to be named for an English watchmaker of the same name who worked early in the 18th century, a gold colored alloy of copper and zinc, sometimes used in jewelry of low quality, e.g., "The 1788 inventory listed a Pinchbeck gold locket." Also see **tombec** and **gold.**

Pine Tree shilling: thought to be the first coinage on this continent, coined in Massachusetts from 1652 until 1684, e.g., "Coin collectors prize their Pine Tree shillings."

pinnace: a light, quick sailboat, usually with one sail, e.g., "Many pinnaces were seen on Chesapeake Bay and Potomac River."

pipe: in some sources, a volume measure of wine, usually 110 gallons, in others, a measure of liquid equal to two **hogsheads** (q.v.); 126 gallons, e.g., "The ship manifest showed 6 pipes of **Madeira** (q.v.)."

piracy, pirates, privateering, privateers: privateering (against enemy shipping) or piracy (against friendly vessels) was common in American waters during the 16th, 17th, and early 18th centuries, e.g., "Of the many pirates, probably the best known in the American colonies were Capt. (William) Kidd, tried and hung in England in 1701, Stede Bonnet (hung in South Carolina in 1718), Blackbeard (William Teach) who was captured, killed, and beheaded in 1718 by a command under Virginia Governor Spottswood, and the privateer Jean Lafitte (1780 - 1825)."

piragua, piraqua: a large canoe with one or two sails, e.g., "Piraguas were common on old Albemarle Sound."

piroque, rowboat: early, small, light open boat, usually with oars, e.g., "Hunt earned money by rowing people to and from Jamestown in a piroque."

pistareen: a Spanish coin of small value, e.g., "Some early references speak of pistareens."

pistole: a coin, variously of France, Spain, and Portugal, having different values at different times, e.g., "His reference to receipt of '12 pistoles' gave little clue as to the value of the goods."

pitapat: a flutter or palpitation, e.g., "The personality of Scarlett's Aunt Pitty Pat was perfectly described by her name."

pitch: thick resin, sap, or tar-like substance that oozes from the bark of pine trees, e.g.,"In the 1720s Thomas Drake sold pitch for ship caulking."

pitcher and bowl: used as a set, a pitcher, usually of 2 to 4 quart capacity, and a bowl of somewhat greater volume and from 10 to 16 inches across by 3 to 6 inches deep; usually placed within a ***bedchamber,*** on a ***commode, basin stand,*** or ***washstand*** (all, q.v.) in order that the occupant might wash, shave, or otherwise be refreshed, e.g., "The pitcher and bowl in the bedchamber were of the finest quality *flowing blue* (q.v.) porcelain."

pitchfork, hayfork: a large, wooden or metal tined, long-handled tool to move hay, straw, etc., e.g., "Every farmer had one or more pitchforks."

pitching pennies: See ***spanfarthing.***

pitkin: a small earthenware container used for boiling liquids, e.g., "The pitkins in the inventory were unusual since all other kettles and pots were of iron or pewter."

pityriasis: any of a number of misunderstood skin diseases where there was a scaling or flaking of skin, e.g., "For pityriasis, he often administered acetic acid, borax, or dilute sulfuric acid."

place: one's home, home place, or residence, e.g., "He wrote that he would not have a bull on the place."

placitum: an agreement, e.g., "Some early records speak of placitum, meaning a bargain or agreement.

Plague of 1874, Locust: the worst grasshopper infestation in American history, ravaged the west from the Canadian border to Texas, e.g., "Virtually every crop on the Great Plains was destroyed by the Plague of 1874."

plaintiff: that person lodging or bringing an action seeking legal remedy or redress, e.g., "The plaintiffs were the ***siblings*** (q.v.) of the defendant." Also see ***defendant.***

plane: as now, a tool for working, shaping, smoothing, or thinning wood, e.g., "Virtually every flat board produced before 1820 was hand planed at great effort."

plankbottom chair, plank bottom chair: a very common, armless, sturdy, simple, utility chair, low and straight backed, with 3 or 4 round, flat, or arrow shaped vertical splats or spindles, and a thick seat often made of a single piece of wood rounded downward at the front, e.g., "During the 18th and 19th centuries, the man of the house made the plankbottom chairs."

plantation house: the main house; the house of the master, e.g., "The servants for the plantation house were literate and well dressed."

planter: very early, one who earned a livelihood through agriculture; later, a title for one of affluence and standing in the community and having substantial agricultural landholdings, e.g., "As a planter, he was expected to support the church, provide men for the militia, and serve in public office as needed."

plasters: cloth or sometimes dough, containing medications and placed over a location of discomfort, e.g., "He advised mustard plasters as a medication for ***pleurisy*** (q.v.)."

plat: a scale drawing of a tract of land, e.g., "The plat revealed that the property was 100 feet wide and 435.6 feet deep, for a total of one acre."

plate warmer: early, a doored, metal box either placed on or attached to a shelf above the cooking surface of a stove, and used to warm plates before serving, e.g., "Her big iron stove had an attached plate warmer."

plate, plating: as now, plating varied in quality and thickness, e.g., "Until about 1840, most plating was done by chemical process; after that, it was accomplished through electrolysis, e.g., "Her silver plated Rogers dinnerware was of very high quality."

platform rocker, spring rocker: any of several styles of rocking chairs mounted a few inches off the floor on a stationary base, said to have been designed to prevent wear of the carpet and the crushing of children's feet by conventional rockers, e.g., "She had a walnut platform rocker of great beauty."

platoon: See ***armies, organization of.***

play horseshoes: See ***horseshoes.***

plead clergy: See ***benefit of clergy.***

pleas and quarter sessions (courts of): courts of general jurisdiction and record; in North Carolina, the lowest courts of record, usually synonymous with terms circuit court and common pleas court, they met quarterly, e.g., "He was charged with hog stealing and was summoned before the April Pleas and Quarter Sessions."

pleasure wagon, market wagon: the former term apparently unknown in the South; a four-wheeled, sturdy vehicle having substantial space for hauling freight, feed, etc., with one seat mounted at the front, and used for both pleasure and utility, e.g., "Most families had only either a buckboard or a pleasure wagon, ***carriages*** (q.v.) being reserved for the more affluent."

plebeyos: farmers or ordinary tradesmen and merchants, e.g., "In the Spanish speaking states references to plebeyos are common."

plethora: unlike now, an excess of blood, e.g., "For the plethora, he advised ***cupping*** (q.v.)."

pleurisy: as now, an inflammation of or infection in the lining of the chest cavity, very often fatal in early times, e.g., "The symptoms of pleurisy having appeared, he was in great fear for his life."

pleurodynia, Devil's grip: sudden chest pain, likely often angina pectoris, supposed to return on the third day after the initial attack, e.g., "For

Devil's Grip, he prescribed ether spray and mustard plasters."

Plough Monday: the Monday after the end of the Christmas season; the Monday after **Twelfth-Day** (q.v.), e.g., "Scarcely observed in the colonies, Plough Monday probably derived from the requirement that work again be undertaken after the holiday season had ended."

plow shares, plow sheers: the leading edge of a plow that cuts the ground, e.g., "Virtually every 17th and 18th century rural home had one or more plow shares."

plow tree: See **horse tree.**

plumcake: a sweet cake made with raisins, e.g., "While the term raisins meant the same in early days as it does today, plumcakes were not made with plums."

plummet: a thin piece of lead, used by early schoolmasters to line paper for the use of their students, e.g., "Lead pencils, as we know them, were too expensive for most students of the 1840s, so the teacher usually had a plummet."

pluries attachment: See **attachment.**

pluries capius: See **capius.**

pluries: a term used to describe a writ, order, or declaration of a court issued for a third time, as in pluries capius or pluries attachment, e.g., "A pluries attachment issued for 'costs and £23/7/10'."

Plymouth colony: that settlement of 101 persons under the authority of the Plymouth Co. (32 "Pilgrims" and 66 others, including Miles Standish and 14 indentured servants), intended to land at the Virginia Co. holdings, but settled at Plymouth, now Massachusetts, in December/January, 1620/21, e.g., "As with the **Jamestown Settlement** (q.v.), fully half the first settlers of the Plymouth colony perished during the first year."

pneumonia: as now, but not understood early, e.g., "For pneumonia, he often administered **blisters** (q.v.), ammonium carbonate, morphine, or mercury salts."

pocket: unlike now, a small pouch or bag, usually with a drawstring and carried attached to the belt or tied around the waist, e.g., "It was said that he always carried a sandwich in his pocket."

pocket book: now, a purse; early, a small record, note, diary, or day book intended to be carried in a **pocket** (q.v.), e.g., "Dr. Drake's Day Book originally was a pocket book."

pocket knife: a medium sized, utility knife with one or more (usually two) folding blades, carried on the person and serving to skin game, cut rope, leather, cloth and other material, whittle, etc., e.g., "He had a **penknife** (q.v.) that remained in the desk, and a pocket knife that he carried at all times."

pocketglass: a small mirror carried on the person, e.g., "The inventory mentioned her clothes and a pocketglass."

podagra: See **gout.**

Point Pleasant, War at: See **Lord Dunmore's War.**

poison bottle: before widespread literacy, and to prevent injury to children, many homemakers stored poisons in bottles having small unpolished bumps or protrusions on the surfaces, thereby warning anyone picking it up of the danger present, e.g., "The medicinal arsenic was always kept in a poison bottle."

poke: originally a Scottish word for sack or pocket; a small to medium sized ***sack*** (q.v.) e.g., "The child said she would share her poke of candy with her brother." Also see ***poke sallet.***

poke sallet, pokeweed sallet: an Appalachian (and Scottish) expression meaning a salad made from tender young shoots of the pokeweed, it a plant of the South having purple/blue berries and thought to have medicinal value, e.g., "She made poke sallet of fresh poke shoots, sugar, vinegar, and bacon grease."

pokeweed: See ***poke sallet.***

pole: in surveying, a measure of length commonly found in early deeds and equalling 16-1/2 feet; a rod or perch; there are forty poles in a furlong and eight furlongs in a mile, e.g., "The town lot was five poles wide and nine poles deep."

polecat: See ***skunk.***

poledavy: a coarse fabric, usually made of flax or wool, e.g., "Poledavy was similar to linsey-woolsey."

polishing iron: a small, light, iron smoothing tool (now, an "iron") for finishing the collars, cuffs, lace, etc., when smoothing clothes, e.g., "Where polishing irons are found, it is likely that the appearance of the man of the family was important."

political subdivision: a division or portion of a larger political and geographical area wherein separate laws and regulations obtain, e.g., "After the Revolution, the colonies gave up much of their authority in order to become political subdivisions of the United States."

poll, polls: originally meant head; people singly considered, as in a ***poll tax*** (q.v.) where a tax is levied on each individual (on each "head") of any class of people; a place where people cast ballots; a voting place, e.g., "The 1694 poll tax exempted only slaves under eight and white children under twelve"; "The polls open at 7:00 a.m."

poll tax: a head tax; literally, a tax on a category of persons within a certain political jurisdiction, usually of a certain minimum age, usually men (or femme sole in some jurisdictions), e.g., "There was a poll tax on all males over sixteen living within the county."

polyandry: the practice of taking more than one husband or male mate. See ***polygamy.***

polygamy: the practice of people of either sex having multiple living mates, where such is legally permissible, but most commonly referring to the status of a man who has more than one wife (***polygyny,*** q.v.); e.g., "***Bigamy*** (q.v.) differs from polygamy, because in the latter, no crime is intended."

polygyny: the practice of taking more than one wife or female mate. See ***polygamy.***

pomade, pomatum: as now, a scented ointment, usually having for cosmetic purposes, e.g., "Her pomatum recipe was simply sweet lard (without salt), to which was added 'any agreeable perfume'."

pomander: unlike now, a ball or clump of scented weeds, spices, perfumes, etc., carried on the person and thought to prevent disease, e.g., "Her pomander was of lilac, rose, and lily petals and **Peruvian bark** (q.v.)." Also see **nosegay.**

pomatum: See **pomade.**

pone, corn pone: corn bread, usually fried, e.g., "Corn pone was a staple of early Ohio and Indiana."

pool checkers: a version of the game of checkers where the pieces may be moved in any direction, thought to have been adapted by early slaves from the French, e.g., "Pool checkers is yet a popular game with many Southerners."

poor farm: those early facilities for the care and keeping of those of little or no estate; a small farm, tended by poor residents where food was grown by them for their own use, e.g., "Martha was residing at the poor farm at the census of 1850."

pop-robin: a batter of eggs and flour boiled in milk, e.g., "Many early New England breakfast consisted of pop-robin and fried pork."

popery: See **papist.**

porch: unlike now, an entryway, e.g., "She came in through the porch."

porridge: early, unlike now, stew or thick broth made by boiling meat until it separated; later, cereal grains cooked in water until soft and thickened, e.g., "The porridge of the 17th century was the stew of the 19th."

porringer: a very common, short-handled, shallow pan or dish, quite usually of wood or metal (often pewter) from which was eaten all manner of foods, including liquids, stews, and cooked cereal grains (hence, the word "porridge"), e.g., "As did virtually every inventory of the 17th and early 18th centuries, his estate included porringers." Also see **trencher.**

port, port side: See **starboard.**

Port, port: a sweet, red wine, originally from Portugal, and very popular in the American colonies, especially with women; e.g., "Very often one would find port being sipped by women while the men were served **sherry (q.v.).** "

porter: a heavy, dark brown ale, e.g., "Until after the **Potato Famine** (q.v.), porter was not commonly found here."

posse, posses: (from the Lat. posse commitatis) any or all of the community that a sheriff may summon to his assistance to aid in capturing criminals or perform service for the public good, e.g. "Unlike the posses of early times, those of the American West usually were deputized volunteers."

posset: an intoxicating drink made from hot milk, sweetening, and spices and curdled by adding wine or ale; probably French and a **syllabub** (q.v.), e.g., "The records of Southern taverns reveal the serving of possets."

post: the public mail service, e.g., "In the 18th century, the post was the only practical way to communicate over a distance."

post and plank fence: See **post and rail fence.**

post and rail fence, post and plank fence, straight fence: a fence of split rails or rough lumber inserted in holes or slots cut into posts that have been driven into the ground at regular intervals, e.g., "Before wire fencing, post and rail fences were very common." Also see **snake fence** and **barbed wire.**

poster bed, four poster bed, canopy bed: beds having posts on each corner to support a framework from which hung the curtains used to keep insects and "drafts" from the sleepers and to provide a measure of privacy, e.g., "The invention of screening meant she no longer needed the side **curtains** (q.v.), so he cut the posts off the poster bed."

posterity: all of one's descendents in a direct line, e.g., "We should all so conduct ourselves that our posterity need not be ashamed."

pot-belly, pot-bellied stove: a small, round heating stove, vented through the wall, designed to burn coal or wood, and usually placed in a central room or parlor, e.g., "With the coming of the Franklin Stove and the iron pot-bellies and cook stoves, the open fireplace became a thing of the past."

pot hook, pothook: simple, iron, "S" shaped hooks used to hang pots in a fireplace, e.g., "Every home had several pot hooks, usually made by the local **blacksmith.**

pot metal: an inexpensive cast metal used for pots, pans, kettles, and similar containers, e.g., "While her pot metal kettles were inexpensive, they usually broke if dropped on the stone **hearth** (q.v.)."

pot rack: as now, a rack, either free-standing or designed to hang on a wall, intended to hold pots and pans when not in use, e.g., "The pot rack hung on the wall near the **bread box** (q.v.)."

potash: the liquid resulting from slowly pouring water through ashes, particularly hickory, e.g., "Potash and lard or other grease cooked together made soap."

Potato Famine: that period of economic distress suffered by the Irish people during the period 1845-1855, during which many emigrated to the United States, e.g., "His ancestors came to New York City at the time of the Potato Famine."

potato scoop: a long-handled tool with 10 to 16 tines placed side by side in the shape of a scoop shovel, e.g., "The potato scoop design made it possible to gather up potatoes with the dirt falling through the tines."

pothecary: See **apothecary.**

poultice, blister: a large patch, usually of cloth, and sometimes of dough, mush, or meal, into which has been placed medication, the whole then applied to a wound, swelling, inflamed or erupted area, e.g., "For the unknown swelling, she made a poultice of turpentine and tobacco juice."

pound: a unit of weight, e.g., "A pound (lb.) avoirdupois is sixteen (16) ounces, however a pound Troy is but twelve (12)." Also see ***Pound.***

Pound (£): a British denomination of money used as a standard in colonial America, the world, and in several of the United States after the Revolution; generally, if a sum was stated in silver or by silver certificate, it was called Pound Sterling; there were and are twenty (20) shillings in a Pound (£), and ten (formerly twelve) ***pence*** (p or d) in a ***shilling*** (S), and four (4) ***farthings*** (q.v.) in a pence, e.g., "The deed related that the ***consideration*** (q.v.) was twenty Pounds Sterling."

poverty: as now, meaning the state of being very poor; in genealogy, usually refers to those legal conclusions concerning assets that were required before pensions were awarded to veterans and others who provided services or material to the government, e.g., "His pension application set forth his infirmities and his condition of poverty."

powder box: usually, a small box for talcum or other powdered cosmetic, e.g., "Her powder box was inlaid with ivory and was ***japanned*** (q.v.)."

powder horn, powder flask: a small waterproof container, often metal or a few inches of the pointed end of an animal horn, with a narrow stoppered opening or neck, used to carry the gunpowder needed for loading ***muzzle loaders*** (q.v.), ***muskets*** (q.v.), etc., e.g., "His powder horn had belonged to his great grandfather."

powdering tub, salting tub, salt tub: a long, deep, large wooden tub or container in which meat was placed for salting or otherwise preserving, e.g., "Their powdering tub was large enough to hold the meat from three hogs."

power of attorney: an instrument by which one has temporary legal authority to act in behalf of another, e.g., "The power of attorney was for the purpose of handling the affairs of his friend who was going abroad."

prayer: that section of a legal pleading where the court is asked to grant some certain relief, money, etc., e.g., "The record stating that she prayed for divorce had nothing to do with religion."

precinct: early, political subdivisions often nearly the equivalent of counties; usually a small area within a town or city, usually now eliminated except for voting purposes, e.g., "Early North Carolina Precincts conducted their affairs as though they were counties, even before they were so declared."

precipe, praecipe: written instructions, usually from a litigant, to the clerk of the court, e.g., "The precipe directed the clerk to summon Jones, thus providing a clue for the researcher that Jones may then have been within that county."

preface: that writing appearing in the front of a literary work that often reveals the rules, discipline, and attitude of the writer as to the subject matter, e.g., "The Preface revealed that the evidence presented would include hearsay and material that could not be substantiated by other records."

prefect, prefet (Fr.): an officer of government charged with the administration of the law in his section or district, e.g., "While a prefect is usually an administrative officer, in New Mexico prefects are probate judges."

preponderance of evidence: a measure of proof; in genealogy, a measure of proof thought insufficient by most scholars, e.g., "When the evidence tending to prove one hypothesis outweighs, even minimally, the evidence tending to prove a contrary view, the first hypothesis is said to prevail 'by a preponderance of evidence'." Also see *clear and convincing.*

prerogative courts: in New Jersey, a court of appeals from decisions of the *orphans' courts* (q.v.), e.g., "While prerogative usually means a peculiar power or authority, when that word appears in New Jersey records the researcher must search out the records of the lower court."

press, to: See *iron (to).*

press: See *clothes press.*

pressbed: what now is called a hide-away bed; a bed designed to be folded up to form a seat or couch, e.g., "Pressbeds are commonly found in early inventories."

pressed, pressed to death, peine forte et dure: a crushing of the naked body by adding iron until the chest cavity collapses, e.g., "One of those charged with witchcraft in old Salem was pressed to death."

pressed glass: glass, some of very high quality (Sandwich, Northwoods, Indiana Tumbler, etc.), with designs impressed while near molten; early, sold as a substitute for the more expensive cut glass, and occasionally then spoken of as "poor man's cut glass", e.g., "The Chrysler Museum has on display some elegant pressed glass."

prest, pressed, were prest: summoned to service by some legal authority, e.g., "Constable Smith prest John and his horse Smith to service of a warrant."

pret, pret oa interet (Fr.): a loan, e.g., "Early Southern records speak of pret a interet, meaning a loan upon which interest was to be charged."

pretermitted heir: a child who has been excluded from a will without mention or provision by a parent, e.g., "In many cases, pretermitted heirs are provided for as though the parent had died *intestate* (q.v.)."

pretty, pretties: See *curios.*

primary sources, primary materials: in genealogy, a term reflecting a view of the user concerning some source; usually refers to those writings thought to be unchanged since originally written; "original" materials, written at or near the time of the event by one who had direct knowledge of the matter and apparently had no reason to be other than candid; sometimes, those materials considered by the user to be more reliable than *secondary sources* (q.v.), e.g., "In his research, he used the court's orders as primary sources."

primer, primmer: very early, a prayer book; 19th and early 20th centuries, a book of fundamental principals and basic facts and numbers, usually used in early schools to teach children the early and first lessons, e.g., "The *McGuffey's First Reader* (q.v.) was also called a primer."

primitive furniture, primitives: furniture made by other than those trained in the art of furniture or cabinet making, e.g., "Most furniture of early rural families was primitive, it having been made by the men of the family."

primogeniture: the ancient, superior, and exclusive right of the first born male to succeed to the family property; a doctrine manifest in many early estates by which the eldest son, or his eldest son, etc., inherited family property to the exclusion of all siblings, the widow, and any other relative without regard to need; an ancient principle, abolished in Georgia in 1777; North Carolina in 1784; Virginia in 1785; Maryland and New York, 1786; South Carolina, 1791; Rhode Island, 1798. Except in RI, land was inherited equally with the eldest son receiving a double portion, e.g., "Even where outlawed, the principles of primogeniture appear in many early wills."

privateers: See ***piracy.***

privy, a necessary: an outdoor toilet; a dug pit, over which a bench with holes and a small, doored shelter were built, and used for personal relief, e.g., "Privies were known to all, rich and poor alike, until the advent of indoor plumbing in the 19th century."

probate, probate courts: as in to "probate a will," that legal process by which a will is given effect; sometimes, those legal processes involving any estate, testate or intestate; relating to proof of wills; presently (in American law) a general term used to refer to any matter in which probate courts have jurisdiction, such as matters of death, orphans, adoption, children, lunacy, guardians' estates, etc.; often called orphans' courts or surrogate courts, e.g., "In most States, a judge of a probate court is elected for a term of years"; "The entry declared the will to have been 'admitted to probate', meaning that it had been ***proven*** (q.v.) and was subject to such proceedings as might be necessary to its purposes."

probative value: that weight or evidentiary worth of a bit of evidence as it relates to some matter in question or being proved, e.g., "The Bible entry had great probative value in determining his age at death."

procedendo (writ of): an ancient and still used writ by which a higher court orders a lower court to proceed in its duty, e.g., "The Supreme Court, by a writ of procedendo, ordered the lower court to proceed with the charge against the defendant."

processioning, processioners: under the ancient authority and guidance of the parish, the walking (processioning) of the boundaries of private lands within the parish by appointed, knowledgeable, and responsible parishioners, in order that boundaries be determined and boundary disputes be resolved, e.g., "The processioners of Newport Parish confirmed the Drake lines in late March of 1723."

Proclamation Money: late 18th-century currency, particularly of North Carolina, the value as a means of settlement said to be established by proclamation, e.g., "He paid for the land with Proclamation money."

professional researcher: those who do genealogical research for others for hire, e.g., "She hired a professional researcher to search in the D.A.R. Library for her veteran ancestor."

profit a prendre: a right to remove something such as minerals or crops from land, e.g., "One of the profits a prendre was the right to harvest the wheat."

progenitor, progeny: a common ancestor; the collective descendants of a common ancestor, e.g., "Her progeny included thirty grandchildren and fifty-four great-grandchildren."

prohibition (writ of): an ancient and still used writ by which a court orders that another arm of government refrain from acting in a certain fashion, e.g., "The writ of prohibition ordered that the assessor discontinue with increases in the assessed value."

Promontory Point (UT): that place in present-day Utah where the Central Pacific and the Union Pacific tracks met to form the first transcontinental railroad, e.g., "It was at Promontory Point, on 10 May, 1869, that the Jupiter and Engine 19 met, ***cowcatcher*** (q.v.) to cowcatcher, signifying the completion of the great railroad."

prones: prunes, e.g., "She crushed and boiled prones for the small children."

proof: in genealogy, that accumulation of evidence sufficient to establish some matter of lineage, e.g., "The proof of his death date came from the death certificate, the family Bible, and the newspaper."

proper English: See ***King's English.***

propres: any property inherited from any blood relative, e.g., "Early Louisiana records sometimes speak of ***propriete*** (q.v.) propres, providing a clue as to a relative."

propriete (Fr.): property, e.g., "Many early records speak of propriete propres, meaning property inherited from a blood relative."

prostatitis: as now, e.g., "For prostatitis, he advised the use of hot enemas and suppositories of opium."

protestants: any religious group that is other than Roman Catholic, e.g., "The word protestant derives from protests by Luther and others against Catholic doctrine."

prothonotary: the principal clerk of courts in some jurisdictions, e.g., "In New York and Pennsylvania the Prothonotary is the counterpart to the Virginia Clerk to the Circuit Court."

prove: the accomplishment of accumulating evidence sufficient to meet the requirements of a discipline as to a matter unproven or at issue; the act of confirming through witnesses that a writing is the valid and subsisting will of a decedent, e.g., "She proved the lineage through Bible entries, censuses, and tax records"; "The witnesses to the will appeared and proved it." Also see ***proof.***

province: in early genealogy, a place or geographical area considered to have a measure of autonomy, government, or body of laws that differentiate it from other places or destinations, e.g., "He went out to the English provinces."

Psalm Book: See ***Bay Psalm Book.***

psalter: a psalm book: the Biblical book of Psalms, e.g., "The psalter of the inventory likely was an ordinary volume of psalms."

pub: an **ordinary** (q.v.); a small tavern dispensing alcoholic beverages, minimal food, and not providing overnight accommodations, e.g., "Early 20th-century Boston was widely known for its neighborhood Irish pubs."

public house: See **tavern.**

public(k) times: apparently used almost exclusively in the South, especially in Jamestown and Williamsburg, meant those days during which the general assembly (House of Burgesses) was in session, e.g., "Publick times were always well attended, especially after Williamsburg became the capital in 1799."

puddings: See **desserts, early.**

puerperal fever, puerperal convulsions, purple fever, childbed fever: early, a seizure during labor or immediately thereafter, often fatal, and generally accompanied by loss of consciousness or mental aberration; a dreaded, usually fatal infection, early thought to be a disease peculiar to those giving birth and not understood to be a likely result of unsanitary conditions, e.g., "Many a young woman was said to have died of puerperal fever."

pummy: apparently, anything left over from farm production that could be fed to livestock, e.g., "Some early writings speak of pummy in association with cattle."

pumps: See **shoes.**

punch: intoxicating beverage; a flavored drink, usually containing fruit juices, and in early times of considerable alcohol content, e.g., "Early punches often were made of wine or rum and fruit juices, hence the expression 'it has a punch'."

puncheon: heavy lumber, roughly dressed, for use as timbers or floors, e.g., "Puncheon floors occasionally were found in early schoolhouses, otherwise the floors were dirt."

punk, spunk: rotten wood taken from the inside of a maple tree, used to **carry fire** (q.v.), e.g., "It was easier to borrow fire from a neighbor by carrying spunk than by carrying a shovel or container of hot ashes."

punt: a small, flat-bottomed, usually two-seated boat with oars or poles, e.g., "There was usually a punt or two waiting at the Jamestown landing."

puny: in a state of poor health, usually of a temporary nature, e.g., "She wrote that her whole family had been puny that winter."

pupillus: in Civil law, one under the age of puberty, often an orphan or ward, e.g., "Early Louisiana records often speak of orphans of pupillus."

pur autre vie: during the life of another, e.g., "Interests in land given to one pur autre vie lapse when that other (autre) person dies."

purchase money mortgage: See **mortgage deed.**

purge, purgatives, cathartics: early thought to be helpful in myriad ailments and complaints; causing the evacuation of the body, especially the bowels, e.g., "In their desperate efforts to affect cures, early physicians often administered violent purges, including mercuric chloride."

Puritans: those who insisted on strict conformity to the doctrines of the Anglican Church, e.g., "During the 17th century the Puritans became a powerful force in both England and the American colonies."

purser: that person charged with keeping the books and accounts of a ship, e.g., "Dan Boucher was once the Purser of the Quaker ship *Blessing.*"

putting on airs: See **airs, putting on.**

Q

quadrangles, quads, topos, USGS topographical maps: very fine and detailed maps of small geographical areas published by the U.S. Geological Survey and available for much of the U.S., e.g., " She found quadrangles for the township at the Chamber of Commerce office." Also see **Geological Survey, U.S.**

quadrille: a five-part square dance for eight people; a card game for four people, e.g., "They danced a quadrille and several *Virginia reels."*

quadroon, quarterone: a person having one negro and three white grandparents, e.g., "While he appeared to be of Caucasian background, he was, in fact, a quadroon."

quads: See **quadrangles.**

Quakers: that religious discipline organized in England about 1650, and best known on the American continent through William Penn and Pennsylvania, e.g., "While early the colonies saw widespread persecution of the Quakers, by 1685 that discipline was active and prospering, including in North Carolina and Tidewater Virginia."

qualify: a recognition that one has met some requirement for admittance, office, or recognition, e.g., "As the widow and relict of the deceased, she qualified as administratrix of her husband's estate."

quantum meruit, quantum valebant: that which he or she deserved; that amount the material or goods were worth, e.g., "Early lawsuits were sometimes styled 'in quantum meruit', meaning that the complainant had not been paid for work or services, and 'in quantum valebant, meaning that he had not been paid for goods sold, in both cases often revealing the occupations of ancestors."

quarter chest: See **chest, chest of tea.**

Quarter Eagle: a U.S. gold coin having a face value of $2.50, e.g., "Every housewife of the 19th century recognized a Quarter Eagle."

quarter houses: slaves quarters or cabins, e.g., "The **overseer** (q.v.) wrote that the quarter houses were in need of repair."

quarter section: See **section.**

quarter sessions, courts of: See **common pleas, courts of.**

quarter sessions of the peace (courts of): Pennsylvania courts of misdemeanor criminal jurisdiction, usually acting at the time of or by the judges of **oyer and terminer** (q.v.), e.g., "The Ohio county court has criminal jurisdiction identical to the Pennsylvania courts of quarter sessions of the peace."

quarter sessions: See **pleas and quarter sessions, courts of.**

quarterly courts: Kentucky courts that hear appeals from the **justices of the peace** (q.v.) and have original jurisdiction in most civil cases, e.g., "The records of the Kentucky Quarterly Courts are excellent research sources."

quarterone: See **mulatto** and **quadroon.**

quarto: usually, the size of a book; about 12" X 9 1/2"; a 19" X 24" sheet folded twice resulting in 8 pages (4 leaves) for printing, e.g., "The book was bound in quarto." See also **folio.**

quay: See **key.**

quean: very early, a whore, e.g., "Our terms 'queenie' and 'queen', meaning a woman of the night, derive from the ancient term quean."

Queen Anne's War, War of Spanish Succession: 1702 - 1713; in the American colonies, those conflicts between New Englanders against Minas, Beaubassin, and Fort Royal brought on by the Abenaki attacks on Deerfield, Massachusetts, and Winter Harbor, Maine, and between armed Carolinians against St. Augustine, all to prevent the alliance of France and Spain, and ending at the Peace of Utrecht (1713), e.g., "But few records remain concerning those who took up arms in Queen Anne's War."

Queen Bess: See **Good Queen Bess.**

queens and kings, reigns of: See **regnal years.**

query: in genealogy, a request for information, accompanied by a brief summary of a research problem, e.g., "Her query read 'Seek those researching the John Meachum family of 1810 Vermont.'"

quick, quickening, quick with child, quick child: alive; first discernible movements of a fetus, e.g., "The expression quick with child meant that the fetus had moved."

quick consumption: See **tuberculosis.**

quietus: acquitted, as in dismissal after completion of a task; the discharge of one after service of payment of obligation, e.g., "The Maryland court ordered a quietus, he having met the obligations."

quill pen: an early writing instrument; the unfeathered end of a tail feather of a bird, usually a goose, split lengthwise to permit a flow upon dipping the same in ink, e.g., "His quill pen writing was difficult to read, probably because of the pen, the quality of the ink, or the texture of the paper."

quilt: as now, e.g., "In early times, all clothing scraps were saved in order that quilts might be made."

quilt frame: a large, usually collapsible wooden framework upon which is stretched cloth to be made into a **quilt** (q.v.), e.g., "The quilt frames were moved to wherever the **quilting bee** (q.v.) was to be held."

quilting bee: a gathering of women for the purpose of making quilts, during which there was social exchange and instruction in the art for young girls, e.g., "Every neighborhood had its quilting bees."

quinsy, quinsey: any severe sore throat or 'strep throat', e.g., "Just prior to the development of the pneumonia that is said to have killed him, George Washington complained of quinsy."

quire: a merchant's measure of writing paper, usually 24 sheets, e.g., "In the mid 18th century, writing paper was very expensive, often the equivalent of $30.00 for a quire."

quit-claim, quitclaim: often imprecisely called "quit-claim deed"; an instrument by which there is transferred whatever interest one may have in property (usually real estate) to someone else, and which contains no warranties concerning the nature of the title being transferred, e.g., "Even though he probably had no interest, the court ordered him to quit-claim whatever he might be found to have."

quit-rents, quitrent: a rent or payment of an annual fee by a *freeholder* (q.v.) for the use of land; a tax, after which one had no further taxes due the state for that period, e.g., "The 1704 list of those Virginians who were chargeable with quit-rents is a very valuable genealogical source."

quoddy boat: a New England fishing boat, usually pointed on both ends with one sail, e.g., "The lobstermen of old Maine often worked from quoddy boats."

R

rabbet plane, rabbet saw: a plane with a sharp edge, used by *joiners* (q.v.), **cabinetmakers** (q.v.) and **carpenters** (q.v.) to make grooves (rabbets) in wood, e.g., "His rabbet plane had a sharp edge, facilitating cutting rabbets."

rack: a device of punishment that slowly pulls the body apart; also, one of several **gaits (q.v.)** of horses, e.g., "Even though we occasionally **pressed** (q.v.) people to death, the rack apparently was not known in the American colonies."

Raleigh's Colony: See **Crotoan Inscription.**

ram: a male sheep, e.g., "The inventory listed a ram and three **ewes** (q.v.)."

rancho: a small group of habitations or persons and their houses; a hamlet or small village, e.g., "The ranchos of early Texas and California writings were not individual houses."

rapine: the forcible taking of one's property, against his or her will, e.g., "Early comments about rapine had nothing to do with sex."

rasp: a large, heavy toothed wood file, e.g., "There were rasps of several sizes in his shop."

rattan furniture: chairs, settees, etc., made of woven rattan (the tough stems of palms), e.g., "The **Gay Nineties** (q.v.) brought to the market the popular rattan furniture."

rattlesnake root: black snakeroot, the common medication for snake bite, e.g., "The 17th-century colonials swore by black snakeroot for bites of any kind."

re, in re: as now, in the matter of, in regard to; e.g., "The record titled 're Susannah Drake,' meant in the matter of certain affairs of that woman."

reader (for microfilm or microfiche): that optical equipment or machine used to view microfilm or microfiche, e.g., "When she arrived at the library, all the readers were in use."

real estate, real property, realty: refers to land or interests or ownership in land; all other property is personalty, e.g., "Her estate consisted of twenty acres of real property and personalty worth $3,000.00."

ream: a measure of paper, usually now 500 sheets, e.g., "The storekeeper had three reams of paper that he usually sold in *quires* (q.v.)."

rebeck: a three-stringed fiddle, e.g., "Early French immigrants sometimes brought their rebecks, often the only musical instrument in the settlement."

Rebels, Rebs: usually referred to Southern soldiers, and occasionally to any Southerner during the Civil War, e.g., "Johnny Reb was the counterpart of Billy Yank."

reck: take heed, be mindful of, as in reckon, e.g., "A Texas court recognized the word reck."

reclusion: incarceration, usually at hard labor, e.g., "A number of Louisiana records speak of imprisonment for crime as reclusion."

Reconstruction: meaning the process by which those states that had seceded again became a part of the Union, e.g., "The congressional acts between 1867 and 1878 by which the former Confederate states again gained representation and voice in the U.S. government were known as the Reconstruction Acts." Also see *Civil War.*

record (to), registrar: the act of entering any document or writing into the public record, whether by a clerk, recorder, register of deeds, or otherwise in accordance with "recording statutes"; an innovation peculiar to the early American colonies and rarely previously found in England, e.g., "Contrary to popular notion, most early transfers of land were recorded."

recorder: in genealogy, an early, common, wooden wind instrument, similar to a flute, e.g., "Among her possessions were a flute and a recorder."

rector: the title given one who is a spiritual head of a Catholic church; a member of the clergy who has been elected to be in charge of a parish, e.g., "Bayley was one of the rectors of Upper Nansemond Parish." Also see *rectory.*

rectory, benefice: in England and the early colonies, the whole of the Episcopal church structures, glebes, lands, tithes, etc., of a parish, e.g., "The rectory of Upper Nansemond consisted of three churches."

Redcoat: a word of contempt for a soldier, e.g., "The term Redcoat, as a means of showing disdain for the soldier, was not unique to the Revolution; it was as common in old England as in the colonies."

Redemptioners, free willers: one who has undertaken to labor for some agreed or specified time period (average 4 years) in order to redeem himself or herself from the obligation owing to another for transportation or training given, e.g., "As a Redemptioner, her ancestor had been required to work for four years to pay the total cost of his transportation." Also see **indentured servant** (q.v.)

redeye: as now, a severe inflammation of the eyes, e.g., "Dr. Lockhart administered a boric acid **collyrium** (q.v.) for the redeye."

redgum: a disease of the newborn, usually characterized by an eruption or by dark coloration of the gums, e.g., "Even though sometimes treated as a symptom of some worse ailment, redgum usually was short-lived and harmless."

redhibition: a suit to set aside a sale for the reason that the goods are worthless or so difficult of use that the buyer would not have purchased it had he known, e.g., "The Louisiana civil code permits suits of redhibition, often leading researchers to customer ancestors."

redware: inexpensive stoneware, red by reason of the iron oxides in the clay, e.g., "She had a pitcher and several other items of redware."

reek: unlike now, steam, smoke, or vapor, e.g., "The comments that the baker's shop reeked of bread did not mean that it had a foul odor."

reel (a dance): See **Virginia reel.**

reel, rele: a device (revolved by hand) upon which yarn or thread was wound usually as it was spun, e.g., "Early inventories showing spinning wheels also usually listed a reel or rele."

regiment: See **armies, organization of.**

Regina: See **Rex.**

registrar: See **record (to).**

regnal years: the years of the reign of a monarch, early used as a means of establishing the dates of instruments and their terms, e.g., "Following are regnal years often encountered by the American genealogist:

>Elizabeth I, Nov. 17, 1553 - March 23, 1603
>James I, March 24, 1603 - March 26, 1625
>Charles I, March 27, 1625 - January 29, 1649
>Commonwealth, January 30, 1649 - May 28, 1660
>Charles II, May 29, 1660 - Feb. 5, 1685
>James II, Feb. 6, 1685 - Feb. 12, 1689
>William and Mary, Feb. 13, 1689 - March 7, 1702
>Anne, March 8, 1702 - July 31, 1714
>George I, August 1, 1714 - June 10, 1727
>George II, June 11, 1727 - Oct. 24, 1760
>George III, Oct. 25, 1760 - Jan 28, 1820
>George IV, Jan. 29, 1820 - June 25, 1830
>William IV, June 26, 1830 - June 19, 1837 and
>Victoria, June 20, 1837 - Jan. 21, 1901

Thus, a document dated the 1st of March during the fourth year of the reign of Queen Anne was executed March 1, 1706."

regular army: that force of armed men maintained over a long period, is usually better trained, and is not assembled for any immediate purpose, e.g., "Units such as the 1st U.S. Sharpshooters, 7th U.S. Cavalry, 19th U.S. Heavy Artillery, etc., were regular army, while volunteer and conscript units, such as the 55th Ohio Volunteer Infantry, were not 'regular' and did not carry the designator 'U.S.'"

Regulators, War of the Regulation: that association of western South Carolina settlers and farmers who (1769-1771) sought schools, roads, churches, courts - government - and refused to pay taxes to far off Charleston until they received the same, e.g., "The Battle of Alamance between the 2000-plus Regulators and the state militia, resulted in the defeat and hanging of six Regulators and the end of their organization."

reinsman: usually, one who drove an animal-drawn stagecoach or passenger vehicle team; sometimes, any driver of a team of multiple animals, e.g., "In 1850 the reinsmen of the Columbus to Pomeroy stage in 1850 were colorfully described."

relationship: in genealogy, the extent to which one is related to another, whether by **affinity** (q.v.), **consanguinity** (q.v.), legal action, or choice, e.g., "Her relationship was unknown until the family Bible record was discovered."

relative: as now, a kinsman or kinswoman, e.g., "A relative may be by blood or affinity."

release, release of mortgage: See **mortgage.**

reliability of source: in genealogy, that measure of certainty to be accorded any bit of evidence as it relates to an issue to be proved, e.g., "Having found a headstone bearing one date and a column in a newspaper stating a different one, she had to consider reliability of sources."

relict: a widow or widower, e.g., "Parker married the relict of William Huntt."

remainder: generally, an interest in land that will take effect upon the termination of some prior interests, e.g., "Through his remainder interest, he gained possession at the death of his father, who had been a life tenant." Also see **life estate.**

render, rendering: cooking down of any substance; usually, the boiling down of fat from hogs, thereby producing lard and **cracklins** (q.v.), e.g., "At **killing time** (q.v.), enough lard was rendered to last the winter."

repertory, repertories: the notes kept by notaries public concerning all contracts acknowledged before them, e.g., "Early repertories yet remain in archives of Southern states, particularly Louisiana."

res: a thing, object, or asset; subject matter, particularly of a lawsuit, e.g., "Many courts' reports and writings refer to the res of the action, usually meaning the subject matter being disputed - a tract of land, a cow, a portfolio of stock certificates."

residence: See **domicile.**

reverse indexes: indexes to deeds compiled alphabetically in the surnames of the grantees/transferees (usually the buyer), e.g., "Since he knew his ancestor had lived in the area, he searched the reverse index to see if the ancestor had bought land there." Also see **direct indexes,** q.v., and **grantor/grantee indexes.**

Revolutionary War: See **War of Independence.**

revolver: a repeating handgun (pistol), so designed as to mechanically move 4 to 9 (usually 6) pre-loaded rounds into firing position; first patented by Samuel Colt in 1835, e.g., "The Colt revolvers are said to have won the West."

Rex, Regina: monarchs, male and female, e.g., "Since monarchs are said to have no surnames, Elizabeth Regina means simply Elizabeth, Queen."

rick: a measure of firewood measuring 4' X 4' X 4'; one-half a **cord** (q.v.), e.g., "They burned nearly a rick of wood per week in their big fireplaces."

riddle: a coarse sieve, e.g., "The inventory listed a colander and a riddle." Also see **colander, searce,** and **tea strainer.**

ridgling: a horse with one testicle removed, e.g., "Texas writings reveal that horses were sometimes half castrated, called ridglings - thereby bringing about a more gentle disposition."

riding chair: a two-wheeled, single-seated vehicle, much like the now-familiar Chinese rickshaw, often used in early cities, pulled by a person, and usually for hire, e.g., "Rather than tie his horse in the sun for the day, he took a riding chair to the capitol building."

rifle, rifling, rifled musket: a hand-held firearm with spiralled grooves in the barrel thereby causing greater accuracy by reason of the spin imparted to the projectile, e.g., "The invention of rifling was the end of the inaccurate old smoothbore **muskets** (q.v.)."

rixdollar: the German (reichsthaler), Dutch (rijksdaalder), or Danish (rigsdaler) coins having a value equal to about 4S, 6p (about $25.00) in the late 18th and early 19th centuries, e.g., "Immigrants often arrived at Philadelphia and New York with rixdollars in their purses, only to be cheated by the **money changers** (q.v.) of the day."

road cart: See **sulky.**

road wagon: a usually inexpensive, topless passenger vehicle or carriage with four large wheels and one seat for two people, e.g., "The ordinary road wagon could be purchased for 25% to 40% less than a better quality one-seated, topless **buggy** (q.v.)."

roadhouse: a business offering food, drink, and entertainment for travellers and food and drink for their animals, and usually without overnight accommodations, e.g., "Settler's roadhouse on the Bucyrus pike at Waldo was well known to Ohioans."

roads, early: Zane's Trace from Wheeling, WV, to Maysville, KY, Braddocks Road from the Potomac to Fort Pitt, Forbes Road from Fort Loudon to Fort Pitt, and Gists Road from Fort Cumberland to the upper Monongahela River were 4 of the earliest roads that served western Pennsylvania and the **Ohio country** (q.v.); shortly thereafter, other famous ways were Philadelphia-Lancaster Turnpike, then Knoxville Road that tied together Wilderness Road (through Cumberland Gap and north into Kentucky) and the Cumberland Mt. settlers, and Walton Road (west and south through Tennessee and beyond); the National Road (Cumberland Rd.) from Cumberland, MD, to Wheeling, now WV; the Territorial Road that opened up southern MI, and the Chicago Road that opened up northern IN and MI.

roan: a color, especially of horses and dogs, e.g., "Dr. Drake gave Mary Alice a roan mare."

Roaring Twenties: that period after World War I during which prosperity was at hand, the stock market seemed to have no ceiling, world dominance by the U.S. seemed apparent, and a measure of personal freedom was felt by reason of high wages, shorter work days and weeks, and inexpensive automobiles, e.g., "The Roaring Twenties came to an abrupt end with the collapse of the stock market in October and November of 1929, particularly marked on Black Thursday, 24 October 1929."

rockaway: a light, 4-wheeled carriage with a permanent top and lowerable, waterproofed side curtains, e.g., "The rockaway was a favorite of those of new affluence who yet thought a doored carriage to be pretentious."

rocker bench, rocker settee, rocking settee: a **mammy bench** (q.v.) with rockers, e.g., "She often sat on the rocker bench, entertaining and rocking the baby while chatting with her guests."

rocker, rocking chair: early, a rocker had much shorter rocker boards than now, especially in front where they extended not much more than an inch; often primitively made by attaching short rockers to straight chairs, e.g., "The very short original bars on the rocker revealed to her that it was very old."

rod: a unit of measure, especially by surveyors, a pole, 16 1/2 feet, e.g., "The lot was 10 rods deep and 6 rods wide; about 165' X 100'.

roles: unknown, "On June 24 Ezekiel Brown bought 8 ells of roles."

roll wagon: a horse-drawn vehicle of commerce, having rollways and bars so mounted as to roll barrels frontward and backward and thereby facilitate loading and unloading, e.g., "Virtually every early brewer had a roll wagon, since beer was universally sold in wooden barrels."

rolltop desk, rolltop, curtain top desk, tambour desk: a common, popular desk of the Victorian period to now, usually of oak or walnut, with a kneehole and drawers on both sides below, a retractable slatted top (the tambour) that was either of quarter circle or "S" shape, behind which were several small drawers and **pigeon holes** (q.v.), e.g., "Her "S" curve rolltop desk was of walnut, and had belonged to her grandfather."

rood: one-fourth acre, e.g., "The lot was a 1 1/2 roods, about 3/8 acres."

room: in genealogy, meant in the place of or instead of, e.g., "As overseer of the road, he served in the room of Peter Smith."

room and board: See **board.**

room freshener: See **vinegar of the 4 thieves.**

rope bed: until the early part of the 19th century, most beds were made with ropes stretched within a frame (**bedstead,** q.v.) to support the **ticks**

(q.v.) or primitive mattresses, after rope beds came slatted beds, e.g., "Even though likely made earlier, some rope beds were still in use in the early twentieth century."

Rosenoble: a very early English coin having a value of 3/4 Pound Sterling, e.g., "There is at least one 17th-century Virginia reference to a Rosenoble."

Rough Riders: that force of cavalry under Col. Theodore Roosevelt (later Pres.) that saw service in the **Spanish American War** (q.v.), e.g., "The Rough Riders were dismounted during the famous San Juan Hill attack."

Roundhead: very early, a Puritan or a follower of Cromwell, so named by reason of the practice of cutting their hair in a short and round style, e.g., "While in early Virginia many were said to be Cavaliers, very few references to Roundheads are found."

Royal Navy: the navy of Great Britain, e.g., "The Royal Navy has been so called since the 17th century."

rubella: See **measles.**

rubican: probably, an early name for what we now know as an the Appaloosa horse; a horse of dark color with a small spots of white or gray on the rump, e.g., "Early New York writings mentioning rubicans likely referred to horses marked like our Appaloosas."

rubstone: See **whetstone.**

ruff: that usually heavily starched, linen, neckpiece commonly worn in the 16th and 17th centuries, e.g., "Queen Elizabeth was commonly portrayed wearing a ruff."

rug: early, any bed or table cover or bedspread; coarse, nappy, large woolen cloth or heavy cloth upholstery; later, as now, a floor covering, e.g., "His 1740 inventory included a **bed and furniture** (q.v.), a ticking bag, and a rug."

rule: a ruler, e.g., "The rule was like another thumb to the **cabinetmaker** (q.v.)."

rule against perpetuities: See **perpetuities, (rule against).**

rule of three: an early measure of one's education; often, the "three Rs"; meaning that one could "read, write, and cast accounts" or "...and cypher," that is, do simple addition, subtraction, multiplication and division; occasionally meant that specific knowledge of mathematics through algebra sufficient to determine an unknown 4th number where the other three were known, e.g., "The plantation owner had provided that his sons were to be educated to the 'rule of three', likely meaning that they were to be taught to read, write, and understand the business accounts of the farm."

rum, Jamaica spirits: a high alcohol content liquor enjoyed by the American colonists, e.g., "The 1694 manifest listed three barrels of Jamaica spirits."

rush bottom chair, cane bottom chair, cane chair, cane back chair: any chair with a woven bottom, back, or sides, usually of rush, cane, or thin wooden strips, e.g., "She had three primitive chairs, two rush bottom, and one **plank bottom** (q.v.)."

Russia leather, Russian leather: a fine, highly polished leather, usually black, burgundy or deep red, and early considered a mark of substantial wealth, e.g., "In 1675, and revealing of her affluence, Mrs. Parker had four Russia leather chairs."

S

saber, sabre: the "sword" of a cavalryman; an early weapon with a long, slightly curved, heavy blade, e.g., "Griffith's will bequeathed to his son his 'sabre and **Buckanear gun** (q.v.)'."

sack: a sweet wine, early from the Canary Islands, e.g., "Many slave traders also carried sack, particularly to the Southern colonies."

sackcloth: as suggested by the word, a coarse material (often hemp) used to make feed, grain, or **tote sacks** (q.v.), e.g., "The very poor often made play clothes for children from sackcloth."

sad: made of iron, e.g., "In the inventory, her skillets were listed as sad." Also see **sad iron** (q.v.).

sad griddle: See **griddle.**

sad iron: by the 18th century and after, tool used to smooth (press) cloth, having a detachable handle, usually weighing from 4 to 6 lbs, and large enough to retain heat longer than a flatiron, e.g., "She had three sizes of sad irons, 4 lbs, 5 1/8 lbs, and 5 3/8 lbs." Also see **flatiron,** and **iron.**

sad ware, sadware: any iron cooking utensil or ware, e.g., "Among the items listed were two large, sad ware kettles."

saddler: one who made saddles, e.g., "Early records frequently speak of harnessmakers and saddlers."

safe: unlike now, a pantry, e.g., "The safe mentioned in the early floor plan had nothing to do with money or jewelry."

safeguard: a long, ladies' outer coat, worn over other apparel to protect the clothing beneath from water, mud, etc., "Her safeguards saw little use after she became too old to ride."

salamander: unlike now, a medium to long handled, flat piece of iron, heated to high temperature and held over any cooking food where the top is to be seared or browned, e.g., "The cook used the salamander to brown her pie crusts after the filling had cooked."

Salem Witch Trials: that series of charges and trials during and immediately before 1692 that culminated in some 14 women and 5 men being hanged, one man being pressed to death, and 4 dying in jail (none were burned), e.g., "The Trasks were among those caught up in the Salem Witch Trials." Also see **witchcraft.**

saleratus: soda, sodium bicarbonate, as now, used in cooking, e.g., "The scarcity of 'soda' in early Pennsylvania, led to the use of corn cobs burned to ashes and settled as a substitute saleratus."

sallet: See **poke sallet.**

saloon table: See **tavern table.**

saloon: See **tavern.**

salt box: See **salt dish.**

salt cellar: See **salt dish.**

salt dish, salt, salt box, salt cellar, dredging box, duster: small, shallow, open dishes; until granulated salt was widely marketed, there were no salt shakers, and salt was placed in open containers, either a larger one in the center of the table for the use of all, or, in refined homes, in smaller dishes at each setting, e.g., "Mrs. Vanderbilt is said to have had leaded, cut glass salt dishes in their retreat in Asheville."

salt: See **salt dish.**

salting tub: See **powdering tub.**

saltpeter, saltpetre: usually potassium nitrate; a nitrate used to make gunpowder and explosives; a compound thought to have medicinal value, e.g., "Saltpeter and other potassium salts were administered as diuretics, and thought valuable in treating heart disease."

salve tins: a small lidded tin or metal container used to keep salves, lotions, etc., e.g., "She washed all old salve tins in order that they might be reused." Also see **ointment pot.**

salver: a tray for serving finger foods; in the colonies, usually a pan to catch drippings, e.g., "She served hors d'oeuvres on a silver salver"; "There was a salver near the fireplace." Also see **dripping pan.**

sampler: a cloth, needlework **picture** (q.v.), and sample of the sewing skills of the maker, usually a young girl, they bore the name of the maker, and also displayed numbers, letters, sayings, proverbs, Biblical verses, and decorations, e.g., "The sampler was dated 1838, and was made by Elizabeth Carner."

sand glass: See **hour glass.**

Santa Claus: See **St. Nicholas.**

Santa Fe Trail: that trail that opened commerce and trade with the east and Missouri from the far southwest, e.g., "William Becknell who must be given considerable credit for the opening of trade over the Santa Fe Trail."

SASE: a self-addressed stamped envelope enclosed with requests made to others for genealogical assistance, e.g., "Good manners require that a SASE be included if response is expected."

sash: a raisable window, usually paned, e.g., "He tore open the shutters and theew up the sash.'"

sash glass: window panes, e.g., "The sash glass was broken by the **gust** (q.v.)."

saucered and blowed: a common expression meaning that preparation is completed; derives from the early practice of pouring hot drinks from a cup or mug into a saucer, blowing across it to cool it, and then pouring the fluid back into the cup for consumption, e.g., "When he said that the little chest was saucered and blowed, he meant that it was completed and ready for use."

saucepan: as now, a small pan in which food was boiled or fried, e.g., "The many inventory references to skillets usually meant saucepans."

sausage gun, sausage stuffer: a rather long, metal tube with a piston in one end and a smaller tube (with an opening) in the other end, into which is loaded bulk sausage, the same forced through the small end into a **casing** (q.v.) to make link sausages, e.g., "At **killing time** (q.v.), nearly all rural families made good use of the sausage gun."

saw set, saw jig: a small, hand-held but often bench-mountable tool designed to hold a saw when sharpening it, and to guide the user as to the angle at which the teeth should be reset, e.g., "Every early **joiner, cooper, carpenter,** and **cabinetmaker** (all, q.v.) had saw sets."

sawbuck table: a very sturdy, large table of the colonial era, usually unfinished, and with X legs on both ends secured by a beam between them, e.g., The sawbuck table often did duty as a **harvest table** (q.v.)."

sawyer: an occupation; one who has the tools and knowledge to accurately saw wood and, especially, make veneers of all kinds for use by furniture and cabinetmakers, e.g., "As a sawyer, he bought raw lumber from the sawmills and sold the finished product to the cabinetmakers."

scald head: a condition where the head of an infant or very small child is covered with scabs and lesions, e.g., "Old Dr. Lockhart applied turpentine or an ointment of sulphur and tar for the scald head."

scales: early, a balance or balance pans used for weighing; now, any device used to weigh anything, e.g., "In the inventory, the scales were distinguished from the **steelyards** (q.v.)"

scaps, skeps, gums: hives of bees, e.g., "Every early Pennsylvania farm had a scap or two of bees."

scarlatina: early, thought to be a mild form of the dreaded **scarlet fever** (q.v.), e.g., "At the first symptoms of scarlatina, Dr. Drake prescribed belladonna and ammonium carbonate."

scarlet fever: a common, greatly feared disease that often was fatal, e.g., "For scarlet fever, he administered mercury, mustard bathes, phosphorus, and sharp purges followed by vapor baths, among other treatments thought then to be effective."

scate: See **skate.**

scattergun: See **shotgun.**

school recores, Catholic: See **Orders of Nuns.**

schools, old field: See **old field schools.**

schoolmaster's desk, master's desk, schoolteacher's desk, clerk's desk: any of several designs of tall, light weight desks with a flat large work surface, often with turned legs and stretchers and occasionally with a fold down writing surface concealing pigeon holes and small drawers, or occasionally with a light roll top and drawers below the writing surface, e.g., "Her schoolmaster's desk was of white oak, with a lockable tambour and small compartments inside." Also see **rolltop desk.**

schooner: a light, fast ship, rigged fore and aft, e.g., "Many were the schooners owned by the merchant princes of New York City."

sciatica: See **lumbago.**

scire facias, writ of: an early court order directing that one show cause why some matter of record should not be enforced or used to advantage, e.g., "Early land patents often were subject to writs of scire facias where one was occupying land patented or granted of record to another person." Also see *scire feci.*

scire feci: the endorsement on a writ of *scire facias* (q.v.) revealing that the sheriff notified the person that he was to come forth and answer the writ, e.g., "The words scire feci written on a document reveal to the researcher that the sheriff of that county found the party named as defendant and gave him notice."

scold: a nagging wife; a woman known to make or encourage trouble or disagreement among neighbors, e.g., "An early court report quoted a husband as saying 'she was but a common scold'."See *common scold.*

sconce: early, a wall-mounted candle holder, usually with a small mirror behind the candles for enhanced illumination or decoration.

scoops: unlike now, usually a large ladle or handled container, e.g., "The scoops in the inventory probably were ladles."

scotch hands, scotch paddles: small, short-handled, wooden paddles, ribbed on one side, for working or handling butter, or mixing color into *oleo* (q.v.), e.g., "Her scotch hands showed many years of use."

Scotch, Scotch whiskey: a highly favored blend of whiskeys made in Scotland from malted barley, e.g., "Scotch has been an American favorite since the mid-18th century."

Scotch-Irish: immigrants, the majority of whom arrived between 1715 and 1775, particularly from the area of Ulster, who either were or were descendants of those Scottish who had migrated from Scotland to Ireland during the preceding decades, e.g., "With the coming of the sturdy Scotch-Irish, a certain wanderlust - 'itchy feet' - was infused into the American personality."

Scotch-Irish influence: many words and expressions arose from our Scotch-Irish ancestry, including 'axe to grind', 'dumb as a wedge', 'dumb as a basket of rocks', 'set on the fence', and the words a-feared, a-fishing, a-going, a-doing, etc., damndest, chaw, injin, picter, clabber, yous (as a plural of you), and the addition of 'all' as a suffix, such as you-all, where all did you go, what all did you do; e.g., "Bog, inch, and whiskey are but three examples of Scotch-Irish influence."

scrapple: a very common, early *Dutch* (q.v.) food made of corn meal, pork, seasoning, and sometimes buckwheat flour, e.g., "Fried scrapple was a favorite at Dutch breakfasts."

scribe, scribble, scribbler, scribner, scrivener: a writer; one trained in the art of writing; one whose occupation was writing for others for hire, e.g., "The surnames Scribner and Scrivner derive from the terms scribe and scribble."

scrip: early, a small writing; later and now in the U.S., usually paper currency of fractions of dollars, e.g., "After the Civil War scrip was printed in many denominations less than a dollar."

scrub brushes: See *clamps.*

scurvy: a disease causing painful joints and mental apathy, peculiar to mariners, recognized and cured from the earliest times, it nevertheless likely affected as many as 30,000 men during the American Civil War, e.g., "In 1610 Dr. Buhun prescribed fresh oranges and lemons for the scurvy of Lord Delaware."

scythe: a long handled tool with a long and sharp blade set nearly perpendicular to the slightly curved handle, and used to cut wheat and other long stemmed grains or cereals, e.g., "Swinging a scythe under an August sun was incredibly tiring."

seal: the act of placing a personal symbol on a document, widely used before literacy was common; an impression of ones seal or sign, usually made in a wax wafer or penetrating the document, for the purpose of confirming the execution of the document by the person whose name appeared; the small metal device bearing the **signet** (q.v.), symbol, or sign of the owner, e.g., "Major Bond noted that the grantor had not used a seal because no wax was available at the time of the signing"; "His seal was carried in his **weskit** (q.v.) and was of gold."

searce, searcer, bolter: a small, fine sieve, e.g., "She had a little silver searce that she used to strain her tea." Also see **tea strainer, colander,** and **riddle.**

seasoning: unlike now, the acclimation by newly arrived slaves and indentured servants particularly, and immigrants in general, to the summer heat and little understood diseases of sub tropical Virginia and the South, e.g., "The need for new arrivals to be seasoned led those who had a choice to arrive in Virginia, the Carolinas, and Georgia in the fall."

seating, seat, seated land: those governmental requirements that granted land be inhabited within certain time limits, before title could be perfectedimplicit in which was a measure of improvement; to satisfy the seating requirement inhabitation by either an "owner" or a tenant usually was adequate, e.g., "The seating requirement caused him to build a cabin for himself and his son's family."

seated land: See **seating.**

secession: those acts by which the Southern states left the American Union to become the Confederacy, e.g., "Commencing with South Carolina on December 24, 1860, Mississippi, Florida, Alabama, Georgia, Louisiana, Texas, Virginia, Arkansas, North Carolina, and Tennessee seceded from the Union and formed the Confederate States Of America.

second cousins: (third, fourth, etc.) those persons who share a common great grandparent; to each "great" in the title of the ancestor, one (1) is added to determine the degree of cousinhood, e.g., "Their great grandmother was their most recent common ancestor, so they were second cousins." (1 "great", so "2nd" cousins); "They shared common great-great-great grand-parents, so were fourth cousins (3 'greats', plus one (1), equals '4th' cousins)."

second day dress: an expression of the upper class, usually of the Old South; a dress to be worn on the day after one's wedding, e.g., "Her mother was careful to select a second day dress appropriate to their travel plans."

secondary sources, secondary materials: in genealogy, terms reflecting a subjective view of the user as to the reliability of some source; usually refers to those research materials that are not "original" and were abstracted or extracted from or are compilations of original sources; materials considered by the researcher to be less reliable than primary sources, e.g., "The abstracts of the original court's orders were considered secondary sources."

secret diseases: venereal diseases, e.g., "The **chancres** described in early medical records were caused by the 'secret diseases.'"

secretary: any of several styles of drop- or fall-front desks with drawers below and doored bookshelves above or, occasionally, to one side, e.g., "The secretary was of walnut and was Victorian."

section: a square mile; 640 acres, e.g., "There are 36 sections in a township." 1/2 section and 1/4 section were also common measurements of parcels of land.

seedcake: a small, sweet pastry, containing aromatic seeds such as caraway, e.g., "Seedcakes were one of the many pastries or **sweetmeats** (q.v.) served in early days."

seed drill: See **drill.**

seignior: from which is derived the Spanish señor, e.g., "The Spanish term Seignior was reserved to gentlemen and men of political position."

seized and possessed: an expression meaning that one is legally in possession of a tract of real estate, e.g., "She was seized and possessed of the tract, even though it was actually occupied by her tenant."

selectman, selectwoman: those municipal officers having executive powers and elected by northeastern towns to conduct day-to-day business of that political subdivision, e.g., "The county administrators or executives of some states have their counterparts in New England selectmen."

Seminole Wars: those conflicts against the negroes and Indians of east Florida that were viewed as a threat to the peace of Georgia, and resulted in the capture of Pensacola and St. Marks, bringing U.S. dominance over all of east Florida, e.g., "Jackson's actions in the 1st Seminole War resulted in his administration having an improved position in foreign affairs."

Senior and Junior: abbreviated "Sr.," and "Jr"; terms that reveal the existence of another person of the same name; early, applied to either males or females, not necessarily related; now, usually father and son, e.g., "Elizabeth Jones, Sr., and Elizabeth Jones, Jr., acted as witnesses to his will."

senorio: usually real property, e.g., "Many early southwestern writings refer to the senorio belonging to someone."

separate examination, separately examined, examined away: questioning of a wife, privately and out of the presence of the husband, by one appointed by a court or by law authorized to take oaths, concerning whether she acted of her own free will in executing and acknowledging a deed or other instrument, e.g., "Early law required separate examinations to assure that husbands did not coerce wives into acts contrary to their interests."

serge: a fine cloth, made of linen or wool, e.g., "The passenger lists revealed that he was a sergemaker from London."

servitude: see **indentured servants.**

settee: any of the many styles of seats with backs, for two people, usually upholstered, with arms, and very widely used, e.g., "Many 19th-century inventories listed settees."

settle, settle bench, settle chair, settle bed: a long wooden seat or bench, with a high wooden back (sometimes spoked), and wooden arms; a chair for one, of "settle" styling; a bed with a tall hinged sideboard or a long hinged head or foot board that could be lowered for use as a table, e.g., "While most were plain and sturdy in appearance, her settle bench appeared very much like Windsor furniture."

sewing table: somewhat of a luxury, a small table of a height appropriate for a woman, usually of better wood, often with a folding extension, and with a cloth bag beneath for scraps, pieces of thread and refuse of sewing, e.g., "Her sewing table was mahogany, and had been a birthday gift."

sexton: the chief administrator of a cemetery, either church or secular; occasionally, a church handyman, e.g., "Offices of sextons often provide genealogical information not available from any other source."

sexual intercourse: See **cover.**

Shakers: that religious sect brought here in the 1770s that advocated common ownership of **realty** (q.v.), celibacy, and an austere life, e.g., "The simplicity of Shaker life was reflected in their magnificent, yet very plain, furniture."

shakes, palsy: any of the several, little-understood nervous disorders, including Parkinson's syndrome, e.g., "He treated the palsy with tonics, aconite and potassium bromide."

shallop: a small boat with one or two sails, used for near shore fishing, and light hauling, e.g., "Many were the shallops on 18th-century Chesapeake Bay."

shaloon: a light woolen cloth, e.g., "It is likely that the shaloon Brown purchased of Mr. Parham was used for the linings in cold weather clothing."

shanker: See **chancre.**

share, plow share, sheers: the metal point of a plow, e.g., "'Beat their swords into plowshares' is intelligible only if one knows what a share was."

shave, drawknife: a two-handled tool used to shape wood by drawing the sharpened edge toward the user, e.g., "A shave used to hollow wood as in making a **porringer** (q.v.) was called a hollow shave, and a hollow shave with a straight blade on the other end was called a jigger or jigger shave."

shaves: those, usually wooden, pole like struts extending forward from the axle of a one horse buggy or **wagon** (q.v.), to the sides of the horse or other draft animal, and between which the animal is hitched for pulling, e.g., "Shaves were used for lighter loads than were **tongues** (q.v.) and **trees** (q.v.)." Also see **swingletrees,** and **collars.**

shaving cup: a handled mug in which was placed shaving soap, the same wetted and agitated with a shaving brush thereby creating a lather with which to shave, e.g., "Virtually every man of the 19th century had a shaving mug and a **straight razor** (q.v.)."

shaving mirror: a small, adjustable, free-standing mirror, of a size to be placed on a **washstand, chest of drawers, commode,** or **bedside table** (all, q.v.) e.g., "Whenever a male guest was in the home for overnight, she placed the shaving mirror in his **bedchamber** (q.v.)."

shawfowl: a decoy, usually to attract ducks or geese, e.g., "While very early commercial duck and goose hunters on Chesapeake Bay often spoke of shawfowls, the term decoy seems to have been preferred by early in the 1800s."

shay: See **chaise.**

Shays' Rebellion: that Massachusetts uprising (summer 1786 - Mar. 1787) by destitute farmers seeking a paper money issue and other financial relief that led to the raising of forces by both Massachusetts and Congress, and finally the death of 5 "Shaysites" and the collapse of the insurgent force, e.g., "As in Bacon's Rebellion, in order that their families not suffer (and to the chagrin of present day genealogists) many of the men of Shays' Rebellion remained anonymous."

sheer, sheers: See **share.**

shellac: a fine and ancient finish for furniture and other wooden objects, made of a resinous substance exuded by an insect (**lac,** q.v.) dissolved in alcohol, e.g., "Most furniture made before 1880 was finished in shellac."

sheriff: very early, shire reeve or high sheriff; an ancient office, recorded in England before the 12th century; a "High Sheriff" had wide authority and jurisdiction within a county, and spoke for the Crown, the courts, and government in general; later and now, the elected chief administrative and peace officer of a county, having duties in assisting all courts of general jurisdiction, summoning juries, serving writs and executing court orders, e.g., "The judge ordered the sheriff to take William West into custody and hold him until the next **term** (q.v.) of court."

sherry: originally, an amber colored wine with an added alcohol content and made in southern Spain, e.g., "Early colonials bought ordinary sherry and then added grain alcohol to fortify it."

Shetland wool: the wool made the fine undercoat of the Scottish Shetland sheep, and pulled by hand from the animals, e.g., "The cloth made from Shetland wool was among the finest **stuffs** (q.v.) available in colonial America."

shift: early, a woman's undergarment; now, a long, straight, unadorned woman's dress, e.g., "Susannah had three shifts when she died."

shilling (S or s): a British denomination of money used as a standard in Colonial America and for years thereafter in some of the states; there are twenty (20) shillings in a pound (L), and ten (10) pence in a shilling (formerly 12), but it was not everywhere of uniform value; e.g., "In Virginia, in 1755, the price of sugar for home use was one shilling, six pence (1s,6p or /1/6) per pound."

shimmey: See **chemise.**

shin-plaster: paper money of greatly diminished worth; paper money having a value of less than a dollar; fractional currency, e.g., "The term shin-plaster arose when certain paper money came to have so little value that it could be used to dress a cut or bruise, as on the shin."

shinney, shinny: homemade Louisiana whiskey, e.g., "A Louisiana court found McClinton guilty of making shinny."

ships (famous): Of the best known ships moving to and from the American colonies and states, surely one would list Columbus' *Nina, Pinta,* and *Santa Maria;* Hudson's *Half Moon;* Drake's *Revenge* and *Golden Hind;* Jamestown's *Susan Constant, Godspeed* and *Discovery; Mayflower* and *Speedwell; Virginia* (first ship built in the American colonies); Jones' *Bon Homme Richard* and *H.M.S. Serapis; U.S.S. Constitution;* Perry's *Lawrence; Monitor* and *Merrimac* of the Civil War, *Maine, Hornet,* and *Arizona.*

shire: early, a political subdivision in England, made up of an indefinite number of **hundreds** (q.v.); now, a county, e.g., "Somersetshire is now Somerset County."

Shire: an English breed of powerful, heavy draft horses, brown or bay with white markings, e.g., "The beautiful Shires and Clydesdales both were predominantly a rich brown color."

shoemaker: one who made shoes and boots, distinguished from a cobbler or harnessmaker, e.g., "Samuel Martin was a shoemaker in Holidaysburg in 1840." Also see **cordwainer** and **cobbler.**

shoemakers lamp, jewelers lamp: by placing a candle behind a clear glass container or bulb of water, the light was diffused broadly and shadows on close work were reduced, hence the name, e.g., "He had a brass shoemakers lamp with two candles and four bulbs mounted around them."

shoes: unlike now, e.g., "Milton called shoes shoons; early poor and rural dwellers tied pieces of leather or heavy cloth to their feet for out of doors, and used lighter cloth for indoors; straight boots (jackboots) and half boots or demi-boots (both heavy and 'dress', and sometimes with very broad, draping tops as portrayed by the "Three Musketeers") have always been worn by men, especially on horseback; by Henry VIII shoes often had thick cork soles (2" plus) and were known as pantofles; for the wealthy, early fashion required very long toes pointed upwards (early, even tied to the knees with chains of tiny links); by 1715, wooden shoes (pattens), open at the back, with metal rings to keep the feet above mud and water were common, and wooden heels were used on all leather shoes, especially among the French and Hollanders; clogs, open at the back (as now) were wooden and without the rings of pattens; goloeshoes (hence the term "galoshes") were thick leather, and as pattens, were open at the heel; knots of flowers or colored cloth decorated the buckled or stringed shoes of 18th century women of means (some strings were jewelled or made of gold and silver thread, and were valuable enough to appear in inventories); leather French fall shoes were low, of better quality, and worn by both men or women, and

women of means also wore highly decorated silk and satin or half leather and
silk; 1825 to 1850 saw shoes with square
toes, and wooden high heels (cross cut
heels) were common; by 1835, as now,
India rubbers and overshoes were worn
over shoes to prevent moisture; and not
until the early 1800s were shoes made for
the left and right foot.

shoo fly rocker: the source is unclear; a rocking toy for children, with a
seat mounted between small silhouettes of small horses, the whole on
double rocker bars, e.g., "The shoo fly rocker had belonged to his father."

shoons: See ***shoes.***

shooting iron: usually, firearms of short barrel held in one hand, e.g.,
"The expression shooting irons probably arose in the days when firearms
were made of iron and locally made."

shooting match, shootin' match: contests of accuracy usually with
rifles, popular during the period 1750-1950, usually attended with prizes
and gambling, e.g., "Sgt. York participated in shootin' matches until well on
in years."

shopboard: a wooden work bench, e.g., "In early times, the word bench
usually meant seat, and shopboard was preferred for a work area at which
one stood."

short ton: See ***long ton.***

shot: lead pellets used in ***shotguns*** (q.v.), made in various sizes from "00
buck" to "#9" and smaller, selected based on the size of the animal being
hunted, e.g., "He used was 00 buck for deer, #2 for turkeys, #4 for ducks
and geese, #6 for grouse and pheasant, and #7 and #8 shot for quail."

shot pouch, powder pouch: a small bag of leather or waterproof cloth,
tied to the belt or worn over the shoulder, used to carry the shot, ***caps*** (q.v.),
balls (q.v.), wadding, etc., needed for operation of the firearms carried for
hunting, e.g., "He had his father's old shot pouch."

shotgun, scattergun, fowling piece, bird gun: of many makes and
models and of various "gauges" (size of load and barrel diameter); a firearm
firing multiple small lead pellets, quite usually used for ducks, geese, wild
fowl, small game, and pests, e.g., "Every fall he took up the old 16 gauge
shotgun and went hunting for grouse and quail."

Shrove Tuesday: the day before Ash Wednesday, e.g., "Early Episcopal
and some court records speak of Shrove Tuesday."

shrubs: a cherry juice liquer, e.g., "Her recipe for cherry shrub called for
finely strained juice from ripe whole cherries cooked in a double boiler, to
which sugar was added, the mixture placed in qt. bottles with 2 ounces of
brandy in each, the bottles then sealed and stored until needed."

shutters: unlike now, hinged covers for windows mounted inside the house behind the windows, and used to seal the house from intruders and severe weather, e.g., "Knowing what a shutter was renders the "Christmas Carol" intelligible: '...away to the window I flew like a flash, tore open the shutters and threw up the sash....'"

sibling: from the Saxon "sibb"; early, any relative or kinsman; later and now, brothers and sisters, e.g., "Having no interest in **collateral lines** (q.v.), she did not research the descendants of her grandfather's siblings."

sick time: the time immediately prior to and immediately after one's delivery of a child, e.g., "Her sick time was not far off."

sickle: a short-handled tool with a curved thin blade used to cut weeds, grasses, and other stemmed vegetation, e.g., "The sickle was a necessity in cleaning **fence rows** (q.v.)."

side by side, bookcase: inexplicably, sometimes called a **buffet** (q.v.); usually, any of several styles of cabinets with a single, paned door and bookshelves on the left, a drop-down writing surface with compartments and **pigeon holes** (q.v.) within and often a doored compartment above on the right, and often with a small mirror above the drop writing surface, e.g., "Her side by side, that she called a bookcase, was mahogany and had bookshelves and a small, paned compartment above."

side chair: chairs of many designs and styles, straight-backed, usually without arms and either upholstered or with padded, woven, or leather seats and no other upholstered surfaces, designed to be placed against a wall and moved to a table or about the room as needed, e.g., "She had pressed-back, oak side chairs that were kept side by side against the **parlor** (q.v.) wall."

side saddle, ladies saddle: a woman's saddle, having both stirrups on one side, and so made as to permit a woman to ride without being astride the animal, e.g., "The 1679 inventory revealed '1 old side-saddle'."

side table: any small to medium-sized table, occasionally with a revolving or folding top, so shaped as to set against a wall in hallways, foyers, etc., e.g., "Her side table was of burl mahogany with a folding top, and also served as a **game table** (q.v.)."

sideboard: a long, usually rather narrow, waist high, serving piece, narrower and with fewer drawers than a **buffet** (q.v.), and usually made of quality, highly finished wood, with a drawer or two and usually doored compartments below the work surface; used to serve refreshments or as a buffet, e.g., "Her Empire sideboard was covered with cookies and every other imaginable dessert." Also see **huntboard** and **butler's sideboard.**

sieve: early, and before wire, hoops were strung with human hair.

signatures (theory of): that early theory of medicine in which every illness had a natural cure, e.g., "Since walnut meats had a shape similar to the brain - its signature - they were prescribed for headaches and any other

distempers (q.v.) of the brain."

signed, sealed, and delivered: an early expression, once restricted to deeds, that stated the three requirements for a deed to be effective; later, and now, meaning an action involving a writing has been accomplished, e.g., "In addition to being executed, very early deeds had to sealed and actually delivered - handed over - to the grantee, hence the expression signed, sealed, and delivered."

signet ring, Jesuit ring: a ring bearing ones initials, and used early to seal documents by pressing it into melted sealing wax, e.g., "The signet ring of Thomas Drake bore the initials 'TD'."

silkmercer: See **mercer.**

sillibub: See **syllabub.**

silver: the word silver often appears in inventories, even though the items were not silver or silverplate, e.g., "African silver was silverplate usually made in Birmingham, Eng., at about the time of our Civil War; Brazil silver was nickle plate; Waldo or Waldo silver was a gold colored ware made in Connecticut in the 1890s; Siberian Silver was silver plate on a copper base metal; Oregon silver was inexpensive plate made in England near the end of the 19th century; and German silver also was not silver, but an alloy of cheaper metals."

simples: any herb, root, or plant used for medicinal purposes, e.g., "The New World provided many new simples around which the Dutch built a substantial trade in Europe."

singletree: See **swingletree.**

Sir and Madam: early, titles referring to noblemen and their ladies; until recently, reserved for gentlemen and their wives, or ladies of accomplishment and standing, e.g., "Francis Drake became Sir Francis upon being knighted by Queen Elizabeth I"; "There being tithables residing there in 1677, the household of Madam Parker was listed."

sire: a male parent animal, usually a **stallion** (q.v.), e.g., "The sire was a beautiful black **thoroughbred** (q.v.)."

sissers, scissors: as now, e.g., "In 1760s Virginia, the value of a pint of good rum or a silk handkerchief was about equal to that of a pair of scissors."

sister: a sibling; a nun; a term often used in the Biblical sense, e.g., "His siblings consisted of four brothers and three sisters"; "Care must be exercised since the records of the old church refer to unrelated members of the congregation as brothers and sisters." Also see **brother.**

sitting, sitting of court: a time limit, the length of time of a session of court, e.g., "The court ordered that during the sitting of the court the sheriff was to give her 21 lashes."

sitting room: See **parlor.**

sixpence, su'pence: an English coin commonly found in the colonies in the 17th, 18th, and 19th centuries, having a value of 1/2 Shilling (6 pence), e.g., "Sixpence coins were common, particularly among seafaring men."

skate, scate, ice skate: unlike now, early skates were shoes with metal plates tied to them, e.g., "Blades on ice skates were uncommon early in other than eastern Europe."

skedaddle: to leave some place on foot at a rapid pace or with urgency, e.g., "While he spoke of skedaddling, his friend said that he had high-tailed it out of there."

skein: usually, a winding of some number of loops of yarn; to mer-chants, a measure of number (often 40) and length of loops of yarn, e.g., "If from her own **wheel** (q.v.) and for her own use, a skein was an indetermi-nate number of loops"; "He sold her three skeins of woolen yarn."

skep: very early, a beehive shaped like an inverted basket and made of coiled rope tied together to prevent its collapse; early, usually a round, 1/2 bushel wooden or reed basket, often with handles, e.g., "Early depictions of beehives almost always show them as skeps"; "The 1751 inventory revealed 'two oaken skeps'."

skewer: as now, a pointed metal utensil for moving pieces of food from one place to another, e.g., "So common were they that very few inventories even mention skewers."

skiff: a rowboat, nearly pointed on both ends, occasionally with a single sail, e.g., "Every early landing had skiffs moving about."

skimmer: a long-handled, metal kitchen utensil, usually shallow and with or without a removable perforated top, used to skim grease, bones and undesirable materials from the surface of fresh milk, and from boiling or cooking stews and foods, e.g., "Skimmers were used in virtually every 18th-century kitchen."

skillet: unlike now, a small kettle used for boiling small quantities of food, e.g., "Early inventories have many references to skillets, meaning saucepans or small kettles."

skins in the limes, in the limes: apparently referred to animal skins being cured for making leather, e.g., "Harris was said to have no estate except for some 'skins in the limes'."

skunk, polecat, fitchew: as now, the common skunk, e.g., "Her refer-ence to the 'dogs being sick from the polecat' meant that a skunk had sprayed them from close distance causing nausea and vomiting."

slant top desk: See **desk.**

slave: one who is owned by and held as property of another, and who may gain personal freedom and liberty only through action by that owner or by law, e.g., "Having been purchased by that family, she was their slave, as were her children."

slaver: an early ship used in the slave trade, e.g., "Many early American port records refer to slavers."

sleepers: early term meaning the large beams under the floor of a barn or other large buildings other than a residence, e.g., "Knowles wrote that the corn crop had been so great that the weight had broken the barn sleepers."

slice: See **peel.**

slicer: very early, a large knife, and if serrated, used to slice bread, if not, used for meats, etc.; later, a mechanical utensil with a revolving blade used to slice meats and cheeses, e.g., "The 1679 Parker inventory included 2 slicers, a **cleaver** (q.v.), and a **pey peel** (q.v.)."

slipper chair: a small, low, upholstered chair without arms, so designed that a woman wearing a bustle might sit and put on or remove slippers or shoes by reaching down to either side of her dress, e.g., "Her Empire slipper chairs were upholstered in red velvet, and were elegant."

slop, slop bucket: usually, a container for table scraps, leftovers, and food remnants or by products (sour milk, etc.) saved for feeding to hogs; that pail or bucket used to carry food to hogs, e.g., "Slopping the hogs was one of the first chores assigned to farm children."

slop bowl: a term apparently of the middle class meaning a small table bowl in which were placed tea dregs, seeds and peelings from fruits, etc., e.g., "She said she placed a slop bowl on the table when big meals were being served."

slut: female dog; a bitch; a very common, quite acceptable, early expression, not considered vulgar until the end of the 19th century, e.g., "Many were the classified ads of the 1870s that told of sluts for sale."

slumps: See **desserts, early.**

smelling salts: of many recipes, thought to revive those who were faint, e.g., "For smelling salts, to 1 oz. potassium acetate (called 'sal diureticus') in a **sniffing bottle** (q.v.), she added 1/2 oz. of sulphuric acid and a few drops of lavender oil."

smith: one who works metal, i.e., tinsmiths, goldsmiths, silversmiths, coppersmiths, blacksmiths (iron), etc., e.g., "His neighbor was Paul Revere, the silver and gold smith."

smoke-jack, chimney jack: a rather ingenious device designed to more or less slowly ratchet or turn a spit as the air and heat flow in a chimney increased or decreased, e.g., "The smoke-jack made it possible for her to be about other **chores** (q.v.) while the meat cooked."

smiths work: iron work done for hire, e.g., "In 1687 the court approved payment for 'smiths work on the jail door.'"

smock: a woman's undergarment; a shift, e.g., "In early times, any women's garments worn under other clothing were called smocks."

smokepipe, pipe: a hand-held pipe for smoking tobacco, e.g., "Will wrote that the tailors were 'warming their noses with their smokepipes'."

smoothbore, smoothbore musket, smoothbore gun: a firearm firing a single shot, as in a **rifle** (q.v.), but without spiral grooves (**rifling,** q.v.) in the barrel, e.g., "The old inaccurate smoothbores were relegated to the gun rack when rifling was invented."

smoothers: See **iron (to).**

snake fence, zigzag fence, waving fence: so called by reason of its appearance; a fence without posts made with split logs laid with the ends overlapping in a zigzag fashion, e.g., "Before wire fencing, snake fences were common where the soil was so rocky as to make driving posts difficult." Also see **post and rail fences,** and **barbed wire.**

snakeroot: any of several roots or plant parts believed to have value in treating venomous snake bites, e.g., "One physician's snakeroot might be different from that of another." Also see **rattlesnake root.**

sniffing bottle, sniff bottle, sniffer, occasionally, tickler bottle: unlike now, a usually glass stoppered bottle for **smelling salts** (q.v.), e.g., "Her sniffing bottles were hand-blown, and of high quality glass."

snow roller: a horse-drawn vehicle having a huge roller instead of front wheels, used to flatten the snow on streets so as to facilitate the use of sleighs and cutters, e.g., "The purchase of a snow roller by the little town was a boon to those who had to move about during the winter."

snuff box, snuff tin, pinch box: a metal box, often **chased** (q.v.), small enough to be placed in one's pocket, and in which is carried chopped smokeless tobacco - **snuff** (q.v.), e.g., "She had a chased silver pinch box."

snuff: powdered or finely chopped tobacco, used by placing a small amount (a **pinch,** q.v.) between the teeth and lips or cheek, e.g., "Snuff has been widely used since early in the 17th century." See also **dip.**

snuffer: as now, a small, long handled, triangular cup used to put out a candle by placing it down over the flame, e.g., "Parker made her a brass snuffer."

soap: as now; early, produced by slowly adding lye (made by adding water slowly to fine ashes - hickory was preferred - and draining off the resulting liquid) to clear boiling lard (made by cooking down pork fat), and stirring and cooking until the mixture thickened, then cooling and slicing into blocks, e.g., "The grease resulting from skimming stews and **rendering** (q.v.) lard was used with lye to make soap."

socer: a man's father-in-law, e.g., "Early southwestern records occasionally speak of a socer."

societies: See **fraternities, sororities, and societies.**

Society Of The Cincinnati (The): (1783) a fraternal organization of officers of the Continental Army, and their descendants, e.g., "George Washington was the first President of The Society of the Cincinnati."

sock darner, sock egg: a handled, glass or wooden ball used to insert in and shape stockings being repaired, e.g., "The sock darner was ceramic and beautifully made."

sofa bed, bed lounge: an upholstered **couch** (q.v.) with a slightly elevated end to be used as a shoulder and headrest and a usually straight, upholstered back shaped like a headboard or the back on a **lounge** (q.v.), e.g., "Sofa beds were common in late Victorian times."

sofa: any upholstered, armed seat for more than one person, e.g., "Johnson defined a sofa as a 'seat covered with **rugs'** (q.v.)."

softening of the brain: See **brain.**

solar: land with a house, e.g., "Early Texas references to one's solar have nothing to do with the sun."

solstice: that point on the vertical, above which the sun does not rise in summer, and below which it does not descend in winter, e.g., "The summer and winter solstices and the vernal and autumnal **equinoxes** (q.v.) were the means by which a precise calendar was drawn."

songs, popular: as now, e.g., "A list of popular and well known early rhymes and songs must include Mother Goose (c. 1715); Beggar's Opera (1752); Messiah (1770); My Days Have Been So Wondrous Free (c. 1760); Yankee Doodle (1767); All Hail The Power Of Jesus' Name (1793); President's March (1793); Hail Columbia (1798); Star Spangled Banner (1814); Old Oaken Bucket (1813); Turkey In The Straw (c. 1834); We Won't Go Home Till Morning (1842); Old Dan Tucker (1843); Jimmy Crack Corn (1846); Oh, Susanna (1848); De Camptown Races (1850); Old Folks At Home (1851); Massa's In De Cold Cold Ground (1852); Frankie and Johnny (1850); Old Kentucky Home (1853); Darling Nelly Grey (1856); Jingle Bells (1857); Dixie (1859); and Old Black Joe in 1860."

Sons of Confederate Veterans, The: a non-profit society of those whose paternal ancestors were Confederate veterans of the Civil War, e.g., "His great grandfather George Drake was in the 43rd North Carolina, making Al eligible for The Sons of Confederate Veterans."

Sons of Liberty: 1765-1766, those groups of men, particularly under Samuel Adams, usually of port cities, who viewed themselves as Patriots and serving the public good, and who undertook to rebel against the Stamp and Townshend Acts, etc., by inciting others to join them in destroying 'stamped' documents, undermining the authority and public regard of servants of the British, and harassing other citizens who did not share their views, e.g., "The best remembered activity of the Sons of Liberty was the Boston Tea Party."

Sons of the American Revolution: (The Society of, S.A.R.) a hereditary and charitable organization of men descended from persons who served honorably in any military unit or performed other valuable service to the cause during the American Revolution, e.g., "Since his fifth-great grandfather was with the **Green Mountain Boys** (q.v.), he was eligible for membership in The Society Of Sons of the American Revolution."

Sons of Union Veterans, The: a non-profit society of those whose paternal ancestors were Union veterans of the Civil War, e.g., "His great grandfather Midlam was in the 55th Ohio, making Ray eligible for The Sons of Union Veterans."

sorghum, sweet sorghum, sugar sorghum, sorgo, molasses: a sweetener made from the plant sorgo, widely used across the mid-South and South, particularly where maple syrup was not commonly produced, e.g., "Many of the old horse-drawn **turnstiles** (q.v.) used to crush sorgo for sorghum are still in use."

soring, soreing: a method of training a horse, especially a **Tennessee Walker** (q.v.), to lift its front feet very high between steps by weighting those feet and shoeing them so as to bring pain when that foot touched the ground, e.g., "The cruelty of soring has caused it to no longer be tolerated nor practiced by horse lovers."

sororities: See *fraternities, sororities, and societies.*

sorrel: usually, a brownish, red to yellow color, particularly of horses or dogs; rarely, a seasoning, e.g., "Jackson's horse was named Old Sorrel by reason of its color."

soundex: a common method of indexing, particularly applicable to censuses after 1870, by which, through the assignment of numbers to vowels and first letters of names, one may search the records, e.g., "The soundex record for Tom James is found through assigning numbers to the letter T and the letters J, M, and S."

Southern Confederacy: See **secession.**

sow: early, to plant by hand casting (**broadcasting,** q.v.) seed from side to side, and later by a crank operated device to similarly cast seed, e.g., "The old method of hand sowing was hard and time consuming." Also see **drill.**

spanfarthing, spanpenny: as now, a game, played by both adults and children, in which coins were tossed at a mark, circle or target, e.g., "In the colonies the terms 'penny pitch' and 'pitching pennies' seem to have taken the place of the English games of spanpenny or spanfarthing."

b **Spanish American War:** that armed conflict that occurred during 1898 and 1899 between Spain and the United States, e.g., "Carl was with the 4th Ohio Volunteers during the Spanish American War."

Spanish Main: the Caribbean Sea; the coastal land surrounding the Caribbean Sea, especially along south Florida, e.g., "The Spanish Main was the haunt of pirates such as **Blackbeard.** (q.v.)."

Spanish people, words gained from: many words arose from our experiences with the Spaniards who settled or maintained commerce with the colonies, e.g., "Conquistadores, barbecue, chocolate, tomato, enchilada, marijuana, plaza, stampede, and tornado are but a few."

Spanish Succession, War of: See **Queen Anne's War.**

spanking, spanking team: smart, quick moving, handsome, e.g., "He had a spanking pair of blacks used only with the sleigh."

spark (a): in the 17th century, a diamond, e.g., "The inventory revealed that among her jewelry was a ring with 'two sparks'."

spark, to, sparking: to court; to engage in romantic activities, physical and otherwise, e.g., "Gazebos were favorite places for sparking."

spark lamp: a small lamp of minimal illumination, first with a candle and later using **lamp oil** (q.v.) as fuel, commonly used as a night light, especially in hallways and in the rooms where small children slept, the name derived from their use during courting (**sparking,** q.v.) e.g., "She kept spark lamps in the foyer and in the nursery." Also see **night lights.**

spatterware: common to 18th- and 19th-century estates and often called "Dutch" or "Pennsylvania Dutch" ware, it was earthen, with stippling, splashed, or dabbed colors over a differing base color, e.g., "Her spatterware was white with blue-green stippling."

specie: coin of precious metal, e.g., "Mention of consideration in specie means that the land was bought with coin money, quite usually silver or gold."

spermaceti, spermacoeti, whale candle wax: a white or nearly color-less wax obtained from the head of a sperm whale, early used to make high quality candles, salves, perfumes, and ointments, e.g., "While the poor used

tallow (q.v.), the rich had spermaceti candles."

spice graters: See **nutmeg graters.**

spider: a skillet or frying pan; usually a shallow, iron cooking pan, often with short legs, e.g., "She made a small pile of coals on the **hearth** (q.v.) and placed the spider over it."

spinal meningitis: a dreaded, very often fatal disease of the nerves of the spine, e.g., "For Helen's spinal meningitis, he administered compounds of mercury, aconite, opium, quinine, and prescribed cold baths, all to no avail."

spinet: early, a small **harpsichord** (q.v.), e.g., "Early inventories of the rich often reveal spinets."

spinning wheel, walking wheel, wool wheel, wheel: a large spinning wheel, common in nearly every home of the early years, and used to make yarn of all sorts except linen, e.g., "In addition to a **flax wheel** (q.v.), they had a spinning wheel she referred to as a walking wheel because it was turned with a short stick while the spinner was standing."

spinster: any woman considered by her peers as having passed the age at which she would be expected to first marry, and only occasionally used to refer to widows, e.g., "Being twenty-eight years old and unmarried, she was identified in the census as a spinster."

spirits of, spirituous: alcohol or alcohol based, e.g., "Spirits of wine was natural alcohol boiled off and retained."

spirituous liquors: See **liquors.**

spit: as now, e.g., "Often the spits were very large, holding as much as an entire hog." Also see **smoke-jack,** q.v.

splint lights: the earliest illumination used in the American colonies, and previously used by the Indians; a simple thin splint of fresh pine 6 or more inches long, which, when lit, burned brightly for 15 to 30 minutes, e.g., "The early splint lights dripped pitch, gave but little light, and the danger of fire was ever-present."

spoke shave: a common, sharp edged tool of the **cabinetmaker** (q.v.), **wagonmaker** (q.v.), and **wheelwright** (q.v.), used to shape and trim round spokes, struts, chair stretchers, etc., e.g., "He had several sizes of spoke shaves."

sponsor: one who presents or stands in ceremonial behalf of another (usually a child) for religious purposes such as baptisms or dedications, e.g., "Her two sisters were sponsors at the baptism of her daughter."

sports (adult): of the many pastimes and sports, perhaps the best known early were fox and raccoon hunting with hounds, quarter horse racing, footraces, **bowls** (q.v.), and gambling; later, shooting ("shootin' matches") thoroughbred and harness racing (see **sulky**), and fishing and boxing matches; and in the early 20th century, as now, baseball and hunting."

sporting house: a house of ill repute, a whorehouse, e.g., "Rhett Butler frequented Belle Watling's sporting house."

spouse: as now, one's wife or husband.

spring rocker: See **platform rocker.**

springerles, springerle cookies, Hartshorn cookies: a hard, German cookie, seasoned with **Hartshorn** (q.v.), and often hung on and eaten from Christmas trees, e.g., "Vera made springerles every December."

spruce: neat, yet without elegance, or to dress in an affected, unusual, or pretentious manner, e.g., "Our expression 'get spruced up' derives from the early definition of spruce."

squad: See **armies, organization of.**

squeezer: See **wringer.**

squire: See **esquire.**

St. Anthony's Fire: any serious skin condition that was eruptive or gangrenous, e.g., "For St. Anthony's Fire, the mother administered turpentine, mustard plasters, or clove oil."

St. Nicholas, Santa Claus, Old Goody: the patron saint of children, early portrayed as a cleric, but by 1860 depicted as an elf covered with chimney dirt and soot, e.g., "The magic reindeer of St. Nicholas were first named in Moore's 'The Night Before Christmas'."

St. Vitus Dance: See **chorea.**

stable: See **livery.**

stack book case, stacked book cases: enclosed book shelves with glass paned, hinged doors that open upward, usually made in increments of one self contained shelf, with a separate detachable bonnet for the entirety, and stacked four to six high, e.g., "The stack book case was four high and of oak."

stacks: any shelves of books or other writings in a library, public or private; may be open to the public - open stacks - or closed to use except through an accountability system, e.g., "The Mormon library maintains generally closed stacks, however, access to the books through the attendants is speedy and efficient."

Staffordshire: very popular, usually fine china, creamware, porcelain, and stoneware of all types and styles, made in Staffordshire, Eng., by a number of makers, and often seen in early inventories in the colonies and the U.S., e.g., "Her Staffordshire Toby Jug was her most prized **curio** (q.v.)."

stage line, stagecoach, stage coach: usually, a business using horse-drawn vehicles - stagecoaches - between distant points at more or less frequent intervals, e.g., "The 'stage line operated between Columbus and Pomeroy, and the stagecoaches ran on Mondays and Thursdays."

stagecoach: See **stage line.**

stallion: See **horse.**

stand, stand for office: to be a candidate for some public office; an early way station, where food and drink for both travellers and their animals might be purchased, most having either the most sparce or no accommodation for overnight sleeping, e.g., "He stood for state senator that year";"By 1795 Johnson's stand was in business on the **Wilderness Road** (q.v.) some twenty miles west of Crab Orchard Inn."

stand-up bath: not until after 1870 were bathtubs in common use, and in rural areas even much later than that, resulting in a need by all to wash from a bucket, basin, or **pitcher and bowl** (q.v.) while standing, giving rise to the expression, e.g., "Many was the lady who, having not been wet all over since childhood, maintained her cleanliness through stand-up bathes."

starboard (larboard) and port: usually pronounced star-bird and port; to one facing forward, the right-hand side of a vessel is starboard, and the left side is the port side, e.g., "As a vessel moves up the James River, Jamestown is to starboard, and Surry courthouse and Hog Island are to port."

state(s), States of the Union: those political subdivisions, previously territories, that were admitted to the Union upon gaining legally sufficient population and approval of application to Congress, e.g., "Since, except for the original thirteen colonies, all other states were admitted by Congress after petition by their residents, the applications often provide valuable information concerning early settlements."

States' Rights: simply stated, that view that the states reserved to themselves any and all powers and privileges not specifically given over to the federal government at the ratification of the Constitution, e.g., "Contrary to the thinking of the States' Rightists, the Union took the view that the federal government had gained all powers and authority necessary to maintain itself and those institutions approved by a majority of its people."

stays: as now, e.g., "Early high quality stays often were made of the cartilage from the mouths of whales." Also see **whalebone.**

steel: unlike now, hardened sharpening rods having a lightly roughened surface for sharpening of knives and other cutting edges, e.g., "The 1737 inventory revealed 'a **slicer** (q.v.) and the steel for it'."

steelyards, stillyards: a weighing scale with an adjustable beam and weights, usually hung from a hook and used to weigh heavy objects, e.g., "The steelyards in the inventory had been used to weigh tobacco."

steer: a male bovine, castrated before sexual maturity, e.g., "The inventory revealed four steers, two calves, and a bull."

steerage: those quarters located in the hind part of a ship, e.g., "Odors from the front of a moving ship passed through steerage, rendering that the least desirable of the ship passengers' quarters, thus the least expensive."

step-back cupboard: See **cupboard.**

Sterling: a standard of value, silver content, and purity of English silver coin, e.g., "In colonial writings, the mention of Pound Sterling meant that the debt, obligation, or payment was to be made either in English silver coin or in other currency having an exchange value equal to such coin."

stick: probably a small measure or roll of cloth goods such as ribbon or heavy cord, e.g., "During 1763, Brown bought three sticks of **twist** (q.v.)."

stiletto: a long, thin bladed, sharp knife used as a weapon, e.g., "He had a stiletto hidden in the carriage."

stillyards: See **steelyards.**

stirpes: See **per stirpes.**

stock: in genealogy, one's ancestry or lineage, from which arises the expression, "The family is from good stock."

stockade, stockade fort: an enclosed fort; an enclosure with walls of heavy timbers or tree trunks pointed at the top and placed in the ground side by side so as to be impenetrable by ordinary means, e.g., "Twelve Unknown Soldiers of the War of 1812 were buried within the Fort Morrow stockade."

stocks and pillories: the former, a device having holes in which to bind the ankles and sometimes the wrists, and the latter, a device designed to bind the hands and head of a condemned; both were usually placed in a public place for all citizens to see and ridicule the criminals, e.g., "The Sussex court promptly ordered that stocks and a pillory be constructed on the courthouse lawn."

stomacher: a highly decorated, often jewelled garment of the 15th, 16th and 17th centuries, worn over the chest, e.g., "**Good Queen Bess** (q.v.) is almost always portrayed wearing a beautiful stomacher."

stone (the), having the stone, having the gravel: kidney, gall, or bladder stones, which brought grievous suffering and for which, until surgery in the mid-18th century, there were no effective cures, e.g., "An Indian remedy for stone was a tea of hydrangeas."

stone: a measure of weight; 14 pounds, e.g., "It was written that he weighed '10 stone' - 140 lbs."

stoneware: any ware made of ceramic, e.g., "Stoneware was very common in the 19th century."

stout: a dark brew made from toasted malt and having a high hops content, e.g., "Stout was popular in Civil War New York City."

straight fence: See **post and rail fence.**

straight razor: a very sharp knife with a folding blade used for shaving, e.g., "Until well into the 20th century, there were no satisfactory shaving tools except the straight razor."

strand: the shore of the sea or a large river, e.g., "A land description mentioning a boundary at a strand means at the edge of the high water of a river or sea."

strangery, stranguary: stricture of the urethra, often perhaps prostatitis or cancer of the prostate; difficulty and pain in urination, not understood by early physicians, e.g., "Dr. Lockhart prescribed opium enemas and hot hip baths for strangery."

street washer: a horse-drawn vehicle that sprayed water on streets during the summer, thereby rinsing away refuse, manure, etc., and keeping down the dust, e.g., "The new street washer kept much of the dust out of the stores along the main streets of 1880 Marion."

streetcars, horsecars, trolleys: public conveyances, usually on tracks, designed for a number of people; streetcars and trolleys usually were powered by electricity, and horsecars by horses, e.g., "Virtually every late 19th-century city of any size had, first, horsecars and, later, streetcars or trolleys."

stretcher: in furniture, those struts or reinforcements between the legs of tables, chairs, and other furniture, so mounted as to add strength and stability to the whole, e.g., "In furniture of the William and Mary period, **turners** (q.v.) usually made stretchers with round ball shapes."

stroking, stroking of a corpse, stroking the body: early judges, coroners, and sheriffs frequently required a person suspected of murder through violence other than the obvious (by gunshot or stabbing) to touch or rub the corpse, it being supposed that it would show signs of life or lividity if the suspect was guilty, e.g., "No signs of life having been witnessed upon stroking, the suspect was released."

strong box: a small to medium box with lock, usually transportable by one or two men, e.g., "The valuables of the passengers often were carried in the stagecoach strong box."

strop, strap, razor strop, razor strap: a very common strap of polished leather used to put a final edge on a very sharp knife or **straight razor** (q.v.) by rubbing the blade against it, e.g., "Every barber chair had a razor strop hanging at the barber's hand height."

stuff: any unfinished cloth or material, e.g., "The 'other stuffs' referred to in the inventory were cloth and fabrics."

subpoena: an order directing one to appear before a court or other body having the authority to summon, e.g., "Since she failed to answer the subpoena delivered by the sheriff, the court found her in contempt."

subscribing witness: one who in writing on a document attests to the signature of another on that document, e.g., "Subscribing witnesses to a will quite usually were present when the decedent signed it."

sucket: candy (q.v.), hard candy; sugar candy; any **sweetmeat** (q.v.) to be dissolved in the mouth, e.g., "There are numerous instances of quantities of suckets being transported."

sudoritick: a purge; any medication that induced sweating, e.g., "Sweating having been considered necessary to a balancing of the humours, numerous plants were used as sudoriticks, especially hot peppers."

suffrage: the right or privilege to vote, e.g., "On August 25, 1920, the 19th Amendment provided suffrage for women."

sugar: a sugar bowl, usually without a lid, e.g., "The inventory revealed eight salts and a sugar." Also see **sugar box** and **salt dish.**

sugar box, sugar pot: early, a box to store and keep cake or loaf sugar dry and free from insects; usually, a sugar bowl, e.g., "The sugar pot was pewter." Also see **sugar,** and **loaf sugar.**

sugar firkin: See **firkin.**

sugar grater, sugar nippers, sugar hatchet, sugar shears, sugar cutter: household tools for dividing or breaking up **loaf sugar** (q.v.), e.g., "In the 17th and early 18th centuries refined sugar was so expensive that every grain was carefully picked from the sugar grater."

sugar house, sugary: the facility or building in which sap from maple trees is boiled down into maple syrup and maple sugar, e.g., "The sugar house on the old Strine property dated from 1845."

sugar, loaf: See **loaf sugar.**

sugar tit: a piece of cloth either soaked in or wrapped around sugar or other sweetener, shaped like a nipple and very commonly given to infants to pacify them, e.g., "She regularly made sugar tits from maple sugar and cotton cloth."

sugary: See **sugar house.**

suit: in furniture, as now, e.g., "A bedroom suit usually consisted of a **wash stand** or **commode, a chest of drawers** or **chiffonier,** and a **bedstead** (all, q.v.), while a parlor suit usually was a **settee** (q.v.) and two matching chairs."

sulky, road cart: a very light, single-seated vehicle for one or two people, having two high wheels and pulled by one horse, commonly upholstered and used for quick trips about a city, or stripped down and pulled by pacers and trotters in racing, e.g., "The famous Houghton Sulky Company of Marion was yet in the business of building sulkies in 1950." Also see **gait.**

summary: in genealogy, a writing of different wording that abbreviates, summarizes, or paraphrases significant or important portions of another writing or source, e.g., "In writing summaries of the abstract works of others, one must be aware of the copyright laws." Also see **abstract, extract, copyright,** and **Fair Use.**

summer kitchen: prior to air conditioning and modern appliances, cast iron stoves created and retained so much heat that for summer use they were moved outside the main house kitchen (winter kitchen) and into an open sided, roofed outside room, e.g., "The annual chore of moving the big stove to the summer kitchen fell to the men of the family."

summer soldiers, sunshine patriots: Revolutionary War expressions, disdainfully referring to those who were willing to serve in the warm months when it was relatively easy, but not during the winter season, e.g., "During the early days, when there was no draft as we know it, men were at liberty to be summer soldiers if they so chose."

summons: a subpoena; an order directing one to appear before a court or other body having the authority to summon; courts issue summons, sheriffs serve them, e.g., "A summons issued ordering John Boortly to appear at the next court in the matter of the claim against him by Richard Parker."

sun time: before the railroad and the invention of the telegraph in the 19th century required an adoption of standard times and time zones, time usually was reckoned by the position of the sun at noon wherever one might be, especially on June 21 and December 21 (the summer and winter solstices), resulting in many different times across the country, e.g., "Until rapid communication from area to area made it necessary, even the President found that sun time served his needs."

Sunday go to meeting clothes: See **_meeting clothes._**

sunshine patriots: See **_summer soldiers._**

Superior Court: a term of varying definition; in some states the lowest court having appellate jurisdiction; elsewhere, a court of original jurisdiction; and in still other jurisdictions, an ordinary court of **_nisi prius_** (q.v.) jurisdiction, e.g., "The family researcher must know the meaning of the words _superior court_ in that state in which research is being done."

Supreme Court: a term of varying definition; our highest Federal court, maintaining ultimate appellate jurisdiction and original jurisdiction in matters of extraordinary writs; in some states, the lowest court having appellate jurisdiction; in other states, the lowest court having original jurisdiction (of record), e.g., "The case was appealed from the Court of Appeals for the Sixth Circuit to the U.S. Supreme Court; "The first appeal from decisions made in California is to the Supreme Court"; "He filed his damage suit in the Supreme Court at Albany, New York."

surety: one who, through a pledge of money or other thing of value, guarantees the truth of some matter or the appearance of himself or another; nearly synonymous with bondsman, e.g., "He acted as surety for the administrator of the James Drake estate."

surfeit: overindulgence in food or drink, e.g., "Surfeit was treated with caffeine and a diet of vegetables and fruit."

surgeon: See **_chirurgeon._**

surname: the family or "last name" of a person, quite usually that of the adoptive or natural father, e.g., "She repeated her surname, Alexander, as the middle name of her son."

surrey: a four-wheeled carriage with two forward-facing seats, usually with a removable top, e.g., "The musical "Oklahoma" accurately depicted a 'surrey with a fringe on top'."

surrogate's court: a court of probate jurisdiction, e.g., "The New York Surrogate's court has the same jurisdiction as do the **_Chancellors_** (q.v.) of Tennessee." See also **_probate court._**

sutler: a person who sells food, drink, newspapers and necessaries to an army, e.g., "Sutlers went everywhere that Grant's armies."

Sutter's Mill: a mill being erected by J. W. Marshall for Johann A. Sutter on a branch of American River in Eldorado County, California, at which site Marshall discovered gold (24 January, 1848), the spread of the news of which sparked the California Gold Rush, e.g., "After his discovery at Sutter's Mill, Marshall waited for days before telling Mr. Sutter and others." Also see **_Forty-niners._**

swage, swag, swagged: a steel tool of the blacksmith used to create bends in unheated iron, e.g., "He had the apprentice hold one end while he swagged the other end."

sweet lard: lard without salt, e.g., "Sweet lard was often used for cooking pastries."

sweet oils: any edible oil, especially as in medications, e.g., "Needing a sweet oil, Dr. Drake used clove oil mixed with chloroform for toothaches."

sweetbreads: the pancreas of a calf or pig; a delicacy, e.g., "Mrs. Randolph's recipe for 'oysters and sweetbreads casserole' is superb, albeit loaded with cholesterol."

sweetmeats: usually, candied fruits; sometimes, any confection or very sweet finger food, e.g., "She made sweetmeats of many varieties, including raspberries, cherries, peaches, and strawberries."

swift: See **yarn swift.**

swing team, swing horses: lead horses or that horse or horses ahead of the wheelers and usually just behind the lead horses, usually younger, strong, and trained to turn as commanded, e.g., "The swing horses were three-year-old black Percherons, just learning to work as commanded."

swine, hogs: early, a pig or shoat was a young hog of either sex, a boar was a grown male, and a sow was a grown, at least once-bred female, e.g., "The inventory listed the swine as '3 sows with ten shoats, 18 pigs, and a boar.'"; "Most early writings speak of swine generally, and of hogs (males), sows (females), and shoats and pigs (young) particularly."

swine plague: See **cholera.**

swing chair: See **hammock chair.**

swing horse: a toy; a model of a horse, saddle, and bridle mounted on springs and a stand, the same used by children in pretending to ride a horse, e.g., "If the family could not afford a swing horse, **hobby horses** (q.v.) were the next best thing."

swingleg table: See **gateleg table.**

swingletree, singletree, doubletree, whippletree, tree: a pivoted crossbar used with one horse, usually of hickory or oak, to which **traces** (q.v.) are connected, thereby delivering the power of horses or other **draft** (q.v.) animals to the load; a doubletree is used when two animals are **hitched** (q.v.), e.g., "As Paul pulled onto the scales, the team pulled the tree in two."

sworn statement: testimony to facts (written or spoken) that involves some legal proceeding, or is done in compliance with a requirement of government, the same usually invoking the name of God and done before an officer empowered to administer oaths, e.g., "To gain her widow's pension, Prudence had to submit a sworn statement that she and the veteran had been married on February 2, 1832."

syllabub, sillibub: a favored, early drink made of milk curdled by the addition of wine (or cider), usually with a sweetener added, e.g., "Syllabubs topped with sweet whipped cream were a favorite of many."

syndic: a burgess or recorder; an agent of a corporation or university, e.g., "The records reveal a finding that a syndic acted as an agent for a Minnesota corporation."

synod: any general meeting of ecclesiastical people concerning religion; a meeting of ecclesiastics within some specific district, e.g., "A synod was held in Pencader Hundred in the state of Delaware."

syphilis, great pox: as now, the dreaded, crippling venereal disease, e.g., "Though none were effective, early physicians strove desperately to cure syphilis." Also see **chancre,** and **clap.**

T

tack: in Scotland, a lease, e.g., "Early Scottish settlers and records occasionally referred to leases as tacks."

tackle: See **blocks and tackle.**

taffeta: a thin, finely woven silk, e.g., "Taffeta appears in many early inventories."

taffy pull: See **candy pull.**

take against: an expression used widely, meaning that one dissents from the terms of a will, and chooses to inherit through the laws of **descent and distribution** (q.v.) or by **intestate succession** (q.v.), e.g., "In 1804, the records reveal that Judith Matheny took against the will of her husband Daniel."

take the waters: usually meaning to go to an inn or resort offering mineral baths for one's health, e.g., "Stonewall Jackson often took the waters in the resorts of Shenandoah Valley."

talesman: a prospective juror summoned from among bystanders or folks about the halls of the courthouse, e.g., "Early references to talesmen are common, since on court days a large portion of the citizenry was near the courthouse."

tallow: animal fat, usually beef, melted, poured into molds, and cooled; as were whale spermaceti, beeswax, and the wax extracted from bayberries, it was used to make candles or burn with a wick for illumination, e.g., "Her tallow candles were the best she had until bayberry season."

tambour desk, tambour: See **rolltop desk.**

taminy: a woolen cloth of medium quality, e.g., "The inventory appearance of a taminy shawl reflects but moderate affluence."

tam-o'-shanter: a tasseled cap, originally from Scotland, usually made of wool and having a berm that falls slightly about the head, e.g., "Tam-o'-shanters were commonly worn by young men of the colonies, especially by **dandies** (q.v.)."

tankard: a large, wooden or metal mug, with a lid and handle, e.g., "The old tavernkeeper still served ale in the big tankards."

taper: a thin wax candle, commonly used in sconces and tapered at the wick end to nearly a point; a string or wick coated with wax sufficient to stiffen it for use in lighting other candles or gas lamps, e.g., "She had a **sconce** (q.v.) that held three tapers."

tavern table: a small, usually square or rectangular, very sturdy table with one or two drawers and occasionally of small drop leaf design, the slightly splayed legs providing stability, typically used by two, three or four people while drinking, e.g., "Her maple tavern table dated from about 1850."

tavern, saloon, tippling house: a place where drinkers are entertained, usually with minimal food and without overnight accommodations, the rates of which were frequently set by a court having county-wide jurisdiction; a saloon usually was a lower class tavern, e.g., "To the dismay of the preachers, every small town had its share of taverns"; "The upper class might speak of having been to a tavern, but not admit to visiting a saloon."

tax lists: lists of taxable persons, the ages of which varied at different time periods and places, e.g., "The 1846 tax lists revealed three men surnamed Martin."

tax office: usually, the office of the local or county tax assessor or tax collector; may also designate a state office of similar purpose, e.g., "They sought the personal property tax records in the tax office."

tea strainer: a very fine sieve, typically used to separate leaves or grounds from tea or coffee, and to strain medications, e.g., "She had all sizes of sieves, a **tea strainer, a searce,** a **colander,** and a **riddle.**" (all, q.v.)

tea table: a table of many designs and periods, small, usually rounded or square, without drawers and used to serve teas, coffee, or chocolate, e.g. "Her tea table was cherry and Victorian in styling." Also see **center table.**

teacher's desk: See **schoolmaster's desk.**

teamster: unlike now, one who earned a livelihood by driving a team of animals, usually horses or mules, e.g., "He worked as a teamster for the Consolidated Milk Company."

Templars, Knights Templar: a religious order of knighthood organized in 1119, and having a modern counterpart in the form of a Masonic Order, e.g., "The original Knights Templar often undertook to protect travellers from harm and be charitable to poor Christians and pilgrims on journeys to religious sites."

tenancy by the entirety: an interest based on the ancient legal fiction that husband and wife were one person; an ownership by a husband and wife in the whole of something by reason of a conveyance or transfer naming both; when the marriage ended by whatever means, the estate or interest went to the survivor, e.g., "Unlike a **joint tenancy** (q.v.), where either party may sell mortgage, devise, or otherwise dispose of his or her interest, in a tenancy by the entirety both husband and wife must join in any action affecting the interest."

tenants in common: those who own land with another, yet gained that ownership by varying means or at different times, e.g., "The tenants in common were John, who gained his 1/3 interest through the will of his father, and James, who purchased his 2/3 from the father before he died."

tender age: early, under fourteen years, e.g., "The court appointed a guardian for the son who yet was of tender age."

tenements: structures situated on a specific tract of land, usually habitable, e.g., "The lease included the tenements and the rentals to be received from them."

Tenerife: See **Canary.**

tenterhooks, tinterhooks, on tenterhooks: hooks, shaped as fish hooks, attached along the sides of a wooden frame, and upon which cloth was tightly stretched in order that it could dry without wrinkles or bends, from whence is derived the expression, e.g., "Saying that 'she was on tenter-hooks' meant that she was in a state of painful stress or anxiety."

term, term of court: in genealogy, that period of time during which a court is regularly in session, e.g., "The Michaelmas term of court began on June 1, 1674, and continued for twenty four days."

terminer: See *oyer and terminer (courts of).*

territory: a political subdivision having the achievement of statehood as its ultimate purpose, e.g., "The Territory of Alaska became a State in 1949."

testamentary, letters testamentary, testamentary capacity, testamentary power, etc.: a common term, pertaining to wills and the execution thereof, and also pertaining to gifts, deeds, appointments, and documents in general that do not take effect until the moment of death, e.g., "Having qualified as *executrix* (q.v.) letters testamentary were issued to her."

testamentary disposition: a conveyance or transfer of property by deed or gift in such a way as to appear like a will, e.g., "His statement that his impending death was the reason for transferring the land to his daughter made it a testamentary disposition." Also see *in contemplation of death.*

testamentary guardian: a guardian named in a will, e.g., "The court recognized the testamentary guardianship of John, who had been named in his brother's will as the person to care for the minor children."

testate: death with an operative (valid) will, e.g., "After her death testate, her executors undertook to execute the provisions of her will."

testator, testatrix: one who makes a will, e.g., "As testator and testra-trix, John and Jane Brown each devised the land to their sons."

teste, teste me, te.: witnessed or confirmed by me, the signer, e.g., "At the bottom of the copy was written, 'teste. G. Williams, Cl. Ct.' meaning that Gary Williams, Clerk to the Court, confirmed that the copy was a true one."

tester, tester bed: a posted bed with a framework for curtains or cano-py, e.g, "The tester bed was listed, as were a *rug, valance,* and *curtains.*"(all, q.v.)

tetanus, lockjaw: a dreaded and much feared, usually fatal disease resulting from bacteria entering the body through wounds, bites, and other penetrations of the skin, and attended by violent spasms and rigidity of certain muscles, e.g., "Early physicians tried even tobacco juice in their futile attempts to cure tetanus."

tetter: any of several breakings out or eruptive diseases of the skin, such as impetigo or eczema, e.g., "Many cures, including ground insects and tar, were used for tetter."

Texas, Republic of: 1836 - 1845, that short-lived republic (Sam Hous-ton, Pres.) based on a constitution (adopted 2 March, 1836) similar to that of the U.S., that after the battles of the Alamo (March 6) and San Jacinto (April 21) signed a peace treaty with Mexico and 8 years thereafter gained admission to the Union under Pres. Tyler, e.g., "The Republic of Texas was being formed during Santa Anna's siege of the Alamo."

thible: See *peel.*

thimble: recently, as now; early, a sleeve mounted in a wall or ceiling, through which the stack or exhaust from a stove passes to the outside, and designed to prevent fires in the walls or ceilings, e.g., "Without a thimble, the danger of fire was very great."

thirds: a rather imprecise manner of referring to that share of a deceased husband's estate to which a widow is entitled if there were children, e.g., "The court ordered the administrator to divide what would have been the widow Parker's thirds between her two surviving sons."

thorn: (𝖄 or 𝕏) an ancient Saxon symbol, common in early writings and in longhand similar to the small case letter "y", it represented the sound and letters "th", e.g., "The thorn (𝖄) often is found preceding 'at' for the word 'that', preceding 'is' for 'this', and preceding 'e' meaning 'the'; our ancestors were not saying 'ye'."

thoroughbred: early, meaning of very fine bloodlines; now, those horses bred primarily for speed and stamina and ridden in contests of jumping, steeplechasing, and flat racing, e.g., "Triple Crown champions Citation and Man O' War are two of the most famous thoroughbreds."

thrall: a servant slave; bondman; serf.

thraldom: slavery; occasionally voluntary **servitude** (q.v.), e.g., "Descriptions of people as in a state of thraldom occasionally appear in 17th-century records of ships' passengers."

threshing, threshing time: at harvest season, that labor-intensive task of harvesting grain, especially wheat, and loading it into the threshing machine that separated the stalks and chaff from the grain, e.g., "At threshing time, as the women prepared huge meals, the men of the neighborhood, all working together and assisting each other, undertook the harvesting and threshing the crop, the following day moving on to the next farm."

throw away, throw away person, throw away animal: a person or animal of little worth, value, or desirability, a **common** (q.v.) person, e.g., "When told that her pet was pretty, she said it had been but a throw away kitten."

throw down: an expression of the South and west, the derivation of which is now unknown, meaning to be critical of one usually while that person is in the presence of others, or to ridicule or chastise one of a group of persons, e.g., "Jones told the innkeeper that he should not throw down on his customer."

thrush (the): sores and white spots in the mouth, usually of infants, e.g., "Dr. Drake prescribed potassium chlorate washes and eucalyptus for the thrush."

tic-tac-toe: See **ticktack**.

ticking bag, tick: an early form of mattress; a bag made of heavy cloth, usually canvas or **oznaburg,** (q.v.) and filled with straw, feathers, or rags (flock), e.g., She had three ticking bags that she referred to as ticks."

tickler bottle: See **sniffing bottle**.

ticktack: tic-tac-toe, as now, e.g., "As now, ticktack was a favorite game of our ancestors." Also see **games**.

tidewater Virginia (or NC, GA, MD, etc.): any of the seaboard counties lying generally in the area below the fall lines and affected by the tides, e.g., "The fishing in the estuaries of tidewater Virginia was superb."

tierce: 1/3 **pipe** (q.v.); 42 gallons, e.g., "He ordered two tierces of Madeira wine."

tiffany, tifany: very sheer, high quality material made of silk, used for better dresses, veils, and occasionally by the wealthy for bed curtains, e.g., "References to tifany are not uncommon in early inventories."

tilt-top table: any of the many styles of small to medium-sized tables with a top that tilted to the vertical position for storage or to conserve space, e.g., "She had a walnut, cloverleaf-shaped tilt-top table."

tin lizzie: an early term for a small, cheaply made and inexpensive automobile, even if new, e.g., "While she referred to their little Chevrolet as a tin lizzie, she referred to her son's old Ford coupe as a *flivver* (q.v.)."

tincture: any medicinal mixture using alcohol as the solvent or vehicle, e.g., "Tincture of Iodine was an antiseptic even very early."

tinder box: a box, usually wooden, used to hold the materials needed to kindle a fire, i.e., flint, a piece of steel, and fine very dry wood shavings (tinder), e.g., "Before matches, only a tinder box saved one from going to a neighbor to **borrow fire.**

tinsmith: one who has knowledge of and makes utensils, toys, lamps, etc., from tin and associated metals, e.g., "The first tinsmith in town did very well financially." Also see **tinware**.

tintype, ferrotype: a photograph made on a piece of sensitized metal, usually tin or iron, e.g., "There are many tintypes yet in family collections." Also see **ambrotype,** and **wet plate process**.

tinware: any of the many utensils and household items made of soldered tin; inexpensive and not very durable, tinware often was sold from door to door, and occasionally came painted, especially in New England, upstate New York, and Pennsylvania, e.g., "She had owned many pieces of tinware, however at her death but few of them remained."

tippling house: See **taverns,** and **ordinaries**.

tire: unlike now, the metal band secured tightly around the circumference of a wheel, the same holding the rim tight against the spokes and hub, and upon which surface the wheel rolled, e.g., "Upon the loss of a tire, the wheel would not last long."

tit-tat-toe: In early PA and NY, same as **ticktack**. Also see **games**.

tithables, tithes: in the church, those portions of income allotted to religious causes; in genealogy, usually those persons subject to taxation by virtue of their age, property owned, or residency; one is tithable when required to pay tithes, e.g., "The total money received as tithes was £220"; "He was shown tithable in the 1676 Surry County lists.

title: rights owned in some property, e.g., "Title in land is said to vest in the devisees at the moment of death."

titled land: See **land grants.**

toaster: a medium-handled, wire or fine wrought iron holder used for toasting one or more slices of bread over an open fire, e.g., "The use of early toasters was a **chore** (q.v.) often assigned to little children."

tobacco knife, tobacco cutter: a large, heavy, wooden-handled, long-bladed knife with a sharp curved tip, used to cut the heavy stems of tobacco for harvest, e.g., "Every Southern farmer had one or more tobacco knives."

tobacconist: an occupation or calling; one who has knowledge of and sells or deals in tobaccos and pipes, and their uses, care, and handling, e.g., "Every city of the 19th century had several tobacconists."

toboggan: a small sled with a flat bottom that extends up and curves backwards in the front; in the southern Appalachians, often a soft knit wool covering for the head and ears, e.g., "In early times, oak or hickory was planed thin and shaped over frames into toboggans for the children"; "Jess insisted that the children wear their toboggans when going out in the cold."

tod: a measure of new wool; 28 lbs of wool, e.g., "The inventory revealed 2 tods of wool."

toffee pull: See **candy pull.**

toilet, toilet articles: as now, grooming ones self; tools and cloth used in shaving or grooming, e.g., "She was at her toilet."

tombac: a mixture of copper and zinc having the color of gold used in inexpensive jewelry, e.g., "The trouble with tombac jewelry was that the copper content left green marks on the skin of the wearer." Also see **Pinchbeck gold,** and **gold.**

tombstone: See **headstone.**

ton: usually, 2,000 lbs, but in recent New York a ton of 2,240 lbs avoirdupois was recognized, e.g., "Early merchants of coal and metals were careful to learn the poundage of the ton being discussed." Also see **long ton.**

tongue: that wooden shaft extending forward between draft animals to which were attached **whiffletrees** (q.v.) through all of which animal power was brought to bear to move the load, e.g., "Tongues were usually oak or hickory."

tonics: as now, elixirs supposed to aid in general health, e.g., "Tonics were made from myriad substances, including alcoholic drinks and teas made of blackhaw root, brier hips, curled mint, dandelion root, gentian, goldenseal root, and St. John's wort."

toothdrawer: one who pulled teeth for hire, e.g., "Dental science (and, thus, dentists) having been unknown, **chirurgeons** (q.v.), toothdrawers, and parents served in their stead."

top buggy: See **buggy.**

top: See **whirligig.**

topos: See **quadrangles,** and **Geological Survey, U.S.**

Tories: in the colonies (including the American), the 18th century political party made up of those who supported the British in their view that the established church, monarchy, and existing form of government and status of colonies should be maintained, e.g., "At every turn, the Tories were rebuked by those colonist who sought independence."

tote sack, gunny sack, feed sack: any large cloth sack or bag made of hemp or other heavy material, e. g, "He referred to the empty feed bags as tote sacks." Also see **sackcloth.**

touching the dead body: See **stroking.**

town: now, usually a small political subdivision without a court of general jurisdiction; in New England, early, a governing authority much like a county that usually received grants of 36 sq. miles (now, a township), e.g., "During the mid 19th century, small towns serving as agricultural centers were scattered throughout the Midwest"; "She went to the Town Meeting in order to be heard on the tax issue."

town crier: early, that person hired by governments of cities to shout or otherwise make public announcements; that calling and person paid for by a community to announce new laws, news, the hour of the day, and affairs of interest to the townspeople, e.g., "In the late 17th and early 18th centuries, before the advent of inexpensive newspapers and clocks, town criers were common, especially in New England."

town meeting: a meeting, usually at regular intervals, of the qualified voters of a New England **town** (q.v.) in order that the affairs of that political subdivision might be carried out, e.g., "In its 'town meeting' of 1987, Fentress County, TN, undertook to copy the Greenwich, CN, model."

township: (abbr. "T") in some states (e.g., OK, UT, KS, IL), a political subdivision and part of a county or precinct, and varying in size; in surveys of public lands of the U.S., 36 square miles (6 miles X 6 miles, 36 **sections** (q.v.) of 1 sq. mi. each), e.g., "In early times, Justices of the Peace and Constables represented the broader law and kept the peace within a township"; "Throughout Ohio and Illinois, most lands that once were public lands are divided into townships of 36 sq. miles."

trace, traces: See **harness.**

trade dollar: a silver coin of 420 grains of silver, **Troy** (q.v.), e.g., "The coinage of trade dollars resulted from a need for a uniform quantity of silver to represent the U.S. dollar."

tradesman: a shopkeeper; one who kept store of common dry and hardware necessities, e.g., "What later were keepers of general stores early were known as tradesmen."

trains, great: as now, e.g., "A list of great passenger trains of the late 19th and early 20th centuries surely would include Royal Blue, Bluebird, Orange Blossom Special, City of San Francisco, 20th Century Limited, Wabash Cannonball, Zephyr, and Chief."

trammel: a fireplace hanger for pots, kettles, etc, e.g., "A stew kettle hung on the trammel most of the winter."

transcript: a verbatim record or exact copy of a portion or all of some proceedings, writings, or words, e.g., "A transcript was made of most of her writings for use by researchers."

Transylvania ('State' of): that temporary state and government formed during the Revolution (1775) by Kentucky settlers, most of whom had Virginia and North Carolina roots, e.g., "As a monument to the efforts of the North Carolinians, Transylvania College thrives today at Lexington, Kentucky."

traslado: a copy, e.g., "Early Texas reports often refer to trasladoes, meaning simply exact copies of some other document."

trebucket: See **ducking stool.**

tree: See **swingletree.**

trencher: early, a very common, small to medium-sized, flat plate, usually made of wood, upon which meat or other food to be cut or carved was served, e.g., "Every home of the 17th and 18th century had one or more trenchers."

trepan: a surgeons' tool used to cut pieces from the skull, e.g., "The trepan and the practice of trepanning were well known even before the Christian era and not uncommon in England in Elizabethan times."

trestle table, trestle bench: a common, usually roughly finished table or bench with two legs shaped like an inverted "T", e.g., "The old trestle table in his shop had stood in the house during harder times."

tricorne: a three-pointed or triangular shaped colonial hat, usually of felt, e.g., "When men wore their tricornes, it often was to draw attention to their natural hair or their dislike for **periwigs** (q.v.); more often they carried their hat."

trinkets: small, decorative items worn on the person, e.g., "Early listings of trinkets often included jewelry."

trivet: a usually small, perforated, flat, iron platform with 2- to 4-inch legs, used to support pots, frying pans, etc., e.g., "She pulled coals out on the hearth with the **oven rake** (q.v.) and placed a trivet over them to heat the pot."

trivet kettle: a lidded iron pot with three legs, used like a **trivet** (q.v.) and pot, e.g., "In addition to her trivet kettle, she had two other kettles."

trolleys: See **streetcars.**

trophies: See **ornaments.**

trot: See **gaits.**

Troy weights: that system of weights by which precious metals and bread were measured in early times, e.g., "Physicians and **apothecaries** (q.v.) from colonial times down to the mid-twentieth century used Troy weight equivalents as follows:

      20 grains = a scruple,

      3 scruples = 1 drachm or dram,

      8 drachms or drams = 1 ounce,

      and, as with all Troy measurements, 12 ounces equal 1 pound."

truckle bed: See **trundle bed.**

trumped up, trumpery: to cause an appearance of value where little is present, e.g., "The old cruet **caster** (q.v.) was painted and trumped up."

trundle bed, truckle bed: as now; a bed, sometimes wheeled, and low enough to be stored beneath another bed, e.g., "Trundle beds were very common in the early days, in order that space might be conserved."

trust deed: often imprecisely called a "mortgage deed of trust"; similar to a mortgage deed, however in trust deeds legal title is conveyed in trust from the borrower to a third party agreeable to both; as with mortgages, if the debt is paid as agreed the land is reconveyed to the borrower, e.g., "His brother-in-law served as the transferee in the trust deed." Also see **mortgage deed.**

tub: early, unlike now, usually a measure of 60 lbs. of tea, e.g., "Camphor often was measured in tubs, however the weight varied from 56 to 86 lbs, unlike tea, where a tub seems to universally have been 60 lbs." Also see **chest.**

tuberculosis, consumption, quick consumption, phthisis: as now, e.g., "In early times and usually to no avail, medications such as arsenic, creosote, **blisters** (q.v.), starch enemas, mercury, and calcium phosphate were administered for consumption." Also see **consumption.**

tucker: a small piece of linen worn out of doors to cover and thus shade the breasts of women wearing low-cut gowns, e.g., "The fear of skin cancer, desirability of pure white skin, and disdain for 'tans' led to the wearing of tuckers in summer by all ladies."

tumbler: usually as now; occasionally, an ornate or highly decorated, rather large earthen, porcelain, or ceramic, nearly cylindrical container without handles, e.g., "Her prize tumbler was cameo cut."

tumbrel: See **ducking stool.**

tun: four (4) hogsheads (256 gallons) of wine or oil, e.g., "The number of **hogsheads** (q.v.) appears more often than tun in early mentions of wine."

tureen: as now, a medium to large glass or earthen container, often with a lid, from which soup, gravy, consomme, or other liquid was served, e.g., "The soup tureen had been a part of Maggie's first dishes."

turf and twig: an ancient expression reflecting a transfer of possession and ownership of real property through the act of handing over to the grantee of a clod, piece of turf, bough, or twig, e.g., "Some very early Virginia deeds carried the expression 'turf and twig' reflecting the symbolic physical delivery of possession of the land."

turnbench: a small lathe, e.g., "From the earliest times turnbenches were made of iron."

turner: an occupation or calling; those who have knowledge and experience in wood lathe and wood shaping operations, and make turned parts for furniture, e.g., "When called upon to make truly fine furniture containing round parts, the **cabinetmaker** (q.v.) relied on the local turner for such shaping."

Turner, Nat, Insurrection: See **Nat Turner Insurrection.**

Turner Thesis: that hypothesis of Frederick Jackson Turner (and Beard) that the American frontier, and not the influences of commerce and the 'old countries', was by far the greatest factor in the molding and shaping of the American personality, character, and government, e.g., "The Turner thesis has been studied by every history student of the 20th century."

turnkey: early, one who worked for a sheriff, tended to prisoners, and had the responsibility of caring for the keys; now, anyone working about the courthouse or jail who has a measure of authority over prisoners, e,. g., "The sheriff referred to the officer then on duty as the turnkey."

turnpike, pike: very common, an early road constructed by laying down trimmed, small trees perpendicular to and across the roadbed, e.g., "Even early turnpikes often retained a ***washboard*** (q.v.) appearance and feel, into the 20th century."

turpentine: a derivative from the sap of pine trees, used very early for its supposed antiseptic properties, and as a vehicle for paint, e.g., "She lanced the boil, and put turpentine on it."

Twelfth Day: January 6; the twelfth day after Christmas, upon which the festival of the Epiphany was celebrated; the end of the Christmas season, e.g., "The twelve days of Christmas and Twelfth Day celebration were but scarcely observed in the colonies after the Revolution."

twiffler: perhaps a dish for hot puddings, e.g., "Twifflers apparently were known only in the American colonies."

twist: heavy string or cord, e.g., "During 1762, Hines bought several ***sticks*** (q.v.) of twist."

two handed: unlike now, large and bulky, e.g., "The chest was two handed."

tyke, tike: a small dog, e.g., "His grandmother called the little boy a cute little tyke."

tympany: flatulence, e.g., "Dr. Richardson administered an herb remedy for tympany."

U

U.C.V.: See ***United Confederate Veterans.***

U.S.G.S.: See ***Geological Survey, U.S.***

ulcers, gastric ulcers: as now, any draining or seeping sore, destruction of the inner wall or lining of the stomach, e.g., "His arm was ulcerated as a result of infection";"Gastric ulcers not being understood, such harsh remedies as arsenic, silver oxide, and lead acetate were employed."

ultimo (ult.): a term used in early writings and correspondence revealing that the writing at hand was being done during the month succeeding some prior act of writing, e.g., "If responding on March 10th to a letter written to you on February 20th, it would be appropriate to say, 'I received your note of the 20th Ultimo'." Also see ***instant.***

ultramarine: a very deep blue dye, e.g., "She used ultramarine, called French blue, to dye her work clothes."

Uncle Tom's Cabin: an 1852 anti-slavery novel by Harriet Beecher

Stowe that sold over 1.25 million copies, and gave rise to enormous anti-slavery feelings across the North, e.g., "Uncle Tom's Cabin did more to bring war than did any other writing."

under eaves bed: a short-legged, very low bed with little or no head or footboard, e.g., "There were two under eaves beds kept in the **garret** (q.v.)."

underground railway: that loose organization of over 3000 anti-slavery citizens that operated from about 1830 until the last days of the Civil War, and provided hiding places and varying measures of transportation and sustenance for negroes making their way to the North, e.g., "What is now the Stengel-True Museum in Marion, Ohio is said to have been a 'station' on the underground railway."

undulant fever, brucellosis: an often fatal disease causing severe remittent fevers in humans and abortions in many animals, e.g., "The occurrence of spontaneous abortions in two ewes caused her to fear the presence of undulant fever."

unfixed, unfixt: See **fixed.**

Union Army: the armed forces of the U.S. (the North) during the Civil War, e.g., "The Union Army often was referred to as the Boys in Blue."

Union Veterans, Sons of: See **Sons of Union Veterans, The.**

union: in genealogy, a marriage - ordained, licensed, or common law - or other legal association of man and woman, e.g., "They were married in 1850, and to that union were born six children."

United Confederate Veterans: (The U.C.V.) a fraternal organization of Confederate Veterans of the Civil War, including those who served in the Navy; as was the **G.A.R.** (q.v.), the U.C.V. was a powerful political force in the last years of the 19th century, e.g., "If one hoped to be elected to Southern office at the turn of the 20th century, he sought the aid of the U. C. V."

United Kingdom, United Kingdom of Great Britain and Ireland: the official title of the kingdom consisting of England, Scotland, Wales, and Ireland, e.g., "The United Kingdom was an ally of the U.S. during World War II."

unnatural will: a will that disposes of an estate to strangers and largely or entirely excludes those who would be expected to benefit therefrom, e.g., "A California court referred to Shay's will as unnatural."

up (a suffix): an ancient expression meaning to accomplish, finish, or complete some effort, e.g., "Expressions using the up suffix, such as grocery up, eat up, wash up, dress up, sew up, beat up, and speak up, were very common."

urban: being within a city, borough, village or concentrated settlement, as opposed to a rural location, e.g., "Records revealing urban lifestyle of the 19th century are common."

uremia, uremic poisoning: a fatal and misunderstood retention of those wastes usually disposed of by the kidneys, e.g., "Diuretics, caffeine, crotan oil, and mustard plasters all were believed to give relief in cases of uremia."

ursicatories: medications used to cover wounds and prevent infection, e.g., "Glycerin was a base for many favorite ursicatories."

USGS topos: See **quadrangles.**

uxor: See **et ux.**

V

valance bed, valence, valons: a bed with draw curtains and often with a fringe surrounding the canopy; the decorative drapery that hangs from the canopy of a bed, e.g., "There was a valance bed and **curtains** (q.v.) in the inventory of her estate"; "The presence of several valances in the inventory is an important clue to relative affluence."

valid: legally sufficient; incapable of being legitimately set aside; binding and of force and effect, e.g., "The deed was valid, it having been properly written, executed, and delivered."

valons: See **valance bed.**

van -: (Du.) a prefix meaning from, originally referred to a town, village,etc., from which the subject person came, e.g., "The name van der Hoffen is revealing of an area in which that family once lived and called home."

vara: a Spanish-American measure of length equalling 33 inches, e.g., "While a meter is about three inches longer than a yard, a vara is about three inches shorter."

varmint, varmit: any animal, especially squirrels, foxes, wolves, hawks, owls, lynx, coyotes, prairie dogs, Carolina Parakeets, etc., early considered to be a menace to settlers or their crops or livestock, and upon which bounties often were paid, e.g., "Bounties were being paid for the ears of wolves and other varmints as early as 1670." Also see **bounty.**

varnish: a fine, very hard finish used on wood, especially fine furniture and musical instruments, and made of natural resins dissolved in spirits, e.g., "The varnish on Stradivarius violins is of the finest natural resins, and has lasted for hundreds of years."

vaudevil: from which arose our vaudeville; Johnson said 'songs sung by the vulgar, a trivial strain', e.g., "The change from disdain of the vulgar called vaudevil to the classification of light and gay humor and dancing as vaudeville did not take place until the late 19th century."

vellum: kid or lamb skin, finely finished and used for important documents, e.g, "Many early land grants were on vellum."

vendee, vendor: a vendee is a buyer, and a vendor is a seller of personal property (**personalty**, q.v.), e.g., "In vendors and vendees the suffixes -or and -ee are from the Latin."

vendue, public vendue: an auction, e.g., "Many early documents speak of matters sold at public vendue."

venereal diseases: See ***chancre, clap, syphilis.***

venire facias, venire, venireman: usually that writ or list of citizens ordered to appear as prospective jurors, e.g., "A notation that an ancestor appeared on the venire or venire facias or was a venireman means that he or she was a prospective juror during that ***term of court*** (q.v.)."

venter: any of the three cavities of the body, i.e., the head, chest, and abdomen, e.g., "Early writings of physicians and ***chirurgeons*** (q.v.) often speak of ***distempers*** (q.v.) within one of the venters."

venue: that county or place where an event is said to have taken place or where one may demand that a lawsuit be heard, e.g., "The property was in Rowan County, so venue for an action in detainer was also there."

vera, vera., ver., vera record: abbreviations for "verified" often found at the conclusion of early documents, and followed by the name of the clerk or other verifying officer, revealing that the document is a true copy or is correct as against another copy or the original, e.g., "In the 1679 inventory, following the words Vera record, the clerk of Surry placed a "crossed p" and then his initials, meaning 'per himself'."

veranda: a covered portico or porch, e.g., "Verandas were a common feature of Victorian houses."

verify, verification: usually, an oath as to the truth or validity of some writing; occasionally, an oath as to an oral statement, e.g., "He verified the complaint of the lawsuit."

vestry, vestrymen: in the American colonies, the entirety of the ministry, elders or church wardens and the parishioners; occasionally, a small room in a church; often, a committee or group of people (early, usually affluent men) appointed to tend to the physical condition and business affairs of the church, e.g., "The vestry register contained notes as to various activities of the church, congregation, and the minister, including baptisms and repairs to the church";"William Hunt was a 17th-century vestryman in Charles City County."

veteran: in genealogy, anyone who served in the military for any period of time - whether the service was by conscription (***draft,*** q.v.) or voluntarily - in any militia unit or in the service of the federal, state, or territorial government or militia, and who was honorably separated from that service unit, e.g., "Matheny was a veteran, having served during the Revolution in the militia from Shenandoah County."

veterinarians: early physicians and ***chirurgeons*** (q.v.) also cared for livestock, especially valuable horses and dogs, e.g., "As early as the 1640s, the records reveal that John Spilman recovered his fees for veterinary care of a horse belonging to Smith."

Victorian period: that name given the period 1840 - 1900 (Queen Victoria's reign) during which the dark colors, massive, often ostentatious, Baroque, Gothic, and geometrically elaborate designs in furniture and architecture dominated, e.g., "Of the 'antiques' being marketed in the last quarter of the 20th century, Victorian pieces are the most common."

victuals, vittles: often, any food; sometimes, ready-to-eat food, e.g., "He was the ship's victualer"; "The many early references of seeing to or gaining the wherewithal for the family vittles referred to ordinary daily foods or nutritional necessities."

victualer: a grocer or seller, usually of unprepared food, e.g., "The ships' victualer made a handsome profit."

videlicet, viz.: "to-wit" and "that is" are videlicets; that symbol or term indicating that the words following are comments or itemizations elucidating the remark, e.g., "His comments that 'the livestock, viz., two cows, three horses, and a mule, were bequeathed to the eldest son' was an example of the use of the videlicet."

vinegar of the 4 thieves: a room freshener, especially for **chambers** (q. v.) of the sick, e.g., "To make vinegar of the 4 thieves, to a gallon of strong vinegar (in an earthenware container) she added a handful each of leaves of lavender, sage, rosemary, wormwood, rue, and mint, the covered container then was left in the hottest sun for 2 weeks, after which it was carefully drained, and the fluid was bottled with a clove of garlic in each bottle."

vinous liquors: See **liquors.**

vintner: one who sells wine, e.g., "Wine shops are operated by vintners."

virginal: a common, small, square or rectangular plucked stringed musical instrument held in the lap, e.g., "Virginals were perhaps the most common of the early stringed instruments found in the colonies."

Virginia cloth, Virginia plain: plain, unbleached, homespun cloth from which work and slaves' clothing were made, e.g., "Many early North Carolina inventories reveal quantities of Virginia cloth."

Virginia reel: from an early Scottish dance (reel) brought to Virginia in the 17th century, modified, and very much enjoyed by colonials, e.g., "At the party they danced several waltzes and as many Virginia reels."

Virginia rum: probably, rum made in Virginia or specifically for Virginia merchants, e.g., "The inventory revealed a half barrel of Virginia Rum."

virtuous: as now, e.g., "A Georgia court once said that a woman is virtuous if '...she has never had sexual intercourse with another, though both her mind and heart be impure.'"

vital statistics: information important to the operation of government; dates of births, deaths, marriages and divorces, etc., e.g., "After 1914, all states were required to maintain an office housing the vital statistics of that state"; "The Ohio Bureau of Vital Statistics is located in Columbus."

vittles: See **victuals.**

vixen: a female fox, early viewed as a **varmint** (q.v.) upon which bounties were paid, e.g., "The vixen had 4 **cubs** (q.v.)."

viz.: See **videlicet.**

vizard: a mask or pretense, e.g., "The court report said that the 'vizard would be taken off and his wickedness plainly demonstrated'."

void, voidable: for genealogical purposes, void meant the intended result never took place or was ineffectual in accomplishing that which was intended; voidable meant that knowledge has been gained or acts done

W

waffle iron: as now, small, hinged, iron griddles with long handles used to bake waffles in a fireplace, e.g., "The waffle irons saw much use on cold winter mornings."

Wagon Road, Great, Great Philadelphia: that heavily travelled route of immigration to the west and south that extended from Philadelphia west to Lancaster, thence through the Shenandoah Valley (the Valley Road) and into the Carolinas, Georgia, etc., especially the area near present Salisbury and Rowan County, NC, e.g., "Many of the Germans of eastern Pennsylvania ended up in central Tennessee by travelling the Great Wagon Road and then the Walton Road."

wagon: a general term for any horse-drawn vehicle used for general, hauling and utility purposes, e.g., "Those of high station had carriages, while the bulk of society rode in wagons." Also see **carriage.**

wagonmaker: an ancient occupation or calling; one who had knowledge of the many parts of a wagon and the methods of best making and assembling them, e.g., "As a wagonmaker, he often needed the services of the **blacksmith, wheelwright,** and **harnessmaker."** All, q.v.

wainscot, wainscotting, wainscot chair: wooden paneling, especially in halls and doorways; a very early, heavy, usually oak, hickory, or chestnut chair with a solid back, e.g., "The wainscotting was walnut and butternut"; "The wainscot chair dated from the 1650s."

wair: a measure of lumber, equaling two yards by one foot by one inch; 6 board feet of lumber, e.g., "By the time of the Revolution, the word wair seems to have been abondoned in favor of 'board feet'."

waistcoat, wescot, weskit: early, a man's vest, later a vest for either man or woman, e.g., "His weskit was of burgundy silk"; "She wore a red velvet waistcoat."

wake: a watching over of a corpse, especially throughout the nights before burial; in America, usually accompanied by celebration, drinking, and partying, e.g., "Wakes came into existence centuries ago to prevent the burial of the 'dead' who were but in a coma."

walk: See **gaits.**

walk the dog: an early superlative among men operating heavy or large machinery, probably derived from the fact that in the early days only the very finest of dogs would be walked, and even then only by people of the upper class, all others fending for themselves, e.g., "When the big steam engine performed beyond the expectations of everybody, Evan smiled broadly and announced that it 'flat out was walking the dog'." Also see **flat.**

Walker, walking horse, Tennessee Walker: a smooth-gaited saddle horse, usually a mix of Morgan and Standardbred, noted for the exaggerated high step of the front feet, e.g., "The Walker had been **sored** (q.v.), hence had a very high step."

walking wheel: See **spinning wheel.**

wall eye, wall-eyed: usually, a horse with an unusual amount of white showing in its eyes, or one with near white or colorless irises, e.g., "He rode a walleyed Morgan." Also see **horses.**

wallet: unlike now, a small bag in which necessaries were carried for a trip of some distance, e.g., "For the requirements of the average work day a **purse** (q.v.) took the place of the wallet." Also see **pocketbook.**

Walton Road: See **roads, early.**

wampum: strung beads made from shell and used as currency by some American Indians; an early medium of exchange, e.g., "Wampum occasionally served as money for the white colonists of New England."

wamus: a short coat of heavy, warm homemade cloth, common to the rural areas of the north, e.g., "The Carners of early Centre County were known for their red or deep blue wamuses."

War Between The States: See **Civil War.**

War for Southern Independence: See **Civil War.**

War of 1812: that armed conflict between the United States and England during the years 1812-1814, e.g., "The British burned Washington during the War of 1812, and destroyed some of the Decennial Census of 1790 and much of the North Carolina militia records."

War of Independence, American Revolution: that armed conflict of the period 1775-1783/5 between the American colonies (with the aid of the French late in the war) and the British, as a result of victory in which the colonies became the United States, e.g., "His service in the Revolution made his descendants eligible for the **D.A.R.** (q.v.) and the **S.A.R.** (q.v.)."

War Of The Rebellion: See **Civil War.**

War of the Regulation: See **Regulators.**

ward: a political subdivision of a city or town having limited jurisdiction in matters of voting and elections, sanitary regulations, fire and police protection, and enumerations, e.g., "The ward and **precinct** (q.v.) leaders of early 20th century New York had wide influence."

wardrobe: a common, tall, wide, deep, often collapsible, usually two doored cabinet of the 19th and early 20th centuries, without legs, and having a divider, hooks, pegs, and often a shelf and drawers, used as a closet for the hanging of coats and clothing in general, especially in the winter; also, a room in which clothes were kept, a closet; e.g., "Her 7 foot wardrobe was of walnut and broke down into 6 pieces for summer storage." Also see **armoire.**

warehouse receipt: a written document providing evidence of the existence of property belonging to one person in the hands of another for hire (warehouseman); often employed as currency by early colonials where tobacco was being used as the medium of settlement, e.g., "He paid for his horse with a warehouse receipt for 2 **hogsheads** (q.v.) of tobacco."

warming pan: a **bedwarmer** (q.v.) or a shallow pan for warming food, e.g., "In association with several other kitchen utensils, the Parker estate of 1679 listed 'a warming pan'."

warrants: in law, an order by a court directing that a person or property be taken into custody; in genealogy, as said, and also, written documents issued to persons in exchange for military service or contributions of goods and services, enabling the recipient to gain lands or assets belonging to the U.S. Government, the states, or the colonies, e.g., "He sold his warrant for land."

warranty deed: a formal written document transferring interests in land and containing warranties concerning the extent of the rights transferred; the most common deeds used, they contain a description of the property, names of the buyers and sellers, are acknowledged ("notarized", "sworn to"), almost always are recorded, and, especially early, contain a recital of the consideration given in exchange, e.g., "Through their descriptions, warranty deeds often make it possible for the researcher to locate the property of an ancestor."

wars: those conflicts, whether declared as war or not, that bring men and women to duty with weapons in the public cause, e.g., "The French and Indian War took place between 1754 and 1763, and the so-called Indian wars were during the last third of the nineteenth century."

wash boiler, wash kettle: a large, oblong, lidded, often copper (early) and later galvanized boiling pan used to boil and wash clothes, e.g., "The old copper wash boilers often were called 'copper kettles'."

washboard: a common household tool consisting of a small board with a ridged surface, one end of which was placed in a tub of water, against which soap and clothes were rubbed to clean or "wash" them, e.g., "Before the 20th century, almost every housewife had used a washboard."

washstand: a small chest used in bed **chambers** (q.v.), usually having 1 to 3 drawers and a doored compartment below, and a splash board and towel rack at the back of and above the work surface, and upon which were placed a **pitcher and bowl** (q.v.), **shaving mirror** (q.v.), etc., to be used for **stand-up bathes** (q.v.) and refreshment after sleeping, e.g., "Her washstands were Victorian in style and made of oak."

wassail, wassailing: a liquor made of apple juice, sugar, and ale; the word "wassail" literally meaning "to be healthy," this drink was and still is typically served in cold weather at Christmastime, often carried and consumed while singing carols from house to house, when the carolers traditionally drink to the health of their neighbors; "The old Christmas song that mentions wassailing was speaking of a favorite liquor of the early colonies and old England."

water course: a running stream, e.g., "Often the use of the word watercourse in a description makes it possible to locate a property that once belonged to an ancestor."

water witch: See **dowser, etc.**

waters, taking the: See **take the waters.**

waving fence: See **snake fence.**

weathercock, weathervane: as now, a movable device, usually placed atop a house or barn, and shaped in the silhouette of a long-tailed rooster (or other animal), that can rotate and thereby show the direction of the wind, e.g., "Early weathercocks usually were made of brass, lead, or wood."

week, a week: refers to a day more than a week in the future, e.g., "On Sunday, he said he would leave Tuesday week, meaning on the Tuesday following the Tuesday that was within the same week as the statement"; "In relating to him on Friday that she was leaving a week from that coming Sunday, she said 'I'll be going Sunday a week.'"

weeper: anything worn as an indication that the wearer is in mourning, e.g., "As weepers, she wore a black veil and black gloves."

weir: a fence set in a flowing stream to catch fish, e.g., "They would set the weir, then go upstream and wade toward it."

Well-born Men: a tribunal of early New York, e.g., "Early New Amsterdam records reveal activities of the Well-born Men.

well laid on: an expression found in court orders directing a sheriff to whip criminals, meaning that the blows should not be softened, e.g., "In 1686, for having an illegitimate 'mulattoe' child, Mary Poore was sentenced to 'tenn lashes on her bare back well layd on'."

Welsh cupboard: a full open cupboard with a shallow work space between shelves above and shelves below, e.g., "Mrs. Roberts' 1838 Welsh cupboard still is in the family."

wen, win: a sebaceous cyst, very often behind the ears or on the cheeks, e.g.., "Paul had several wens behind his right ear."

wench: on this continent, a slave woman, usually young, e.g., "Unlike in England, early Virginia records seem to reveal the word wench only when the reference was to slave women."

wescot: See ***waistcoat.***

Westward Movement: that mass immigration of families to the western frontier of the American colonies and states that took place throughout the 16th, 17th, 18th, and 19th centuries; the phenomenon resulting from the availability of opportunity and inexpensive land on the western edge of settlement over a period of some three hundred years, e.g., "One of the main routes of the Westward Movement was up the St. Lawrence River, thence through the Great Lakes to Minnesota, Wisconsin, and beyond."

wet nurse: a woman employed to provide breast milk to the child of another, e.g., "During the nineteenth century, women whose infants had died often sought employment by advertising to be a wet nurse."

wet plate photography, wet plate process: an early process by which plates coated with light sensitive materials were exposed and processed into "negatives," after which photographic prints were made therefrom, e.g., "The wet plate process so well known from Mathew Brady's work was still actively pursued by W. L. Midlam as late as 1915." Also see ***what's it wagon.***

wether: a castrated male sheep less than a year old, so rendered to improve the quality of the meat, e.g., "The early inventory listed a ram, three ewes, and a wether."

whalebone: cartilage from the mouths of certain whales, often early used for corset **stays** (q.v.), e.g., "In addition to the oil and **spermaceti** (q.v.), he also sold whalebone."

what's it wagon: a wagon used by early travelling photographers and equipped to serve as a "dark room," e.g., "Many Old West letters and newspapers refer to the arrival of Alexander Gardner's what's it wagon."

wheel: a bicycle, usually one with a tall front wheel, e.g., "It was said that Billy was very proficient on the wheel." Also see **spinning wheel.**

wheel barrow, wheelbarrow, wheel barra: a single-wheeled, handled device to carry any heavy item, especially earth, stone, etc., e.g., "The fully loaded wheelbarrow was more than the boy could handle."

wheel lock: See **flintlock.**

wheel stick: a short, simple stick used to move the wheel on a **spinning wheel** (q.v.), e.g., "Any short dried piece of wood served as a wheel stick."

wheelers, wheel horses: that horse or horses harnessed closest to the front wheels of the vehicle, usually the more powerful of the animals in the hitch, e.g., "Old Lew Wickersham had a pair of blacks as the wheelers, a pair of grays as the **swing horses** (q.v.), and a pair of whites as the **leaders.**

wheelwright, wheelmaker: an ancient occupation or calling; one having the knowledge needed to make spokes, hubs, axles, **tires** (q.v.), etc., needed for spinning wheels, wagons, carriages, turnstiles, and the like, e.g., "Charles Carner was an early Pennsylvania wheelwright."

whelp: a recently weaned puppy; occasionally, a word of gentle reprimand for children, e.g., "Maggie often smiled and called the boys whelps as she corrected their errant ways."

whetstone, rubstone: a stone, found in many grits and sizes, used to sharpen knives, edged instruments, and weapons, e.g., "He had two sharpening stones, one for his **hatchet** (q.v.) and axe, and another for his wives scissors and his **penknife** (q.v.)."

Whigs: in the U.S., an early political party of Patriots favoring the **War of Independence** (q.v.); later, as opposed to the **Democrats** (q.v.), they sought high tariffs and liberal construction of the Constitution, e.g., "Jefferson, especially in light of his work in framing the Constitution, had little tolerance for the views of the early Whigs." Also see **Tories.**

whip: one who drove a stagecoach or other animal-drawn, passenger vehicle including a trolley or horsecar, e.g., "When carrying valuable goods or money, in addition to the whip, an Overland Stage crew also included one or more men who 'rode shotgun.'" Also see **yahoo.**

whipping: a method of punishing by use of a whipping post and a harsh leather strap - a "whipping strap", e.g., "Whipping was not outlawed in the U.S. until February 28, 1839."

whippletree: See **swingletree.**

whirligig, top: a "top"; a toy that could be spun with the hands or a string, e.g., "A many-colored whirligig was a highly favored toy to be given at special occasions."

whish broom: See **whisk broom.**

whisk, whisk broom, whish broom: as now, a small, hand-held broom used to sweep crumbs, small bits of debris, etc., e.g., "Because of the gentle sound it made, Maggie called the little broom a whish broom."

Whiskey Insurrection, Whiskey Rebellion: that 1794 revolt by western Pennsylvania citizens over taxes on whiskey that resulted in Washington calling up the militia to quell the uprising; two participants were convicted of treason and later were pardoned by Washington, e.g., "Many participants in the Whiskey Insurrection have descendents living today."

white lightning: See **corn whiskey.**

white mule: See **corn whiskey.**

Whitecaps: an organization of racists first formed in Tennessee and outlawed in 1896, e.g., "In practice, the Whitecaps did not differ from the **Ku Klux Klan** (q.v.)."

whiteware: any white pottery, e.g., "She had several whiteware bowls."

Whitsuntide: the feast of the Pentecost, held the 5th day after Easter Sunday, e.g., "For the most part, Whitsuntide was observed only by members of the Church of England."

Whole Duty of Man, The: a book of duties and responsibilities of a Church of England Christian, first published in London in 1694, and thereafter in several editions, e.g., "Next to the Bible and the **Book of Common Prayer** (q.v.), *The Whole Duty of Man* perhaps was the most well known book in the early South."

whooping cough, hooping cough: as now, a deep, racking cough, e.g., "Whooping cough often was treated with chloroform, cod liver oil, tannin, or musk."

wicker, wicker furniture: furniture, usually woven of pliant willow branches; **rattan furniture,** is also sometimes referred to as "wickerwork."

widows' pensions: in genealogy, those sums of money and other benefits awarded widows and (later) widowers by reason of prior military service of or contributions of time, services, or supplies by their deceased spouses, e.g., "As a result of his War of 1812 service, Martha received $8.00 per month as a widow's pension.

wig block: as now, a rounded form upon which wigs are shaped and stored, e.g., "There are many wig blocks shown in early households."

wildcat, lynx: as now, e.g., "By reason of their depredations of chickens, ducks, and young and small farm animals, wildcats were perceived as perhaps the worst of the predators."

Wilderness Road: that rather ill-defined and well used route of substantial westward movement extending westward from the area of Salisbury, North Carolina, through the several gaps in the Blue Ridge and the Smokey Mts., thence through Cumberland Gap to Kentucky and north, or through Crab Orchard Gap to Nashville and beyond, e.g., "Part of the family moved from Tidewater Virginia to western Tennessee across the Wilderness Road." Also see **roads, early.**

will: that writing that sets forth the last wishes and intended **devises** (q.v.) (real estate) and **bequests** (q.v.) (personal property) of a person; to be a will, the document must precisely comply with the law of the jurisdiction or state, and all states require at least two witnesses, e.g., "His will named three persons as devisees and was executed on 2 December 1769." Also see **nuncupative will,** and **holographic will.**

wimple: a head scarf tied under the chin, similar to that worn by nuns, e.g., "Wimples were common in early times."

windgun: a very early term meaning a "B.B. gun" or air rifle, e.g., "Windguns as toys for affluent children were known well before 1800."

Windsor chair: a chair of original American styling (c1700-1825), simple in design, light, and very strong, with a back of 5 to 9 spindles (the more, the older), usually made of hickory, pine, maple, ash, or of other hard wood that was on hand, often with a shallow saddle-shaped seat, and almost always painted and decorated, e.g., "As was typical, her Windsor side chairs had seven spindles and were painted."

wingback chairs: a common design, first seen in the side pieces of colonial chairs and still popular, armed, upholstered, with 6 to 8 inch legs, the back wrapping around to the sides of one's head, thereby preventing **drafts** (q.v.), e.g., "She had two tufted wingback chairs, each with a **center table** (q.v.) to accompany it."

winnowing, winnow: to separate grain from chaff, e.g., "Early winnowing was done by hand by agitating a large, shallow, sieve-like basket."

winter kitchen: See **summer kitchen.**

witch ball: an open glass ball, often with a nipple or hole in the side, containing potpourri, colored paper or string, or flowers, and hung in windows, supposedly to ward off evil spirits, e.g., "While most women of the nineteenth century used witch balls as decoration, a few still believed that they warded off evil."

witch trials: See **Salem Witch Trials.**

witchcraft: the practice of sorcery, magic (especially "black magic") and the casting of spells, etc., e.g., "Charges of engaging in witchcraft in the American colonies largely ended with the **Salem Witch Trials** (q.v.) of 1691 and 1692."

witness: attestation; one who gives testimony, e.g., "Since she was present when the event occurred, she was summoned to be a witness to the facts."

wooden hammer: See **mallet.**

woodsrider: a superintendent of cutting or lumbering of trees or in the woods, e.g., "An early Florida court recognized the title of woodsrider as an occupation or calling."

wool wheel: See **spinning wheel.**

woolmercer: See **mercer.**

words, colonial, derived from other sources: See **Spanish people, influence of; New World influence; Scotch-Irish influence; Indians, American, influence of; French influence, German influence, Italian influence, Irish influence.**

work beast: any draft animal, e.g., "His work beasts were well harnessed." Also see **draft horses.**

work horses: See **draft horses.**

work table: unlike now, any of many styles of small to medium, square, usually singly or doubly drawered tables, either with or without knee space beneath, e.g., "Her cherry work table was of Sheraton styling."

World War I: that armed conflict that took place between 1914 and 1919 and involved nations from across the globe; armed participation by the U.S. troops was during 1918 and 1919, e.g., "He was a part of the American Expeditionary Force (A.E.F.) in World War I."

World War II: that massive, worldwide, armed conflict that took place between 1938 and 1945 and involved nearly the entire world; armed participation by the U.S. was from December 1941 till August 1945, e.g., "Leonard was with Patton's Third Army in World War II."

worsted: a fabric, usually of high quality, made entirely from wool or wool yarn, and originally made in the town of Worsted, England, e.g., "Griffith was said to be a maker of worsted"; "Worsted had gained a reputation for its fine woolen goods by the 16th century."

wringer, clothes wringer, clothes squeezer: with the coming of the Industrial Revolution myriad new time savers were devised, including mechanical washing machines and cranked wringers for wet clothes, e.g., "The 1870s newspapers spoke glowingly of the newly available metal and rubber 'clothes squeezers' - wringers."

writ: in genealogy, any order by a court in the name of a government - federal, state or local - addressed to a sheriff or other law officer; often used to direct an officer of the law to take some thing or person into custody or to see to the accomplishment of some requirement of the court, e.g., "Writs ordering that action be taken against ancestors are often very revealing, and are commonly found in 'loose papers' and archival collections."

writ of estrepement: See **estrepement, writ of.**

writ of scire facias: See **scire facias.**

writing chair: any of many styles and shapes of chairs having a writing arm or surface mounted to one side, e.g., "Original Windsor writing chairs in decent condition are valued at several thousands of dollars."

writing desk: a small box with a hinged, raisable lid on which one might write, and beneath which paper and writing supplies were kept, often held in the lap, but sometimes on legs or a pedestal, e.g., "The Empire writing desk was of *flame grain* (q.v.) walnut and mounted on a pedestal." Also see **desk.**

writs (extraordinary): See **certiorari, habeus corpus, procedendo, mandamus,** and **prohibition.**

writs of error: See **error, writs of.**

written law: the law as stated by legislatures, as opposed to the **common law** (q.v.), i.e., case law, e.g., "The foundation of the French legal system is the written law - Civil Law - and that system followed their people to Louisiana."

X, Y, Z

yahoo: an uncouth or vulgar person; one who drove a stagecoach or other animal-drawn passenger vehicle other than a trolley or horsecar. Also see *whip.*

Yamassee War: 1715 - c.1718; that series of conflicts pitting South Carolina settlers against the Yamassees and Creeks, and resulting in the ouster of the Whites from the area west of Savannah River, following which the settlers and the Cherokees drove the other Indians from the area and built forts at present Columbia and Port Royal, e.g., "The genealogist will yet find a few records of those Carolinians who took up arms in the Yamassee War."

Yankees: originally, a person from New England; after about 1855, those who declared allegiance to or lived in a Northern state, e.g., "Yankee Doodle was an expression well known in Revolutionary New England"; "The 'damned Yankees' was expressive of a common view of the Civil War and Reconstruction South."

Yankee cakes: doughnuts, e.g., "The Yankee cake cutters listed in the early 19th century likely were tin doughnut cutters."

yarn swift, yarn reel: a revolving reel for yarn, mounted on a pedestal, and usually short to accommodate a sitting spinner; occasionally three to four feet in height for those who stand at a *spinning wheel* (q.v.) and called a standing yarn swift, e.g., "She had a cherry Shaker standing yarn swift that had belonged to her great grandmother." Also see *reel.*

yaws, frambisia: severe, excreting lesions of the skin caused by a parasite, red to burgundy in color, and peculiar to the South and Caribbean Islands, e.g., "When yaws appeared, early physicians routinely applied turpentine, quinine, and various Indian ointments."

yearling: any animal, but usually an equine or bovine, that has passed its first birthday, but not yet its second, e.g., "Since imperfections were not yet apparent to most eyes, he always sold his colts as yearlings."

years allowance, yearly support, yearly provision: that sum in cash or assets allowed at various early times (not until 1796 in North Carolina) to a widow for the support, food, and provisions needed by herself and her children during the year following her husband's death, e.g., "The court approved 630 pounds of tobacco as her year's allowance."

yellow fever: See *calenture.*

yeoman: in the early days, quite usually one who owned or had previously owned land in small quantity, e.g., "He owned three acres and spoke of himself as a yeoman."

Yiddish: that language of Germanized Hebrew words, e.g., "It was said that many New Yorkers spoke Yiddish as early as 1740."

yoke, yoake, yoke and irons: a sturdy contrivance used to tie together two draft animals, and consisting of two padded wooden collars and a connecting iron arm, e.g., "The old yoke was retired when he got rid of the oxen."

Yom Kippur: the most solemn and sacred holiday in the Jewish calendar, celebrated on the 10th day of the first month of the Jewish calendar - Tishri, e.g., "In 1993, Yom Kippur was on September 25."

yonder: an early Scotch-Irish and English expression carried to the South and indicative of relative distance from the speaker; a remnant of those references to distance such as expressed in the words "hither, thither and yon" - here, there, and beyond, e.g., "When she said 'look yonder', the listener knew to turn his eyes not to 'here' or 'there', but rather to look beyond those imaginary parameters."

References

The number of historical terms is unlimited, as is the amount of re-source material available to the researcher. In compiling this dictionary, the author consulted numerous sources, many of which line the shelves of his own private collection of rare and antique books. The following books are highly recommended to those wishing to do further historical research.

Bassett, J.S., ed. *Writings of Colonel William Byrd.* New York. Burt Franklin. 1970.

Bruce, Philip A. *Economic History of Virginia in The Seventeenth Century.* 2 vols. New York. McMillan & Co. 1896.

____. *Institutional History of Virginia in the Seventeenth Century.* 2 vols., New York. G.P. Putnam's Sons. 1910.

____. *Social Life of Virginia in the Seventeenth Century.* Richmond. Whittet & Shepperson. 1907.

Drake, Paul, ed. *The Day Book of Dr. William Kitchen Drake, 1841-1856.* Crossville, Tennessee. Published by the editor. 1984.

Fletcher, S.W. *Pennsylvania Agriculture and Country Life, 1640-1840.* Harrisburg. Pennsylvania Hist. & Museum Comm. 1971.

Hall, Wilmer, ed. *Vestry Book of the Upper Parish, Nansemond County, 1743-1793.* Richmond. Virginia State Library. 1969.

Hopkins, W.L., abstractor. *Suffolk Parish Vestry Book, 1749-1784, Nansemond County, VA, and Newport Parish BVestry Book 1742-1772, Isle of Wight County, VA.* Richmond. Published by the abstractor. 1988.

Johnson, Samuel, LLD. *Dictionary of the English Language.* Edinburgh. D. Buchanan. 1802.

Morgan, Edmund S. *Virginians At Home; Family Life in the Eighteenth Century.* Colonial Williamsburg Foundation. 1952.

Phillips, Ulrich B. *Life and Labor in the Old South.* Boston. Little Brown & Co. 1963.

Withington, Lathrop. *Virginia Gleanings in England.* Baltimore. Genealogical Publishing Co. 1980.